日本海軍

THE
JAPANESE
NAVY
IN
WORLD
WAR
II

*In the Words
of Former
Japanese
Naval
Officers*

SECOND EDITION

*Introduction
and Commentary
by
Dr. Raymond O'Connor*

*Editor
and Translator
of the Second Edition,
Dr. David C. Evans*

*Naval Institute Press
Annapolis, Maryland*

Copyright © 1969, 1986
by the United States Naval Institute
Annapolis, Maryland

Published 1969. Second Edition 1986

All rights reserved. No part of this book may be reproduced without written permission from the publisher.

All but two of the chapters herein were originally published in the United States Naval Institute *Proceedings* and copyrighted in 1952, 1953, 1954, 1955, 1956, 1957, 1958, 1960, 1961, and 1979.

Chapter 4 was translated, with permission, from Toshikazu Ohmae, "Die japanischen Operationen im Bereich des Indischen Ozeans," *Marine Rundschau* 55 (April 1958).

Chapter 9 was translated, with permission, from Minoru Nomura, *Rekishi no naka no Nihon kaigun* (Tokyo: Hara Shobō, 1980).

Library of Congress Cataloging-in-Publication Data
The Japanese Navy in World War II.
    Includes index.
    1. Japan. Kaigun—History—World War, 1939–45.
2. World War, 1939–1945—Naval operations, Japanese.
3. World War, 1939–1945—Aerial operations, Japanese.
I. O'Connor, Raymond Gish. II. Evans, David C.
D777.J3 1986   940.54′5952   86-8537
ISBN 0-87021-316-4

Printed in the United States of America

Preface to the Second Edition

Well over fifteen years have passed since the popular first edition of this book appeared. Yet interest in the Japanese navy's role in World War II has, if anything, increased in the meantime.

This new edition is a response to that interest. It incorporates five more articles: three from the Naval Institute *Proceedings,* one from the German journal of maritime affairs *Marine Rundschau,* and one from Minoru Nomura's book *Rekishi no naka no Nihon kaigun.* I have translated the last two and provided short introductions for all five. They fill gaps in the previous edition by discussing operations in the Indian Ocean, the Battle of the Philippine Sea, the protection of merchant shipping, submarine warfare, and Japan's general naval strategy.

As in the first edition, a brief introduction precedes each chapter. Minor errors in the first edition have been corrected and new photographs and maps added. I have updated the biographical sketches of authors and editors wherever possible. All notes at the back of the book are those of the editors and translators rather than the authors. In the text I have retained the first edition's practice of listing Japanese names in Western order, surname last, and without macrons to indicate long vowels. The index, however, lists each Japanese name in the native order and with phonetically accurate romanization. Proper transliterations for Japanese ship names and technical terms are also provided in the index.

DAVID C. EVANS

Publisher's Preface to the Original Edition

In presenting this anthology of articles on Japanese naval participation in World War II, the publisher wishes to acknowledge the contribution of those persons whose interest in naval history made it possible:

Herman O. Werner, professor emeritus of the U.S. Naval Academy's Department of English, History, and Government and senior associate editor of the U.S. Naval Institute *Proceedings* from 1948 to 1960, first proposed the project. He was preparing introductory material at the time of his death in 1967.

Robert M. Langdon, associate professor in the same department and an associate editor of the *Proceedings* from 1951 to 1957, worked briefly on the book until his death that same year.

Credit for the idea of obtaining Japanese views on the war goes to Commander Roy de S. Horn, U.S. Navy (Retired), who was managing editor of the Naval Institute from 1945 to 1959.

Roger Pineau edited and prepared most of the chapters for

publication in the *Proceedings;* part of the work was done by Clark Kawakami. English translations of the Japanese texts were supplied by Masataka Chihaya, Masaru Chikuami, and Toshikazu Ohmae.

Contents

ix

Introduction

The Japanese task force attack on the American fleet at Pearl Harbor, Hawaii, on 7 December 1941 was the first engagement in what became the greatest naval war in history, marking the culmination of a rivalry in the Pacific that had endured for generations. The initial hostility to the United States that followed the opening of Japan to Western trade by Commodore Perry and his squadron in 1854 was succeeded by an era of friendship and close commercial ties, marred only occasionally by American resistance to Japanese attempts to gain hegemony over portions of the Asian mainland in the early years of the twentieth century.

After World War I, during which Japan had taken steps to extend and consolidate her influence in China, the situation was aggravated by naval competition among the United States, Japan, and Great Britain. Realizing that armaments were expressions and instruments of political objectives, the leading powers met in Washington in 1921 to discuss Far Eastern problems and try to halt the weapons race. Agreement was reached on the preservation of the territorial and commercial integrity of China—the Open Door policy as formulated by Secretary of State John Hay in 1899–1900—which thwarted Japanese ambitions in that country; on the nonfortification of certain bases; and on a limitation of two categories of naval vessels, namely, capital ships and aircraft carriers. The ratio of strength established allowed Japan to build up to 60 percent of the quota allocated to both the United States and Great Britain—the 5:5:3 formula. Regarded by some as the equivalent of "Rolls-Royce, Rolls-Royce, Ford," this ratio, which relegated Japan to the category of a second-class power, was resented by many Japanese, especially members of the armed forces, who believed the agreement was made by civilian leaders who did not understand the imperatives of imperial defense.

A subsequent conference in London in 1930 extended limitations to all types of naval vessels with some improvement in the ratio for Japan, but the resulting furor over the treaty helped spur Japanese military action in Manchuria the following year. American attempts to halt the aggression provoked the Stimson-Hoover Doctrine, which declared that the United States would not recognize the acquisition of territory by the use of force. A condemnation of the Manchurian invasion by the League of Nations led to Japanese withdrawal from that body. In 1934, when the government in Tokyo announced that it would reject an extension of the naval limitation treaties unless Japan was given parity in warships with the United States and Great Britain, the stage was set for renewed naval competition and, ostensibly, for further Japanese aggressive moves in the Far East.

American resistance to Japanese aggression was reaffirmed when President-elect Franklin D. Roosevelt accepted the principle of the Stimson-Hoover Doctrine, and his former affiliation with and sympathy for the navy became apparent when he utilized relief funds for new construction to bring the fleet to treaty strength. The increasingly belligerent conduct of Hitler's Germany and Mussolini's Italy alarmed the president, who was fearful of the impact on world peace and American security. Confirmation of the worst fears about Japanese motives came in 1937, when Japan began a full-scale invasion of China, euphemistically called the China Incident. This conflict, which ultimately grew to mammoth proportions, brought stiff American protests. In January 1938, after the unprovoked attack by Japanese aircraft against the USS *Panay* on the Yangtze River the previous month, Roosevelt asked and received from Congress a special appropriation for naval construction. Both the United States and Great Britain announced a resumption of competitive building to counter the accelerated naval program in Japan. The equilibrium of naval power that had been created by the various treaties was being upset, and a further deterioration of the power relationships could not be tolerated with aggressive nations on the move in Asia and Europe.

When Hitler violated the Munich pact by absorbing the remainder of Czechoslovakia in the spring of 1939, it became apparent that Great Britain would be required to concentrate her resources on the effort to stem aggression in Europe, and the outbreak of war with Germany in September further weakened British influence in Asia. To help fill the vacuum left in the Far East by the British commitment in Europe, the president began to exert economic pressure on Japan, first by announcing the abrogation of the commercial treaty of 1911 and subsequently by imposing other sanctions as the Japanese authorities exploited the European war to further their designs in Asia. The U.S. Navy, in 1940, conducted its annual fleet problem in the Pacific under vigorous protests from the Japanese press, and the fleet was retained at Pearl Harbor to serve as a deterrent to Japanese expansion. Responding to a recommendation by the navy's General Board, the president requested legislation for the construction of a two-ocean navy, and he authorized the preparation of plans envisioning war with the Axis nations in both the Pacific and the Atlantic.

The naval strategies contemplated by the major powers

were based on decades of study and experience and were more explicitly defined and incorporated into training exercises during the 1920s and 1930s. Great Britain was committed to an essentially defensive strategy in what was deemed the initial period, for a three-year conflict was assumed and it was believed that time was on her side. The fleet air arm had been weakened by its placement under the Air Ministry until 1937, and even then the Admiralty was not given control of research and development. Also, as Lieutenant Commander P. K. Kemp, RN, Ret., has pointed out in *Key to Victory: The Triumph of British Sea Power in World War II* (Boston: Little, Brown & Co., 1957), "The convoy lessons of 1917 had never been fully digested, indeed to some extent had been forgotten," and a critical shortage of escort vessels existed. A significant portion of the British navy was deployed in the Mediterranean in anticipation of Italy joining Germany as an ally, and command of this area was deemed essential. The remainder of the British naval forces were deployed to protect the Isles from a German invasion, to blockade Germany, and to protect British commerce on the high seas— commerce without which the nation would collapse in a matter of weeks. And protection involved, according to the thinking of that day, cruiser defense against surface raiders, not escorts for convoys. The British navy was also affected by what might be called the Jutland syndrome. As the British naval historian Stephen Roskill puts it, during much of the interwar period "the British admiralty's thinking was directed more to the causes of the Royal Navy's lack of success at Jutland than to the question whether such lessons had any validity for the future."[1] The shortcomings of British naval planning were revealed in the abortive Norwegian amphibious operation, the inadequacies of hunter-killer groups in countering German U-boat depredations, and the tragic decision to deploy the *Prince of Wales* and the *Repulse* without adequate air support.

American naval strategy between the wars had been predicated on a view of Japan as the most probable enemy. Strategists envisioned a fleet engagement that would destroy the major Japanese forces and a subsequent blockade of the home islands that would strangle the nation and induce capitulation. The battleship was generally regarded as the "backbone of the fleet," and carrier aircraft were to serve primarily for scouting and spotting. A major part of the curriculum at the Naval War College consisted of a Pacific war game, and Fleet Admiral Chester W. Nimitz later remarked that "the course was so complete that when the war in the Pacific actually started, nothing that happened surprised us at all except the kamikaze attacks."[2] Of course the versatility and decisive nature of the fast carrier task force had been foreseen by few, but fortunately in America naval air doctrine had progressed more than in Britain, although it lagged behind that of the Japanese.

Japanese authorities had sought British assistance in developing their naval air arm after World War I and soon outstripped their mentors in carrier utilization. The United States was regarded as the most probable enemy, and training was designed to prepare for this contingency throughout the interwar period. As American economic pressure accelerated during 1941 and culminated in the oil embargo, key Japanese naval leaders came to agree with their more militant army colleagues that the nation had to choose between war with the United States or a dissolution of the empire. After consideration of four separate military strategic concepts, a plan representing a compromise between those advocated by the separate services was adopted. Simultaneous attacks were to be launched against the Philippines and Malaya, to be followed by an advance against the Dutch East Indies. Military and logistic considerations were combined with the desperate need for those natural resources which had been denied by economic sanctions and without which Japanese industry would be paralyzed and the military machine could not function. Most controversial was Admiral Isoroku Yamamoto's proposal to attack the U.S. Fleet at Pearl Harbor. There was the danger that this bastion protected by major naval units might prove too formidable, but a naval encounter in the western Pacific, close to Japanese land-based planes, could provide circumstances more conducive to success.

By mid-October Admiral Yamamoto's daring plan had been adopted. With the collapse of negotiations between the two governments, the task force was directed to carry out its orders. The Japanese grand design envisioned the immobilization of the American fleet and its consequent inability to contest Japanese advances. Territory would be occupied, bases established, and a veritable fortress area created in the southwest Pacific incorporating all the resources necessary to sustain Japanese military and civilian activities. The United States—faced in the Pacific with the enormous and lengthy task of replacing its decimated navy and carrying the war to the virtually impregnable defense perimeter in the Far East, and faced in Europe with what Japan considered the assured Axis victory—would be induced to settle for a negotiated peace that would leave the Japanese with many of the fruits of conquest.

Prior to America's formal entry into the war, joint Anglo-American discussions had led to agreement that in the event of a two-ocean conflict Germany should be defeated first. Resources, it was felt, would simply not permit the mounting of full-fledged campaigns against both major antagonists at the same time, and Germany was regarded as the most dangerous foe. Soon after the attack at Pearl Harbor and a declaration of war by the other Axis powers, American naval command relationships were changed. Admiral Ernest J. King was appointed commander in chief of the U.S. Fleet and chief of naval operations. Admiral Nimitz succeeded Admiral Husband Kimmel and became commander in chief of the Pacific Fleet. The American high command became a unified body in the Joint Chiefs of Staff; collaboration between American and British military leaders, which had begun some time earlier,

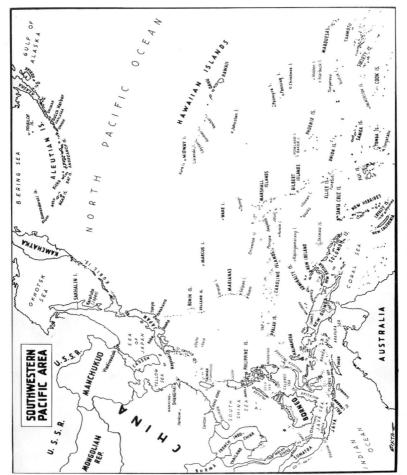

On the Eve of the Pacific War. *Official U.S. Navy photograph*

was formalized by the creation of the Combined Chiefs of Staff. In March 1942 the two nations reached an understanding on the strategic control of operations whereby the United States assumed principal responsibility for the entire Pacific area and China; Great Britain for the Middle East and Far East areas except China; and the Combined Chiefs of Staff for grand strategy in both zones and all operations in the Atlantic-European area, with a division of naval responsibilities in the Atlantic. While the heads of state retained the final decision-making power for major operations, they interfered very little with the conduct of the war in the Pacific.

The Japanese, meanwhile, intoxicated by their naval successes at Pearl Harbor and in the Java Sea and their commensurate accomplishments in land campaigns, succumbed to what has been called victory disease. Instead of consolidating their remarkable achievements of the early months of the war and concentrating on a defensive strategy, they embarked on a new program of conquests. Their first move was aimed at the capture of Tulagi in the Solomon Islands and Port Moresby in New Guinea. These secured, the Japanese would dominate the Coral Sea and threaten Australia and the Allied line of communications. But their attempt was thwarted by the first naval engagement between carriers in the Battle of the Coral Sea, which was a tactical draw but a strategic defeat for the Japanese. Their second and more ambitious venture was to capture Midway Island and the western Aleutians in order to enlarge the defense perimeter, to bring the U.S. Pacific Fleet to a decisive engagement, and to destroy what had remained after Pearl Harbor. The outcome of the ensuing battle altered the course of the war in the Pacific and gave Admiral King the opportunity to press for more support for the Pacific theater. Although King had been in agreement with the Europe-first strategy, he waged a constant struggle to obtain sufficient resources to keep pressure on the Japanese and prevent them from establishing a virtually impregnable position. After the Battle of Midway, the Joint Chiefs of Staff finally accepted King's arguments for a defensive-offensive strategy—as he put it, tactically offensive, strategically defensive—and he was able to secure authorization for a move on Tulagi and Guadalcanal. Thus, the Solomons were invaded to resist the Japanese advance to the southeast against the United States–Australia communication line.

During the Solomons campaign the Japanese naval air force suffered such severe losses in aircraft and trained pilots that it never again was able to exercise a decisive influence in the Pacific War, and the Imperial Navy withdrew to a new defense line that extended from Tokyo through the Marianas and Truk. Allied strategy now moved to the purely offensive phase with the aid of the newly created two-ocean navy. Admiral Nimitz now commanded the most formidable naval force in history, structured around the Fast Carrier Task Force. A dispute among army, navy, and air force planners over the most desirable strategy to be followed was resolved by the recognition that all three methods could be pursued, for by 1944 the United States possessed sufficient resources to combine them. Implementing a parallel advance, the southwest Pacific forces continued to move along the island route from New Guinea to the Philippines, while the Fifth Fleet cleared a path across the central Pacific under ideal conditions for the employment of the carrier task force. The navy profited from experience, notably that at Tarawa, which revealed the dangers of inadequate preparatory bombing and bombardment, and consequently the Kwajalein assault became the model of a "perfect invasion." This landing, as Stephen Roskill has observed, "punched a hole right in the center of the 'defensive perimeter' which the Japanese had hoped to hold."[3] The Fifth Fleet assault on the Marianas in mid-1944 drew the Japanese fleet out of the Java Sea area, and in the Battle of the Philippine Sea the imperial fleet was repulsed with significant losses from submarine and carrier-based plane attacks. With the capture of the Marianas, air force B-29s were able to raid the Japanese home islands, and bases were provided for an intensification of the submarine campaign. The interdiction of shipping by submarine operations and the laying of mines in Japan's home waters became so effective that they threatened to suffocate the nation.

The campaign for the recapture of the Philippines was approved after a lengthy dispute among the top commanders, and factors influencing the decision included political and moral considerations as well as the army's conviction that the Philippines were needed as a staging area for the projected invasion of the Japanese homeland. The controversial aspects of the ensuing Battle of Leyte Gulf are best left to more detailed accounts. The bloody Okinawa operation that followed witnessed the appearance in full force of the kamikaze suicide planes, marking the last desperate effort by the Japanese to halt what had become a virtual American avalanche. With the dropping of the atomic bombs and the entry of the Soviet Union into the war, the Japanese government sued for peace. The degree to which either or both factors were responsible for the decision to surrender will long be argued by historians and strategists.

There were many heroes on both sides in this gigantic conflict, and enmity did not prevent respect for the adversary or at times a grudging admiration for his abilities. During the Pacific War the American naval commanders enjoyed certain advantages in terms of information, technology, and—in the later stages—quantitative superiority. Each may have proved decisive in some cases, although fundamental throughout was what Mahan called the personal equation, namely, the fighting qualities of the men and the proficiency of their leaders. One of the most impressive and determinant aspects of the war was, as the British put it, "what the Americans call 'logistics.'"[4] In fact, some British authorities contend that the creation and successful employment of the "fleet train" ranks with effective utilization of the carrier task force as one of the two greatest American accomplishments of the naval war. In convincing the Japanese that this conflict was a "mistaken war," the American navy profited by the success of the Japanese carrier task force at Pearl Harbor and developed this concept of naval warfare to such a degree of perfection that it drove the Imperial Navy from the Pacific and established control of the sea, the essential ingredient for victory.

The following articles present a Japanese view of significant strategic and tactical operations during the Pacific War. The authors provide a different perspective for these events and clarify many hitherto confusing episodes by combining firsthand knowledge with subsequent interviews and painstaking research in the records. Understanding the erstwhile enemy—his aspirations, the reasons for his decisions, the disagreements, the mistakes, and the repercussions of success and failure—adds dimensions to the study of war and of human activity. It is not necessary to accept the adage that more is learned from a defeat than from a victory in order to profit from these moving and authoritative accounts by the vanquished foe.

RAYMOND O'CONNOR

日本海軍

1

The
Hawaii
Operation

SHIGERU
FUKUDOME

The lengthy negotiations between the United States
and Japan over a solution to the Far East altercation
reached an impasse in November 1941, when it became apparent that neither government would accept the terms of
the other. Pressures exerted by the United States and other
friendly governments to induce the Japanese to cease aggression in China and French Indochina had convinced the Tokyo statesmen that their nation must fight or die. The presence of the U.S. Pacific Fleet at Pearl Harbor was a threat to
Japan, although some Japanese authorities believed that it
was in an exposed and vulnerable position and lacked the
logistic support for distant operations. A transfer of major
segments of the fleet to the Atlantic in May 1941 to support
the British effort against the German navy further weakened
the American position in the Pacific and made Pearl Harbor
more inviting as a target.

In Japan, government officials debated the desirability of
moving north to attack Russia or moving south to cut the
British lifeline and take over the rich resources of Southeast

Asia. Either enterprise would aid the Axis partners engaged in the European war, but with the removal from office of Foreign Minister Matsuoka the issue was resolved in favor of the rich lands to the south. Then the primary strategic question arose: whether to launch the operation against British and Dutch holdings, an action that would soon lure the American fleet to the area, or to risk a bold assault on Pearl Harbor to cripple that fleet and permit a consolidation of the Japanese position in the western Pacific.

In the following article, the author presents the strategic problem as it was seen by Japanese naval leaders, and the factors that determined their final decision. The Imperial Navy, which had been preparing for years to engage the American fleet in its home waters, violated conventional theory by making an offensive thrust into enemy territory. Admiral Fukudome ardently defends the attack as strategically and tactically sound and eminently successful in light of its objectives, though he is mildly critical of the Japanese failure to launch one more attack. He points out the disappointing results of the submarine arm of the operation without fully exploring the reasons for them, and he does not deal with the overlooked opportunity for the task force to follow up its impressive strike by seeking out and destroying the remaining American naval units in the area. Still, such an effort was not part of the plan for the Hawaii Operation, the Imperial General Headquarters' official name for the Pearl Harbor attack. The Japanese fulfilled their purpose by immobilizing the Pacific Fleet and preventing it from interfering with their moves in the southwest Pacific.

One item of special interest is the Japanese estimate of the strength of the American fleet. Admiral Fukudome emphasizes the element of surprise, which was deemed essential for the success of the mission. Yet it has been noted by such an authority as Fleet Admiral Nimitz that it was fortunate that the United States did not know of the approach of the Japanese task force toward Hawaii, for Admiral Kimmel would

2

have steamed forth to meet it, and in Admiral Nimitz's words, "The Japanese would have sunk every one of our ships in deep water," primarily because of superior air power.[1] Conjecture, of course, but such a fate probably would have met the U.S. Pacific Fleet if it had sailed into the western Pacific to encounter the Imperial Navy within the shelter of its land-based aircraft.

NUMEROUS criticisms have been voiced since the end of the war, both at home and abroad, regarding the Hawaii Operation. As far as the writer's knowledge goes, however, domestic criticism appears to be restricted to the political arena and is aimed solely at blaming the Hawaii Operation for having ignited a rash war. In other words, there seem to be no attempts yet to analyze and criticize the operation from a purely strategic or tactical standpoint.

Naturally enough, this subject has been given the most serious attention by the United States. In his work *The Rising Sun in the Pacific*, volume 3 of *History of U.S. Naval Operations in World War II*, Dr. Samuel Eliot Morison bitterly criticizes the Hawaii Operation in the following manner: "It would be impossible for anyone to find in the annals of history an operational precedent having brought about a more fatal blow upon the aggressor himself than this attack. Tactically speaking, the Japanese committed the blunder in the Pearl Harbor attack of concentrating their attacks only on warships instead of directing them on land installations and fuel tanks. Not only was it strategically a folly, but politically too, it was an unredeemable blunder."[2]

Dr. Morison goes on to remark: "Although they [the Japanese] succeeded in destroying the [U.S.] battleship fleet and wiping out the land air force, they overlooked various naval installations in Pearl Harbor. Among them were repair shops

3

Crewmen aboard a Japanese aircraft carrier cheer as a fighter takes off for the Pearl Harbor attack. *Courtesy of the National Archives*

which later were able to repair those ships damaged in the attack within an astoundingly short space of time. They furthermore did not make attacks upon power facilities and fuel tank dumps which were stored up to their huge capacity. As duly expressed in the opinion of Admiral Thomas S. Hart, commander in chief of the Asiatic Fleet, at the time, the loss of those installations would probably have delayed the U.S. counter-offensive in the Pacific more than did the actual damage to the U.S. vessels."[3]

Dr. Morison explains his contention that, strategically, it was a ridiculous and stupid operation: "If the Japanese forces had not carried out their attack on Pearl Harbor, the Rainbow 5 operational plan, which was to be started with the declaration of war, would have been carried out, and the U.S. Pacific Fleet would have attacked Japanese posts in the Marshall and Caroline archipelagoes, including Truk Island."[4]

This meant that, had the Hawaii Operation not been conducted by the Japanese, the U.S. Fleet would have launched an offensive, and the Japanese navy could accordingly have launched its long-cherished countering operations by calmly remaining in waiting. The Japanese navy had for thirty years been arduously studying and training for the so-called "counter-attack decisive battle against the U.S. Fleet," in which an American onslaught was to be countered and destroyed in the seas adjacent to Japan. This was seen as the only sure way of gaining a victory. No offensive operation against Hawaii had ever been contemplated in the past.

Dr. Morison's contention, therefore, may mean that by carrying out the Hawaii Operation, the Japanese navy committed the folly of forever losing an opportunity to realize its fundamental operational plan. In contending that it was an unredeemable political blunder, moreover, Dr. Morison points out that the Pearl Harbor attack served to arouse the united determination of the American people, fighting under the slogan "Remember Pearl Harbor!," to crush the Japanese Empire.

At complete variance with this view of Dr. Morison's, however, is that held by Admiral William V. Pratt, one of the most illustrious figures of the modern U.S. Navy. In commenting upon the Hawaii Operation in a letter to former Admiral Kichisaburo Nomura, who is his intimate Japanese friend, the American admiral described the Japanese attack upon Pearl Harbor as a most thoroughly planned and daring project—a strategic success with few precedents in history. The question as to which of the two, the historian or the strategist, holds the more correct view will be left to the good judgment of the reader.

Because the Pacific War ended so tragically for the Japanese people, there seem to be some among them who do not wish even to be reminded of the Hawaii Operation, feeling that the entire prosecution of the war was an act of folly. On the other hand, there are a considerable number who feel that those actually concerned in the operation should compile a true and unbiased historical account of it. This essay is a contribution toward that end.

Admiral Shigetaro Shimada, the navy minister at the time Japan went to war, wanted by all means to prevent the United States from becoming an enemy and taxed himself to find some means of enabling Japan to declare war only after the United States had opened hostilities. His idea was for Japan to declare war on Britain and the Netherlands, but to resort to arms against the United States only after being challenged by the latter.

Admiral Shimada had long been with the Naval General Staff when he was appointed navy minister, and he had a profound knowledge of naval operations. He advocated passive operations against the United States, but at the same time requested the Naval General Staff, the office responsible for operations, to make a study of the problem. He preferred, if worst came to worst, to let the United States strike first, enabling Japan to declare war with honor. Had things turned out as Shimada wished, not only would there have been no cry of "Remember Pearl Harbor!" but the political developments pointed out by Dr. Morison would have taken a different course.

Shimada believed there would be little chance to exploit a conquest of Southeast Asia if our long Southern Operation line, stretching far below the equator, was flanked by a dominant American fleet, prepared to strike at the best time and in a manner of its own choosing. A political guarantee of nonintervention by the United States was a desired prerequisite for launching the Southern Operation, but that was out of the question in the situation prevailing both at home and abroad. Since there was no sure political guarantee, it was obvious that the United States would sooner or later join on the side of Britain and the Netherlands in a war against Japan, even if she could be prevented from entry in its early stage.

In reply to the Japanese government's inquiry about its

6

attitude toward Germany, the U.S. government stated in a note dated 16 July 1941, "The use of our right of self-defense against Germany is our own proper responsibility," and moreover, "any state attempting, at this juncture, to compel the United States to remain neutral shall be regarded as belonging to the same camp of aggressors." From its extremely scathing tone, one could readily surmise that the note not only indicated the stern stand of the United States toward Germany but also clarified her attitude toward Japan.

Even though the United States could be kept out of the war for a while, it was absolutely certain that she would not remain an idle spectator forever. Therefore, the final judgment reached in 1941 was that there was no other way for Japan to gain victory except by forestalling America's armed intervention, for a war with the United States had already been deemed inevitable.

Because the Japanese realized that there was no means of isolating the United States from operations in Southeast Asia, the main target of the Japanese navy from the outset was to be the U.S. Fleet, and all other objectives were to be treated as secondary. How to accomplish the destruction of the U.S. Fleet was the grave responsibility entrusted to Admiral Yamamoto, the commander in chief of the Combined Fleet.

During basic maneuvers of the Combined Fleet, held sometime between April and May 1940, I was Admiral Yamamoto's chief of staff. One feature of the exercises was a mock air attack. The fleet skillfully eluded the first and second assault waves of imaginary torpedo bombers but sustained theoretical heavy damage, reducing its strength to one half, when the "enemy" successfully launched aerial torpedoes from both flanks in spite of the skillful elusive action of the fleet.

"There is no means for a surface fleet to elude aerial torpedoes simultaneously launched from both sides," I said to Admiral Yamamoto. "It seems to me that the time is now ripe for a decisive fleet engagement with aerial torpedo attacks as the main striking power."

7

Fleet Admiral Isoroku Yamamoto, commander in chief of the Combined Fleet, who originated the idea of an aerial surprise attack on Pearl Harbor. *Official U.S. Navy photograph*

"Well," replied Yamamoto, "it appears that a crushing blow could be struck on an enemy surface force by mass aerial torpedo attacks executed jointly with shore-based air forces." The admiral was undoubtedly thinking at that moment of the powerful U.S. Fleet concentrated in Pearl Harbor.

Ever since 1909, the Japanese navy had made the U.S. Navy its sole imaginary enemy. It was natural that in the fleet training of 1940, due consideration was given to the strategic situation in which the U.S. Fleet was concentrated in Hawaii and steadily making preparations for war, thus showing its determination to resort to armed intervention in opposition to Japan's policy toward China. The Japanese fleet had for thirty years studied and trained for a decisive fleet counter-offensive as its basic evolution, but such an operation, whose nature was in the final analysis passive, involved the great disadvantage of leaving the initiative in the enemy's hands. Moreover, the situation was such that, as time passed, the balance of naval strength between the two would gradually favor the United States, steadily diminishing Japan's chance to gain a victory. The Japanese navy was accordingly compelled to find some means for assuring an early decisive engagement. Now, with the U.S. Fleet already advanced to its Hawaiian base, it could readily continue to the western Pacific, thus creating a definite threat to Japan. As long as it remained at its Hawaiian base, it created a strategic situation incomparably more tense and threatening to the Japanese than when it was based on the Pacific coast. Every Japanese naval officer realized that a crushing blow would be inflicted if a successful attack was launched on distant Hawaii, depriving the enemy of the initiative and assuring us an impregnable position. It was believed that the Japanese navy, because of the operational limitations of its warships, could not attack Hawaii. But Fleet Admiral Yamamoto, the "father of naval aviation," had long believed that future wars would be decided by air power, and he had improved and developed the Japanese navy's air arm to that end. In consequence, he alone originated the idea of an aerial surprise attack—and thus made the impossible possible.

Upon promotion to rear admiral on 1 November 1939, I was transferred from command of the fleet flagship, the *Nagato,* to duty as chief of staff of the Combined Fleet, under Admiral Yamamoto. In April 1941 I was transferred to duty as chief of the First Bureau of the Naval General Staff. Since my position as chief of the First Bureau placed me in charge of operations, my duties in both capacities associated me with the Hawaii Operation from beginning to end. It may be said that except for the late Admiral Yamamoto, I was the only

9

person acquainted with detailed plans of the operation from the moment of its conception.

"I want a flier whose past career has not influenced him in conventional operations to study this problem," Commander in Chief Yamamoto said, and then asked me what I thought about it. This occurred toward the close of 1940, after the annual fleet training exercises had been completed.

"It is a fine idea, sir," I replied.

"For the time being, I will keep the matter secret from other fleet staff officers, except for the aviator assigned to the problem, and would like to ask you to keep it for your personal study," he said. Thereupon the admiral secretly summoned his selected naval aviator, Rear Admiral Takijiro Ohnishi, and entrusted him with planning the Hawaii Operation.

Ohnishi had long been an airman to the core and had much practical experience, unlike Admiral Yamamoto, whose main experience had been in naval air organization and administration. They were congenial friends of long standing. Since Ohnishi had not been long with the Naval General Staff, there was little fear that he might be hampered by conventional operational doctrine. Moreover, he was noted for his cautious and logical thinking as well as for his vast experience. Admiral Yamamoto could not have made a better choice in his selection of an officer to whom to entrust this important study.

Toward the end of April 1941, Admiral Ohnishi completed the general plan. He called on me at my office in the Naval General Staff and explained his plan: "This operation involves two difficult problems. One of them is the technical difficulty of launching aerial torpedo attacks in Pearl Harbor, which is so shallow that aerial torpedoes launched by ordinary methods would strike the bottom. The other concerns the tactical problem—whether a surprise can be made successfully. This operation apparently cannot be carried out without a surprise element."

Even though he pointed out numerous difficulties involved in the operation, Ohnishi estimated, in the early stage of planning, that it had a sixty percent chance of success. I thought its chance to be forty percent, since I took operational difficulties more seriously than did Ohnishi. Opposition to the operation that was later expressed by the Naval General Staff arose mainly because of my opinion. Had I from the very beginning been entrusted with the study of the idea instead of Ohnishi, I would certainly have recommended to Commander in Chief Yamamoto that the Hawaii Operation be abandoned.

I remember that Ohnishi called on me again in the early part of September 1941 in the Naval General Staff and said that the Hawaii Operation now seemed too risky and he wanted to recommend to Admiral Yamamoto that it be given up. Later Ohnishi, accompanied by Rear Admiral Ryunosuke Kusaka, then chief of staff to Vice Admiral Chuichi Nagumo, who later commanded the Hawaii Operation Force, called on Admiral Yamamoto on board the flagship *Nagato* and earnestly advised him to give up the operation. But Admiral Yamamoto stuck to his guns.

With Japan's resolution to go to war with the United States when necessary—a decision made at the Imperial Conference held on 6 September 1941—war preparations were put in full swing.

Previously, Admiral Yamamoto had received Ohnishi's plan for the Pearl Harbor attack and had made it one of his fleet's operational studies, and his staff continued to work on it. As a result, the admiral succeeded in drafting an operation plan in which he could place full confidence. From about the middle of September, earnest discussions were held between the Naval General Staff and the Combined Fleet headquarters about the general operational plan that was to be carried out in the event of war. With it, the problem of the Hawaii Operation inevitably came to the fore.

11

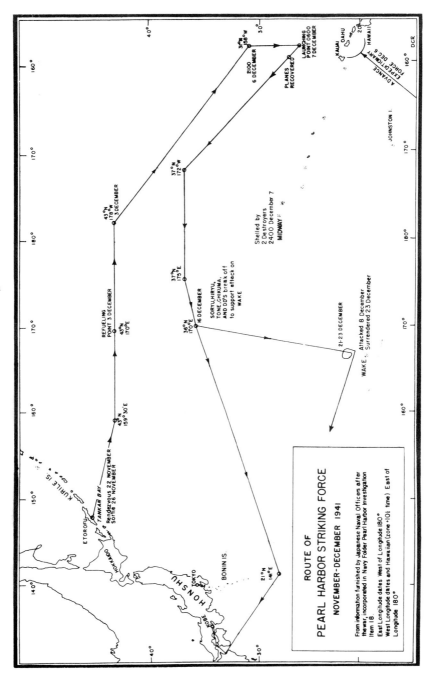

Drawn by David C. Redding for The Rising Sun in the Pacific, *courtesy of Naval Historical Center*

ROUTE OF
PEARL HARBOR STRIKING FORCE
NOVEMBER–DECEMBER 1941

From information furnished by Japanese Naval Officers after the war, incorporated in Navy Folder Pearl Harbor Investigation Item 18.
East Longitude dates West of Longitude 180°
West Longitude dates and Hawaiian (zone +10½ time) East of Longitude 180°

ETOROFU
TANKAN BAY
Rendezvous 22 NOVEMBER
Sortie 26 NOVEMBER

HOKKAIDO
KURILE IS.

HONSHU
TOKYO
KOBE
BONIN IS.

43° N
159° 30' E

43° N
170° E
REFUELING
POINT 3 DECEMBER

43° N
178° W
REFUELING POINT 3 DECEMBER

2100
6 DECEMBER

37° 58' W
35°N

PLANES
RECOVERED

LAUNCHING
POINT 0600
7 DECEMBER

37° N
172° W

37° N
175° E

36° N
170° E
16 DECEMBER

SORYU, HIRYU,
TONE, CHIKUMA,
AND DD'S break off
to support attack on
WAKE

21-23 DECEMBER
WAKE: Attacked 8 December
Surrendered 23 December

Shelled by
2 Destroyers
2400 December 7
MIDWAY

JOHNSTON I.

KAUAI OAHU
HAWAII
ADVANCE
EXPEDITIONARY
FORCE DEC. 6

21° N
141° E

In early October, staff officers of the Combined Fleet went to Tokyo under orders of Admiral Yamamoto and reported to the General Staff that they wanted to launch an attack on Hawaii at the outset of war, if and when it should start. But the General Staff did not approve the proposal, on the ground that the Hawaii Operation was inadvisable from the standpoint of the overall operational concept. The Naval General Staff doubted that the Hawaii Operation would succeed and feared that much would be lost if it failed. Moreover, the staff feared that the operation might have an unfavorable effect on the negotiations then being conducted between the United States and Japan because initiation of the operation was necessary prior to the termination of the negotiations.

The essential objections of the Naval General Staff were five in number:

1) Success of the Hawaii Operation was dependent upon the achievement of surprise.

The powerful American fleet concentrated in Hawaii was too strong for conventional attack by our task force. Without surprise, our fleet could never achieve success. The prerequisite for a successful surprise attack was the secrecy of the movements of its task force. Since the operation was large scale, employing as many as sixty ships that had to be dispatched one month before the outbreak of war in the eastern Pacific, it was likely to attract attention, especially because the southerly advance was generally felt to be Japan's chief strategy in the event of war. In view of the tense international situation, it was believed that the close intelligence network of the United States and Great Britain had been widely extended, and that of their ally, Soviet Russia, was also thought to be dangerous. Therefore, much apprehension centered on whether the secrecy of the operation could be maintained.

Besides, there was the fear that the task force might meet hostile or neutral ships en route to the point of attack. All would be lost if our task force were to meet a ship at sea that sent a radio dispatch stating, "Japanese fleet proceeding eastward in great strength."

13

2) The Hawaii Operation was not so indispensable as to be executed regardless of risk.

Unless a blow was dealt at the outset of war by carrying out the daring Hawaii attack, the American fleet would certainly come out to attack us. It seemed unlikely that the enemy would come straight to our homeland seeking a decisive battle; rather, he would first establish advance bases in the Marshall Islands and then attempt the island-hopping strategy by gradually advancing his bases.

In that case, we would be given ample time to concentrate all our available strength in the decisive contact engagement for which our navy had long studied and trained. It would be wiser to seek a decisive battle in familiar waters than to attempt the Hawaii Operation with its risk of failure.

3) Almost all naval vessels participating in the Hawaii Operation would have to be refueled at sea en route, destroyers at least twice.

Since the establishment of the Imperial Defense Policy in 1909, the Japanese navy had accepted defensive operations against the United States as its fundamental policy, so that the radius of action of our ships and planes was generally short. Meteorological statistics showed that on only seven days during the month were conditions favorable for refueling destroyers at sea on the north Pacific route the fleet would have to take to avoid commercial traffic lanes. If refueling could not be carried out, not only would the Hawaii Operation fail, but all the units involved would have been uselessly diverted from other planned operations.

Last, one hitch was apt to lead to another. If refueling at sea met with difficulties, radio dispatches would have to be transmitted. Radio transmission would immediately break the secrecy of the operational force's movement, thus tragically spoiling the elaborately planned operation at the last moment. A good example of this was seen later in the Battle of Midway. Should the secrecy of the Hawaii Operation be broken en route to the attack, not only would the Hawaii

14

attack force itself be endangered, but the indispensable Southern Operation as a whole would be adversely affected.

4) There was a high probability that the task force would be spotted by enemy patrol planes at the point from which the attacking planes were to be launched, with consequent enemy interdiction.

Alertness around the Hawaiian Islands had gradually been intensified. The radio intelligence section of the Naval General Staff knew that the daily air patrol had been extended to six hundred miles from Oahu. Since our carrier force had to close to within two hundred miles of the target, there was a considerable risk that it might be counterattacked by the enemy before launching its attacks.

5) The operation would break down the negotiations between the United States and Japan.

The navy did not give up hope of success in the negotiations until the last moment. Admiral Osami Nagano, chief of the Naval General Staff, had placed much hope in Admiral Kichisaburo Nomura, the ambassador in Washington, who was one of his close friends. Nagano, who had believed that "nothing can be done here in Japan with the negotiations between the United States and Japan, and that only Admiral Nomura could break the deadlock," rejoiced greatly at the news received from Ambassador Nomura about 20 October to the effect that there was some hope of solving the stalemate. The chief of staff repeatedly told me, "Nomura is a great fellow, and no one but he could succeed." The firm confidence Nagano had in Nomura may well be seen from the fact that, even when Admiral Yamamoto came up to Tokyo on 1 December on his last visit, the policy of withdrawing all forces in the event of a favorable turn to the negotiations was confirmed between Nagano and Yamamoto.

In the meantime, Admiral Yamamoto, as commander in chief of the Combined Fleet, had trained his fleet in the Inland Sea and had drawn up emergency operational plans. After

15

receiving his staff's report that they had failed to secure the approval of the Naval General Staff for the Hawaii Operation, upon which he placed the utmost importance, the admiral elaborated on his plan. Rear Admiral Ugaki, chief of staff, and other staff officers went up to Tokyo again to submit his recommendation to the General Staff. Salient points stressed on that occasion were as follows:

> The present situation, i.e., that of the U.S. Fleet in the Hawaiian Islands, is, strategically speaking, tantamount to a dagger pointed at our throat. Should war be declared under these circumstances, the length and breadth of our Southern Operation would immediately be exposed to a serious threat on its flank. In short, the Hawaii Operation is absolutely indispensable for successful accomplishment of the Southern Operation.
>
> Moreover, when we consider the naval strength ratio between the United States and Japan, we see that we would have no chance of victory unless a decisive attack was launched at the earliest possible opportunity. Therefore, the Hawaii Operation is truly indispensable to the accomplishment of the mission assigned the Japanese navy. Unless it is carried out, the commander in chief of the Combined Fleet has no confidence that he can fulfill his assigned responsibility.
>
> This operation is beset with numerous difficulties, none of which, however, makes it impossible. What concerns us most is the weather; but if there are seven days in a month when refueling at sea is possible, the chance of success is by no means small. If good fortune is bestowed on us, we will be assured of success. Should the Hawaii Operation by chance end in failure, that would merely imply that fortune is not on our side. That should also be the time for definitely halting all operations.

An extremely grim resolution could be clearly read between those lines.

After carefully listening to the vice chief of staff's detailed explanation of Yamamoto's real intention and his practical

16

The *Kaga* launched planes for the Pearl Harbor attack. She was later sunk by U.S. carrier aircraft in the Battle of Midway, 4 June 1942.

plan, Nagano, as chief of staff, finally gave his verdict on the issue: "If he has that much confidence, it's better to let Yamamoto go ahead."

As far as the navy was concerned, with these words the Hawaii Operation was formally approved as a plan. Needless to say, the Naval General Staff thereafter did its best to make this operation successful. At the same time, it also drew up a plan whereby the Hawaii Operation force would turn back immediately in the event that a setback or hitch occurred en route.

At the Imperial Conference held on 6 September 1941 it was decided that, "in view of the potentiality of the empire's national strength, Japan is determined without delay to go to war with the United States (and Great Britain and the Netherlands) in the event that there is little prospect of achieving our aims by as late as early October." This decision meant that, considering the possible severance of the flow of essential imports because of the embargo against this country by the so-called ABCD (American-British-Chinese-Dutch) ring, no time should be wasted if and when war was finally deemed unavoidable. Of those essential materials, particular importance was placed on oil.

"One of the major causes for this war, I think," said Admiral Nagano in the U.S. Strategic Bombing Survey's interrogation conducted after the war, "was the oil problem. Not

17

only the army and navy, but the government also, showed a great concern over this problem, because this country faced a serious oil shortage, since the United States, Britain, and the Netherlands refused to sell oil to our country."

"We believed that we would be able to get oil from the southern region," stated Ambassador Nomura during the same interrogation. "Our oil resources were so limited that we had to secure oil from those islands at all costs."

The Japanese navy's operational plan called for a stockpile of oil for two years' consumption as the minimum prerequisite for going to war. Thanks to its oil policy, which had been followed for a long time, the Japanese navy had stored up enough oil to meet that demand, but the army had barely done so. Therefore, a further continuation of the oil import embargo was considered intolerable for maintaining Japan's fighting strength. War should be avoided, if possible; but if and when war was finally deemed unavoidable, the sooner it was started, the better.

Of course, the oil problem was not the only factor determining the time for going to war. There were many other factors, both political and military. One was the possibility that the operation might well be hampered by foul weather during the northeast monsoon season. Another was preserving the secrecy of the operation prior to the outbreak of the war. From the operational standpoint, it was apparent that "one day's delay would mean one day's disadvantage." Reflecting the tense international situation, war preparations in the ABCD ring were rapidly going forward. The U.S. Fleet standing by at Hawaii was improving its war preparations, and the U.S. Army Air Force in the Philippines and British air strength in Singapore were rapidly being augmented.

When the Ogikubo Conference was held, on 12 October 1941, in which the final attitude of the third Konoye Cabinet toward "peace or war" was decided, Admiral Oikawa, the navy minister, stated the navy's view:

"Now we have reached a crossroads where a choice for

18

peace or war should be made. Speaking for the navy, we will find ourselves at a complete loss, if asked to go to war, until such time as the current negotiations between the U.S. and Japan reach a deadlock."

Believing that an early commencement of operations would be advantageous for the aforementioned reasons, the Imperial General Headquarters originally intended to go to war on 1 December. But when top-ranking army and navy officers, including General Terauchi and Admiral Yamamoto, assembled in Tokyo at the beginning of November 1941 for a briefing on the Southern Operation, the date was postponed to 8 December (Tokyo time) by request of Yamamoto, who considered a successful execution of the Hawaii Operation a prerequisite. Yamamoto indicated complete accord with the idea of attacking the U.S. fleet on Sunday, when the ships were more likely to be in Pearl Harbor for the weekend, but he preferred the second Sunday of December over the first because his fleet would not have sufficient time to prepare for the original date. The Imperial General Headquarters approved his request.

Thus it was decided to raise the curtain of the Pacific War, with the first attack on Hawaii to be launched at 0830 of 8 December (7 December, Hawaii time).

Because approval of Yamamoto's Hawaii attack plan by Nagano, chief of the General Staff, meant no more than an informal decision within the naval command, various procedures had to be worked out before a formal decision could be made. Under the old Japanese constitution, the opening of hostilities was the prerogative of the emperor's supreme command. The chief of the Naval General Staff was responsible to the throne for naval operations. After the China Incident in 1937, the Imperial General Headquarters had been established, its membership being the chiefs of the army and navy general staffs and the ministers of both the war and the navy departments. It was, therefore, necessary for the chief of the

Naval General Staff to propose the plan of the Hawaii Operation to the chief of the Army General Staff and also to the ministers of the war and the navy departments.

The operation plan had also to be discussed at the Liaison Conference between the government and the high command. The Liaison Conference had been established about a year before, when the need for a supreme body to maintain close and smooth relations between military strategy and politics was keenly felt as a result of the China Incident. The first meeting of the conference was held on 27 July 1940. This body, which later became the Supreme War Conference, was composed of the premier, the foreign minister, the war minister, the navy minister, and the chiefs of the army and navy general staffs as regular members. When necessary, the finance minister and the minister of the interior also attended the conference. But since the Hawaii Operation was an important operation that required top-secret security, it was disclosed only to the premier and the foreign minister in addition to the army and navy members of the conference.

After the above procedures were followed, the chief of the Naval General Staff asked for imperial sanction, thus formally acknowledging it as the Japanese navy's operational plan. This occurred on 5 November 1941.

On the same day, Imperial Naval General Staff Order No. 1 was issued ordering the Combined Fleet to make operational preparations:

Imperial Naval General Staff Order No. 1

5 Nov. 1941

To: Commander in Chief, Combined Fleet, Isoroku Yamamoto

Via: Chief of Naval General Staff Osami Nagano

By Imperial Order

1) The Empire has decided to schedule various operational preparations for completion in the early part of December in view of great fears that she will be obliged to go

to war with the United States, Britain, and the Netherlands for her self-existence and self-defense.

2) The commander in chief, Combined Fleet, will make necessary operational preparations.

3) Detailed instructions will be given by the chief of the Naval General Staff.

How to integrate diplomatic policies and military operations is a problem of the utmost importance. The case of the last Pacific War was no exception. Since the war was to be started by the attack upon Hawaii, the manner in which Japan timed the commencement of that attack and the sending of the ultimatum to the United States still leaves much room for discussion as an important subject related both to government administration and to the high command.

The Hawaii Operation obviously could not be conducted without surprise. This is the reason it was decided that the war was to be started with that operation. Under no circumstances should diplomatic steps be taken that would give the United States time to prepare countermeasures to our surprise attack.

Because international law experts maintained that it is legal to declare war if the declaration precedes the commencement of hostilities—even if only one or one-half second in advance (the interval of time is of no concern)— it was believed that the operation could be carried out in accordance with diplomatic usage if the declaration could be sent to the United States at such a time as to prevent her from making preparations. In this way, it was expected, no hitch in the execution of the operations would occur. Thus the government and the high command mutually decided to send the declaration in accordance with international law.

The issue of Japan's sending the declaration after the attack is a complicated one. After the war, the late declaration was one of the important charges made by the Far East Interna-

21

tional Military Tribunal. To this day, even after this country has regained her sovereignty, some people still seem to entertain doubts about the declaration.

The indictment filed in the Far East International Military Tribunal included three categories of charges: first, offense against peace (charges 1 to 36); second, offense of murder (charges 37 to 52); and third, ordinary war crimes and offense against humanity (charges 53 to 55).

To these charges Mr. Kiyose, a lawyer representing the defense counsel, delivered a refutation in his introductory argument. He pointed out that article 10 of the Potsdam Declaration stated, "We do not intend that the Japanese shall be enslaved as a race or destroyed as a nation, but stern justice shall be meted out to all war criminals, including those who have visited cruelties upon our prisoners." Accordingly, the terms laid down at Potsdam, Kiyose asserted, "constituted the only grounds for the war crime tribunal. Since Japan accepted that declaration because she was defeated in the Pacific War, the crime tribunal should be limited to those crimes committed in the course of that war, but not to such cases in 1928 as were included in the indictment." Kiyose pointed out six additional areas in which Japan should be beyond the jurisdiction of the military tribunal. As one of those seven points, Kiyose strongly insisted that the offense of murder should not exist in war—not only from the point of view of international law, but also from that of custom.

Murder was charged in the indictment from the beginning, with the Pearl Harbor attack as its case in point. Since that attack was made without a declaration of war, it disregarded international law. The prosecution charged, therefore, that the attack constituted murder.

At 2:20 P.M. on 7 December (Washington time), Japan's declaration addressed to the U.S. government was formally delivered by Ambassadors Nomura and Kurusu to Secretary of State Cordell Hull at the State Department. The original schedule called for its delivery at 1:00 P.M. (Washington time), which was 8:00 P.M. Hawaii time, thirty minutes before the scheduled time of the attack upon Hawaii.

As it turned out, the declaration was not delivered until 2:20 P.M., due to a mishap. This caused the declaration, which should have been delivered thirty minutes *before* the commencement of the attack, to be given to the U.S. government about one hour *after* the actual attack. The prosecution charged that the attack launched before the delivery of the declaration was an unlawful one that constituted the crime of murder. The prosecution furthermore contended that sending the declaration was nothing but a trick conceived by the Japanese government and the military, which had from the outset no intention of sending it before the commencement of the attack but used it as an excuse for their disregard of international law. The prosecution even branded it as the same kind of trick as the dispatching of Ambassador Kurusu to the United States just before the outbreak of war in an attempt to camouflage the intention of going to war.

If the Pearl Harbor attack was judged to constitute murder, many top military leaders at the time of the outbreak of war, including Admiral Nagano, would have to be indicted for murder. The development of the controversy was accordingly watched with keen attention by all Japanese officials.

From November to December 1945 I was questioned about the Hawaii attack by Mr. Keenan and four other prosecutors. A surprise attack cannot be censured of itself, as it is a tactic that has been most ardently advocated both in Japan and abroad. The issue under dispute was whether the attack on Pearl Harbor violated international law because it had been launched without a previous declaration of war. Although I explained the situation in as much detail as I could, the prosecutors seemed to be prejudiced by their first suspicion, i.e., that the attack was a trick planned by the Japanese, who had no real intention of declaring war before the commencement of hostilities. Examinations on this point were also made of other persons concerned with the Pearl Harbor attack, but the indictment presented to the tribunal showed that the prosecutors refused to change their previous view. Prosecutor Higgins severely attacked the Hawaii Operation as treacherous.

All charges of murder (charges 37 to 52), however, were dismissed by the ruling that only offenses against peace would be subject to the judgment of the tribunal. In effect, the court made the decision that it had no jurisdiction in connection with the murder charge.

The operational units employed in the Hawaii Operation were divided into two groups: the Task Force, whose main objective was aerial attacks, and the Submarine Force, whose main objective was submarine attacks. Vice Admiral Chuichi Nagumo, commander in chief of the First Air Fleet, was appointed as the overall commander.

The units of the Task Force were organized as follows: After completing their war preparation at the Kure Naval Station, the thirty-three warships—six carriers, two battleships, two heavy cruisers, one light cruiser, eleven destroyers, three submarines, and eight tankers—left their bases in several groups during the period from 10 to 18 November 1941. By 22 November they had assembled at Hitokappu (Tankan) Bay, on the southern coast of Etorofu Island in the Kurile Islands. The crews were informed for the first time of their grave mission of launching attacks upon Hawaii, and they exhibited excellent morale. Presumably there had been no discovery of the plan by foreign agents.

On 25 November Yamamoto issued an order that "the Task Force will proceed to Hawaiian waters and, under a separate order to be issued later, operate in such manner as to destroy the U.S. Fleet at the outset of war." The order was supplemented by instructions calling for an immediate withdrawal of all Hawaii Operation forces in case diplomatic negotiations were successfully concluded between Japan and the United States.

At 6:00 P.M. on 26 November, in a dense fog, the Task Force sortied from Hitokappu Bay into the northern Pacific en route to its historic attack.

In conjunction with the movements of the Task Force, submarines of the Submarine Force were stealthily converging on Hawaii from other directions.

The Submarine Force was organized as follows: These twenty-seven submarines, the cream of the Combined Fleet, had undergone the most rigid training over a long period. As the General Staff estimated the chance of a successful aerial attack by the Task Force to be fifty percent, they considered it necessary to have the Submarine Force participate in the Hawaii Operation and launch underwater attacks coordinated with the aerial attacks. A plan was accordingly made to encircle Oahu Island with all available crack submarines at the time of the aerial attack on the U.S. Fleet in Pearl Harbor. These submarines were not only to sink enemy vessels confused by the aerial attack, but also to intercept enemy reinforcements and supplies from the West Coast. The submarines had to be sent to their assigned positions in advance

Mitsubishi dive-bombers warm up before takeoff. *Courtesy of the National Archives*

Units	Mission	Commander
First Carrier Div. (*Akagi* and *Kaga*) Second Carrier Div. (*Soryu* and *Hiryu*) Fifth Carrier Div. (*Zuikaku* and *Shokaku*)	Aerial attack	Vice Adm. Nagumo, CinC, First Air Fleet
First Des. Sqd. (*Abukuma*) Seventeenth Des. Div. (*Tanikaze, Urakaze, Isokaze,* and *Hamakaze*) Eighteenth Des. Div. (*Kazumi, Arare, Kagero,* and *Shiranuhi*)	Guard and escort	Rear Adm. Sentaro Omori, First Des. Sqd. commander
Third BB Div. (*Hiei* and *Kirishima*) Eighth Cruiser Div. (*Tone* and *Chikuma*)	Guard and support	Vice Adm. Gun'ichi Mikawa, Third BB Div. commander
Second Sub. Div. (*I-19, I-21, I-23*)	Patrol	Capt. Kijiro Imaizumi, Second Sub. Div. commander
Seventh Des. Div. (*Sazanami, Ushio*)	Bombardment of Midway Island	Capt. Kaname Konishi, Seventh Des. Div. commander

First Supply Train (*Kyokuto Maru, Ken'yo Maru, Kokuyo Maru, Shinkoku Maru, Akebono Maru*)	Supply	
Second Supply Train (*Toho Maru, Toei Maru,* and *Nihon Maru*)		
Katori (cruiser)	Flagship of Sixth Fleet	Vice Adm. Mitsumi Shimizu, Sixth Fleet commander
First Sub Sqd. (*I-9, I-15, I-17, I-25*)	Blockade of Oahu and raiding operations	Rear Adm. Tsutomu Sato, First Sub. Sqd. commander
Second Sub. Sqd. (*I-7, I-1, I-2, I-3, I-4, I-5, I-6*)	Same as above	Rear Adm. Shigeaki Yamazaki, Second Sub. Sqd. commander
Third Sub. Sqd. (*I-8, I-74, I-75, I-68, I-69, I-71, I-72, I-73*)	Same as above	Rear Adm. Shigeyoshi Miwa, Third Sub. Sqd. commander
(*I-16, I-18, I-20, I-22, I-24*)	Special attack unit*	Capt. Hanku Sasaki
(*I-10, I-26*)	Reconnaissance of key points	Cdr. Yasuchika Kashihara

*Each submarine of the Special Attack Unit took a midget sub on board.

of the Task Force in order to reconnoiter Hawaiian waters. That is why the submarine force was named the Advance Force.

Among those responsible for the operation, I counted heavily on the activities of the Submarine Force. It was my belief that, even if the Task Force's aerial attack ended in failure, the Submarine Force's operation would not fail. My belief was based on the expectation that no hitch would arise in the submarines' operations. The submarines had a cruising radius of ten thousand miles and no need of refueling at sea. Besides, they were best suited for stealthy movements, and a blockading operation of Hawaii would be very easy for the highly trained Japanese submariners. Furthermore, I expected that more damage would be inflicted by submarine attacks, which would be continued over a longer period, than by the air attacks, which would be of comparatively short duration.

The Submarine Force left Kure and Yokosuka between 18 and 20 November and proceeded to Kwajalein in the Marshall Islands, where the final refueling was carried out. Then they headed straight for their operational positions.

Thus, the Hawaii attack force proceeded eastward, the Task Force taking the northern course and the Submarine Force the southern. The strictest radio silence was maintained all the way.

On 2 December the famous code-word telegram, "Climb Mount Niitaka," was received from Admiral Yamamoto. It meant that the date for opening hostilities had been set for 8 December as scheduled, and that the attacks would be made as planned.

No obstacles were encountered in the movements of any of the operational forces. The weather, which the General Staff and the operational forces feared most, eventually turned out favorably, and the secrecy of the operation was safely maintained by the grace of Heaven. Although fear no longer existed that a change of plan would be necessary, there was one factor that we could not determine until the last moment. It was whether the U.S. Fleet would be in Pearl Harbor at the time the attack was launched. If it was not there or within the limits of our attack radius after it had departed for maneuvers and training, the operational objective would be lost. By means of secret intelligence, designated "A" information, we could learn of the daily activities of the U.S. Fleet in Pearl Harbor until the day before the attack. The last information on the enemy that the attack force received was:

> Received 2050, 7 December
> "A" Information (issued 1800, 7 December)
> *Utah* and a seaplane tender entered harbor the evening of 5 December.
> Ships in harbor as of 6 December:
> 9 BB, 3 CL, 3 seaplane tender, 17 DD
> In docks: 4 CL, 3 DD
> All carriers and heavy cruisers at sea. No special reports on the fleet. Oahu is quiet and Imperial General Staff is fully convinced of success.

This last information gave us confidence that the enemy fleet would be in the harbor, and therefore everyone concerned with the Hawaii Operation felt relieved. But at the same time it worried me that there were no enemy carriers in the harbor. This was of the utmost importance. Not only would our force be unable to destroy them, but we might in turn be attacked by them. Carriers and cruisers had been going in and out of the harbor for several days, and it was thought that they were at sea for training; but at the same time there was the possibility that they might be in Lahaina, a customary training anchorage. If so, it was estimated that those enemy carriers and cruisers would be discovered by submarine reconnaissance prior to the aerial attack, and that they could be attacked and destroyed by submarines even if the aerial attack failed to get them.

But actual events were entirely contrary to this estimate. Except for the USS *Enterprise*, which was then steaming two hundred miles off Oahu Island, the carriers and heavy cruisers were far away in waters near Wake Island for training exercises against the Japanese. It was only learned after the war that the Nagumo force, on its return to Japan after the attack, passed those ships at a distance of about five hundred miles to the north. Had these forces met, the first engagement in history between carriers would have occurred.

Although the "A" information of the day before the attack reported, as already mentioned, the presence of nine battleships, seven light cruisers, three seaplane tenders, and twenty destroyers in the harbor, there were actually eight battleships, two heavy cruisers, six light cruisers, twenty-nine destroyers, five submarines, one gunboat, nine minelayers, ten minesweepers, ten seaplane tenders, three repair ships, two oilers, two ocean tugs, one hospital ship, one surveying ship, one supply vessel, one ammunition vessel, one submarine rescue ship, one antique cruiser, and one submarine tender—totaling ninety-four vessels—in harbor when the air attack hit. As a result of the attack, six battleships were sunk, two others were seriously damaged, and one heavy cruiser and two oilers were sunk. Heavy damages were also inflicted upon one heavy cruiser, six light cruisers, three destroyers, and three auxiliary vessels.

Damages inflicted upon the enemy air force were no less heavy. The United States admitted that in the Pearl Harbor attack heavier damages were inflicted on the air force than on the surface force. When attacked from the air by surprise, warships can retaliate, as they actually did, but planes lined up wing to wing were absolutely defenseless. Maintenance crews and fliers at several bases on Oahu did all they could, and bravely fought even by mounting displaced airplane machine-guns on work benches and trash boxes. But most of the U.S. air force on the islands was destroyed before such makeshift defense measures became effective. Ninety-nine navy and sixty-five army planes were destroyed and many others damaged.

30

As a result of the attack, a total of 2,403 navy, army, and civilian personnel were killed and 1,178 wounded.

It was most noteworthy that all this damage was inflicted by the air attack, not by the submarine attack, upon which so much hope had originally been placed.

In comparison with the damages inflicted, our attack force lost eight fighters, fifteen dive-bombers, and five bombers. In addition, one flier was killed in a plane and several were wounded. Seventy-four planes were holed. One submarine and five midget subs of the Submarine Force failed to return.

Few could doubt the tactical success of the Hawaii Operation after comparing damages inflicted on both sides. Dr. Morison's criticism of the Hawaii Operation was focused on the point that in undertaking the attack, the Japanese overlooked a greater victory that they could easily have gained.

When it is recalled that the success of this air attack upon Pearl Harbor nullified the U.S. Navy's Rainbow No. 5 operational plan, and that it took two full years for that navy to recover its strength, and further, that our forces in the meantime were able to complete without interruption the occupation of the Southern Resources Area, we who are students of strategy cannot agree with Dr. Morison's criticism that assailed the tactics employed by the Japanese. If the Japanese navy had not launched the Hawaii attack and had consequently encountered the U.S. Fleet advancing on the Marshall and West Caroline Islands in pursuance of their Rainbow No. 5 operational plan, it would have been impossible for the Japanese navy to have inflicted greater damage than it did in the Pearl Harbor attack, however favorable an estimate may be applied to the case.

Dr. Morison's view maintains that, from the political standpoint as well, the operation was a foolish one, for the attack incited the Americans to adopt the slogan "Remember Pearl Harbor!" Their firm determination to defeat Japan made the idea of a negotiated peace absolutely untenable to them. But does this really hit the nail on the head? Although the Pearl Harbor attack really angered the Americans, it is

31

inconceivable that their fighting spirit depended on the point on which the first attack was made, since Japan in any case would have declared war, attacked U.S. forces, and occupied enemy territory. I cannot agree with Dr. Morison's view.

Everyone knows that the Japanese submarines were a total failure in the Pearl Harbor attack. There are many descriptions and discussions of the air operations at Pearl Harbor, as well as of the special attack kamikaze at the last stage of World War II, but there is almost no mention made of the special attack forces' midget submarines. For this reason I should like to describe their operations in particular.

Toward evening on 18 November 1941, five large submarines—*I-16, I-18, I-20, I-22,* and *I-24* of the Special Attack Unit under the command of Captain Hanku Sasaki—secretly left the Kure Naval Station and headed eastward. Each of them carried a secret weapon called Target A, which was stored in a large tube on deck. These secret weapons were the midget submarines that tried to penetrate deep into Pearl Harbor on 7 December with the air attack.

Incidentally, the midget submarine was not a weapon that was produced overnight for use in the Pearl Harbor attack but a product of the tireless work of technicians over a period of many years. Back in 1933, a group of torpedo technicians got a hint from "A Sure Hit with Human-Piloted Torpedo," advocated by Captain Noriyoshi Yokoo, who distinguished himself as one of the heroes of the Port Arthur Blockade Unit in the Russo-Japanese War, and started to study a method of "assuring a hit by releasing a torpedo piloted by one man from a mother torpedo."[5] For security reasons, this mother torpedo was named Target A, and it was this midget submarine that participated in the Pearl Harbor attack.

Why, then, was such a weapon produced? The mission assigned the Japanese navy since the establishment of the national policy in 1909 was to safeguard the national security by using inferior strength against the superior strength of our potential enemy, the U.S. Navy. Since then, all aspects of strategy, tactics, preparations, education, and training had been concerned with the principal objective of gaining a victory over the U.S. Navy. Particular emphasis was placed on the use of submarines and long-range torpedoes in a decisive fleet engagement as a method to be employed by our inferior naval strength. A weakness inherent to the submarine was her slow submerged speed, a disadvantage that often made her miss an opportunity to attack. The limited range of torpedoes often made them unsuccessful in attacks. The answer to the problem of how to utilize the advantages of both submarines and torpedoes and overcome their defects in a decisive battle materialized in this Target A.

Its characteristics, which showed a considerable enlargement over the early types, were in general as follows:

Total length	2 meters
Diameter	2 meters
Underwater displacement	50 tons
Torpedo tubes	2
Torpedoes	2
Underwater speed	19 knots
Radius of action	Capable of making 8-hour run at low speed after 50-minute underwater run at 19 knots
Crew	2

In shape it was an enlarged replica of a torpedo, to which a small conning tower was attached. Midget submarines were successfully constructed about one year after work on them was started. Then the building of their three tenders, the *Chitose, Mizuho,* and *Nisshin,* was begun with the objective of using them in a decisive battle against the main body of the enemy's forces. In the spring of 1941, the first test launching of a midget sub from the *Chitose* was successfully conducted.

Although those midget submarines were originally built for use in a decisive engagement, a study was conducted of various methods of employing them in other operations, and we

33

became convinced that they could be effectively used against vessels at anchor in a harbor. Since studies and preparation for the Hawaii aerial attack were being made at that time, all Target A personnel ardently wished to volunteer for a special attack. Their requests were granted, and some eventually penetrated Pearl Harbor on 7 December. At the start of hostilities, twenty midget subs had been completed, of which five participated in the Hawaii Operation as the special attack unit.

Since the success of the aerial attack was of primary importance for the Hawaii Operation, those midget submarines were directed to first lie in wait outside the harbor and then stealthily enter to attack after the air strike began. It was extremely difficult to determine the results of the midget submarine attacks because of the confusion that followed the aerial attack, and also because none of the five subs returned to report. But the Japanese military, and the people as well, believed in their success before the facts were uncovered after the war. These erroneous opinions were principally based on the fact that one of our submarines on watch outside the harbor entrance the night of 7 December observed a huge explosion inside the harbor at 2101 Hawaii time, and also on the fact that a secret message that stated "succeeded to make attack" was received from one of the midget subs at 2241 that night. According to records made public by the United States after the war, however, only two of them finally succeeded in entering the harbor, and no torpedo hits were scored.

Similar attacks by midget submarines were later made in Sydney Harbor, Australia, and Diego Suarez, Madagascar Island. Each was recognized as a valiant and glorious act of warfare conducted in the name of special attacks and excelling all the former deeds of the so-called suicide bands.

In a strict sense, however, there was some distinction between the midget submarine special attack and the special attacks widely conducted toward the end of the war. The difference was that a means for rescuing crews was provided in the midget sub special attack, while in the later attacks there were actual body crashes in which there was no hope of returning alive. For example, when the plan of Target A was advanced in the early part of 1933, Fleet Admiral Prince Fushimi, then chief of the Naval General Staff, gave his approval only after he was assured that "this weapon is not to be used for body-crashing." And when midget sub attacks were planned for the Pearl Harbor attack, Admiral Yamamoto, commander in chief of the Combined Fleet, gave his consent only after his staffs had exhaustively studied the feasibility of rescuing crews of midget subs as well as their chances of survival. As a matter of fact, those midget subs possessed sufficient cruising radius to return to a safe point outside the harbor after completing their attacks in the harbor. Upon reaching this point, they were to be picked up by the waiting mother submarines.

But none of the ten men who participated in the attack expected to return alive. They were determined to hit by ramming themselves, their spirit being identical with that of later special attack units. Ensign Sakamaki, whose boat went aground outside the bay owing to engine trouble, had the misfortune of becoming the first POW of the war. Mr. Matsura Hashimoto, who was the torpedo officer of the *I-16*, which released Sakamaki's midget sub outside Pearl Harbor, wrote in his book *I-58 Safely Returns to Base:*

> When Ensign Sakamaki's personal effects which were left behind were checked, his hair and nails were found carefully wrapped up together with a letter of farewell addressed to his parents. Even the required postage was attached to the list of addresses to whom these keepsakes were to be forwarded. The balance of his money had been given to his boy. The special precaution he took to prevent matches (to be used for destroying his boat) from getting wet by wrapping them in oil paper was proof of the grim

determination of this young officer who did not expect to return alive.

As previously stated, Dr. Morison severely criticized the Japanese aerial attack for committing a strategic blunder in selecting its targets. He even said that it was the height of folly for Japan not to have attacked land military installations, especially oil tanks, since much more damage would have been inflicted by setting those oil tanks on fire than by directing attacks on battleships in the harbor.

I think that if Vice Admiral Nagumo had executed two or more air attacks, he would undoubtedly have ordered those oil tanks and other military installations on land attacked. But Nagumo had planned from the beginning only one wave of air attacks on Pearl Harbor, and he selected for his targets the direct battle forces rather than the indirect military elements, and decided to concentrate all air attacks on ships and planes. In my opinion, Nagumo made the best choice of targets for the simple attack he launched.

Another argument among military students both at home and abroad about this aerial attack concerns the number of attacks. Why did the Japanese air force, blessed with such a rare opportunity, discontinue its attacks after launching only a single one? Why didn't it exploit the gains made by repeating attacks upon the enemy two or three times? These criticisms, in other words, implied that had the Japanese repeated their attacks several times for two days, as the U.S. task forces did later in the war, almost all of the naval craft in Pearl Harbor, numbering one hundred, would have been completely destroyed, and land military installations also would have been wiped out.

But I do not agree with this view. It was not before 1944, three years after the war started, that U.S. task forces could gain control of the sea; by this time the Japanese navy had lost its integral fighting strength tactically as well as strategically. U.S. forces had become so powerful that they no longer

36

encountered a rival anywhere. There was no need for them to risk a surprise attack, as the Japanese navy had in the Hawaii Operation. They could launch an attack in strength anytime and anywhere they wished. To compare those attacks of the U.S. task forces with our Hawaii Operation can only be called irrational.

No greater surprise attack could have been planned than the Hawaii Operation. Our estimate of the available strength and state of preparation of the American forces precluded any advance plan for launching repeated attacks lasting two or three days.

But a war situation is liable to undergo kaleidoscopic changes. To alter original plans to meet the actual circumstances of an engagement, therefore, is left entirely to the discretion of the commander in the area.

This is a criticism that does not hit the mark. The fact that there were no enemy carriers in the harbor meant that enemy carrier-borne air forces might suddenly come out to attack our force while our planes were attacking Pearl Harbor. Since our force achieved much greater results in its initial attack than had been expected, Nagumo might even be credited with wisdom in his decision to terminate the attacks instead of going too far with them.

One thing I regret is that Nagumo's aerial reconnaissance over the entire area within the radius of his attacks was not sufficient. Because he had already been informed by the "A" information the night before that there were no enemy carriers in the harbor, he should have conducted a thorough and close air reconnaissance over the whole area to locate targets of attack as well as to safeguard his own force from their attacks. Had such air reconnaissance been carried out, the *Enterprise*, which was then sailing within two hundred miles of Hawaii, should have been discovered. I think there would have been no occasion for criticism of Nagumo's conduct in the Hawaii Operation if he had repeated the attack on Pearl Harbor just once more while carrying out air reconnaissance over the entire area more closely. At the same time, he would have gone too far under the circumstances had he repeated attacks more than three times.

Admiral Nagumo's insufficient air reconnaissance around his force was not limited to this case. In the Midway operation in May 1942 he committed the same blunder, as a result of which the Japanese navy sustained fatal damage and a crippling blow to subsequent naval operations. Although those facts were kept secret at the time in the interests of the war's direction, they are now well known to the public.

2

The
Air
Attack
on
Pearl
Harbor

MITSUO
FUCHIDA

An eyewitness account of an event often provides insights for which there is no substitute. On the other hand, such reports often suffer from a kind of myopia, which results in a distorted view of the actual situation. In the following selection, Captain Fuchida presents a highly personal but comprehensive description of the tactical aspects of the daring raid on the U.S. Fleet and American installations at Pearl Harbor. Although troubled by doubts about the wisdom of the operation, he threw himself wholeheartedly into the task and worked devotedly to overcome the technical difficulties that at times seemed insuperable.

The narrative portrays the participant's anxieties and his feeling of relief as successive anticipated obstacles failed to materialize and it appeared that fate, providence, or chance had conspired to provide every opportunity for success. The morale of the officers and men, excellent at the start, improved with each favorable omen, and anticipation mounted to a fever pitch as the task force approached its target. Yet not until the last moment was Captain Fuchida able to feel "the bitterness of war," that extra motivation which has inspired men to almost superhuman performance in battle.

Errors in execution during the bombing runs, primarily due to faulty communications, apparently had little effect on the outcome. Defects in formation and approach that should have been foreseen could not be modified after they were detected, and these shortcomings in planning and implementation could have proved fatal if the Japanese had been confronted with a more alert adversary. And the merits of another strike, urged by Captain Fuchida and others but rejected by Admiral Nagumo for understandable if not overwhelming reasons, continue to be debated. But it became evident that never again would the Imperial Japanese Navy have such an opportunity to administer a real death blow to the U.S. Pacific Fleet.

IN SEPTEMBER 1941 I was transferred from the staff of the Third Carrier Division to the aircraft carrier *Akagi,* a position I had left just one year earlier. Shortly after joining my old comrades in the *Akagi,* I was given additional duty as commander of all air groups of the First Air Fleet. This was an assignment beyond my wildest dreams. I felt that something big must be afoot.

It was at Kagoshima, on the southern tip of Kyushu, that I first learned the magnitude of events in store for me. My good friend Commander Genda, air operations officer on the staff of the First Air Fleet, came to see me at the air base and said, "Now, don't be alarmed, Fuchida, but we want you to lead our air force in the event that we attack Pearl Harbor!"

Don't be alarmed? It was all I could do to catch my breath, and almost before I had done so we were on our way out to board the *Akagi,* then anchored in Ariake Bay, for a conference with the First Air Fleet commander, Vice Admiral Chui-

chi Nagumo, and his staff, including the chief of staff, Rear
Admiral Ryunosuke Kusaka.

The more I heard about the plan, the more astonishing it
seemed. Genda kept urging that torpedoes be used against
ships in Pearl Harbor, a feat that seemed next to impossible
in view of the water depth of only twelve meters, and the
harbor's width of not more than five hundred meters. When
I pointed this out, Genda merely grew more determined, insisting that if we could launch torpedoes, they would not be
expected, adding to the surprise of the attack and multiplying
its effectiveness. This line of argument won me over, and,
despite the technical difficulties that would have to be overcome, I agreed to include torpedoes in our attack plans.

Shallow-water torpedo launching was not the only difficult
problem I had to cope with. From ordinary fleet practice we
had to shift our energies to specific training for this all-
important mission calling for vast and intensive preparations;
and, moreover, everything had to be done in haste. It was
already late September, and the attack plan called for execution in December!

There was no time to lose. Our fliers had to work at the
hardest kind of training. An added handicap to our efforts
was that, for security reasons, the pilots could not be told
about the plans. Our progress was slow, especially with the
problem of launching torpedoes in shallow water. Against my
will I had to demand more and more of every man, yet none
complained. They seemed to sense the intensification of the
international situation and gave of themselves unquestion-
ingly.

It was not until early November that the torpedo problem
was finally solved by fixing additional fins to the torpedoes,
and then my greatest worry was over. I was indeed proud of
my men and felt honored to be their commander and participate in this great attack.

In mid-November First Air Fleet planes were taken on
board their respective carriers, which then headed for the

41

Kuriles, traveling singly and taking separate courses to avoid attention. By 22 November the entire force had assembled in isolated Tankan Bay on Etorofu, the second island from the southern end of the chain extending northeast from Hokkaido. This force consisted of the carriers *Akagi, Kaga, Soryu, Hiryu, Shokaku,* and *Zuikaku;* the battleships *Hiei* and *Kirishima;* the heavy cruisers *Tone* and *Chikuma;* the light cruiser *Abukuma;* the destroyers *Urakaze, Isokaze, Tanikaze, Hamakaze, Kazumi, Arare, Kagero, Shiranuhi,* and *Akigumo;* the submarines *I-19, I-21,* and *I-23;* and the tankers *Kyokuto Maru, Ken'yo Maru, Kokuyo Maru, Shinkoku Maru, Akebono Maru, Toho Maru, Toei Maru,* and *Nihon Maru.*

The following order was issued from Tokyo on the day that the *Akagi* sailed into Tankan Bay:

Imperial General Headquarters
Navy Order No. 5

21 November 1941

To: Commander in Chief, Combined Fleet, Isoroku Yamamoto

Via: Chief of Naval General Staff Osami Nagano

By Imperial Order

1. Commander in chief, Combined Fleet, will, at an appropriate time, dispatch to standby points necessary forces for execution of operations.

2. Commander in chief, Combined Fleet, is empowered to use force in self-defense in case his fleet is challenged by American, British, or Dutch forces during the process of carrying out military preparations.

3. Detailed instructions will be given by the chief of the Naval General Staff.

Four days later Admiral Yamamoto accordingly issued an operation order from his flagship *Nagato* at Hiroshima to Vice Admiral Nagumo, in command of the Pearl Harbor attack force:

The task force will leave Tankan Bay on 26 November and, making every effort to conceal its movements, advance to the standby point, where fueling will be quickly completed.

The designated standby point was 42°N 170°W, over a thousand miles to the north of the Hawaiian Islands chain.

At 0600 on the dark and cloudy morning of 26 November our twenty-eight-ship task force weighed anchor and sailed out into the waters of the North Pacific Ocean. [East longitude dates and Tokyo time, Zone minus 9, are used primarily here.] The sortie was cloaked in complete secrecy. A patrol boat guarding the bay entrance flashed a message, "Good luck on your mission." But even that boat was unaware of our assignment. The *Akagi* signaled, "Thanks," and passed by, her ensign fluttering in the morning breeze. It would not be long before this ensign was replaced by a combat flag.

But this did not mean that the arrow had already been loosed from the bow. "In case negotiations with the United States reach a successful conclusion," Nagumo had been instructed, "the task force will put about immediately and return to the homeland." Unaware of this, however, the crews shouted "*Banzai!*" as they took what might be their last look at Japan.

On the *Akagi's* bridge, Commander Gishiro Miura, the navigation officer, was concentrating all his energies on controlling the ship. The responsibility for successfully reaching the scheduled launching point rested entirely upon his shoulders. He appeared so tense that he seemed a completely different man. His usual jovial attitude had disappeared. He now wore shoes instead of his usual slippers, and he was neatly dressed, a decided change from his customary dirty, worn-out uniform. Captain Hasegawa, the skipper of the ship, stood beside him. Sitting at the flight desk control post under the bridge, I watched the gradually receding mountains of the Kuriles.

Young boys of the flying crews were boiling over with fighting spirit. Hard nights and days of training had been followed by hasty preparations, and now the sortie, which meant that they were going to war.

I felt their keen enthusiasm and was reassured. Still, I could not help doubting whether Japan had the proper confidence to carry out a war. At the same time, however, I fully realized my duty as a warrior to fight and win victory for my country.

Personally, I was opposed to the operational policy. The idea of an attack on Pearl Harbor was a good one, but I thought the plan should have called for complete destruction of the U.S. Pacific Fleet at the outset, followed by an invasion of the Hawaiian Islands to push America entirely out of the central Pacific. The plan covered expansion to the south—the Philippines, Malaya, Hong Kong, Guam, and other such vulnerable positions. It was my opinion that if Pacific operations to the east proved successful, there would be no need for military operations in the south.

Since the United States was our main foe, I could not understand why operations were not aimed directly toward the east. Admiral Yamamoto was quoted as having said that he had no confidence in the outcome of war after the first year. Why, then, did he not press and press the enemy in that first year to force an early conclusion to the war? Anyway, the immediate mission was to strike a telling blow, and my assignment carried a grave responsibility. At the time I thought, "Who could be luckier than I?"

My thoughts continued: What if the fleet is not in Pearl Harbor? In that case we would seek out the enemy en route to the attack. If we should meet the enemy tomorrow, would Nagumo withdraw? No, we should attack and destroy him, I thought, and if the admiral showed any hesitation, I would volunteer my views on these matters.

Such thoughts came one after another, but one remained uppermost. I was determined to do my utmost for victory.

In the meantime, the fleet had assumed formation. The carriers sailed in parallel columns of three followed by the tankers. On the outside two battleships and two heavy cruisers took positions, the whole group encircled by a screen of the light cruiser and destroyers. The submarines patrolled about two hundred miles ahead of our force. The course was direct to the standby point; speed was fourteen knots. The first fueling at sea was carried out five days after our sortie, on 30 November.

Since our departure from Tankan Bay, we had kept a strict alert against U.S. submarines. Our course was chosen to pass between the Aleutians and Midway Island so as to keep out of range of air patrols, some of which were supposed to extend six hundred miles. Another concern during the cruise was how to avoid a chance meeting with foreign merchant ships. The three submarines sent ahead of the fleet were to report any ships sighted to the fleet, which would then change course to avoid them.

If an enemy fleet was sighted before X day minus two, our force was to reverse course immediately and abandon the operation. On the other hand, if it was one day before X day, whether to reverse course or launch the attack was left to the discretion of the task force commander.

Meanwhile, deceptive measures were being taken elsewhere to cover up our movements. On 5, 6, and 7 December sailors of the Yokosuka Naval Barracks were sent to Tokyo on a sightseeing tour. In early December, the *Tatsuta Maru* of the N.Y.K. Line had even left Yokohama heading for Honolulu, and she reversed course only upon receipt of the news that hostilities had begun.

Since leaving Tankan Bay we had maintained our eastward course in complete secrecy, thanks to thick, low-hanging clouds. Moreover, on 30 November and 6 and 7 December, the sea, which we feared might be rough, was calm enough for easy fueling. The not-too-rough sea also made it easy to maintain and prepare planes, and gave the men, especially the flying crews, a much-needed chance to relax.

The fleet observed strict radio silence, but concentrated on

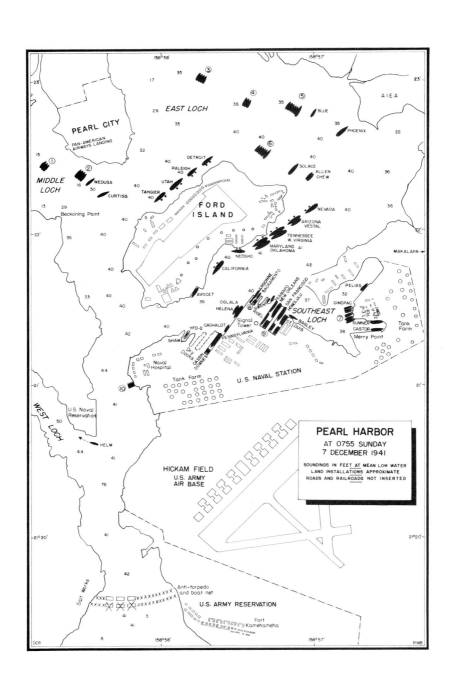

listening for broadcasts from Tokyo or Honolulu. Our predominant concern was to catch any word about the outbreak of war.

In Tokyo a liaison conference between the government and the high command was held every day from 27 to 30 November to discuss the U.S. proposal of the twenty-sixth. It was concluded that the proposal was an ultimatum tending to subjugate Japan and making war inevitable. At the liaison conference of 30 November the decision was made to go to war. This conference also concluded that a message declaring the end of negotiations would be sent to the U.S., but that efforts would be continued to the last moment. The final decision for war was made at an imperial conference on 1 December.

The next day the General Staff issued the long-awaited order and our task force received the Combined Fleet dispatch of 1730, which said, "X day will be 8 December."

Now the die was cast and our duty was clear. The fleet drove headlong to the east.

Why was 8 December chosen as X day? That was 7 December and Sunday, a day of rest, in Hawaii. Was this merely a bright idea to hit the U.S. Fleet off duty? No, it was not so

(*Left*) Key to chart of Pearl Harbor (reading NW to SE in nests of ships): 1. Destroyer-minecraft *Ramsay, Gamble, Montgomery;* 2. Destroyer-minecraft *Trever, Breese, Zane, Perry, Wasmuth;* 3. Destroyers *Monaghan, Farragut, Dale, Aylwin;* 4. Destroyers *Henley, Patterson, Ralph Talbot;* 5. Destroyers *Selfridge, Case, Tucker, Reid, Conyngham;* tender *Whitney;* 6. Destroyers *Phelps, Macdonough, Worden, Dewey, Hull;* tender *Dobbin;* 7. Submarines *Narwhal, Dolphin, Tautog;* seaplane tenders *Thornton, Hulbert;* 8. Destroyers *Jarvis* and *Mugford* (inside *Argonne* and *Sacramento*); 9. Destroyer *Cummings;* destroyer-minelayers *Preble, Tracy, Pruitt, Sicard;* destroyer *Schley;* minesweeper *Grebe;* 10. Minesweepers *Bobolink, Vireo, Turkey, Rail, Tern.* Other auxiliaries, not shown, were moored up West Loch. There were also several tugs and yard craft, not shown, in the area of the chart. *Drawn by Robert M. Berish for* The Rising Sun in the Pacific, *courtesy of Naval Historical Center*

simple as that. The date of the opening of hostilities had been coordinated with the time of the Malayan operations, where air raids and landings were scheduled for dawn. Favorable moonlight was a major consideration, three or four days after the full moon being the most desirable time, and on 8 December the moon was nineteen days old.

There was another reason for choosing 8 December. Our information indicated that the fleet returned to harbor on weekends after training periods at sea, so there was great likelihood that it would be in Pearl Harbor on Sunday morning. All things considered, 8 December was the logical day for the attack.

Long before the planning of the Pearl Harbor attack, we had been interested in fleet activities in the Hawaiian area. Our information showed:

> 1) The fleet either went out on Tuesday and returned on Friday, or went out on Friday and returned on Saturday of the next week. In either case, it stayed in harbor about a week. When it went out for two weeks, it would usually return by Sunday.
>
> 2) The fleet trained to the southeast of Pearl Harbor. Intercepted radio messages from planes flying between this training area and Pearl Harbor showed that these planes were in flight for forty to sixty minutes. Accordingly, the training area was estimated to be near Maui, and probably north of 19°N latitude.
>
> 3) It was hard to determine whether the fleet put in to any other port during training periods, and if so, where. There were some indications that it might go to Lahaina or Maalaea for a short while.

After Japan's decision to go to war had been sent to the attack force, intelligence reports on U.S. Fleet activities continued to be relayed to us from Tokyo. The information was thorough, but the news was often delayed two or three days in reaching Tokyo. These reports from the Imperial General Staff were generally as follows:

48

Issued 2200, 2 December; received 0017, 3 December

Activities in Pearl Harbor as of 0800/28 November:
  Departed: 2 BB (*Oklahoma* and *Nevada*), 1 CV (*Enterprise*), 2 CA, 12 DD.
  Arrived: 5 BB, 3 CA, 3 CL, 12 DD, 1 tanker.
Ships making port today are those which departed 22 November.
Ships in port on afternoon of 28 November estimated as follows:
  6 BB (2 *Maryland* class, 2 *California* class, 2 *Pennsylvania* class)
  1 CV (*Lexington*)
  9 CA (5 *San Francisco* class, 3 *Chicago* class, and *Salt Lake City*)
  5 CL (4 *Honolulu* class and *Omaha*)

Issued 2300, 3 December; received 0035, 4 December

Ships present Pearl Harbor on afternoon of 29 November:
  District A (between Naval Yard and Ford Island)
    KT (docks northwest of Naval Yard): *Pennsylvania* and *Arizona*
    FV (mooring pillars): *California, Tennessee, Maryland,* and *West Virginia*
    KS (naval yard repair dock): *Portland*
    In docks: 2 CA, 1 DD
    Elsewhere: 4 SS, 1 DD tender, 2 patrol ships, 2 tankers, 2 repair ships, 1 minesweeper
  District B (sea area northwest of Ford Island)
    FV (mooring pillars): *Lexington*
    Elsewhere: *Utah,* 1 CA (*San Francisco* class), 2 CL (*Omaha* class), 3 gunboats
  District C (East Loch)
    3 CA, 2 CL (*Honolulu* class), 17 DD, 2 DD tenders
  District D (Middle Loch)
    12 minesweepers
  District E (West Loch)
    No ships
No changes observed by afternoon of 2 December. So

far they do not seem to have been alerted. Shore leaves as usual.

Issued 2030, 4 December; received 0420, 5 December

So far no indications of sea patrol flights being conducted. It seems that occasional patrols are being made to Palmyra, Johnston, and Midway Islands. Pearl Harbor patrols unknown.

Issued 2200, 6 December; received 1036, 7 December

Activities in Pearl Harbor on the morning of 5 December:
Arrived: *Oklahoma* and *Nevada* (having been out for eight days)
Departed: *Lexington* and five heavy cruisers
Ships in harbor as of 1800, 5 December:
8 BB, 3 CL, 16 DD
In docks: 4 CL (*Honolulu* class), 5 DD

Issued 1700, 7 December; received 1900, 7 December

No balloons, no torpedo-defense nets deployed around battleships. No indications observed from enemy radio activity that ocean patrol flights are being made in Hawaiian area. *Lexington* left harbor yesterday (5 December, local time) and recovered planes. *Enterprise* is also thought to be operating at sea with her planes on board.

Issued 1800, 7 December; received 2050, 7 December

Utah and a seaplane tender entered harbor in the evening of 5 December. (They had left harbor on 4 December.)
Ships in harbor as of 6 December:
9 BB, 3 CL, 3 seaplane tenders, 17 DD
In docks: 4 CL, 3 DD
All carriers and heavy cruisers are at sea. No special reports on the fleet. Oahu is quiet and Imperial General Staff is fully convinced of success.

These reports had presumably been sent from Honolulu, but I do not know the details.

On 6 December, after fueling the Second Carrier Division and the Screening Force, the Second Tanker Train broke off

Smoke from burning ships nearly obliterates the battleship *California* as she settles to the bottom. A portion of the capsized *Oklahoma* is visible at right. *Courtesy of the National Archives*

from the task force. On the next day the First Tanker Train fueled the screen again and departed. Our force then increased speed to twenty-four knots and raced toward Pearl Harbor. On the carrier decks planes were lined up wing to wing for their final check. Maintenance crews and flying crews worked assiduously to complete final preparation of their planes.

About this time we received Admiral Yamamoto's message for going to war: "The rise or fall of the empire depends upon this battle; everyone will do his duty with utmost efforts." The message was immediately relayed to all hands, and the "Z" flag was hoisted on the *Akagi*'s mast. This was the same signal flag that had been run up on the *Mikasa* almost thirty years before in the Straits of Tsushima.

At 1225 on 7 December (1725, 6 December in Honolulu) a message came in from the submarine *I-72:* "American fleet is not in Lahaina anchorage."

This anchorage was used for training because it was open and deep. If the Pacific Fleet had been there, we would have

51

had our best chance for success, and we had hoped accordingly. Receipt of the negative information, however, blasted our hopes for such an opportunity.

It was now obvious that the warships were either in Pearl Harbor or at sea. Admiral Nagumo was thumbing through the message log to check on battleships reported to be in Pearl Harbor. Completing the count, he looked up and said to the staff members, "All of their battleships are now in. Will any of them leave today?"

The intelligence officer, Lieutenant Commander Ono, was the first to reply: "Five of their eight battleships reached port on the twenty-ninth, and two others left that day, returning on the sixth. There is one more that has remained in harbor all this time, supposedly under repair, or perhaps in dry dock. The five ships that arrived on the twenty-ninth have been there eight days, and it is time for them to leave. I suspect they may go out today."

"Today is Saturday, 6 December," said Chief of Staff Kusaka. "Their general practice is to leave on Tuesday, which would be the ninth."

"It is most regrettable," said Genda, the operations officer, "that no carriers are in."

"On 29 November," Ono explained, "the *Enterprise* left harbor accompanied by two battleships, two heavy cruisers, and twelve destroyers. The two battleships returned on the sixth, but the rest have not yet come back. The *Lexington* came in on the twenty-ninth and left with five heavy cruisers on the sixth. Thus, the *Enterprise* ought to return today. The *Saratoga* is under repair at San Diego, and the *Wasp* is in the Atlantic. But the *Yorktown* and the *Hornet* belonging to the Pacific Fleet must be out here. They may have arrived with the *Enterprise* today."

"If that happens," said Genda, "I don't care if all eight of the battleships are away."

"As an airman," remarked Oishi, "you naturally place much importance on carriers. Of course it would be good if we could get three of them, but I think it would be better if we get all eight of the battleships."

Then Chief of Staff Kusaka, who had always been strong on statistical studies of the U.S. Pacific Fleet, spoke: "There is only a slight chance that carriers may enter the harbor on Saturday, and it seems unlikely that the battleships would leave on Saturday or Sunday. We may take it for granted that all eight battleships will be in the harbor tomorrow. We can't do anything about carriers that are not there. I think we should attack Pearl Harbor tomorrow."

Thus he set the stage for the decision of the task force commander, which was made known on the evening of 7 December, when Admiral Nagumo gave his appraisal of the enemy situation:

> 1) Enemy strength in the Hawaiian area consists of eight battleships, two carriers, and about ten heavy and six light cruisers. The carriers and heavy cruisers seem to be at sea, but the others are in the harbor. Those operating at sea are most likely in the training area south of Maui; they are not in Lahaina.
>
> 2) Unless an unforeseen situation develops tonight, our attack will be launched upon Pearl Harbor.
>
> 3) So far there is no indication that the enemy has been alerted, but that is no reason to relax our security.

At 0530 on 7 December [here and henceforth, West longitude date and Hawaiian time, Zone plus 10½, are used], the *Chikuma* and *Tone* each catapulted a Zero float plane for a preattack reconnaissance of Pearl Harbor. On carrier flight decks readied fighter and attack planes were lined up. The flying crews, also primed for the operation, were gathered in the briefing room. The ships pitched and rolled in the rough sea, kicking up white surf from the predawn blackness of the water. At times wave spray came over the flight deck, and crews clung desperately to their planes to keep them from going into the sea.

In my flying togs I entered the operation room and reported to the commander in chief, "I am ready for the mission." Nagumo stood up, grasped my hand firmly, and said, "I have confidence in you." He followed me to the dimly lit briefing room where the *Akagi*'s captain was waiting with the pilots. The room was not large enough for all of the men, some of whom had to stand out in the passageway. On a blackboard were written the positions of ships in Pearl Harbor as of 0600, 7 December. We were 230 miles due north of Oahu.

Calling the men to attention, I saluted Captain Hasegawa, who issued a brief final order, "Take off according to plan."

The crews went out hurriedly to their waiting planes. Last to leave, I climbed to the flight deck command post, where Genda put his hand on my shoulder. We smiled without speaking, well aware of each other's thoughts.

Turning to me, Air Officer Masuda said, "There is a heavy pitch and roll. What do you think about taking off in the dark?" The sea was rough, and there was a strong wind blowing. The sky was completely dark, and as yet the horizon was not visible.

"The pitch is greater than the roll," I replied. "Were this a training flight, the takeoff would be delayed until dawn. But if we coordinate the takeoffs with the pitching, we can launch successfully." I saluted the officers and went to my plane, the tail of which was striped with red and yellow to distinguish it as the commander's.

The senior petty officer of the maintenance gang handed me a white *hachimaki* [cloth headband], saying, "This is a present from the maintenance crews. May I ask that you take it along to Pearl Harbor?" I nodded and fastened the gift to my flying cap.

The carrier turned to port and headed into the northerly wind. The battle flag was now added to the "Z" flag flying at the masthead. Lighted flying lamps shivered with the vibration of engines as planes completed their warm-up.

On the flight deck a green lamp was waved in a circle to signal "Take off!" The engine of the foremost fighter plane began to roar. With the ship still pitching and rolling, the plane started its run, slowly at first but with steadily increasing speed. Men lining the flight deck held their breath as the first plane took off successfully just before the ship took a downward pitch. The next plane was already moving forward. There were loud cheers as each plane rose into the air.

Thus the first wave of 183 fighters, bombers, and torpedo planes took off from the six carriers. Within fifteen minutes they had all been launched and were forming up in the still-dark sky, guided only by the signal lights of the lead planes. After making one great circle over the fleet, the planes set their course due south for Oahu Island and Pearl Harbor. It was 0615.

Under my direct command were forty-nine level bombers. About five hundred meters to my right and slightly below me were forty torpedo planes. The same distance to my left, but about two hundred meters above me, were fifty-one dive-bombers, and flying cover for the formation were forty-three fighters. These other three groups were led by Lieutenant Commanders Murata, Takahashi, and Itaya, respectively.

We flew through and over the thick clouds, which were at two thousand meters, up to where day was ready to dawn. And the clouds began gradually to brighten below us after the brilliant sun burst into the eastern sky. I opened the cockpit canopy and looked back at the large formation of planes. The wings glittered in the bright morning sunlight.

The speedometer indicated 125 knots and we were favored by a tail wind. At 0700 I figured that we should reach Oahu in less than an hour. But flying over the clouds, we could not see the surface of the water and consequently had no check on our drift. I switched on the radio direction-finder to tune in the Honolulu radio station and soon picked up some light music. By turning the antenna I found the exact direction from which the broadcast was coming and corrected our course, which had been five degrees off.

Continuing to listen to the program, I was wondering how

55

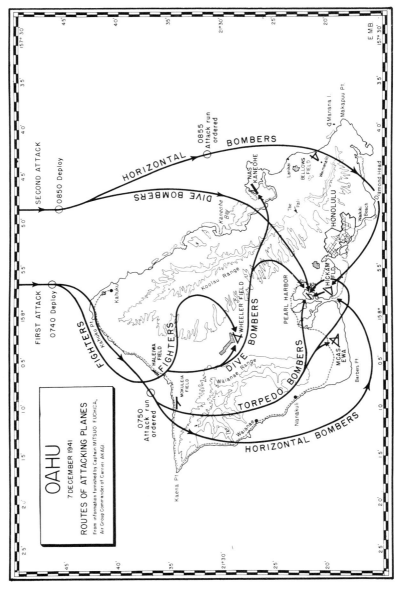

OAHU
7 DECEMBER 1941

ROUTES OF ATTACKING PLANES

From information furnished by Captain MITSUO FUCHIDA,
Air Group Commander of Carrier AKAGI

Drawn by Robert M. Berish for *The Rising Sun in the Pacific, courtesy of Naval Historical Center*

to get below the clouds after reaching Oahu. If the island was covered by thick clouds like those below us, the level bombing would be difficult; and we had not yet had reports from the reconnaissance planes.

In tuning the radio a little finer, I heard, along with the music, what seemed to be a weather report. Holding my breath, I adjusted the dial and listened intently. Then I heard it come through a second time, slowly and distinctly: "Averaging partly cloudy, with clouds mostly over the mountains. Cloud base at 3,500 feet. Visibility good. Wind north, ten knots."

What a windfall for us! No matter how careful the planning, a more favorable situation could not have been imagined. Weather conditions over Pearl Harbor had been worrying me greatly, but now with this information I could turn my attention to other problems. Since Honolulu was only partly cloudy, there must be breaks in the clouds over the island. But since the clouds over the mountains were at one thousand meters altitude, it would not be wise to attack from the northeast, flying over the eastern mountains, as previously planned. The wind was north and visibility good. It would be better to pass to the west of the island and make our approach from the south.

At 0730 we had been in the air for about an hour and a half. It was time for us to see land, but there was only a solid layer of clouds below. All of a sudden the clouds broke, and a long white coastline appeared. We were over Kahuku Point, the northern tip of the island, and now it was time for our deployment.

There were alternate plans for the attack: If we were making a surprise attack, the torpedo planes were to strike first, followed by the level bombers and then the dive-bombers, which were to attack the air bases, including Hickam and Ford Island near the anchorage. If these bases were first hit by the dive-bombers, it was feared that the resultant smoke might hinder torpedo and level-bombing attacks on the ships.

On the other hand, if enemy resistance was expected, the

57

dive-bombers would attack first to cause confusion and attract enemy fire. Level bombers, coming next, were to bomb and destroy enemy antiaircraft guns, followed by the torpedo planes, which would attack the ships.

The selection of attack method was my decision, to be indicated by signal pistol: one "black dragon" for a surprise attack, two "black dragons" if it appeared that surprise was lost. Upon either order the fighters were immediately to dash in as cover.

There was still no news from the reconnaissance planes, but I had made up my mind that we could make a surprise attack, and thereupon ordered the deployment by raising my signal pistol outside the canopy and firing one "black dragon." The time was 0740.

With this order the dive-bombers rose to four thousand meters, the torpedo bombers went down almost to sea level, and the level bombers came down just under the clouds. The only group that failed to deploy was the fighters. Flying above the rest of the formation, they seemed to have missed the signal because of the clouds. Realizing this, I fired another shot toward the fighter group. This time they noticed the signal immediately and sped toward Oahu.

This second shot, however, was taken by the commander of the dive-bomber group as the second of two "black dragons," signifying a nonsurprise attack that would mean that his group should attack first, and this error served to confuse some of the pilots who had understood the original signal.

Meanwhile a reconnaissance report came in from the *Chikuma*'s plane giving the locations of ten battleships, one heavy cruiser, and ten light cruisers in the harbor. It also reported a fourteen-meter wind from bearing 080, and clouds over the U.S. Fleet at 1,700 meters with a scale 7 density. The *Tone* plane also reported that "the enemy fleet is not in Lahaina anchorage." Now I knew for sure that there were no carriers in the harbor. The sky cleared as we moved in on the target, and Pearl Harbor was plainly visible from the northwest valley of the island. I studied our objective through binoculars. They were there all right, all eight of them. "Notify all planes to launch attacks," I ordered my radio man, who immediately began tapping the key. The order went in plain code: "*To, to, to, to. . . .*" The time was 0749.

When Lieutenant Commander Takahashi and his dive-bombing group mistook my signal and thought we were making a nonsurprise attack, his fifty-one planes lost no time in dashing forward. His command was divided into two groups: one led by himself, which headed for Ford Island and Hickam Field, and the other led by Lieutenant Sakamoto, which headed for Wheeler Field.

The dive-bombers over Hickam Field saw heavy bombers lined up on the apron. Takahashi rolled his plane sharply and went into a dive, followed immediately by the rest of his planes, and the first bombs fell at Hickam. The next places hit were Ford Island and Wheeler Field. In a very short time huge billows of black smoke were rising from these bases. The lead torpedo planes were to have started their run to the Navy Yard from over Hickam, coming from south of the bay entrance. But the sudden burst of bombs at Hickam surprised Lieutenant Commander Murata, who had understood that his torpedo planes were to have attacked first. Hence he took a short cut lest the smoke from those bases cover up his targets, and the first torpedo was actually launched some five minutes ahead of the scheduled 0800. The time of each attack was as follows:

0755 Dive-bombers at Hickam and Wheeler
0757 Torpedo planes at battleships
0800 Fighters strafing air bases
0805 Level bombers at battleships

After issuance of the attack order, my level-bomber group kept east of Oahu, going past the southern tip of the island. On our left was the Barbers Point airfield, but as we had been informed, no planes were there. Our information indicated that a powerful antiaircraft battery was stationed there, but we saw no evidence of it.

I continued to watch the sky over the harbor as well as the activities on the ground. None but Japanese planes were in the air, and there were no indications of air combat. Ships in the harbor still appeared to be asleep, and the Honolulu radio broadcast continued normally. I felt that surprise was now assured, and that my men would succeed in their missions.

Knowing that Admirals Nagumo and Yamamoto and the General Staff were anxious about the attack, I decided that they should be informed. I ordered the following message sent to the fleet: "We have succeeded in making a surprise attack. Request you relay this report to Tokyo." The radio man reported shortly that the message had been received by the *Akagi*.

The code for a successful surprise attack was "*Tora, tora, tora. . . .*" Before the *Akagi's* relay of this message reached Japan, it was received by the *Nagato* in Hiroshima Bay and the General Staff in Tokyo, directly from my plane! This was surely a long-distance record for such a low-powered transmission from an airplane, and might be attributed to the use of the word "*Tora*" as our code. There is a Japanese saying, "A tiger (*tora*) goes out one thousand *ri* (two thousand miles) and returns without fail."

I saw clouds of black smoke rising from Hickam and soon thereafter from Ford Island. This bothered me, and I wondered what had happened. It was not long before I saw waterspouts rising alongside the battleships, followed by more and more waterspouts. It was time to launch our level-bombing attacks, so I ordered my pilot to bank sharply, which was the attack signal for the planes following us. All ten of my squadrons then formed a single column with intervals of two hundred meters. It was indeed a gorgeous formation.

The lead plane in each squadron was manned by a specially trained pilot and bombardier. The pilot and bombardier of my squadron had won numerous fleet contests and were considered the best in the Japanese navy. I approved when Lieutenant Matsuzaki asked if the lead plane should trade positions with us, and he lifted our plane a little as a signal. The new leader came forward quickly, and I could see the smiling round face of the bombardier when he saluted. In returning the salute I entrusted the command to them for the bombing mission.

As my group made its bomb run, enemy antiaircraft suddenly came to life. Dark gray bursts blossomed here and there until the sky was clouded with shattering near misses, which made our plane tremble. Shipboard guns seemed to open fire before the shore batteries. I was startled by the rapidity of the counterattack, which came less than five minutes after the first bomb had fallen. Had it been the Japanese Fleet, the reaction would not have been so quick, because although

As the attack continued, navy antiaircraft guns put up a barrage. The heavy smoke is from battleship row. *Courtesy of the National Archives*

the Japanese character is suitable for offensives, it does not readily adjust to the defensive.

Suddenly the plane bounced as if struck by a huge club. "The fuselage is holed to port," reported the radio man behind me, "and a steering-control wire is damaged." I asked hurriedly if the plane was under control, and the pilot assured me that it was.

No sooner were we feeling relieved than another burst shook the plane. My squadron was headed for the *Nevada*'s mooring at the northern end of battleship row on the east side of Ford Island. We were just passing over the bay entrance and it was almost time to release our bombs. It was not easy to pass through the concentrated antiaircraft fire. Flying at only three thousand meters, we thought that this might well be a date with eternity.

I further saw that it was not wise to have deployed in this long single-column formation. The whole level bomber group could be destroyed like ducks in a shooting gallery. It would also have been better if we had approached the targets from the direction of Diamond Head. But here we were at our targets, and there was a job to be done.

It was now a matter of utmost importance to stay on course, and the lead plane kept to its line of flight like a homing pigeon. Ignoring the barrage of shells bursting around us, I concentrated on the bomb loaded under the lead plane, pulled the safety bolt from the bomb release lever, and grasped the handle. It seemed as if time were standing still.

Again we were shaken terrifically and our planes were buffeted about. When I looked out, the third plane of my group was abeam of us, and I saw its bomb fall! That pilot had a reputation for being careless. In training his bomb releases were poorly timed, and he had often been cautioned.

I thought, "That damn fellow has done it again!" and shook my fist in his direction. But I soon realized that there was something wrong with his plane and he was losing gasoline. I wrote on a small blackboard, "What happened?" and held it toward his plane. He explained, "Underside of fuselage hit."

Now I saw his bomb cinch lines fluttering wildly, and, sorry for having scolded him, I ordered that he return to the carrier. He answered, "Fuel tank destroyed, will follow you," asking permission to stay with the group. Knowing the feelings of the pilot and crew, I gave permission, although I knew it was useless to try taking that crippled and bombless plane through the enemy fire. It was nearly time for bomb release when we ran into clouds that obscured the target, and I made out the round face of the lead bombardier, who was waving his hands back and forth to indicate that we had passed the release point. Banking slightly, we turned right toward Honolulu, and I studied the antiaircraft fire, knowing that we would have to run through it again. It was now concentrated on the second squadron.

While circling for another try, I looked toward the area in which the bomb from the third plane had fallen. Just outside the bay entrance I saw a large water ring close to what looked like a destroyer. The ship seemed to be standing in a floating dock, attached to both sides of the entrance like a gate boat. I was suddenly reminded of the midget submarines that were to have entered the bay for a special attack.

At the time of our sortie I was aware of these midget submarines, but knew nothing of their characteristics, operational objectives, or force organization, or the reason for their participation in the attack. In the *Akagi*, Commander Shibuya, a staff officer in charge of submarine operations, had explained that they were to penetrate the harbor the night before our attack, but no matter how good an opportunity might arise, they were not to strike until after the planes had done so.

Even now the submarines were probably concealed in the bay, awaiting the air attack. Had the entrance been left open, there would have been some opportunity for them to get out of the harbor. But in light of what I had just seen, there

63

seemed little chance of that, and feeling now the bitterness of war, I vowed to do my best in the assigned mission.

While my group was circling over Honolulu for another bombing attempt, other groups made their runs, some making three tries before succeeding. Suddenly a colossal explosion occurred in battleship row. A huge column of dark red smoke rose to one thousand feet and a stiff shock wave reached our plane. I called the pilot's attention to the spectacle, and he observed, "Yes, Commander, the powder magazine must have exploded. Terrible indeed!" The attack was in full swing, and smoke from fires and explosions filled most of the sky over Pearl Harbor.

My group now entered on a bombing course again. Studying battleship row through binoculars, I saw that the big explosion had been on the *Arizona*. She was still flaming fiercely and her smoke was covering the *Nevada*, the target of my group. Since the heavy smoke would hinder our bomber accuracy, I looked for some other ship to attack. The *Tennessee*, third in the left row, was already on fire; but next in the row was the *Maryland*, which had not yet been attacked. I gave an order changing our target to this ship, and once again we headed into the antiaircraft fire. Then came the "ready" signal and I took a firm grip on the bomb release handle, holding my breath and staring at the bomb of the lead plane.

Pilots, observers, and radio men all shouted, "Release!" on seeing the bomb drop from the lead plane, and all the others let go their bombs. I immediately lay flat on the floor to watch the fall of bombs through a peephole. Four bombs in perfect pattern plummeted like devils of doom. The target was so far away that I wondered for a moment if they would reach it. The bombs grew smaller and smaller until I was holding my breath for fear of losing them. I forgot everything in the thrill of watching them fall toward the target. They became small as poppy seeds and finally disappeared just as tiny white flashes of smoke appeared on and near the ship.

From a great altitude near misses are much more obvious

than direct hits because they create wave rings in the water that are plain to see. Observing only two such rings plus two tiny flashes, I shouted, "Two hits!" and rose from the floor of the plane. These minute flashes were the only evidence we had of hits at that time, but I felt sure that they had done considerable damage. I ordered the bombers that had completed their runs to return to the carriers, but my own plane remained over Pearl Harbor to observe our successes and conduct operations still in progress.

After our bomb run I ordered my pilot to fly over each of the air bases, where our fighters were strafing, before returning over Pearl Harbor to observe the result of our attacks on the warships. Pearl Harbor and vicinity had been turned into complete chaos in a very short time.

The target ship *Utah,* on the western side of Ford Island, had already capsized. On the other side of the island the *West Virginia* and *Oklahoma* had received concentrated torpedo attacks as a result of their exposed positions in the outer row. Their sides were almost blasted off and they listed steeply in a flood of heavy oil. The *Arizona* was in miserable shape, her magazine apparently having blown up; she was listing badly and burning furiously.

Two other battleships, the *Maryland* and *Tennessee,* were on fire, especially the latter, whose smoke emerged in a heavy black column that towered into the sky. The *Pennsylvania,* unscathed in the dry dock, seemed to be the only battleship that had not been attacked.

Most of our torpedo planes, under Lieutenant Commander Murata, flew around the Navy Yard area and concentrated their attacks on the ships moored east of Ford Island. A summary of their reports, made upon return to our carriers, indicated the following hits: one on the *Nevada,* nine on the *West Virginia,* twelve on the *Oklahoma,* and three on the *California.*

Elements of the torpedo bombers attacked ships west of

the island, but they found only the *Utah* and attacked her, claiming six hits. Other torpedo planes headed for the *Pennsylvania*, but seeing that she was in dry dock, they shifted their attack to a cruiser and destroyer tied up at Pier 1010. Five torpedo hits were claimed on these targets, which were the *Helena* and *Oglala*.

As I observed the damage done by the first attack wave, the effectiveness of the torpedoes seemed remarkable, and I was struck with the shortsightedness of the United States in being so generally unprepared and in not using torpedo nets. I also thought of our long, hard training in Kagoshima Bay and the efforts of those who had labored to accomplish a seemingly impossible task. A warm feeling came with the realization that the reward of those efforts was unfolded here before my eyes.

During the attack many of our pilots noted the brave efforts of the American flyers able to take off, who, though greatly outnumbered, flew straight in to engage our planes. Their effect was negligible, but their courage commanded the admiration and respect of our pilots.

It took the planes of the first attack wave about one hour to complete their mission. By the time they were headed back to our carriers, having lost three fighters, one dive-bomber, and five torpedo planes, the second wave of 171 planes commanded by Lieutenant Commander Shimazaki was over the target area. Arriving off Kahuku Point at 0840, they were ordered to attack fourteen minutes later, and they swept in, making every effort to avoid the billowing clouds of smoke as well as the now-intensified antiaircraft fire.

In this second wave there were thirty-six fighters to control the air over Pearl Harbor and fifty-four high-level bombers led by Shimazaki to attack Hickam Field and the Naval Air Stations at Kaneohe, while eighty-one dive-bombers led by Lieutenant Commander Egusa flew over the mountains to the east and dashed in to hit the warships.

By the time these last arrived, the sky was so covered with

U.S. battleships under air attack at Pearl Harbor, as photographed by a Japanese pilot. *Official U.S. Navy photograph*

clouds and smoke that planes had difficulty in locating their targets. To further complicate the problems of this attack, the ship and ground antiaircraft fire was now very heavy. But Egusa was undaunted in leading his dive-bombers through the fierce barrage. The planes chose as their targets the ships that were putting up the stiffest repelling fire. This choice proved effective, since these ships had suffered least from the first attack. Thus the second attack achieved a nice spread, hitting the least damaged battleships as well as previously undamaged cruisers and destroyers. This attack also lasted about one hour, but due to the increased return fire, it suffered higher casualties, six fighters and fourteen dive-bombers being lost.

After the second wave was headed back to the carriers, I circled Pearl Harbor once more to observe and photograph the results. I counted four battleships definitely sunk and three severely damaged. Still another battleship appeared to be slightly damaged, and extensive damage had also been inflicted upon other types of ships. The seaplane base at Ford Island was all in flames, as were the airfields, especially Wheeler Field.

A detailed survey of damage was impossible because of the dense pall of black smoke. Damage to the airfields was not determinable, but it was readily apparent that no planes on the fields were operational. In the three hours that my plane was in the area, we did not encounter a single enemy plane. It seemed that at least half the island's air strength must have been destroyed. Several hangars remained untouched, however, and it was possible that some of them held planes that were still operational.

Such were my conclusions as I prepared to return to our carrier. I was startled from these thoughts by the sudden approach of a fighter plane banking from side to side. We were greatly relieved to see the Rising Sun on its wings. As it came closer we saw that it was a *Zuikaku* fighter, which must have been here since the first attack wave. I wondered if any other fighters had been left behind, and ordered my pilot to go to the rendezvous point for a final check. Sure enough, there we found a second fighter plane who also followed joyfully after us.

It was extremely difficult for fighter planes to fly long distances at sea. They were not equipped with homing devices and radar as were the larger planes. It was therefore planned to have the bombers, upon completion of their missions, rendezvous with the fighters at a designated point and lead them back to the carriers. Some of the fighters, however, such as these two, must have missed the time of rendezvous, and they were indeed fortunate to find our plane, which could lead them safely back to the task force and their carriers.

My plane was just about the last one to get back to the *Akagi,* where refueled and rearmed planes were being lined up on the busy flight deck in preparation for yet another attack. I was called to the bridge as soon as the plane stopped, and could tell on arriving there that Admiral Nagumo's staff had been engaged in heated discussions about the advisability of launching the next attack. They were waiting for my account of the battle.

"Four battleships definitely sunk," I reported. "One sank instantly, another capsized, and the other two settled to the bottom of the bay and may have capsized." This seemed to please Admiral Nagumo, who observed, "We may then conclude that anticipated results have been achieved."

Discussion next centered upon the extent of damage inflicted at airfields and air bases, and I expressed my views, saying, "All things considered, we have achieved a great amount of destruction, but it would be unwise to assume that we have destroyed everything. There are still many targets remaining that should be hit. Therefore I recommend that another attack be launched."

The factors that influenced Admiral Nagumo's decision—the target of much criticism by naval experts, and an interesting subject for naval historians—have long been unknown, since the man who made it died in the summer of 1944 when U.S. forces invaded the Marianas. I know of only one document in which Admiral Nagumo's reasons are set forth, and there they are given as follows:

> 1) The first attack had inflicted all the damage we had hoped for, and another attack could not be expected to greatly increase the extent of that damage.
>
> 2) Enemy return fire had been surprisingly prompt even though we took them by surprise; another attack would meet stronger opposition and our losses would certainly be disproportionate to the additional destruction that might be inflicted.
>
> 3) Intercepted enemy messages indicated at least fifty large planes still operational, and we did not know the whereabouts of the enemy's carriers, cruisers, and submarines.
>
> 4) To remain within range of enemy land-based planes was distinctly to our disadvantage, especially since the effectiveness of our air reconnaissance was extremely limited.

I had done all I could to urge another attack, but the decision rested entirely with Admiral Nagumo, and he chose to retire without launching the next attack. Immediately flag signals were hoisted ordering the course change, and our ships headed northward at high speed.

3

The Opening Air Offensive Against the Philippines

KOICHI
SHIMADA

American war planning during the 1920s and 1930s was based on the expectation that one of Japan's initial moves would be an invasion of the Philippine Islands. Since the token Asiatic Fleet could offer no effective resistance, the army was assigned the task of holding Manila Bay until the U.S. Pacific Fleet arrived. The stunning blow at Pearl Harbor upset American strategy, and lengthy debates in Washington over the wisdom of an effort to reinforce the defenders of the Philippines were resolved by the realization that such an attempt was impracticable in view of the "Europe First" commitment.

The Japanese planners had envisioned a series of assaults, which by their daring and precision would use to the fullest the element of surprise, gain the maximum effect of the initiative, and exploit those advantages that were essential for victory by a fundamentally weaker nation. The ambitious schedule projected by the Japanese was predicated on a number of imponderables. They allocated their resources on their assessment of Allied strength and predictable Allied reactions, as well as their grand design for bringing the war to a successful conclusion. In this context the Philippine occupation played a major role in the overall program of conquest, and control of the air was deemed the indispensable first phase of the undertaking.

Because of a difference in time zones and daylight hours, the air assault on the American air forces in the Philippines could not be launched at the same time as the Pearl Harbor attack; weather conditions further delayed the Philippine air offensive. Yet, although the element of surprise had been lost, the Japanese pilots found to their amazement that American defenses were not prepared.

Japan's apprehension about an American attack on its airfields in Taiwan was well founded, for the American commander had sought permission to take such action only to be denied it until too late.

The technical obstacles encountered and overcome in mounting and carrying out this successful effort to crush American air resistance are recounted in the following article. Weather, the Zero's fighting ability, and Japanese determination were all potent factors in the outcome. While the occupation of the Philippines took longer than Japan had expected, it was not unduly delayed. The Japanese navy's Eleventh Air Fleet successfully destroyed all American opposition in a matter of days.

IN THE FALL of 1941 the Japanese army and navy high commands were urgently formulating plans for war against the United States, Great Britain, and the Netherlands in the event that diplomacy failed to achieve a speedy solution to the Pacific crisis. A basic stipulation of these plans was that Japan must attack her primary objectives in the southern area during the coming winter, when climatic conditions in Siberia would preclude a possible offensive from the rear by Soviet Russia. Specifically, this meant that the Philippines, Malaya, and the Dutch East Indies must be securely in Japanese hands by the end of February 1942. Accordingly, an imperial conference on 6 September resolved that Japan's decision for war or peace must be made by mid-October at the latest so that, if it was to be war, final preparations might be made in time to launch hostilities in the first part of November. At the mid-October deadline, however, the nation's leaders were still hesitant to take the fateful plunge, and it was not until 5 November that they definitely decided to go to war in early December if no diplomatic settlement was reached in the interim. The armed forces immediately began girding themselves for battle, and D day was set at 8 December. [Unless otherwise noted, East longitude date and Philippines-Taiwan time, Zone minus 8, are used in this article.]

There was thus a delay of one month in the opening of hostilities. But in spite of this delay, the war planners did not alter the stipulation that the conquest of all "first-stage" objectives must be completed by the end of the following February. As a consequence the final invasion timetable imposed on the armed forces the stupendous task of occupying the Philippines in only fifty days and securing the whole southern area in ninety days from the start of hostilities. Although this exacting schedule was primarily intended as a precaution against possible Soviet interference, tactical considerations also argued in favor of the Japanese conquering their initial objectives with maximum possible speed. Not only would this facilitate the operations themselves, but it would also reduce the enemy's chances of moving in the reinforcements that would render the task of our expeditionary forces more difficult.

Of the various forms of reinforcement that might be attempted, the first our planners had to consider was the dispatch of additional American air strength. This was judged especially probable if the surprise attack on Pearl Harbor should prove successful, for the United States would then be incapable of sending major fleet strength to Asiatic waters and would be limited largely to air reinforcement. It was estimated, however, that the danger of such reinforcement would be safely averted if we succeeded in occupying our objectives within the time limits set by the war plan.

Particularly heavy responsibility for the successful execution of the invasion schedule rested on the shoulders of our own air forces, which were to spearhead and support the amphibious advance. As the bulk of our carrier strength was assigned to the Pearl Harbor attack, support of the southern invasions would have to be provided mainly by shore-based air. The initial moves against Luzon and Malaya would be supported by planes operating from Taiwan and southern French Indochina, and subsequent advances would be carried out in stages, a primary objective of each stage being to secure air bases to which our planes could move forward to support the next stage. In order that this step-by-step process might be completed on schedule, it was decided that the advance southward from Luzon must in no case be delayed even if ground operations on that island were not complete.

In the Philippines, we estimated that our only serious opposition would come from the U.S. armed forces stationed there, and that they, in all probability, would not be augmented after the outbreak of the war. The strength of these forces was estimated as follows:

Ground: Approximately 20,000 regular U.S. Army troops.
Naval: Heavy cruiser *Houston,* seaplane tender *Langley,* 2 light cruisers, 15 destroyers, 15 submarines.
Air: 110 fighters, 40 bombers, 20 scout planes, 10 light seaplanes, and 35 flying boats, for a total of 215 planes. In addition there were believed to be some light aircraft, including trainers of the Philippine Air Force.

To deal with this enemy strength, the following Japanese army and navy forces were assigned to the invasion of the Philippines:

74

Ground: Fourteenth Army, comprising two and a half infantry divisions plus supporting and service troops.

Naval: a) For direct participation in amphibious operations: 5 heavy cruisers, 5 light cruisers, 29 destroyers, 2 seaplane tenders, and a large number of small craft of various types, with the light carrier *Ryujo* to be incorporated as circumstances might require.

b) To operate in nearby waters as a covering force: 2 battleships, 2 heavy cruisers, and 9 destroyers under direct command of the theater naval commander.

Air: a) Army: Fifth Air Group, comprising 72 fighters, 27 twin-engined bombers, 54 light bombers, 27 reconnaissance planes, and 12 liaison planes, for a total of 192 planes.

b) Navy: Eleventh Air Fleet main strength, comprising the Twenty-first and Twenty-third Air Flotillas with 108 Zero fighters, 13 old-type fighters, 81 new-type bombers, 36 old-type bombers, 15 reconnaissance planes, 24 flying boats, and 27 transport planes, for a total of 304 planes. (This was about 60 percent of Eleventh Air Fleet strength; the remainder was assigned to operations in Southeast Asia.)

As indicated by the respective numbers of army and navy aircraft assigned, the major role in the air phase of the Philippines invasion was allotted to the navy. This was mainly because of the much shorter combat range of army planes, which had been designed primarily for a continental war against Russia, in which they would operate against Siberian targets from nearby bases in Manchuria. Consequently, army fighters at this time had a radius of less than three hundred miles, while army bombers carrying a normal bomb load could not cover the round-trip distance between southern Taiwan bases and Lingayen Gulf, the principal invasion landing point on Luzon.

Owing to these considerations, it was agreed that in the air offensive planned to precede the initial landings on northern Luzon, army planes would be responsible only for hitting targets north of the sixteenth parallel, while navy air forces would take care of targets south of that line. This meant that the major concentrations of enemy air strength, which the offensive was intended to knock out, lay within the navy zone. In addition, the naval air forces were charged with combat air and antisubmarine patrol for the invasion convoys at sea, with covering landings on eastern and southern Luzon and Mindanao, and even with support of ground operations on the other islands. Navy and army planes jointly were to cover the preliminary landings on northern Luzon and the later main landing at Lingayen Gulf (with army planes then to be operating from occupied northern Luzon bases), but army aircraft alone would be responsible for supporting ground operations on Luzon subsequent to the landings. Quite frankly, it was only in this last-mentioned mission that the navy air force was counting upon any real contribution by army air.

With regard to the employment of Philippine air bases earmarked for early seizure, it was agreed that Legaspi, Davao, and Jolo would be used by the navy, Aparri jointly by the army and navy, and Vigan and Laoag by army air forces.

Of special significance in the makeup of the navy air contingent assigned to the Philippines invasion was the fact that it included virtually every Zero fighter plane the navy then possessed except those allocated to the Carrier Striking Force for the attack on Pearl Harbor. This was because the Zero, though designed primarily as a carrier-borne fighter, possessed an exceptionally long range. In 1940 a group of Zero fighters based at Hankow, in central China, had made a record flight in attacking Chungking, 420 miles distant. We thus knew that their action radius was in excess of 420 miles, but there was serious doubt whether they could operate successfully from shore bases on southern Taiwan to support attacks on targets in the Manila area, a full 550 miles away.

The navy's air operation planners consequently found themselves confronted by an urgent problem for which there appeared to be only two solutions. Either aircraft carriers would have to be employed to serve as a base of operations for the Zeros, or means would have to be found of augmenting the range of these planes so that they could achieve the required 550-mile radius.

Although all six of the navy's big fleet carriers had been reserved for the vitally important attack on Pearl Harbor, there were three other ships of smaller size that could be used in the Philippines invasion. These were the *Ryujo*, displacing 9,400 tons and carrying twenty-four planes; the *Zuiho*, of 11,200 tons and a twenty-eight-plane capacity; and the *Kasuga Maru*, a converted merchant ship of 17,000 tons, which could carry twenty-three planes. At first glance employment of these carriers seemed to offer the simplest solution to the problem, but more careful consideration indicated that there were also some serious drawbacks.

In the first place, these three ships were inadequate for the task, since, all told, they could not carry more than seventy-five fighters, and the number that actually could be used for attack operations would be substantially less because some planes would have to be reserved for combat air patrol over the carriers. Furthermore, the ships were so slow that—unless the wind velocity exceeded twenty miles per hour—planes taking off had to run almost the full length of the flight deck. Consequently, at such times none of these carriers could launch with more than half its planes on deck, and a ship's air group had to be flown off in two divisions.

Much more serious than the deficiencies of the carriers, however, was the difficulty that would be encountered in coordinating the attack operations of Taiwan-based bombers with those of carrier-based fighters far off at sea. The respective times of takeoff would have to be carefully scheduled in advance to assure that bomber and fighter formations would meet at the proper time and place to attack in concert. Yet the schedule might be completely thrown off by differing weather conditions at Taiwan bases and around the carriers, or by other unforeseen developments affecting either the bombers or the fighters. Last-minute readjustments of the plan to meet such contingencies would be hard to effect.

The difficulties of achieving proper air coordination and generally of maintaining tight control of all the invasion forces would inevitably be increased by the fact that the carrier group would have to observe strict radio silence in order to conceal its whereabouts from the enemy. This weakening of coordination and control was viewed as particularly risky in the Philippines attack because here, owing to the 5½-hour time difference between the Philippines and Hawaii, the Americans would already have been alerted for several hours before our air forces delivered their first blow shortly after daybreak on 8 December. Enemy countermeasures therefore had to be considered a definite probability, and to cope with them it was vitally necessary that the tightest possible coordination and control of our forces be maintained. The radio silence under which the carrier group would have to operate, if it were employed, would clearly not be conducive toward this end.

The use of carriers also seemed undesirable from two further standpoints. One was the risk of forewarning the enemy of our intentions prior to the outbreak of hostilities, as the carriers would have to maneuver close to launch Zeros for the opening attack. The other was the loss of efficiency that would result from splitting up our scarce air maintenance personnel to station some on board the carriers.

Because of these considerations, the conclusion of the navy's air planners was that the second alternative, namely, to find means of augmenting the range of the Zeros enough to permit them to operate from shore bases, should be vigorously explored. At the same time, however, the use of carriers could not be definitely abandoned pending some assurance that the efforts to expand the Zeros' range would succeed. Therefore, parallel with these efforts, it was decided that preparations for the eventual employment of carriers should also be carried out.

Evacuating its former base at Hankow in central China, the Eleventh Air Fleet concentrated its main strength at Taiwan bases early in September 1941 and began war preparations late the same month. Experimental studies got under way immediately, looking toward extension of the Zero's combat radius. There was also training in such basics as air fighting, strafing land targets, and night formation flying. And when carriers were dispatched to Taiwan in mid-October, flight-deck training was begun for the Zero pilots.

JAPANESE AIR POWER
TAICHU—navy air base

    Eleventh Air Transport—9 planes—army
    Element of Kanoya Air Group—27 Type 1 medium bombers—navy

KAGI—army air base

    ½ Airfield Bn. of Fourteenth Air Regt.—army
    27 transport planes—navy

TAINAN—army air base

    Element of Thirteenth Airfield Co.—army
    Twenty-first Air Flotilla Hq.—navy
    First Air Group—36 Type 96 medium bombers—navy
    Tainan Air Group—50 Zero fighters and 8 recon. planes—navy

TAKAO—navy air base

    Eleventh Air Fleet Hq.—navy
    Twenty-third Air Flotilla Hq.—navy
    Third Air Group—50 Zero fighters and 7 recon. planes—navy
    Takao Air Group—54 Type 1 medium bombers—navy

HEITO—army air base

    Fifth Air Division Hq.—army
    Fourth Air Brigade Hq.—army
    One Co. of Twenty-fourth Air Regt.—12 Type 97 fighters—army
    Fifty-second Ind. Air Co.—9 recon. planes—army

Seventy-fourth Ind. Air Co.—12 direct support planes—army
Seventy-sixth Ind. Air Co.—9 headquarters recon. planes—army

CHOSHU—army air base

Fourteenth Air Regt.—27 Type 97 heavy bombers—army
Twenty-fourth Air Regt.—24 Type 97 fighters—army

KATO—army air base

Eighth Air Regt.—9 Type 97 headquarters recon. planes and 27 Type 99 light bombers—army
Sixteenth Air Regt.—27 Type 97 light bombers—army

KOSHUN—army air base

Fiftieth Air Regt.—108 Type 97 fighters—army
½ Airfield Bn. of Fiftieth Air Regt.—army
⅔ Thirty-second Airfield Co.—army

GARAMPI—Meteorological Observation Sect.

UNITED STATES AIR POWER

(As reported by Japanese Intelligence)

CAMP CHINIO

Twenty-eighth Bombing Squadron
Seventh Air Squadron—12 reconnaissance fighter planes

CLARK FIELD

Twentieth Pursuit Squadron
Second Reconnaissance Squadron
Second Observation Squadron

ZABLAN FIELD

First Air Squadron
Second Air Squadron
Third Air Squadron
Fourth Air Squadron
Fifth Air Squadron
Seventeenth Training planes

NICHOLS FIELD

Fourth Composite Air Regiment
Twentieth Air Base Unit

80

Third Pursuit Squadron
Seventeenth Pursuit Squadron
Twentieth Pursuit Squadron

RAIYUS FIELD

Ninth Reconnaissance Squadron
Sixteenth Air Squadron
12 reconnaissance and fighter planes

It was just about this time that I joined Eleventh Air Fleet headquarters in Takao as a junior staff officer. The air fleet's strength in Taiwan had nearly tripled by that time as a result of the feeding in of reinforcements. These included a large proportion of fliers insufficiently trained for combat, and virtually none who had had any training in carrier operations. Consequently, with less than two months in which to prepare, the burden of training the fighter pilots so that they could operate either from land bases or from carriers, as eventual circumstances might require, was exceedingly heavy.

This unsatisfactory situation spurred the already strenuous efforts being made to extend the combat range of the Zeros. The air fleet commander, Vice Admiral Nishizo Tsukahara, and his staff, as well as staff officers of the subordinate air flotillas, conferred frequently on this problem, and experts were called in from air technical arsenals to assist. On the lower levels, pilots and maintenance crews likewise worked unremittingly at various means of improving plane performance.

By late October a combat radius of five hundred miles had been achieved for the Zeros without any modification in plane engine or equipment. This was accomplished by reducing the engine cruising speed from the previously established 1,850 RPM to 1,650–1,700 RPM with corresponding adjustment of the propeller pitch, and setting the fuel mixture as lean as possible. Thus, reduced fuel consumption was achieved without any sacrifice in plane speed. This assured a five-hundred-mile radius, allowing a maximum of fifteen

81

The fast and maneuverable Zero played a major role in the attack on the Philippines. Its initially long range was extended to allow it to operate from Japanese fields on Taiwan.

minutes over the target, but it was still fifty miles short of the radius required to operate against objectives in the Manila area. The further fifty-mile extension in combat radius would have to be achieved through pilot skill and discipline to ensure constant flight speed, especially in night formation flying. This demanded even more extensive and severe training.

While no one was certain that the required goal could be achieved in time, a final choice between using carriers and not using them could no longer be delayed. Little more than a month remained before D day, and if our forces were to be ready, we could not continue to train and prepare for both carrier-based and shore-based operations; we had to concentrate on one or the other. Accordingly, a staff conference was held early in November to decide the issue. The consensus of the staff was overwhelmingly in favor of unified bomber-fighter operations from shore bases rather than flying the fighters from carriers. Vice Admiral Tsukahara's decision followed the staff view, and an order was issued to limit future training to shore-based operations.

Even with this limitation, the training program throughout November was the most rigorous the air fleet had ever been through. Every effort was made to bring the flying crews up to peak combat efficiency, and daily fuel consumption rose to such a high level that the supply corps was astonished. Meanwhile, since the use of carriers had been abandoned and further extension of the Zero's range was problematical, other alternatives had to be considered. Tentative plans were made for the occupation on the morning of D day of Batan Island, midway between Taiwan and Luzon, so that our Zeros could make an emergency fueling stop there, if necessary, on their way back from Luzon.

We had known for several years that there was an airfield on Batan Island, but as no recent or detailed information was available about it, a secret air reconnaissance was carried out over the island on 25 October. Similar reconnaissance of key areas on Luzon was not attempted until 20 November, owing to the risk of alerting the enemy to our intentions. Starting on that date, a series of sporadic flights was carried out over a period of four or five days, every possible precaution being taken to guard against enemy discovery of our planes. Final reconnaissance missions were flown on 5 December in order to ascertain any changes in the enemy situation just prior to the opening of hostilities.

We recognized that such limited reconnaissance would not provide all the information we needed, but this penalty was readily accepted in preference to the far graver consequences that would have resulted from premature divulgence of our intentions. The prudent attitude of the navy air force, however, was not duplicated everywhere. For example, the concentration of scores of transport vessels in the south Taiwan port of Takao and at Mako, in the Pescadores, was—if the enemy learned of it—an almost unmistakable tip-off that a large-scale amphibious move toward the south impended.

The Eleventh Air Fleet nevertheless continued, for its own part, to exercise the utmost caution. Following the first clandestine reconnaissance missions over Luzon, the air fleet on 25 November began sending out weather observation planes over the waters flanking the island's east and west coasts to

83

obtain necessary weather data for the areas our attack groups would traverse en route to their targets on D day. Parallel with all these preparatory activities, detailed planning of the air operations went ahead. The rigorous schedule that had been fixed for the conquest of the Philippines was postulated on the assumption that our forces would win complete control of the air at the outset, and this therefore became our primary mission. As its fulfillment would depend upon the effectiveness of our operations during the first few days of hostilities, it was to these operations that we naturally devoted the most attention.

Annihilation of the enemy's air strength had to be the central goal of the initial air offensive, but some members of the air fleet staff were dubious that bomber attacks against enemy air bases would contribute much toward this end. Experience in China had shown that amazingly little damage was inflicted even when scores of bombers in tight formation virtually blanketed an enemy airfield with bombs. Consequently, the emphasis in our air tactics had tended to shift to the offensive use of fighters, especially since the Zero fighter had emerged as the dominant factor in Chinese skies in the fall of 1940. The prevalent view thereafter was that bombers should be employed against surface ships and submarines rather than against land air bases, where they were relatively ineffective.

Nevertheless, despite these considerations, the air fleet staff finally came to the conclusion that our opening offensive in the Philippines, by both bombers and fighters, should be directed exclusively against the enemy air force. There were three reasons for this decision: First, the enemy's air strength was a much greater menace to our amphibious convoys than his relatively weak surface strength. Second, strafing attacks by our fighters on enemy airfields would be easier and more effective if preceded by bomber attacks to knock out ground defenses. Third, if we attacked early enough on D day there might be some chance of gaining tactical surprise and catching enemy planes parked on their fields, in which event concerted attacks might succeed in crippling the enemy air force at a single blow. It was further decided that, in these attacks, the top-priority target at enemy bases would be heavy bombers, since they constituted the biggest offensive threat to the invasion forces.

Shortly after these decisions were made, the aerial reconnaissance of Luzon carried out on 20–25 November revealed that several American submarines were tied up alongside a tender in Manila Bay. The undersea craft were considered a worthwhile target despite the earlier decisions, for although the enemy's surface strength gave us no real concern, the same was not true of his submarines, which might well inflict telling damage on our invasion convoys. Consequently, the plan to send our entire strength against enemy air bases was modified in favor of employing fifteen to twenty percent of our bombers to attack the submarine concentration in Manila Bay. This modification proved short-lived, however, because the final reconnaissance on 5 December showed that most of the submarines spotted earlier had disappeared and that the few remaining were widely dispersed around the bay. Under these circumstances, the diversion of part of our bombers to attack them no longer seemed worthwhile, and the original plan was reinstated.

Next to be determined was H hour, the time for launching the air offensive. Obviously, the closer the time of our initial attack to the Pearl Harbor air strike, the greater would be our chances of achieving surprise with all its attendant advantages. But Japanese planes were to hit Pearl Harbor shortly after sunrise on 7 December, Hawaii time, which was several hours before daylight, 8 December, in the Philippines. Thus, we had given early consideration to a plan by which our bombers would open hostilities with a night attack in the small hours of 8 December, after which a second wave, mostly fighters, would deliver a postdawn attack, taking advantage of the confusion caused by the bombers. But since experience in China showed that our night bombsight was not sufficiently reliable, a night attack was rejected, and it was determined that H hour should be the earliest time at which successful bombing results could be expected.

In accordance with this decision, the final plan issued on 6 December for the first attack on Luzon fixed departure time for Eleventh Air Fleet attack groups from Taiwan bases at 0230 on 8 December. Fifteen minutes after an 0615 sunrise, Nichols Field was to be hit by one force of fifty-four bombers and fifty fighters from Takao, and Clark Field by another of fifty-four bombers and thirty-six fighters from Tainan. These two targets were selected because they were the main concentration points of the enemy's heavy bomber strength. The fighter groups, in addition to knocking down any air opposition, were to execute strafing attacks on both fields as well as on adjacent subsidiary bases. Bombers and fighters not employed in attack operations were assigned to combat air patrol over our Taiwan bases and to combat air and antisubmarine patrol for the convoys carrying the northern Luzon advance landing forces. Flying boats were assigned to patrol the waters east of the Philippines.

The overall plan of air operations also called for an attack on Davao, in southern Mindanao, to be executed at dawn on D day. This mission, however, was assigned to planes of the light carrier *Ryujo*, which it had been decided to employ in support of operations in the southern Philippines. The *Ryujo* was not a powerful carrier but, since no significant enemy air strength was located in the Davao area, she was considered adequate for this mission.

Prior to its final adoption, the Eleventh Air Fleet's operation plan was carried to Tokyo by special courier and submitted to the navy high command for approval. All radio communications that might risk tipping off the enemy to our intentions were naturally being avoided at this time. Consequently, it was with no little amazement—and annoyance—that we shortly received a radio message from Imperial General Headquarters in Tokyo, which said:

Imperial General Headquarters is quite confident of success in jamming the enemy's radio frequencies so that any warning dispatched to the Philippines as a result of the Carrier Striking Force's attack on Hawaii will not get through. Meanwhile, in order to assure the success of the Hawaii attack, it is imperative that the Eleventh Air Fleet in Taiwan take every precaution to guard against the enemy's learning of our military movements before that attack takes place.

Here was the highest headquarters instructing us to take precautions when, by sending out a message filled with such ultra-secret information, it was itself guilty of a most flagrant breach of security!

When the operations plan was issued on 6 December, our knowledge of the enemy situation, as pieced together from radio and other intelligence and from the reports of our air reconnaissance missions through 5 December, was roughly as follows:

1) Most of the enemy surface units and submarines observed in Manila Bay in late November were no longer there. It was estimated that the surface units had moved to southern Philippine waters, while the submarines appeared to be widely scattered. Several submarines had been located by radio to the east of the Philippines and around the Palau Islands, and others were believed to be maneuvering off western Luzon near Lingayen Gulf. Also, on several occasions subsequent to early November, American submarines had been reported to the east and west of Taiwan.

2) Most of the enemy's heavy bombers were based on Clark and Nichols, with a few scattered at Nielson, Murphy, Iba, Del Carmen, and other minor airfields situated around the two major bases. Starting in mid-November, daily routine air patrols had been carried out over the waters west of Luzon. On 5 December enemy air units in the Philippines had been ordered to a fifteen-minute standby alert.

In addition, our reconnaissance planes had succeeded in obtaining good photographic coverage of Lingayen Gulf, the northern Luzon invasion beaches, and the Bataan Peninsula. The photos of Bataan attracted keen attention, as they indicated the existence of extensive fortifications, but no one in our headquarters was capable of interpreting them accurately, and they were immediately sent to the Fourteenth Army for more careful study. Actually, it was not until our ground forces fought their way through these defenses in the spring of 1942 that their full extent and formidableness were realized.

On 5 December the arduous training program of the past two and a half months came to a close, and the succeeding two days were devoted to overhauling and servicing all planes. On the eve of hostilities the disposition of Eleventh Air Fleet forces was as follows:

Air Base	Units
Takao	Headquarters, Eleventh Air Fleet
	Headquarters, Twenty-third Air Flotilla
	54 medium bombers ("Betty")
	50 (approx.) Zero fighters
	7 land reconnaissance planes
Tainan	Headquarters, Twenty-first Air Flotilla
	36 medium bombers ("Nell")
	50 (approx.) Zero fighters
	8 land reconnaissance planes
Taichu	27 medium bombers ("Betty")
Kagi (army base)	27 transport planes (for possible use by paratroopers)

During the planning stage there had been a proposal that a part of our strength be shifted to bases on Hainan Island, off the South China coast, in order to avoid possible congestion at Takao and Tainan fields after D day. This proposal had been rejected for much the same reasons that had prevailed against splitting up our bombers and fighters in order to base the latter on carriers; but, as a precautionary measure, bases at Taihoku and Shinchiku in northern Taiwan, and at Karenko, on the east coast, were prepared to accommodate our planes in case congestion should develop at Takao and Tainan.

In addition to the strength enumerated above, the Eleventh Air Fleet also had twenty-four flying boats and thirteen old-type fighters ("Claude"), which were based on Palau. Army planes that were to participate in the Philippines invasion were based at Heito, Choshu, Kato, and Koshun, all on southern Taiwan.

On 7 December orders were issued restricting all Eleventh Air Fleet personnel to their bases, and the men were assembled and told for the first time that Japan would go to war with the United States and its allies the following day. The same afternoon the commanders of the army and navy air forces, together with their staffs, met in a joint conference at navy headquarters in Takao and decided, after studying the weather forecasts for the next day, that the planned air offensive against the Philippines should be initiated as scheduled. Orders to this effect were promptly issued to all subordinate air commands.

As the last hours of peace rapidly ticked away, there must have been many whose thoughts, like my own, were shadowed by misgiving. On seeing the outline for first-phase operations I had been struck by its resemblance to a railroad timetable and had wondered if a war could really be fought in this manner, so completely at the will of one side. These doubts had eased somewhat as we proceeded to tackle and solve each difficulty in planning and preparing for our own segment of the operation, but now, when the time for execution was at hand, I was once again assailed by apprehension that our grandiose plan of conquest might be just a castle in the air.

It was too late, however, for futile misgivings. Far to the east our Carrier Striking Force was already making its final run toward Oahu. The die of war was cast, and there remained naught but for each man to carry out his assigned role with courage and determination.

Since the attack groups were scheduled to take off at 0230 and cover the greater part of the outward flight in darkness, it was important that the pilots have all possible information about the weather along their line of flight. To obtain weather data, one scout plane was launched at 2030 and another at 2230 on 7 December. So important was this mission that it was decided to send a staff officer to fly as observer in the second plane, and I was chosen.

The weather that we encountered, while not ideal, was not so bad that the attack would have to be postponed. I gave my opinion, in brief radio reports, that our planes could take off on schedule. Use of the radio was kept to a minimum so as not to alert the enemy; nevertheless, there were clear indications that either my plane or the earlier one had been detected. At 2315 our radio monitoring center at Takao overheard Manila sending warnings to Iba and Clark Fields, and at the same time the enemy began jamming the frequencies our weather planes were using.

Just at this critical moment a completely unseasonal mist began to settle over the southern part of Taiwan, threatening to upset everything. By midnight the fog was so thick around Tainan that the air fleet operations staff was forced to postpone the Clark Field attack from that base. Nevertheless, it was decided to carry out the Nichols Field attack from Takao on schedule. Thirty minutes later, however, the bad weather had reached Takao; the planes there were also grounded. Under these circumstances it was necessary to modify the attack plan for execution as soon as the weather permitted.

Every minute's delay in our attack would render the enemy more prepared. If we still followed our original plan to attack

Clark and Nichols Fields, enemy fighter planes based at Iba would be ready for us and could strike the flanks of our squadrons coming and going. Therefore, the attack planned for Nichols Field was diverted to Iba, even though it meant that all of the heavy bombers based at Nichols (about half of the enemy's heavy bomber strength in the Philippines) would be left temporarily intact.

The plan was further modified to provide a diversion. A group of twenty-seven bombers was to be launched early and maneuver close to Iba in order to draw off intercepting fighters based there. After two hours of these tactics, the bombers would join the rest of our striking force in all-out attacks on Iba and Clark fields just as the intercepting fighters had to land for fuel.

At 0200 the fog over our Taiwan bases still showed no sign of clearing, but the entire air striking force was alerted to stand by on two-hour notice after 0400. Reports soon began coming in of successful Japanese attacks in other parts of the Pacific. At 0220 came word that the Pearl Harbor Striking Force had attacked the American naval base at Oahu. A United States declaration of war against Japan was reported at 0315. Forty-five minutes later a monitored enemy message from Guam announced attacks on that island. Next came a report that some of our air groups stationed in French Indochina had delivered strikes on Singapore.

Shortly thereafter the heavy weather in Taiwan seemed to be clearing, but by 0500 it had again closed in. At air fleet headquarters, anxiety mounted with each passing hour. Finally at 0700 the fog gave way to clearing mist, and the sortie was ordered, far behind schedule. As the projected diversionary feint by our bombers would cause a delay of two additional hours, with the result that the entire attack force would not return to base until after dark, the plan was again altered to eliminate that deception. All attack squadrons were in the air and heading south by 0845, and by 0900 the fog had

91

cleared completely. A radio report announced shortly that Batan Island had been occupied and that its airstrip was available for our use.

My weather plane, its mission completed, had arrived back over Takao at 0600. A heavy overcast seemed to cover all of southern Taiwan, and we had to go on to Taichu and land there until the weather cleared. Accordingly, I did not get back to Takao until after the attack squadrons had taken off, but was soon filled in on the changes that had taken place in my absence. Imperial General Headquarters in Tokyo had been making frequent inquiries about developments in Taiwan. It must have been a great relief to them to learn that the Philippine strikes had at last been launched.

Our entire operation plan had been based upon seizing the initiative, and here we were six hours behind schedule. What if the enemy got off an attack on Taiwan before their own bases were hit? Were we prepared for it?

Indeed, our defenses were far from complete. The air raid warning system and antiaircraft defenses were totally inadequate. Moreover, we had little air strength left, since in addition to the attack groups sent against Luzon, we had dispatched planes to provide antisubmarine patrol for the invasion convoys heading for Aparri and Vigan. A few planes had been held in reserve—some bombers for offshore patrol and fighters for combat air patrol over our airfields—but these were barely enough to compensate for our lack of search radar and would have been ineffective against a determined enemy attack.

Our apprehension over the possibility of an enemy attack on our bases persisted until our squadrons returned from their mission. It was certainly strange that no such attack developed. We were at war with the United States, expecting action at any minute, yet the atmosphere on Taiwan remained peaceful and serene almost to the point of unreality.

The sun was lowering to the horizon when the first returning bomber group came into sight, followed by a number of fighter planes. The speedy fighters were behind because they had remained to strafe ground objectives after the slower bombers had completed their work.

As the first plane landed and rolled to a stop, I stood by to listen to the remarks of the crew. Clambering down from their plane, they said in great bewilderment, "Are we really at war?" "We met no opposition." "What is the matter with the enemy?" When similar remarks were heard from other participants in the attack, a fearful suspicion occurred to me. Had the enemy fields been cleared of planes in advance, making our attack completely fruitless? We had frequently experienced this sort of frustration during the war in China, but we had been convinced that our attack on the Philippines would meet with strong opposition.

When the returning crews had reported in greater detail, however, it became apparent that the lack of opposition was not deliberate. There had been some slight reaction from anti-aircraft guns but no interception by enemy fighters. Even more astonishing was the fact that our fliers had found the enemy's planes lined up on the target fields as if in peacetime. Small wonder that the crews had been bewildered! We were bewildered too, for it seemed almost as if the enemy did not know that war had started. Could it be that no warnings from Pearl Harbor had yet gotten through to the Philippines?[1]

When action reports were in from all the squadrons, it was apparent that both our fighters and our bombers had scored great successes. The reports, of course, had to be very carefully studied to guard against duplication of enemy losses and to ensure accuracy of the final assessment. Aerial photos taken after the attacks were of limited assistance because there were no preattack photos with which to compare them. Indeed, this serious defect in our practice was not corrected until the last year of the Pacific War, and it largely accounts for the constant overestimation of attack results, which so gravely handicapped our operational planning. Perhaps the explanation of this failure lies in the fact that, during the

China Incident, the overestimation of attack results had never produced ill effects to make us more careful. In World War II we awoke to the danger, but only when it was too late.

Our final tally for the first day of war showed enemy losses to be 102 planes. This number included heavily damaged planes as well as those which had been totally destroyed.

Again there was a rash of urgent inquiries from top-level headquarters in Tokyo, especially anxious to learn the outcome of the first attack because they knew that it had been carried out far behind schedule. In answer, our successes as well as our losses—only seven Zero fighters and one bomber—were duly reported. Within minutes after this message had been filed, the information was being proudly broadcast to the Japanese public.

Since the first day's offensive had departed from the original plan, the attacks scheduled for 9 December also had to be modified. Nichols Field, which was to have been hit the first day but had been dropped in favor of attacking Iba, was now designated the primary target of the second day's offensive. It was decided to open the assault on Nichols with a small-scale night bombing attack, following with heavier strikes after dawn. Accordingly, a force of nine bombers took off around midnight on 8 December. Two planes had to turn back because of engine trouble, but the rest struck Nichols Field at 0303 on the ninth, destroying two hangars and setting another afire.

So far so good, but as dawn neared, our bases were again enveloped in mist. Around 0600 it appeared to be clearing and the main attack groups were readied for takeoff. Once more, however, the fog thickened and the attack had to be finally abandoned. Search flights, attacks on enemy shipping in the waters around Luzon, and all other scheduled missions were canceled as the foul weather persisted throughout the day. Our air bases, jammed with planes armed and fueled for the offensive, would have been perfect targets for an enemy attack. But the weather that rendered us immobile served also to protect us from attack.

During 9 December our radio intelligence center repeatedly picked up transmissions from American planes searching off the west coast of Luzon, and this activity continued for several days. We surmised that the enemy must be searching for possible invasion convoys and, quite likely, also for aircraft carriers, suspecting that our fighters must have taken off from ships to take part in the Luzon attacks. Such suspicion would have been natural, since the enemy, though probably aware that our Zeros had attacked over a distance of 420 miles in China, could hardly have expected that they were capable of flying from Formosa to attack the Philippines and return.

The third day, 10 December, brought a drizzling rain that started around 0300. The same weather officer who had forecast good weather for the opening day of hostilities now predicted that the rain would clear shortly and give way to fine flying conditions. The operations staff, though somewhat skeptical, decided to proceed on the basis of this prediction and made plans to send out all attack groups except our bombers based at Taichu, where the weather was too bad. The time of sortie for the first planes was set at 0830.

Before any planes took off, however, reports were received from the Vigan and Aparri invasion convoys, now standing off the landing beaches, that they had been under attack by American bombers and fighters since 0700. These raids were sporadic and did not inflict serious damage, but they were rather trying for some of the troops and naval crews who were receiving their baptism of fire. At any rate, eighteen Zeros were promptly detached from the attack groups to reinforce the air cover of the advance landing forces.

The attack groups that finally took off were thus somewhat smaller than we had originally planned. One group of twenty-seven bombers and thirty-six fighters went out to attack Nielson, Murphy, and other strips around Nichols Field; eighteen fighters headed for Del Carmen and its satellite bases; and fifty-four bombers flew to strike at Cavite Naval Base and shipping in Manila Bay. There was undoubtedly some special reason for this departure from the policy of concentrating everything on the destruction of enemy air forces, but I do not now recall what it was.

Despite the weather officer's optimistic forecast, the weather at our bases got worse instead of better after the attack groups took off. By dusk, when the squadrons should have been returning, visibility had dropped, and the ceiling was down to 100–150 meters. At every field anxiety mounted, and even the sensational news that Eleventh Air Fleet planes based in French Indochina had sunk two British battleships[2] off the coast of the Malay Peninsula failed to lighten our concern.

At last a heartening report came in that most of our fighters had made forced landings on Koshun airfield near the southern tip of Formosa. The headquarters wished to verify this report immediately, and as communications were bad between that field and Takao, I was ordered to proceed to Koshun by automobile and investigate. Upon arrival I found that nearly all of our Zeros had returned safely. They had for the first time engaged in aerial combat with American fighter planes, mostly P-40s, and had acquitted themselves well. The morale of the pilots was high.

After consolidating the action reports of the fighter pilots at Koshun, I headed back to Takao, arriving about midnight. By then, our bomber squadrons had also returned to their bases and reported on their successes. The combined results showed a total of 104 enemy planes destroyed, of which 43 had been shot down in air combat; direct bomb hits on two destroyers, two submarines, two small transports, and three other surface vessels; and severe damage to fuel dumps and other installations at Cavite Naval Base, where the bomber crews reported several blazing fires.

We did not learn until after the war that one of the most

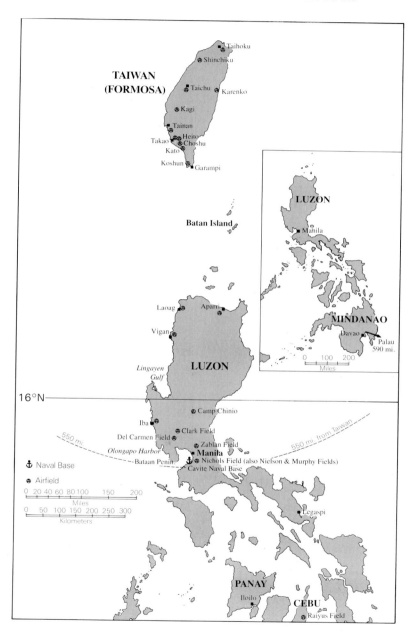

telling blows delivered by our bombers in the Cavite attack was the destruction of the enemy's supply of submarine torpedoes stored there. This severely restricted enemy submarine activity for the remainder of the battle for the Philippines.

The end of operations on 10 December found our planes so widely scattered that it was necessary to reassemble them before we could resume the air offensive. Consequently, no attacks were mounted on the eleventh, although search missions were flown to the west of Luzon and fighters were sent out to maintain combat air patrol over the northern Luzon anchorages where our advance forces had landed the preceding day.

The primary purpose of these landings was to gain possession of the airfields at Vigan and Aparri, so that they might be used as fighter bases for support of the later main landings on Luzon. The first echelon of army fighters moved up to Vigan on 11 December, and other army air units advanced to Aparri within the next few days. The Eleventh Air Fleet had also planned to move some of its Zeros to the Aparri field, which had been designated for joint use, but our observers with the landing force reported that the field was unfit for our planes, and the plan was dropped. The navy was habitually opposed to risking operational damage to its planes on poor fields and, in fact, was quite fastidious on this point. The army, on the contrary, because of the short range of its aircraft, necessarily pursued a policy of moving its air strength forward as far and as rapidly as possible, even though its planes might be jeopardized by poor airfield conditions.

After the one-day interruption of attack operations to permit reassembly of our planes, the air offensive was resumed with a vengeance on 12 December. Every one of the enemy's principal air bases on Luzon came under attack by either navy or army planes during that day, and more than forty enemy aircraft were shot down or destroyed. Aerial reconnaissance in the late afternoon indicated that the enemy had fewer than fifty operational planes left scattered about the island, and only about thirty ships still remained afloat in Manila Bay, as compared with almost fifty on 10 December.

Thus far we had been able to launch attacks only every other day, but on 13 December, for a change, the weather continued favorable, permitting the offensive to go on unabated. The attacks carried out during this day administered the coup de grâce to the U.S. air force in the Philippines and marked the successful conclusion of the initial air offensive. The next day, back on Taiwan, air fleet personnel were allowed to leave their bases for the first time since 7 December. This relaxation, however, did not extend to mechanics and maintenance men, who continued to work double shifts until the seventeenth to put all planes back into tip-top condition.

Our Zero pilots were now combat tested and had developed confidence that their fighters were superior to any that the enemy had. Some of them had previously fought in China, where most of the opposing fighter planes were Russian-built and flown by Chinese pilots. They had fully anticipated that American fighters would be more formidable adversaries, but during the first week of war they had met and successfully engaged the P-40s, which seemed to be the best fighter planes the enemy had in the Philippines, and had found them inferior to their own Zeros in everything except diving acceleration. Throughout the seventy days of action in this area, the confidence of our fighter pilots continued to grow, nurtured by the absence of effective opposition.

On 12 December, two days after the first landings on northern Luzon, a Japanese amphibious force from Palau made another advance landing at Legaspi, on southern Luzon, and quickly seized the airfield there. As at Aparri, the landing strip was found to be in poor condition, but since the navy alone was responsible for manning this base, nine Eleventh Air Fleet fighters were reluctantly ordered to move up to it on the fourteenth. Bad field conditions caused two of these planes to overturn in landing, resulting in their destruction, and further misfortune occurred the same day when an enemy P-40 sneaked in to strafe our planes, slightly damaging two more fighters and five bombers (the latter being used for transport) parked on the ground. Our combat air patrol over the base at the time was flying high and did not see the enemy fighter skim in low for his attack.

In spite of these setbacks, the Eleventh Air Fleet promptly dispatched additional fighters to Legaspi as replacements, and this group played an important part thereafter in assuring Japanese air supremacy over the Philippines. The detachment moved forward again to the island of Jolo, in the Sulu Archipelago, on 7 January and continued its good work, which was recognized in a unit citation by our commander in chief.

Thus, by 15 December, enemy air power in the Philippines had been smashed, and the job had been accomplished almost entirely by planes of the Eleventh Air Fleet. Army planes, after moving up to Vigan and Aparri, had carried out one strike on Iba and another on Clark Field, but outside of these two attacks they had left the destruction of the enemy air force to navy planes, since their own primary mission was direct support of ground troops. A consolidation of the battle results achieved by the Eleventh Air Fleet during the first week of war in the Philippines follows:

American losses		Japanese losses (from all causes)	
Aerial combat			
Fighters	63	Fighters	23
Bombers	4	Bombers	10
Flying boats	3	Flying boats	1
	70		34
Destroyed on ground			
Fighters	59		
Bombers and recon.	62		
Flying boats	9		
	130		

The American losses given in this tabulation were compiled at the time on the basis of a careful evaluation and synthesis of the reports of our air crews, but they are admittedly subject to the overestimation inherent in such a process.

After 14 December our offensive operations were greatly curtailed by a lack of indicated targets, although many worthwhile targets did, in fact, remain. There were still, for example, enemy cargo ships at anchor in Manila Bay, but they were ignored for the most part, since they did not constitute a direct menace to Japanese operations. Our only concern with these ships was the possibility that they might be used to evacuate enemy troops, and it was felt that we could deal with such an eventuality when and if it arose. Only one strike was made on them (on 14 December) by a flight of twenty-six bombers, and no damage was inflicted because the squadron leader's attack plan was inadequately prepared.

On the other hand, both the air fleet headquarters and the Combined Fleet were greatly concerned over the whereabouts of enemy warships that had suddenly disappeared from the Manila area. A photographic reconnaissance of central Luzon on 5 December had disclosed the presence of two cruisers, two destroyers, and a submarine in Manila Harbor; a seaplane tender, three destroyers, and six submarines in Cavite Harbor; and several warships in Olongapo Harbor. After hostilities were opened, these ships could not be located and it was presumed that they had taken refuge at Iloilo, on the coast of Panay, which was a good central position for strategic defense, as it lay outside the radius of Japanese reconnaissance flights. Accordingly, we planned a bomber attack on this locality from our Taiwan bases, a distance of 750 miles. The strike would have to be made without further information, as we could not reconnoiter the area. Furthermore, the bombers would be able to take only half their normal bomb load in order to carry the extra fuel required to fly the distance involved.

Combined Fleet Headquarters did not consider this plan adequate. A surprising message received by the Eleventh Air

Fleet from the Combined Fleet chief of staff stated: "Enemy surface craft are believed to be closing in with the intention of blocking our seizure of Davao. The Eleventh Air Fleet is advised to dispatch a part of its planes to Palau in anticipation of expected enemy action."

It should be noted that a powerful Japanese surface force, centered around three heavy cruisers, was then stationed at Palau, ready to sortie. This group was more than adequate to cope with any makeshift force that the enemy could assemble in the southern Philippines, yet the implication of the chief of staff's message was that our air force must run interference to eliminate every possible obstacle before the surface force moved into action. This was the first indication we had of such an attitude on the part of the Combined Fleet, and unfortunately it was not the last. But, like it or not, the "advice" of the chief of staff had to be honored the same as if it had come from the commander in chief of the Combined Fleet.

Accordingly, we prepared twenty-seven bombers to proceed to Palau on 17 December. The movement was actually delayed one day because of a request from the Japanese forces besieging Hong Kong for a bombing of that city and because of damage suffered in a typhoon that hit Taiwan on the seventeenth. The transfer, however, was carried out on the eighteenth, and the bomber group began operating from Palau the next day.

On the same day that the transfer was effected, the air fleet also carried out its own planned atack on Iloilo from Taiwan. The bombers found no enemy naval force, however, so the results were negative. Two days later, armed bombers searched a broad sector of the southern Philippines and the Celebes Sea hoping to find some trace of the vanished U.S. Asiatic Fleet, but these searches, too, proved unavailing.

With the occupation of Davao, the focus of our operations shifted southward. Our flying boat group advanced its base to Davao on the twenty-second, and fighter groups followed the next day. This enabled us to intensify our efforts to wipe out the last remnants of enemy air strength in the Philippines, and searches for the elusive enemy surface forces were also stepped up.

On 25 December Jolo was taken and again the field of battle shifted to the south. Although we were supreme in the air, enemy planes continued to make occasional attacks on our newly won bases both on Jolo and at Davao. Neither of these fields was large enough to accommodate a sufficient number of planes, and in addition the landing strips were extremely poor. That of the Davao field was too soft, and the one at Jolo was set on an incline, which meant that planes had to take off uphill and land downhill regardless of the direction of the wind.

Indeed, few of the air bases we occupied, not only in the Philippines but also in Borneo and the Celebes, were in satisfactory condition—a fact that made the planned southward advance of our air squadrons much more difficult than had been anticipated. Although navy planes did not use it, even Nichols Field, one of the two main enemy bases on Luzon, was found to have some of the roughest airstrips we had ever seen on a big operational base. At Davao and Jolo it took an inordinately long time before the fields were repaired and enlarged sufficiently to permit the bulk of our air squadrons to move forward to them. As an interim measure, small groups of fighter planes were moved up first, following temporary repairs, while the bombers stayed far behind on Taiwan until the fields were put in shape for their use.

In the latter part of December, the bomber squadrons were at last ordered to carry out intensive attacks on shipping in Manila Harbor, as well as on the fortifications of Corregidor. These attacks were begun on 25 December and continued for six days, involving a total of more than three hundred individual sorties. The results were not commensurate with the effort expended, but direct hits were registered on some thirty merchant vessels and two destroyers. On the day that Manila fell, we observed a great number of vessels that had settled to the bottom with only their superstructures visible above the surface of the water.

By the end of December the missions of the navy air forces in the Philippines had been fully accomplished, and the Eleventh Air Fleet's offensive action was thereafter directed toward the Celebes and the Dutch East Indies. But the complete occupation of the Philippines, which was supposed to be accomplished in fifty days, was actually not realized until the surrender of Bataan and Corregidor on 7 May 1942. Thus, compared with the slow progress of the land forces in this area, it must be conceded that the operations of the naval air forces were remarkably successful.

These air operations were unquestionably small in scale when compared with operations in the European theater and with later air campaigns in the Pacific. Nevertheless, the navy's shore-based air forces, which spearheaded the invasion of the Philippines, must be given due credit that, despite being opposed by approximately equal numbers of American planes at the outset, they never lost the initiative and accomplished their missions with exceedingly small losses in both personnel and aircraft.

In my opinion, our Zero fighters were most responsible for our success. In the Philippines campaign the Eleventh Air Fleet functioned like a smooth-running locomotive, and the Zeros were the pistons that propelled it forward. Like the infantryman of land warfare, they moved forward step by step, advancing their bases to keep up with the combat areas, and covering the entire zone of battle with their offensive might.

In his book *Strategic Air Power,* Stefan T. Possony observed, "Much as the battleship was the queen of the sea, the heavy bomber is the king of the skies."[3] Such, however, was not the case in the Japanese invasion of the Philippines. There our sword, shield, and buckler was the Zero fighter.

104

4

Japanese Operations in the Indian Ocean

TOSHIKAZU
OHMAE

After crippling the American fleet at Pearl Harbor, Japanese forces moved rapidly into the southwest Pacific to occupy key British, Dutch, and American territory. A desperate attempt by Allied naval forces to check the Japanese advance was foiled between 27 February and 1 March 1942 in the Battle of the Java Sea, which virtually eliminated Allied sea power in that area and left the Netherlands East Indies open for invasion. Japan stood on the verge of complete success in Southeast Asia and the Pacific. Her objectives for the "first stage" of the war—the occupation of those areas and the establishment of a defensive perimeter behind which to await the capitulation of her enemies—were largely achieved.

Yet Imperial General Headquarters found it hard to assume a passive stance after the brilliant victories of the first months of the war. Since Japan was ultimately in a position of material inferiority vis-à-vis her enemies, she had to retain the initiative. Her task was to concentrate forces and achieve decisive victories that would whittle down Allied

105

strength. An offensive could go in any one of three directions: toward the Central Pacific, toward Australia, or toward the Indian Ocean.

The Japanese high command chose first to move eastward against the British. As the emperor's soldiers marched into Burma, the Japanese navy advanced into the Indian Ocean for a series of devastating raids on British bases and shipping in April 1942. The following article describes these actions, sets them in the context of overall military planning, and explores the larger issue of India in Japanese strategic thinking.

Americans tend to ignore the early events of the war beyond the Strait of Malacca. Yet this article reminds us that the naval struggle was of vast extent, ranging over 120° of longitude from Pearl Harbor eastward through the Pacific and beyond it all the way to Colombo. It also reminds us that the naval war against Japan was not entirely an American enterprise. (Later in the war, the Royal Navy struck energetically against the Andamans and Sumatra in 1944 and took part in the Okinawan invasion of 1945.) Further, it reminds us what might have been. The catastrophe for the Allies of a British collapse in India was not so remote as hindsight would have it. Japanese leaders understood the weakness of Britain's position in India and, as the article shows, the rich possibilities a link-up with Germany in the Middle East would provide. H. P. Willmott writes, "Had the Japanese risked everything on a major military and naval effort in the Indian Ocean, then both Britain and the U.S.S.R. *might* have been forced out of the war."[1]

The reasons for Japan's halfhearted effort in the Indian Ocean are varied. As the article stresses, there was no Axis high command to implement a global strategy. The army-navy rivalry in Japan prevented coherent war planning. A more proximate cause, though only hinted at in the article, was that Japan did not focus on just one of the targets for a new "second-stage" offensive but tried all three. Soon after the Indian Ocean actions, operations were undertaken against Port Moresby in the Australian area and Midway in the Central Pacific. When one encountered stiff opposition and the other brought a serious defeat, further planning for India was halted.

THE JAPANESE considered a plan for military co-operation with Germany in the area of the Indian Ocean before the war, but those deliberations were destined to assume no concrete form. Japanese plans for the Greater East Asia War drawn up in 1941 did provide for the conquest of Burma, which was to serve several purposes. The action would secure a firm anchor for the right flank of the Japanese line of defense in the Indian Ocean. It would also cut off the Burma Road and, with it, Allied aid to the Nationalist Chinese regime at Chungking. The planners assumed as a matter of course that as a consequence of the Burma operation the Indians would rise up against British rule in greater and greater numbers, helping the Japanese military leadership achieve its declared goal of defeating England in partnership with Germany and Italy. Such a defeat would also accomplish the liberation of India. But it was beyond Japan's capacity to take direct military measures against India, and therefore no plan for such actions was drawn up in the prewar period.

It was only when the favorable development of the war became obvious that plans concerning India were broached. The Liaison Conference between Imperial General Head-quarters and the government drafted a resolution on 10 January 1942, which stated:

> With regard to India, certain measures should be under-taken together with the severance of India's communica-

107

tions with England and America and in synchronization with the progress of military operations. These measures will aim at undermining Indian cooperation with England and also at activating an anti-British movement.

Basing their discussions on this resolution, the army and navy staffs at Imperial General Headquarters reached an agreement on 15 January concerning the most important assignments to be carried out with regard to India. This meeting, however, was largely an affair of the Army Section of Imperial General Headquarters.

Contrary to expectation, the military agreement between Japan, Italy, and Germany concluded in Berlin on 19 January contained no concrete declarations about a common strategy in the area of the Indian Ocean aside from several vague hints about a German thrust eastward and a Japanese one westward. Agreement was reached only on using the line of 70°E longitude to mark off the German and Italian area of operations from that of the Japanese, meaning that India and most of the Indian Ocean fell into the Japanese area.

At this time the staff of the Combined Fleet began, independently of the Naval General Staff and Imperial General Headquarters, to make second-stage war plans to follow the obviously successful conclusion of the first stage. The fleet staff concerned itself initially with the possibility of a conquest of Hawaii, which, it was hoped, would force the Americans into the much-desired decisive battle. When it became apparent that this project could not be carried out, the staff turned to the Indian Ocean. On 27 January it adopted a suggestion made by Captain Kuroshima, chief of the Operations Division of the Naval General Staff, and drew up a plan to employ superior forces to destroy the British Eastern Fleet, take Ceylon, and establish contact with the Germans in the Middle East. But this far-reaching operations plan was not approved by the Naval General Staff and the Navy Section of Imperial General Headquarters, who considered it premature. Another objection was that the army could not place

108

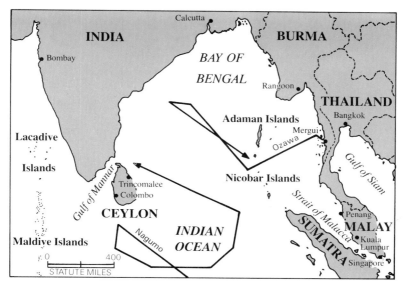

The Indian Ocean Sortie, April 1942

the necessary troops at the disposal of the navy. Only a limited operation, the occupation of the Nicobar and the Andaman Islands, was ordered on 4 February.

In place of the conquest of Ceylon, the Combined Fleet decided on 14 February to carry out a fleet operation in the Indian Ocean that would include a carrier strike on that island. Since the British fleet was expected to interfere with the operations in the Andamans and Burma, the planners wanted their carrier fleet to operate east of Ceylon in the Indian Ocean and wait for a favorable opportunity to launch a surprise attack on that island and the British fleet. The Combined Fleet conducted war games from 20 to 22 February and afterward worked out a concrete plan for the operation, the execution of which was ordered on 9 March.

The operation had two goals. One was to smash the British Eastern Fleet, which was reckoned at two carriers, two battleships, three heavy cruisers, four to seven light cruisers, and a

109

number of destroyers. The other was to destroy the British air forces in the vicinity of the Bay of Bengal, which were estimated to consist of about three hundred aircraft. These blows, together with the rapid advance of the army in Burma, were to provide the first impetus for India's eventual disengagement from Britain. An attack of army troops against the Indian front would follow. This attack, it was hoped, would relieve the pressure on Axis forces fighting in the Middle East. Consequently, the operations that were taking place in step with the progress of the German army were to constitute the first move toward cooperation of Japanese and German forces.

Operations of the Combined Fleet in the vicinity of Ceylon and the Bay of Bengal proceeded as follows in broad outline: In the latter half of March, while weaker Japanese forces occupied the Andaman Islands, the Second Submarine Squadron, with six submarine-cruisers, put to sea from Penang.[2] Its objectives were to reconnoiter waters near Ceylon and take up positions in the most important passages through the Laccadive and Maldive Islands, providing a degree of protection for the western flank of the Japanese fleet. Vice Admiral Nobutake Kondo, commander of the Second Fleet, led the entire operation. He ordered the carrier fleet under Vice Admiral Nagumo to sortie from Staring Bay in the south of Celebes on 26 March. This fleet, including five large fleet carriers, four fast battleships, two heavy cruisers, one light cruiser, and eight destroyers, took a course south of Java and pushed forward into the Indian Ocean.

Various indications led the British to believe that the Japanese would attack Ceylon on 1 April. The British Eastern Fleet under Vice Admiral Somerville cruised in the waters south of Ceylon from 31 March until 2 April. This fleet was made up of a fast division of two carriers, one battleship, two cruisers, and six destroyers, and a slow division of four older battleships, three cruisers, and five destroyers. On 2 April both divisions formed up for the run to Addu Atoll, a base

110

that had been kept secret up to that time. There the fleet refueled from 4 to 5 April.

A British reconnaissance seaplane observed the advancing Japanese carrier group in the afternoon of 4 April. This gave the British commander on Ceylon, Admiral Layton, time to prepare his defenses and disperse the great aggregation of ships in Colombo harbor. Japanese carrier aircraft attacked on the morning of 5 April and, after overcoming British fighters and antiaircraft fire, did heavy damage to land installations. But they sank only a destroyer, an armed merchant cruiser, and a tanker, besides damaging two other ships. Jap-

The heavy cruiser HMS *Cornwall*, sunk by Japanese carrier aircraft south of Ceylon on 5 April 1942. *Courtesy of Ted Silberstein*

The HMS *Dorsetshire*, sister ship of the *Cornwall*, shared her fate off Ceylon. *Courtesy of Jay Launer*

111

anese search planes, however, detected the British cruisers
Dorsetshire and *Cornwall,* which were seeking to join the
British Eastern Fleet. Japanese dive bombers sank the two
ships with many direct hits.

British formations put out from Addu Atoll again and for
a time were as close as two hundred nautical miles to the
Japanese carriers, yet neither side made contact with the
other.

Admiral Nagumo made a great curve to the southeast to
prepare for a second attack, this time against Trincomalee,
scheduled for the morning of 9 April. On this occasion as
well, British aerial reconnaissance made an early discovery of
the attacking forces. They sighted the Japanese forces in the
afternoon of 8 April, which allowed the harbor of Trincomalee to be largely emptied of shipping. The vessels that had
put to sea, however, were summoned back too soon after the
first Japanese carrier aircraft raid, and Japanese search planes
located them about noon. In the course of the afternoon,
Japanese dive-bombers sank the British carrier *Hermes,* a destroyer, a corvette, two tankers, and two transports.

Although Japanese aircraft losses had totaled only seventeen up to that point, as opposed to about forty on the British

The British light carrier *Hermes,* destroyed by Nagumo's dive-
bombers south of Trincomalee.

side, Admiral Nagumo broke off action in the afternoon of the ninth. In his opinion, the expected results had been achieved. In retrospect it is clear, however, that the main goal of these operations should have been to engage the British Eastern Fleet and destroy it with the superior Japanese forces at hand.

While the operations of the carrier group off Ceylon proceeded, a smaller force under Vice Admiral Ozawa sallied from the Strait of Malacca toward the Indian coast and the Bay of Bengal. Dividing into three groups, this force—consisting of a light carrier, six cruisers, and four destroyers—attacked Allied shipping between Calcutta and Madras, sinking twenty-one ships totaling 93,247 tons and damaging four more ships between 3 and 6 April. During the same period Japanese submarine-cruisers sank five ships totaling 32,404 tons and torpedoed an additional transport.

Thus, at the cost of seventeen Japanese aircraft, operations in the Indian Ocean produced British losses of one carrier, two heavy cruisers, two destroyers, one corvette, and one armed cruiser, as well as damage to thirty-one merchant ships of 153,603 tons and seven additional transports. Yet, because the British Eastern Fleet had escaped destruction, the actual aim of the operation was not attained.

In the course of studies that began in early February relating to second-stage operation plans, the Army General Staff and the Naval General Staff had both concluded that the destruction of British power in the Indian Ocean and the conquest of Ceylon were not possible for the time being. Thus they had directed that planning for such operations be halted. But starting in May 1942 the favorable actions of the German army in North Africa placed the British Near Eastern Army in an extremely critical situation, which the Army General Staff interpreted as now offering the possibility to realize the dream of uniting Japanese and German forces by a thrust through the Indian area. Debates over a landing on Ceylon were revived at the end of May and the beginning of June.

Just at this time, however, the Japanese navy was suffering from a shortage of battle-ready ships for the Ceylon operation. It had lost four of its best carriers during the first days of June in the fateful Battle of Midway. Yet the army, spurred by the great success of the Germans in North Africa, ignored the setback at Midway and took the position that the Ceylon operation was an absolute necessity. The Army General Staff ordered preparations in Directive No. 1196 of 29 June. In brief, it contained the following points:

> 1) The goal of the operation was the destruction of enemy forces in the area of the Indian Ocean. Ceylon was to be captured first to provide Japanese forces with bases for further operations.
>
> 2) Participation of one to two army divisions and most of the Combined Fleet would be necessary for the capture of Ceylon.
>
> 3) Commencement of the operation seemed feasible when the enemy was pinned down in the west by the progress of German forces in North Africa and the Near East.
>
> 4) In preparation for this operation:
>
> a) The Thirty-eighth and Forty-eighth divisions, located in Java and northern Sumatra, would be brought together and emphasis placed on training them for amphibious operations in the tropics.
>
> b) All attainable information on the enemy would be energetically collected.
>
> c) The major problems of the operation would be investigated in separate studies.
>
> 5) The operation was called Operation Number Eleven.

Today it is difficult to form a clear picture of the circumstances and the estimates of the situation at that time. The documentary evidence that remains is full of gaps. Descriptions from memory of those who participated contain an element of uncertainty. Yet with all due caution the following can be established.

The Situation of the Japanese Army

The army was unable to grasp the magnitude of the blow caused by the defeat at Midway. It understood that for the time being the navy was not ready to carry out the operation against Ceylon, yet it regarded offensive operations in this area as within the realm of possibility. A further consideration was important in the army's commitment to the Ceylon operation. There was a real fear that front-line units could easily sink into idleness now that the first stage of the war had been successfully concluded. It was considered necessary to revive the fighting spirit of the soldiers by clearly defining goals for future operations; training would be goal-oriented. The supreme command thus considered the task of maintaining morale to be no less critical than other aspects of military preparations. Testimony from various members of the Southern Army staff also refers to the necessity for goal-conscious training and thorough psychological preparation.

Orders for the preparation of this operation were issued without any accompanying orders for its execution. This meant that if other exigencies compelled the army to cancel it, little harm would have been done.

Planning for the action against Ceylon rested fundamentally on the extent of German successes in the North African

A war painting by Shori Arai. A Val receives the acclaim of the carrier crew as it leaves on a mission. *U.S. Army photograph*

115

battles. There was no plan for the Japanese army in the area of the Indian Ocean that did not depend on German success. Doubtless, the Ceylon action would have been allowed to proceed only if the German army in the Near East had stood on the brink of decisive victories. The army believed that with favorable developments of that kind, the navy would give up its negative attitude regarding Ceylon.

The Situation of the Japanese Navy

Although the navy took a different view of landing on Ceylon after the Battle of Midway, it greatly appreciated the need to defeat the British Eastern Fleet in the Indian Ocean. Admiral Nagano, chief of the Naval General Staff, expressed this position in a memorandum to the throne on 7 July: "The plans drawn up in agreement with Germany and Italy for interrupting enemy resupply and destroying the enemy fleet in the western part of the Indian Ocean would bring about a generally most favorable situation."

In July 1942, when the Combined Fleet became aware of German-Italian plans for the occupation of Alexandria and Malta, it began to study actions in the Indian Ocean. As a result of these studies, the First Southern Expeditionary Fleet was given the mission of carrying out offensive actions in the Bay of Bengal. This fleet, which consisted of a training cruiser, three destroyers, and a large number of frigates, minelayers, torpedo boats, and some smaller escort vessels, had the primary task of protecting the Strait of Malacca and the reinforcements going to Burma and the Andamans. For the purposes of this new mission, the Seventh Cruiser Squadron (two heavy cruisers) and the Third Destroyer Squadron (one light cruiser and twelve large *Fubuki*-class destroyers) were allotted to the First Southern Expeditionary Fleet and formed up with it at Mergui, on the west coast of the Malayan Peninsula. Preparations were also made for the participation of twenty naval reconnaissance planes based at Singapore, Sabang, and Rangoon, as well as sixteen planes that could be catapulted from shipboard. The operation was planned for August and September but had to be postponed several times because of poor weather conditions. During August the situation in the South Pacific became critical after the American landing on Guadalcanal. The result was that the forces allotted for the Indian Ocean had to be transferred to the Solomons, and the plans for offensive operations in the Bay of Bengal had to be abandoned. Only submarines actually put out to sea. Two submarine-cruisers reconnoitered the Arabian Sea and the east coast of Africa. Three large fleet submarines operated in the area of Ceylon and on the Indian coast between Ceylon and Calcutta. They sank nine ships totaling 43,218 tons, but these actions had little effect on relative force levels in the Indian Ocean.

These plans suggest that the navy was in full agreement with the army on the important aspect of concurrent timing. On the contrary, the navy gave its consent only reluctantly, continuing to resist because of the large scale of the army's contemplated actions. Its own plans were considerably more modest and did not by any means envision a landing on Ceylon.

Because of the progress of the war in the south Pacific in August and September, further planning for India naturally came to a halt. Yet no formal directive was issued canceling preparations for an operation against Ceylon.

The above account distinctly demonstrates what an enormous influence the serious defeat of the Japanese fleet at Midway had on the global strategic situation. The nations of the Tripartite Pact neglected to create an institution of planning and leadership for grand strategy with powers comparable to those of the Anglo-American Combined Chiefs of Staff. Today we can clearly see that an institution that directed a grand strategy would have been of the greatest importance. It is certainly a coincidence that Field Marshal Rommel began his offensive in North Africa at the same time as the Japanese fleet sortied for its attack on Midway. But what prospects would have arisen if the German attack had been combined with a powerful Japanese offensive in the Indian Ocean! Neither in Japan nor in Germany was there a timely and manifest recognition of these possibilities. The German leadership and the Japanese army thought in continental rather than global terms. The Japanese navy closed its eyes to modern total war and remained a prisoner of the idea of a traditional decisive battle, wanting to exploit to the utmost its superiority of forces to bring about such a battle. The possibilities that lay in the interruption of the enemy's sea supply lines were not recognized.

5

The Battle of Midway

MITSUO
FUCHIDA
and
MASATAKE
OKUMIYA
with an Appendix

After the Japanese victories at Pearl Harbor and in the southwest Pacific, the only remaining obstacle to their surge was the American carrier task force, and the first significant interruption of the Japanese grand design occurred in May 1942, when their Port Moresby Invasion Group was halted in the Battle of the Coral Sea. This epochal encounter between carriers marked a new era in naval combat, constituted a strategic victory for the United States, and forced the Japanese to modify their original plans. Convinced that an effective consolidation of conquests and the creation of a viable defense perimeter could not be achieved so long as major elements of the American fleet continued to control the central Pacific, the Japanese authorities embarked on the Midway operation, which was designed to eliminate this troublesome obstacle and enlarge the defense perimeter.

Admiral Nimitz, commander in chief of the Pacific Ocean Area, was charged with the seemingly impossible task of containing the Japanese thrust with what remained of the decimated American fleet. Since carriers constituted his only effective weapon, he conserved them carefully, realizing that an improper allocation or a serious reversal could prove disastrous. He was able to benefit from some unusual and brilliant intelligence work that appeared to reveal the enemy's intentions, and he made what turned out to be the proper decision by shifting his carriers from the southwest to the central Pacific. Measures to bolster the defense at Midway and emergency repairs on damaged ships brought the American defenders to maximum readiness.

The Japanese, initially unaware that their plans had been discovered, soon realized that the element of surprise had been lost. Yet they remained confident, in part due to a mistaken impression that the American carriers were still in the southwest Pacific. Errors in estimating American naval strength were compounded by faulty air and submarine reconnaissance. The task force hit bad weather, missed a fueling rendezvous, broke radio silence, and approached its objective with a misconception of American intentions and capabilities.

The initial stage of this crucial battle favored the Japanese, but soon they were repulsed and lost their carrier striking force. This engagement, which represented maximum Japanese aggressiveness, gave the American forces time to build up their strength and provided Admiral King with cogent arguments for a greater allocation of resources to the Pacific. Historians will continue to debate the extent to which chance, Japanese mistakes, and American combat performance affected the outcome, though all influenced the course of the battle.

The following chapter is in three sections: "Prelude to Battle," "Five Fateful Minutes at Midway," and an appendix, "America Deciphered Our Code." The first places the operation in the context of the Japanese strategic design and cites the Japanese errors of omission and commission. The second vividly re-creates events aboard a mortally wounded carrier as the prospective victory turned into certain defeat.

In both of these, which were co-written by Fuchida and Okumiya, Fuchida is the narrator; he was present at Midway, although only as an observer, as he was recovering from an appendectomy.

The third section gives the present-day Japanese understanding of how Americans learned of the Midway attack in advance. From 1966 to 1980 the War History Section of the Japan Defense Agency published a 102-volume history of the Japanese part in World War II, the *Senshi Sosho*, or War History Series. Volume 43 of the series, *Middowee kaisen* (The Battle of Midway), contains an account of Japanese naval codes in relation to the battle. The late Edwin T. Layton, rear admiral, U.S. Navy, ret., a former intelligence officer and one of the foremost Japanologists in the navy, translated this section. Comments by Admiral Layton are enclosed in brackets.

PRELUDE TO BATTLE

THE MIDWAY operation had two central objectives. The first and more limited one was the seizure of Midway as an advance air base to facilitate early detection of enemy carrier forces operating toward the homeland from Hawaii, with the attack on the Aleutians as a diversion. The second, much broader objective was to draw out what was left of the U.S. Pacific Fleet so that it could be engaged and destroyed in a decisive battle. If both these objectives were achieved, the invasion of Hawaii itself would become possible, if not easy.

To carry out the invasion plan, the Combined Fleet mustered the mightiest force in Japanese naval history. The task force embraced more than two hundred ships, including eleven battleships, eight aircraft carriers, twenty-two cruisers, sixty-five destroyers, and twenty-one submarines, as well as almost seven hundred planes, carrier- and shore-based. These forces were organized as follows:

121

Main Force—Admiral I. Yamamoto
First Carrier Striking Force—Vice Admiral C. Nagumo
Midway Invasion Force—Vice Admiral N. Kondo
Northern (Aleutians) Force—Vice Admiral M. Hosogaya
Advance Submarine Force—Vice Admiral T. Komatsu
Shore-Based Air Force—Vice Admiral N. Tsukahara

Between 26 and 29 May these forces sortied from three widely separate takeoff points: Ominato, on northern Honshu; Hashirajima, in the western Inland Sea; and Saipan and Guam, in the Marianas. All cleared port uneventfully, evading the prying eyes of enemy submarines, and headed for the battle areas.

[In the following account, Japanese and East longitude times and dates are used unless otherwise noted.]

On 29 May 1942, at the end of the day, the various Japanese forces were forging ahead toward their objectives without any hitch other than the fog still plaguing the Second Carrier Striking Force of the Aleutians Force under Rear Admiral Kakuji Kakuta. On the thirtieth, however, the weather also began to deteriorate over that part of the central Pacific now being traversed by the Yamamoto and Kondo forces. In the afternoon the Yamamoto force encountered rain and increasingly strong winds, which caused the destroyers and cruisers to ship occasional seas over their bows. The formation cut its speed to fourteen knots, and zigzagging was discontinued.

It was not only the weather that was ominous. The *Yamato*'s radio crew, which was keeping a close watch on enemy communications traffic, intercepted a long urgent message sent by an enemy submarine from a position directly ahead of the Japanese transport group. The message was addressed to Midway. It was in code, and we could not decipher it, but it suggested the possibility that the transport group had been discovered. If so, it would be logical for the enemy to surmise that the transports were heading for Midway for the purpose of an invasion attempt, since so large a convoy sailing east-

A Japanese bomber makes a direct hit on the USS *Yorktown*. The crippled carrier was sunk by a Japanese submarine three days later. *Official U.S. Navy photograph*

northeast from Saipan could hardly be taken as merely a supply force destined for Wake Island. Admiral Yamamoto's staff officers, however, were not greatly concerned. They nonchalantly took the view that if the enemy had guessed our purpose and now sent his fleet out to oppose the invasion, the primary Japanese objective of drawing out the enemy forces to be destroyed in decisive battle would be achieved.

Bad weather continued in the central Pacific on 31 May. Not only the Yamamoto and Kondo forces but also Vice Admiral Nagumo's carriers, which were a few hundred miles farther east, encountered strong winds and occasional rain. Meanwhile, the *Yamato*'s radio intelligence unit observed further signs of enemy activity, especially of aircraft and submarines, in the vicinities of both Hawaii and the Aleutians. Admiral Yamamoto and his staff surmised that the activity around Hawaii might presage a sortie by an enemy task force, and they waited eagerly for reports of the flying boat reconnaissance that was to have been carried out over Hawaii.

The two Type 2 flying boats assigned to this mission, designated the second Operation K, had duly moved up to Wotje

123

and were scheduled to take off at 2400 on 30 May (Tokyo time) to reach French Frigate Shoals by 1430 (1730 local time) shortly before sunset, refuel there from submarines, and take off within an hour and a half for Hawaii. If all went well, they would arrive over Hawaii at 2045 (0115 on 31 May, local time). After completing their reconnaissance, they would fly nonstop back to Wotje, reaching there about 0920 (Tokyo time) on 1 June. Vice Admiral Komatsu, commander of the Submarine Force, had assigned six submarines to the operation. Three of them were to refuel the flying boats at French Frigate Shoals. Another was to take station on a line between Wotje and French Frigate Shoals, about 550 miles from the latter, to serve as a radio picket ship. The fifth was to lie off Keahole Point, Hawaii, as a rescue boat in case of mishap, and the sixth was to be stationed eighty miles southwest of Oahu for patrol and weather observation.

The carefully laid plan, however, had already gone awry. On 30 May one of the fueling subs (the *I-123*) reached French Frigate Shoals and, to its dismay, found two enemy ships lying at anchor.[1] It urgently radioed this information back to Kwajalein, adding that there appeared to be little prospect of carrying out the refueling operation at the shoals as planned. Vice Admiral Goto, Twenty-fourth Air Flotilla commander at Kwajalein, who was responsible for directing the second Operation K, accordingly ordered a twenty-four-hour postponement, instructing the *I-123* to keep watching the shoals in the hope that the enemy ships would depart.

This forlorn hope was blasted the following day, when the *I-123* reported that she had sighted two enemy flying boats near the entrance to the shoals. This made it apparent that the enemy was already using the shoals as a seaplane base, and there consequently was no alternative but to abandon Operation K altogether.

These disappointing developments were promptly communicated to Admiral Yamamoto in the *Yamato*. The failure of Operation K meant that there was no way of ascertaining what enemy strength actually was present at Pearl Harbor. Nevertheless, Combined Fleet Headquarters still hoped that if an enemy force did sortie from that base to oppose the Midway invasion, the submarine cordons scheduled to be established by Vice Admiral Komatsu's command between Hawaii and Midway by 2 June would suffice to provide advance warning as well as knowledge of the enemy's strength.

The first of June found the Yamamoto force still surrounded by dark, forbidding weather, although the rain had ceased. Low-lying clouds made visibility so poor that it was barely possible from the *Yamato*'s bridge to make out the phantom shapes of the destroyer screen 1,500 meters away.

It was now time for the Main Force to rendezvous with its tanker train and refuel. The oilers were not found at the prearranged rendezvous point, however, and the *Hosho* launched planes to look for them. The search proved unsuccessful because of the poor visibility, but at this point the tanker train radioed its position to the *Yamato*, making it possible to effect a rendezvous. At the same time, because radio silence had been broken, it had to be assumed that the enemy was now aware of the position of the Main Force.

Evidence that the enemy had already discovered or, at the very least, strongly suspected the Japanese advance toward Midway mounted sharply during the day. Radio intelligence disclosed a marked intensification of communications traffic out of Hawaii, and 72 out of 180 intercepted messages were "urgent," indicating an unusually tense situation. A chance encounter five hundred miles north-northeast of Wotje between a Japanese patrol plane from that island and an American flying boat, which exchanged brief machine-gun bursts, also showed that the enemy had extended his Midway-based air patrols out to a radius of seven hundred miles. There were still further reports to the effect that enemy submarines had been sighted about five hundred miles northeast and north-northeast of Wake Island, which indicated the existence of an

125

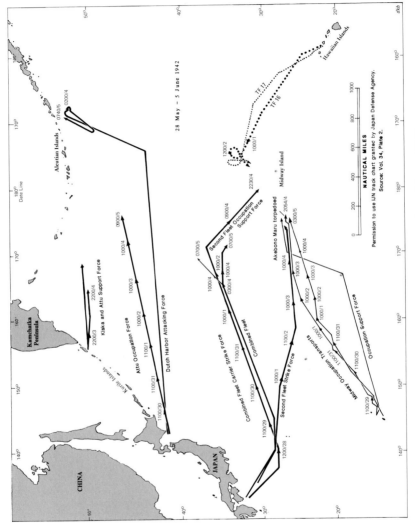

Approach Routes to Midway and the Aleutians, 28 May–5 June 1942

American submarine patrol line about six hundred miles southwest of Midway.

By this time the Midway transport convoy had reached a point about one thousand miles to the west of Midway and was proceeding on a northeast course. Advancing at a rate of 240 miles in 24 hours, the convoy would enter the seven-hundred-mile patrol radius of American planes from Midway on 3 June, two days before the date set for the preinvasion air strike on the island by the Nagumo force. It looked as if the transports were advancing too fast for their own safety.

Cloudy weather, with occasional rain, persisted in the vicinity of the Yamamoto force on 2 June. Fueling operations, which had started the preceding day after the delayed rendezvous with the tanker train, were resumed in the morning but had to be discontinued again when visibility became so poor that the ships could no longer maneuver safely.

Still another hitch now developed in the operation plan. Owing to overhauls, which had delayed their departure from the homeland, the submarines of Subron 5 assigned to the B cordon line scheduled to be established on this date to the northwest of Hawaii failed to reach their assigned positions. Boats of Subron 3 assigned to the A cordon line to the west of Hawaii were also unable to reach their stations because of delays resulting from the miscarriage of Operation K. Actually, it was not until 4 June that the submarines arrived on station.

With the submarine cordons not yet established, Admiral Yamamoto and his staff remained completely in the dark regarding enemy task force activities. During 2 June, however, the submarine I-168, reconnoitering the Midway area, sent in a few bits of information regarding the situation there. Its report stated that no ships had been observed other than a picket ship south of Sand Island; that the enemy appeared to be flying intensive air patrols to the southwest, probably to a distance of six hundred miles; that a strict alert seemed to be in force, with numerous aircraft on defensive patrol day and

127

night; and that many cranes were visible on the island, suggesting that the installations were being expanded. This eventually turned out to be the only significant reconnaissance report sent in by a submarine during the Midway operation.

On 2 June the Nagumo force, cruising some six hundred miles ahead of the Yamamoto force, entered an area enveloped in thick mist. Clouds hovered low over the ocean, and light rain began to fall. Fog seemed likely to follow. Already visibility was so restricted that neighboring ships in the formation could scarcely see each other.

Vice Admiral Nagumo in the flagship *Akagi* was as much in the dark about enemy fleet movements and intentions as was Combined Fleet Headquarters. Indeed, because of the *Akagi*'s limited radio-receiving capacity, coupled with the radio silence being observed by the advancing Japanese forces, he lacked much of the information that had been received by Admiral Yamamoto in the fleet flagship and which strongly suggested that the enemy was already aware or highly suspicious of a Japanese advance toward Midway and was preparing to counter it. This was precisely the situation that Rear Admiral Kusaka, chief of staff of the Nagumo force, had feared might develop. Prior to the sortie, he had repeatedly requested that the *Yamato* relay all important radio intelligence information to the *Akagi*, but it was apparent that Admiral Yamamoto and his staff still hoped that surprise had not been lost and felt it advisable to continue radio silence.

Thus, as 2 June ended, the Japanese forces were steadily approaching their objectives through adverse weather. Thus far there was no certain indication that any of them had actually been detected by the enemy, and every man from Admiral Yamamoto on down hoped that the precious advantage of surprise was still in Japanese hands.

By dawn on 3 June the mist that the Nagumo force had encountered the previous afternoon had become a heavy blanket of fog. Steaming at fog navigation quarters, adjoining ships in the formation were often unable to see each

other across their scant six-hundred-yard intervals. Powerful searchlights were turned on, but they scarcely showed
through the gloom.

The task of maintaining zigzag courses through this endless
veil, with only momentary and infrequent glimpses of con-
sorting ships, was arduous and nerve-racking. Yet it had to
be done, for we were entering waters patrolled by enemy
submarines. While the fog was advantageous in keeping us
hidden from prying scout planes, this benefit was canceled by
the increased hazards of navigation. And the enemy's radar-
equipped submarines would be little affected by the fog that
at the same time prevented us from launching antisubmarine
patrol planes. To cope with these and other problems that
beset us, all ships were at full alert and double watches were
posted at submarine lookout stations.

The starboard side of the *Akagi's* bridge was occupied by
Admiral Nagumo and his entire staff. They stared silently at
the impenetrable curtain surrounding the ship, and every face
was tense with anxiety. Captain Aoki and his navigation officer, Commander Miura, on the other side of the bridge,
devoted all their energies to keeping the ship on course and
maintaining position in the formation. From time to time they
leaned out of the window in an effort to peer through the all-
encompassing fog.

A change in course was scheduled for 1030, and it had to
be executed if our timetable was to be carried out. Yet prior
to execution of such a course change in heavy fog, confirmation would have to be communicated to all ships in the formation lest some stray and become lost. With visibility so
limited, flag signals obviously could not be employed, and
even searchlights would be ineffective to transmit the required
orders. Nothing remained but to use radio, which was sure
to reveal our presence to the enemy.

This distressing situation brought out the fact that the Nagumo force had been assigned two tactical missions that were
essentially incompatible. The assignment to attack Midway

on 5 June in preparation for the landing operation put the task force under rigid limitations of movement. The other mission—to contact and destroy enemy naval forces—required that Nagumo be entirely free to move as the situation required, and it also made it absolutely essential to keep our whereabouts secret while searching for the enemy.

A decision obviously had to be made as to which of these missions should be given precedence. Nagumo's staff had pondered this problem hypothetically for a long time, but now the task force commander faced a situation requiring a definitive choice. And still there was not a scrap of information about enemy naval forces. In this critical situation the senior member of the staff, Captain Oishi, was the first to speak up.

"The Combined Fleet operation order gives first priority to the destruction of enemy forces. Cooperation with the landing operation is secondary. But the same order specifically calls for our air attack on Midway Island on 5 June. This means that the air attack must be carried out exactly as scheduled, provided that nothing is heard about enemy task forces by the time we are ready to launch.

"If we do not neutralize the Midway-based air forces as planned, our landing operations two days later will be strongly opposed and the entire invasion schedule will be upset."

With his usual directness Admiral Nagumo voiced the question in everyone's mind: "But where is the enemy fleet?"

In answer Oishi continued, "We know nothing of the enemy's whereabouts because we failed to reconnoiter Pearl Harbor. But if his forces are now in Pearl Harbor, we shall have plenty of time to prepare to meet them should they sortie following our strike at Midway. They will have over 1,100 miles to cover.

"Even if they are already aware of our movements and have sortied to meet us, they cannot be far out from base at this moment and certainly can't be near us. I think the first thing for us to do is to carry out the scheduled raid on Midway."

At this, Chief of Staff Kusaka turned to the intelligence officer and asked if radio intercepts had given any indication of enemy movements. Informed that nothing had been picked up, Kusaka asked if any information had been received from the Combined Fleet flagship *Yamato*. Receiving another negative response, he addressed a suggestion to Admiral Nagumo. "Since we must maintain the schedule at all costs, would you approve the use of our low-powered interfleet radio for sending the order to change course?"

The commander assented to this as the only feasible solution, and the order was sent accordingly by medium-wave transmitter. A reduced-power transmission would reach out to the fringe of our force and, it was hoped, not farther. This method was not entirely safe, but it had worked on occasion in the past, thanks to enemy carelessness. In this case, however, the message was received clearly even by the *Yamato*, which was six hundred miles to the rear. Inasmuch as an enemy task force was then only a few hundred miles distant—a fact of which we were totally unaware—it was highly probable that it, too, intercepted this signal.[2]

From the first, the planners of the Midway operation calculated that the enemy naval forces would be lured out by the strike at Midway Island and not before. We had not the slightest idea that the enemy had already sortied, much less that a powerful enemy task force was lying in wait, ready to pounce upon us at any moment.

Dense fog still hung over the Nagumo force throughout the afternoon and on into the night. In contrast to the tenseness prevailing on the *Akagi's* bridge, her wardroom hummed with the lusty chatter and laughter of carefree flyers whose only job was to jump into their planes and roar off at a moment's notice. Everything was ready for the scheduled air raid two days hence, and no flight missions had been ordered because of the adverse weather.

THE BATTLE OF MIDWAY

Meanwhile, the weather around the Yamamoto force, six hundred miles astern, improved somewhat in the afternoon, and refueling, which had been suspended on the preceding day, was resumed.

The worst thing about the persistent fog was that it kept enemy movements completely secret. As previously mentioned, the plan for a flying boat reconnaissance of Pearl Harbor on 31 May, using French Frigate Shoals as a refueling point, had been thwarted. Nor did our submarines provide any information. The sole remaining source of information was radio intelligence. As early as 30 May, such intelligence picked up by Admiral Yamamoto's flagship, the *Yamato*, had pointed to brisk enemy activity in the Hawaii area, especially of patrol planes. This strongly suggested the possibility of a sortie by an enemy force from the Hawaiian base, but the Combined Fleet sent no warning whatever to Admiral Nagumo!

Admiral Nagumo and his staff were deeply chagrined when they learned after the battle that Combined Fleet Headquarters had suspected an enemy sortie because of this radio intelligence. Why did the Combined Fleet not transmit this vital information to the Carrier Striking Force so that any danger of its being taken by surprise might be averted?

There were two reasons behind this unfortunate failure. First, Combined Fleet Headquarters thoughtlessly believed that the *Akagi*, closer to the enemy than the *Yamato*, would naturally have obtained the same information, and that Admiral Nagumo was formulating his decisions accordingly. Second, they feared that radio communication between the two forces would reveal their positions to the enemy.

At any rate, Admiral Yamamoto's failure to issue necessary precautionary instructions to the forces under his command was an important cause of the Midway fiasco. He was to blame for being too preoccupied with the idea of "radio silence." It is easy to imagine what angry and bitter emotions must have welled up inside Rear Admiral Kusaka when he went on board the *Yamato* after the battle to report on the near annihilation of the Nagumo force and learned for the first time of the Combined Fleet's negligence. He might well have said, "How often I told them not to let this happen!"

Combined Fleet Headquarters, however, was not alone to blame. The Naval General Staff back in Tokyo was also partially responsible, for it again sent a radio message to the Combined Fleet concerning enemy fleet activity in the Solomon Islands area. The message carried the strong implication that the movement of the Japanese forces toward Midway was not yet suspected by the enemy.

The Naval General Staff had originally opposed the Midway operation, but once having given its approval, it was responsible for the whole operation even more than was Combined Fleet Headquarters. With the decisive battle only a few days off, it was engaged in gathering all available intelligence regarding enemy activity. What particularly attracted the attention of the intelligence staff were indications that an American carrier task force still was operating in the Solomons area. If this was true, as the Naval General Staff believed, it constituted powerful evidence that the enemy did not yet suspect our intention, for if he did, he would obviously have called all his few remaining carriers back from the southwest Pacific. Even after intercepting a number of "urgent" calls from American radios in the Hawaii-Midway area, the Naval General Staff still stuck fast to its first conclusion.

The storm of battle was about to break, and for the first time in six months, fate did not seem to be smiling upon us. No change, however, was made in the operational plan. All forces plunged on through the boundless fog like stagecoach horses driven blindly forward by a cracking whip.

[From this point, West longitude dates and Midway times, Zone plus 12, are used.]

133

At about 0300 on the morning of 4 June the noisy drone of plane engines warming up roused me from slumber. I got out of bed and attempted to stand, but my legs were still unsteady. The engines alternately hummed and then rose to a whining roar. The *Akagi* was preparing to launch her planes for the attack on Midway.

Unable to resist the desire to be topside at takeoff time, I slipped out of the sick bay. The watertight doors of every bulkhead had been closed, leaving only a small manhole in each door open for passage. It was an arduous task to squeeze through these small openings in my weakened condition, and cold sweat soon ran down my forehead. I frequently felt exhausted and dizzy and had to squat on the floor to rest.

The passageways were empty. All hands were at their stations. Lights were dimmed for combat condition, and one could see a distance of only a few feet. With great effort I finally climbed the ladders up to my cabin just below the flight deck, clutching the handrails every step of the way. There I paused long enough to catch my breath and put on a uniform before going on to the flight control post. The first-wave attack planes were all lined up on the flight deck. The warm-up was completed, and the roar of the engines subsided. I found Commander Masuda, air officer of the *Akagi*, in charge of flight preparations.

My colleagues expressed concern over my getting out of bed, but they understood when I explained that I could not bear to hear the sound of the engines and remain below in sick bay. I looked up at the dark sky. The dawn still seemed far off. The sky was cloudy, and the weather, while not good, was not bad enough to prevent flying. The sea was calm.

I asked Lieutenant Furukawa when sunrise would be.

"At 0500, sir," was the reply.

"Have search planes already been set out?"

"No, sir. They will be launched at the same time as the first attack wave."

"Are we using the single-phase search system?"

"Yes, sir. As usual."

I recalled the attacks on Colombo and Trincomalee in the Indian Ocean, two months earlier, when single-phase search had been employed. It had not been a wise tactic. In both instances, the searches had spotted enemy surface forces while our attack groups were away hitting the enemy bases, and this had caused our carriers some anxious moments. With this in mind, I inquired what plans had been made for the eventuality that our search planes might sight an enemy fleet during the Midway attack.

"No need to worry about that," Lieutenant Commander Murata replied. "After the first attack wave departs, the second wave, consisting of Lieutenant Commander Egusa's dive-bombers, my torpedo bombers, and Lieutenant Commander Itaya's Zeros, will be available to attack an enemy surface force, if discovered."

"I see. Well, that's a good team, and we can just hope that the enemy fleet does come out so we can destroy it. What searches are scheduled?"

Furukawa explained them to me on the map board. "There are seven lines extending east and south, with Midway lying within the search arc. We are using one plane each from the *Akagi* and *Kaga*, two seaplanes each from the *Tone* and *Chikuma*, and one from the *Haruna*. The search radius is three hundred miles for all planes except the *Haruna*'s, which is a Type 95 and can do only half that."

Although the coverage appeared adequate, I still felt that a two-phase search would have been wiser. A single-phase search might be sufficient if we wished only to confirm our assumption that no enemy fleet was in the vicinity. However, if we recognized the possibility that this assumption might be wrong and that an enemy force might be present, our searches should have been such as to assure that we could locate and attack it before it could strike at us. For this purpose a two-phase dawn search was the logical answer.

As the term indicates, a two-phase search employs two sets

135

A 1933 view of the battleship *Haruna,* which took part in the Battle of Midway. She was sunk by carrier aircraft in the Inland Sea, 24 July 1945. *Courtesy of Hajime Fukaya*

of planes that fly the same search lines, with a given time interval between them. Since our planes were not equipped with radar at this time, they were completely reliant on visual observation and could search effectively only by daylight. Consequently, to spot an enemy force as soon as possible after dawn, it was necessary to have one set of planes (the first phase) launched in time to reach the end of their search radius as day was breaking. This meant that the areas traversed in darkness on their outbound flight remained unsearched. Hence, a second-phase search was required over these same lines by planes taking off about one hour later.

Men assigned to the first phase of such a search obviously had to be well trained in night flying. Nagumo had such pilots and could have used this method, but it would have required twice as many planes as a single-phase search. Despite the importance of conducting adequate searches, our naval strategists were congenitally reluctant to devote more than a bare minimum of their limited plane strength to such missions. Ten percent of total strength was all they were willing to spare for search operations, feeling that the rest should be reserved for offensive use. But such overemphasis on offensive strength had proven detrimental to our purposes before this, and it would again.

Naturally enough, Admiral Nagumo was eager to devote maximum strength to the Midway attack and did not want to use any more planes for the search than seemed absolutely necessary. Since he had no reason to suspect the presence of an enemy force in the area, he was satisfied that a single-phase search was an adequate precaution.

Search planes from the *Akagi* and *Kaga* were launched at 0430, simultaneously with the departure of the first Midway attack wave. The *Haruna*'s seaplane was also catapulted at that time. But the *Tone* and *Chikuma* planes, which were covering the center lines of the search pattern, were delayed. Watching the two cruisers, I noticed that the last of their search planes did not get off until just before sunrise, nearly half an hour behind schedule. It was later learned that the *Tone*'s planes had been held up by catapult trouble, while one of the *Chikuma*'s planes had a balky engine. This last plane was forced to turn back at 0635, when the engine trouble recurred and it ran into foul weather.

Although poorly advised, a one-phase search dispatched half an hour before sunrise would still have been helpful if everything had worked out as planned. But the delay in launching the *Tone*'s planes sowed a seed that bore fatal fruit for the Japanese in the ensuing naval action. Reviewing the full story of the battle on both sides, we now know that the enemy task force was missed by the *Chikuma*'s search plane, which, according to the plan, should have flown directly over it. The enemy force was discovered only when the belated *Tone* plane, on the line south of the *Chikuma* plane, was on the dogleg of its search. Had Admiral Nagumo carried out an earlier and more carefully planned two-phase search, had the observer of the *Chikuma* plane been more watchful on the outward leg of his search, or had the seaplanes been on schedule, the disaster that followed might have been avoided.

137

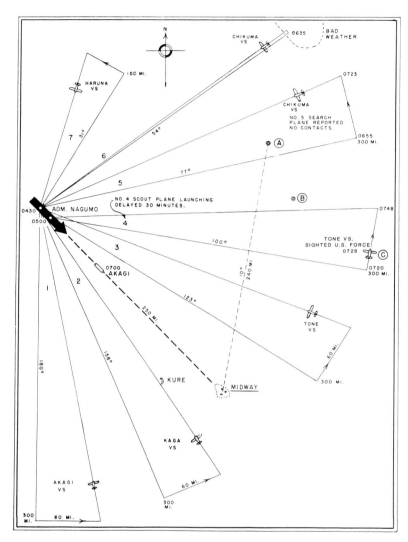

The Japanese Search for the American Task Force: At 0728 a Japanese reconnaissance pilot sighted the U.S. force under Admiral Spruance. The pilot thought that he was at point C and located the American ships at 240 miles from Midway on a ten-degree bearing, which would have placed them at point A. Actually, the U.S. force was at point B. Presumably the Japanese pilot had made an error in navigation.

The fundamental cause of this failure, again, lay in the Japanese navy's overemphasis on attack, which resulted in inadequate attention to search and reconnaissance. In both the training and the organization of our naval aviators, too much importance and effort were devoted to attack. Reconnaissance was taught only as part of the regular curriculum, and no subsequent special training was given. Also, there were no organic reconnaissance units of any appreciable size in the Japanese navy. When reconnaissance missions were required, attack planes were usually refitted and assigned to perform them. There were no carrier-borne planes designed solely for search. In the Pearl Harbor attack, every carrier-borne bomber of Nagumo's six carriers was assigned to the attack, leaving for search only some ten-odd float planes from the accompanying battleships and cruisers. This had been perhaps the basic reason for Admiral Nagumo's decision to withdraw upon that occasion without exploiting his advantage. At the critical moment, when he had to decide whether to launch another attack on Pearl Harbor, he did not have the vital information that reconnaissance planes could have provided. The Nagumo force continued to suffer from this same lack of aerial reconnaissance in every action that followed.

While searching for the British fleet in the Indian Ocean earlier in the year, our search planes often lost their way and the carriers had to send out radio signals on which they could home. This, however, also alerted the enemy to our positions, and the result was an understandable reluctance on the part of Admiral Nagumo and his staff to send out search planes if it could possibly be avoided. This reluctance was still present in the Midway operation and, coupled with the erroneous estimate of the enemy situation, was responsible for the inadequate searches ordered by Admiral Nagumo.

One small step toward remedying the search weakness of the Nagumo force had been taken prior to the sortie for Midway. After prolonged negotiations with the authorities, Nagumo had succeeded in getting two carrier-based reconnaissance planes of a new type, on which experiments had just been completed. This type had been designed originally as a dive-bomber, but was altered for use as a search plane. It was later designated the Type 2 carrier-borne reconnaissance plane, or *Suisei* ("Judy") dive-bomber, and there were high expectations for its success in reconnoitering powerful enemy task forces. Two of these planes had been loaded on board the *Soryu*.

At the time his search and attack groups took off from the carriers on 4 June, Admiral Nagumo was unaware that the Japanese Transport Group had already been sighted and attacked by planes from Midway. The *Akebono Maru,* the only ship hit, was not damaged enough to hinder her progress, but the important thing was that the enemy was fully alerted to the presence of Japanese ships approaching Midway. And we did not know that they knew.

FIVE FATEFUL MINUTES AT MIDWAY

Preparations for a counterstrike against the enemy had continued on board our four carriers throughout the enemy torpedo attacks. One after another, planes were hoisted from the hangar and quickly arranged on the flight deck. There was no time to lose. At 1020 Admiral Nagumo gave the order to launch when ready. On the *Akagi*'s flight deck all planes were in position with engines warming up. The big ship began turning into the wind. Within five minutes all her planes would be launched.

Five minutes! Who would have dreamed that the tide of battle would shift completely in that brief interval?

Visibility was good. Clouds were gathering at about three thousand meters, however, and though there were occasional breaks, they afforded good concealment for approaching enemy planes. At 1024 the order to start launching came from the bridge by voice-tube. The air officer flapped a white flag, and the first Zero fighter gathered speed and whizzed off

140

the deck. At that instant a lookout screamed: "Hell-divers!" I looked up to see three black enemy planes plummeting toward our ship. Some of our machine guns managed to fire a few frantic bursts at them, but it was too late. The plump silhouettes of the American Dauntless dive-bombers quickly grew larger, and then a number of black objects suddenly floated eerily from their wings. Bombs! Down they came straight toward me! I fell instinctively to the deck and crawled behind a command post mantelet.

The terrifying scream of the dive-bombers reached me first, followed by the crashing explosion of a direct hit. There was a blinding flash and then a second explosion, much louder than the first. I was shaken by a weird blast of warm air. There was still another shock, but less severe, apparently a near miss. Then followed a startling quiet as the barking of guns suddenly ceased. I got up and looked at the sky. The enemy planes were already out of sight.

The attackers had gotten in unimpeded because our fighters, which had engaged the preceding wave of torpedo planes only a few moments earlier, had not yet had time to regain altitude. Consequently, it may be said that the American dive-bombers' success was made possible by the earlier martyrdom of their torpedo planes. Also, our carriers had no time to evade because clouds hid the enemy's approach until he dove down to attack. We had been caught flatfooted in the most vulnerable condition possible—decks loaded with planes armed and fueled for an attack.

Looking about, I was horrified at the destruction that had been wrought in a matter of seconds. There was a huge hole in the flight deck just behind the amidship elevator. The elevator itself, twisted like molten glass, was drooping into the hangar. Deck plates reeled upward in grotesque configurations. Planes stood tail up, belching livid flame and jet-black smoke. Reluctant tears streamed down my cheeks as I watched the fires spread, and I was terrified at the prospect of induced explosions, which would surely doom the ship. I

141

heard Masuda yelling, "Inside! Get inside! Everybody who isn't working, get inside!"

Unable to help, I staggered down a ladder and into the ready room. It was already jammed with badly burned victims from the hangar deck. A new explosion was followed quickly by several more, each causing the bridge structure to tremble. Smoke from the burning hangar gushed through passageways and into the bridge and ready room, forcing us to seek other refuge. Climbing back to the bridge, I could see that the *Kaga* and *Soryu* had also been hit and were giving off heavy columns of black smoke. The scene was horrible to behold.

The *Akagi* had taken two direct hits, one on the after rim of the amidship elevator, the other on the rear guard on the port side of the flight deck. Normally neither would have been fatal to the giant carrier, but induced explosions of fuel and munitions devastated whole sections of the ship, shaking the bridge and filling the air with deadly splinters. As the fire spread among planes lined up wing to wing on the after flight deck, their torpedoes began to explode, making it impossible to bring the fires under control. The entire hangar area was a blazing inferno, and the flames moved swiftly toward the bridge.

Because of the spreading fire, our general loss of combat efficiency, and especially the severance of external communications, Nagumo's chief of staff, Rear Admiral Kusaka, urged that the flag be transferred at once to the light cruiser *Nagara*. Admiral Nagumo gave only a halfhearted nod, but Kusaka patiently continued his entreaty: "Sir, most of our ships are still intact. You must command them."

The situation demanded immediate action, but Admiral Nagumo was reluctant to leave his beloved flagship. Most of all he was loath to leave behind the officers and men of the *Akagi,* with whom he had shared every joy and sorrow of war. With tears in his eyes, Captain Aoki spoke up: "Admiral,

142

I will take care of the ship. Please, we all implore you, shift your flag to the *Nagara* and resume command of the fleet."

At this moment Lieutenant Commander Nishibayashi, the flag secretary, came up and reported to Kusaka: "All passages below are afire, sir. The only means of escape is by rope from the forward window of the bridge down the deck, then by the outboard passage to the anchor deck. The *Nagara*'s boat will come alongside the anchor deck port, and you can reach it by rope ladder."

Kusaka made a final plea to Admiral Nagumo to leave the doomed ship. At last convinced that there was no possibility of maintaining command from the *Akagi*, Nagumo bade the captain good-bye and climbed from the bridge window with the aid of Nishibayashi. The chief of staff and other staff and headquarters officers followed. The time was 1046.

On the bridge there remained only Captain Aoki, his navigator, the air officer, a few enlisted men, and myself. Aoki was trying desperately to get in touch with the engine room. The chief navigator was struggling to see if anything could be done to regain rudder control. The others were gathered on the anchor deck fighting the raging fire as best they could. But the unchecked flames were already licking at the bridge. Hammock mantelets around the bridge structure were beginning to burn. The air officer looked back at me and said, "Fuchida, we won't be able to stay on the bridge much longer. You'd better get to the anchor deck before it's too late."

In my condition this was no easy task. Helped by some sailors, I managed to get out of the bridge window and slid down the already smoldering rope to the gun deck. There I was still ten feet above the flight deck. The connecting monkey ladder was red hot, as was the iron plate on which I stood. There was nothing to do but jump, which I did. At the same moment another explosion occurred in the hangar, and the resultant blast sent me sprawling. Luckily the deck on which I landed was not yet afire, for the force of the fall

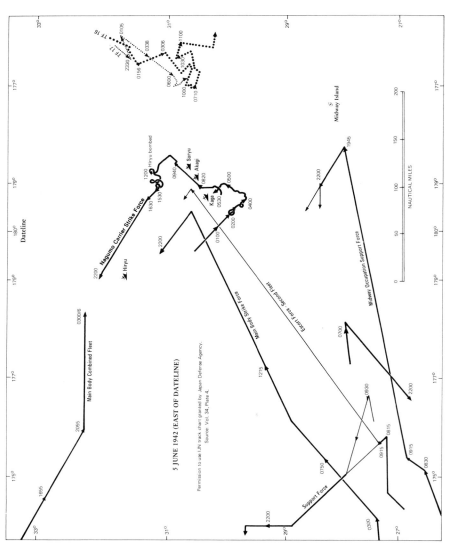

Battle of Midway, 5 June 1942

5 JUNE 1942 (EAST OF DATELINE)

Permission to use IJN track chart granted by Japan Defense Agency.
Source: Vol. 34, Plate 4.

Main Body Combined Fleet

Nagumo Carrier Strike Force

Dateline

Hiryu bombed

Soryu
Akagi
Kaga

Hiryu

Main Body Strike Force

Escort Force, Second Fleet

Midway Occupation Support Force

Midway Island

Support Force

TF 16
TF 17

NAUTICAL MILES

0   50   100   150   200

33°   31°   29°   27°

175°   177°   179°   180°   179°   177°

knocked me out momentarily. Returning to consciousness, I struggled to rise to my feet, but both of my ankles were broken.

Crewmen finally came to my assistance and took me to the anchor deck, which was already jammed. There I was strapped into a bamboo stretcher and lowered to a boat, which carried me, along with other wounded, to the light cruiser *Nagara*. The transfer of Nagumo's staff and of the wounded was completed at 1130. The cruiser got under way, flying Admiral Nagumo's flag at her mast.

Meanwhile, efforts to bring the *Akagi*'s fires under control continued, but it became increasingly obvious that this would be impossible. As the ship came to a halt, her bow was still pointed into the wind, and pilots and crew had retreated to the anchor to escape the flames, which were reaching down to the lower hangar deck. When the dynamos went out, the ship was deprived not only of illumination but of pumps for combating the conflagration as well. The fireproof hangar doors had been destroyed, and in this dire emergency even the chemical fire extinguishers failed to work.

The valiant crew located several hand pumps, brought them to the anchor deck, and managed to force water through long hoses into the lower hangar and the decks below. Firefighting parties, wearing gas masks, carried cumbersome pieces of equipment and fought the flames courageously. But every induced explosion overhead penetrated to the deck below, injuring men and interrupting their desperate efforts. Stepping over fallen comrades, another damage-control party would dash in to continue the struggle, only to be mowed down by the next explosion. Corpsmen and volunteers carried out the dead and wounded from the lower first aid station, which was jammed with injured men. Doctors and surgeons worked like machines.

The engine rooms were still undamaged, but fires in the middle deck sections had cut off all communication between the bridge and the lower levels of the ship. Despite this, the explosions, shocks, and crashes above, plus the telegraph indicator, which had rung up "Stop," told the engine-room crews in the bowels of the ship that something must be wrong. Still, as long as the engines were undamaged and full propulsive power was available, they had no choice but to stay at General Quarters. Repeated efforts were made to communicate with the bridge, but every channel of contact, including the numerous auxiliary ones, had been knocked out.

The intensity of the spreading fires increased until the heat-laden air invaded the ship's lowest sections through the intakes, and men working there began dropping from suffocation. In a desperate effort to save his men, the chief engineer, Commander K. Tampo, made his way up through the flaming decks until he was able to get a message to the captain, reporting conditions below. An order was promptly given for all men in the engine spaces to come up on deck. But it was too late. The orderly who tried to carry the order down through the blazing hell never returned, and not a man escaped from the engine rooms.

As the number of dead and wounded increased and the fires got further out of control, Captain Aoki finally decided at 1800 that the ship must be abandoned. The injured were lowered into boats and cutters sent alongside by the screening destroyers. Many uninjured men leapt into the sea and swam away from the stricken ship. The destroyers *Arashi* and *Nowaki* picked up all survivors. When the rescue work was completed, Captain Aoki radioed to Admiral Nagumo at 1920 from one of the destroyers, asking permission to sink the crippled carrier. This inquiry was monitored by the Combined Fleet flagship, whence Admiral Yamamoto dispatched an order at 2225 to delay the carrier's disposition. Upon receipt of this instruction, the captain returned to his carrier alone. He reached the anchor deck, which was still free from fire, and there lashed himself to an anchor to await the end.

The standby destroyer *Arashi* received word at midnight that an enemy task force was ninety miles to the east of the

Akagi's and her own position. One hour later a lookout sighted several warships through the darkness, and the commander of the destroyer division, Captain K. Ariga, gave chase with all four of his ships: the *Arashi, Nowaki, Hagikaze,* and *Maikaze*. He failed to catch up with or identify these shadows, however, and returned to stand by the carrier. It later turned out that the mysterious ships belonged to Rear Admiral Tanaka's Desron 2.

When Admiral Yamamoto ordered the delay in disposing of the *Akagi,* it was because he saw no need for haste in this action since his force was then proceeding eastward to make a night attack on the enemy. Now, however, as defeat became apparent and the prospect of a night engagement grew dim, a quick decision became necessary. At 0350 on 5 June, Admiral Yamamoto finally gave the fateful order to scuttle the great carrier. Admiral Nagumo relayed the order to Captain Ariga, directing him to rejoin the force when his mission had been accomplished. Ariga in turn ordered his four destroyers to fire torpedoes at the doomed ship. The *Nowaki's* skipper, Commander Magotaro Koga, later described how painful it was for him to fire the powerful new Type 93 torpedo into the carrier, which was his first target of the war. Within twenty minutes all four destroyers had fired. Seven minutes later the sea closed over the mighty ship, and a terrific underwater explosion occurred, sending out shocks that were felt in each destroyer. The carrier's final resting place was at latitude 30°30′N, longitude 179°08′W. The time was 0455, just minutes before the sun rose on 5 June.

All but 263 members of the carrier's crew survived this last of her great battles. Before the fatal torpedoes were fired, the *Akagi's* navigator, Commander Y. Miura, had boarded the carrier and persuaded Captain Aoki to give up his determination to go down with the ship. Both men finally moved safely to one of the destroyers.

The *Kaga,* which had been hit almost simultaneously with the *Akagi* in the sudden dive-bombing attack, did not last as long as the flagship. Nine enemy planes had swooped down on her at 1024, each dropping a single bomb. The first three were near misses, which sent up geysers of water around her without doing any damage. But no fewer than four of the next six bombs scored direct hits on the forward, middle, and after sections of the flight deck. The bomb that struck closest to the bow landed just forward of the bridge, blowing up a small gasoline truck that was standing there and spreading fire and death throughout the bridge and the surrounding deck area. Captain Jisaku Okada and most of the other occupants of the ship's nerve center were killed on the spot. The senior officer to survive the holocaust was Commander Takahisa Amagai, the air officer, who immediately took command of the carrier.

Furious fires broke out, seemingly everywhere. During the succeeding hours damage-control crews fought desperately to check the spreading flames, but their efforts were largely unavailing, and there was scarcely a place of shelter left in the entire ship. Commander Amagai was forced to seek refuge on the starboard boat deck, where he was joined by many of the men. The carrier's doom seemed imminent.

Some three and a half hours after the bombing attack, a new menace appeared. The flame-racked carrier now lay dead in the water and had begun to list. Commander Amagai, scanning the adjacent sea, suddenly discerned the telltale periscope of a submarine a few thousand meters from the ship. Minutes later, at 1410, Lieutenant Commander Yoshio Kunisada, a damage-control officer, saw three white torpedo wakes streaking toward the carrier. They seemed sure to hit, and Kunisada closed his eyes and prayed as he waited for the explosions. None came. Two of the torpedoes barely missed the ship, and the third, though it struck, miraculously failed to explode. Instead, it glanced off the side and broke into two sections, the warhead sinking into the depths while the buoyant after section remained floating nearby. Several of the *Kaga*'s crew, who were swimming about in the water after having jumped or been blown overboard when the bombs struck the carrier, grabbed onto the floating section and used it as a support while awaiting rescue. Thus did a weapon of death become instead a lifesaver in one of the curious twists of war.

The *Kaga*'s protecting destroyers, the *Hagikaze* and *Maikaze*, were unaware of the submarine's presence until the torpedo attack. Immediately they sped out to its suspected location and delivered a heavy depth-charge attack, the results of which were not known. The submarine failed to reappear, so the destroyers turned back to the crippled carrier and resumed rescue operations.

Meanwhile, uncontrollable fires were raging throughout the *Kaga*'s length, and finally, at 1640, Commander Amagai gave the order to abandon ship. Survivors were transferred to the two destroyers standing by. Two hours later the conflagration subsided enough to enable Commander Amagai to lead a damage-control party back on board in the hope of saving the ship. Their valiant efforts proved futile, however, and they again withdrew. The once crack carrier, now a burning hulk, was wrenched by two terrific explosions before sinking into the depths at 1925 in position 30°20'N, 179°17'W. In this battle eight hundred men of the *Kaga*'s crew, one third of her complement, were lost.

The *Soryu*, the third victim of the enemy dive-bombing attack, received one hit fewer than the *Kaga*, but the devastation was just as great. When the attack broke, deck parties were busily preparing the carrier's planes for takeoff, and their first awareness of the onslaught came when great flashes of fire were seen spouting from the *Kaga*, some distance off to port, followed by explosions and tremendous columns of black smoke. Eyes instinctively looked skyward just in time to see a spear of thirteen American planes plummeting down on the *Soryu*. It was 1025.

Three hits were scored in as many minutes. The first blasted the flight deck in front of the forward elevator, and the next two straddled the amidship elevator, completely

149

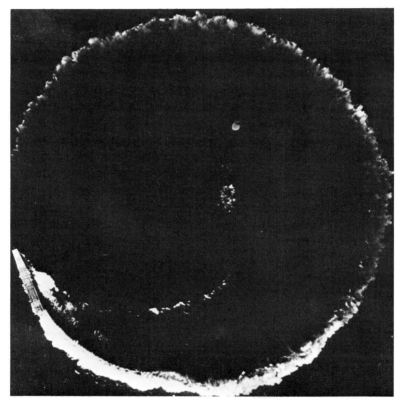

The Japanese carrier *Soryu* maneuvering to avoid bombs in the Battle of Midway. *Courtesy of the National Archives*

wrecking the deck and spreading fire to gasoline tanks and munition storage rooms. By 1030 the ship was transformed into a hell of smoke and flames, and induced explosions followed shortly.

In the next ten minutes the main engines stopped, the steering system went out, and fire mains were destroyed. Crewmen forced by the flames to leave their posts had just arrived on deck when a mighty explosion blasted many of them into the water. Within twenty minutes of the first bomb hit, the ship was such a mass of fire that Captain Ryusaku Yanagimoto ordered "Abandon ship!" Many men jumped into the water to escape the searing flames and were picked up by the destroyers *Hamakaze* and *Isokaze*. Others made more orderly transfers to the destroyers.

It was soon discovered, however, that Captain Yanagimoto had remained on the bridge of the blazing carrier. No ship commander in the Japanese navy was more beloved by his men. His popularity was such that whenever he was going to address the assembled crew, they would gather an hour or more in advance to be sure of getting a place up front. Now they were determined to rescue him at all costs.

Chief Petty Officer Abe, a navy wrestling champion, was chosen to return and rescue the captain, because it had been decided to bring him to safety by force if he refused to come willingly. When Abe climbed to the *Soryu's* bridge, he found Captain Yanagimoto standing there motionless, sword in hand, gazing resolutely toward the ship's bow. Stepping forward, Abe said, "Captain, I have come on behalf of all your men to take you to safety. They are waiting for you. Please come with me to the destroyer, sir."

When this entreaty met with silence, Abe guessed the captain's thoughts and started toward him with the intention of carrying him bodily to the waiting boat. But the sheer strength of will and determination of his grim-faced commander stopped him short. He turned tearfully away, and as he left the bridge he heard Captain Yanagimoto calmly singing "*Kimigayo*," the national anthem.

At 1913, while her survivors watched from the nearby destroyers, the *Soryu* finally disappeared into a watery grave, carrying with her the bodies of 718 men, including her captain.

Not one of the many observers who witnessed the last hours of this great carrier saw any sign of an enemy submarine or of submarine torpedoes. There was a succession of explosions in the carrier before she sank, but these were so

151

unquestionably induced explosions that they could not have been mistaken for anything else. It seems beyond doubt, therefore, that American accounts that credit the U.S. submarine *Nautilus* with delivering the coup de grâce to the *Soryu* have confused her with the *Kaga*.

Appendix: America Deciphered Our Code

Our navy used many different codes/ciphers, but an examination of their message texts indicates that the system most certainly broken was in all probability Navy Code D. Of all our regular codes, it was the one used principally for strategic matters. It was a five-digit mixed code made up in two volumes, one for sending and one for receiving, and was also provided with a separate table of five-digit random additives, which, when applied in accordance with special rules for use with Code D, completely altered the original code text. Navy Code D was first placed in effect on 1 December 1940; Random Additive Table No. 8 was put into use on 4 December 1941, just before the start of the war. [Dates and times are Tokyo standard (Zone minus 9).]

Three other separate tables were also used in conjunction with Code D: 1) a table of grid positions (in latitude and longitude), 2) a table of geographic designators, and 3) a table for enciphering dates (of events). The first of these used three *kana* [a syllabary representing the fifty basic sounds in the Japanese language: essentially the vowels *A*, *I*, *U*, *E*, and *O* alone or in combination following the consonants *K*, *S*, *T*, *N*, *M*, *Y*, *R*, and *W*] plus two numerals. The initial *kana* designated the selected fifteen-degree-by-fifteen-degree square (of the earth) of latitude and longitude, while the second and third *kana* (using the fifty *kana*) indicated the selected latitude and longitude within the above square, to the nearest twenty minutes; the two numerals further refined the designated position in the above twenty-minute square to the nearest two minutes of latitude and longitude [less than a two-mile square in the middle of the ocean].

The second table, for geographic designators, consisted of

152

two or three Roman letters, which were used to indicate a specific place, geographically. The first letter represented a common geographic entity (for example, *A* represented America; *P* stood for Japan's Mandated Islands [which they called their South Sea Islands]; the second letter stood for a specific geographic place name; and if there was a third letter, that place was near the geographic place designated by the second letter (for example, *PS* stood for Saipan, and *PST* represented Tinian).

The third table was a different type of three-*kana* table and was used for enciphering the date of an event or action; this table was arranged in *kana* sequence [analogous to our a, b, c, . . . etc.]. Both these latter tables were used without change from the beginning of the war.

After the plain text of a message was written out, all the dates, grid locations, and geographic names were then enciphered by using their respective tables, and this modified text of the message was then encoded into a series of five-digit code groups taken from the transmission volume of Code D. Now, following the special rules for the use of the random additive table with Code D, another series of five-digit code groups were selected from the random additive table and placed in sequence under each corresponding five-digit code group, and using false addition—i.e., without carrying forward tens—the final code was arrived at, e.g.:

A. Assume the text begins:	["Enemy"	"Sighted"]	etc.
B. Code text from Code D:	52194	73442	etc.
C. Random additives from table:	39682	44189	etc.
Coded and enciphered message:	81776	17521	etc.

[According to *Double-Edged Secrets*, all code groups and all random additives were specifically divisible by three, so all message code groups were also to assist in clearing garbles.[3] Note that the Japanese apparently were not aware of this requirement.]

Since the random additive table consisted of five hundred

pages, each containing one hundred random five-digit groups, the (false) addition of these additives to the code groups completely altered the original/modified code text of the original text, making it extremely complicated and very difficult to break. It is said that our experts in cryptanalysis, and others connected with code and cipher matters, were unable to break it.

The Japanese navy issued orders to replace Code Book D with Code Book D-1 and to replace Random Additive Tables Nos. 7 and 8 with new Table No. 9 on 1 May 1942, although it is said that this had been originally planned for 1 April. According to the postwar statement of the officer in charge of code changes, this change in code could not be carried out because of the delays in distribution of the new code books, and this change was made just before the sortie of the fleet for the Midway operation [27 May 1942—Japanese "Navy Day"—the anniversary of Admiral Togo's victory in the Battle of Tsushima Straits, and the date the Japanese Carrier Striking Force sortied from the Inland Sea for Midway]. . . .

Breaking our code, even partially, undoubtedly increased the reliability of America's strategic estimates, gave them some definitive intelligence on our concepts of operations, and furnished them with a substantial outline of our plans for operations in the future. There is no doubt that from early May onward a great many of our radio messages dealt with operational matters. As there is very little of that material now available, it is not possible to speculate as to which of those messages were broken, but subordinate forces undoubtedly communicated their intended movements to other forces concerned, based on the overall plan. There is no doubt that there were many radio messages concerning the MI [Midway] operation during the early days of May, but we have no reference material containing the geographic designators AF [Midway], AO [Aleutians], or AOB [Kiska]; undoubtedly, there were radio messages concerning future reconnaissance operations by the [auxiliary seaplane carrier/

tender] *Kimikawa Maru* and Submarine Squadron 1 that contained the geographic designators AO and AOB. We have no radio files to show how the enemy confirmed AF to be Midway, but the diary of Commander Sanagi of the Naval General Staff contains the entry "MIDWAY IS SHORT OF FRESH WATER," and a radio message to that effect was indeed transmitted. [This is apparently the author's answer to the assertions of David Kahn (in *The Code Breakers*) and Walter Lord (in *Incredible Victory*) about how U.S. intelligence learned in advance that the Japanese objectives were Midway and Kiska.]

Our navy was not able to break the American military's code(s); our intelligence appreciations and strategic estimates were primarily based on communications intelligence that was derived from enemy traffic analysis, call sign identification, direction-finder bearings, and the interception of plain-language transmissions [particularly those of aviators when airborne]. For example, we could estimate when a strong American force sortied from port or was operating, because their air patrols in that area intensified and expanded and many patrol planes' messages then came up on the air; we could also ascertain the general area of the enemy's intended attack because of their custom of stationing submarines there in advance of the planned attack.

However, it is said that from the beginning of the war, only a few of our many intelligence estimates based on communications intelligence really hit the mark, and our navy's confidence in them was, therefore, relatively low.

6

The
Struggle
for
Guadalcanal

RAIZO
TANAKA

The Japanese surge into the southwest Pacific, frustrated by the Battle of the Coral Sea, was resumed after the abortive Midway venture. Vigorous preparations were made to support another thrust on Port Moresby, this time by land. To counter this offensive, which threatened Allied communications with Australia and the remaining outposts in the area, and to take the first steps on the road to Tokyo, Admiral King secured permission to seize Tulagi and Guadalcanal. A huge U.S. amphibious expedition supported by substantial naval forces achieved complete surprise and gained the initial objectives, only to be stung by a vigorous and determined Japanese reaction that demanded the utmost American efforts to retain the foothold. Each side, aware of the strategic issue at stake, resolved to prevail.

The following article illuminates many facets of Japanese thinking and performance that eluded the ultimate victors during this long and bitter struggle. Here are inadequate reconnaissance, defective communications, conflicting orders, disagreement within the naval command and with its army

156

counterparts, as well as the imperatives of intelligence and logistic support. The refrain "too little and too late" echoes throughout as the author finds little to commend in the Japanese conduct of this operation to retrieve a vital position.

IT CAME as a surprise to me in mid-August 1942 to learn that, as commander of Destroyer Squadron 2, I had been chosen to assume command of a force to bring troops and supplies to Guadalcanal. The reader may appreciate the impact of this new responsibility when I say in all candor that neither I nor any of my staff had the slightest knowledge of or experience in the Solomon Islands. Of Guadalcanal itself we knew no more than its location on a chart. We had much to learn, in little time, of the plan and scope of the operations to be carried out.

As an escort force commander, I had, since the beginning of the war, participated in landing operations in the Philippines and Celebes, at Ambon and Timor. These experiences had taught me that the seizure of a strategic point is no simple matter. Detailed preliminary study of the target area and close liaison between the landing forces and their escorts are vital. And to ensure success, the landing operation must either take the enemy by surprise or must be preceded by powerful naval and air bombardment to neutralize enemy defenses. Knowing that neither of these possibilities would be available to me, I foresaw grave difficulties in my task and knew that we would suffer heavy losses. I resolved, nevertheless, to do everything in my power to succeed.

Japan's string of victories in the five months following the attack on Pearl Harbor gave her control over a vast expanse of territory reaching from the homeland through Southeast Asia, the Netherlands Indies, Melanesia, and Micronesia. Her first failure to attain an objective in World War II occurred in the Battle of the Coral Sea in May 1942. This was followed

Tracers line the night sky as U.S. cruisers and destroyers bombard a Japanese airfield. *U.S. Army photograph*

a month later by her disastrous defeat in the Battle of Midway.

Among the naval forces that limped shamefully from this historic battle was my Destroyer Squadron 2, which had been assigned to escort the transport group of the Midway Invasion Force. Desron 2 consisted of the light cruiser *Jintsu*, my flagship, and ten *Fubuki*-class destroyers organized as follows:

Desdiv 15:	*Kuroshio, Oyashio*
Desdiv 16:	*Yukikaze, Amatsukaze, Tokitsukaze, Hatsukaze*
Desdiv 18:	*Shiranuhi, Kasumi, Arare, Kagero*

On our way back to the homeland the transports and their loads were dropped off: the Airfield Construction Unit at Truk, the Ichiki Army Detachment at Guam, and the two battalions of Special Naval Landing Forces at Yokosuka. The escorting warships went on to an assembly point in the western Inland Sea.

By July my squadron was ordered by the Second Fleet to Tokyo Bay. There we joined forces of the Yokosuka Naval District in antisubmarine operations.

During this time Japan's naval activities in the Solomon

Islands were intensified, with the aim of intercepting the line of communication between the United States and Australia. For this purpose the Eighth Fleet was organized on 14 July 1942, to operate in the southeast area. It was commanded by Vice Admiral Gun'ichi Mikawa, who flew his flag in the heavy cruiser *Chokai*, and contained the following forces:

Crudiv 6:   *Aoba, Kinugasa, Kako, Furutaka*
Crudiv 18:   *Tenryu, Tatsuta*

This fleet advanced in late July to Rabaul, where it took over command of the area from the Fourth Fleet. In addition to these surface forces, the Twenty-fifth Air Flotilla was sent to Rabaul to conduct air operations under the Eleventh Air Fleet.

In May 1942 a few special naval landing forces and airfield construction units had been sent to the southeastern part of New Guinea and the Solomons. They had succeeded in building a seaplane base at Tulagi by the end of July and were making slow progress on an airfield at Guadalcanal. The latter was scheduled to be occupied by land-based planes of the Twenty-fifth Air Flotilla from Rabaul, but the enemy had already reconnoitered the southern Solomons, and he was aware of our intended advance to these new bases.

Accordingly, U.S. forces, whose morale had been lifted by the victory at Midway, ventured their first full-scale invasion of the war by sending the First Marine Division to Guadalcanal. Carried in some forty transports and escorted by powerful U.S. and Australian naval forces, eleven thousand marines successfully landed (7 August) on Guadalcanal and Tulagi, where they overwhelmed the outnumbered Japanese garrisons and took possession of the seaplane base and the partially completed airfield. Several days of bad flying weather that preceded the American landings had prevented any reconnaissance by our Tulagi-based flying boats, and we were taken completely by surprise.

Shocked by news of this enemy success, Admiral Mikawa

159

hastily assembled seven cruisers and a destroyer and sped southward to deliver a surprise attack on the enemy at Guadalcanal in the early morning of 9 August. This was the famous First Sea Battle of the Solomons, and considerable results were achieved.[1]

Despite the heavy damage inflicted on the enemy's warships, his unmolested transports were able to unload all troops and munitions. Thus the enemy landing succeeded, and his foothold in the southern Solomons was established.

While these important events were taking place, Desron 2 continued in antisubmarine operations for the Yokosuka Naval District. The *Arare* was sunk[2] and the *Kasumi* and *Shiranuhi* severely damaged in the Aleutians by enemy submarines. Other destroyers were transferred from my squadron, with few if any replacements, so that by early August the once-powerful Desron 2 consisted of only the flagship *Jintsu* and the destroyers *Kagero, Umikaze, Kawakaze,* and *Suzukaze* (the latter three of Desdiv 24).

As a result of the enemy's invasion of Guadalcanal, the Japanese Second (Advance Force) and Third (Carrier Task Force) fleets were ordered to Truk. At the same time I also received orders to rush to Truk and await further instructions. We departed from Yokosuka on 11 August with only my flagship and the destroyer *Kagero,* Desdiv 24 having been called to Hiroshima Bay to augment the escorts of the Second Fleet. Even before reaching Truk, however, I was informed that my two ships had been incorporated into the Eighth Fleet and that I had been designated by Combined Fleet order as commander of the Guadalcanal Reinforcement Force.

On the evening of 15 August, while my ships were loading supplies at Truk, I received an important and detailed order from the Eighth Fleet commander at Rabaul. The gist of this order follows:

> a) Desdiv 4 (2 DD) plus Desdiv 17 (3 DD) and Patrol Boats No. 1, 2, 34, 35[3] will be assigned to the Reinforcement Force.

The heavy cruiser *Kako*, built 1922–26, was sunk by the USS-44, 10 August 1942. *Courtesy of Hajime Fukaya*

b) The first landing force will consist of nine hundred officers and men of the army's Ichiki Detachment.

c) In the early morning of 16 August six destroyers carrying the landing force will advance to Guadalcanal, where the troops will be unloaded on the night of the eighteenth in the vicinity of Cape Taivu, to the east of Lunga Roads. Each soldier will carry a light pack of seven days' supply.

d) The *Jintsu* and Patrol Boats No. 34 and 35 will escort two slow (nine-knot) transports carrying the remainder of the landing forces, consisting mainly of service units. These transports will also carry additional supplies and munitions for use by the earlier landing forces.

Patrol Boats No. 1 and 2 will escort the fast (thirteen-knot) transport *Kinryu Maru*, carrying the Yokosuka Fifth Special Naval Landing Force, and join with the above group. All will unload in the vicinity of Cape Taivu on the night of the twenty-third.

With no regard for my opinion, as commander of the reinforcement force, this order called for the most difficult operation in war—landing in the face of the enemy—to be carried out by mixed units that had no opportunity for rehearsal or even preliminary study. It must be clear to anyone with knowledge of military operations that such an undertaking could never succeed. In military strategy expedience sometimes takes precedence over prudence, but this order was utterly unreasonable.

I could see that there must be great confusion in the headquarters of the Eighth Fleet. Yet the operation was ordained and under way, and so there was no time to argue about it.

There was not a moment to lose. During the night of 15 August ships had to be supplied, troops loaded on destroyers, operation orders prepared, and all forces readied to sortie early the next morning. Every member of my headquarters worked through the night to complete the complicated and endless details that precede a naval sortie. Somehow, at 0500, the designated hour, six destroyers of the Ichiki Detachment put bravely to sea under the command of Captain Yasuo Sato. Next out of the anchorage were the army transports *Boston Maru* and *Daifuku Maru*, escorted by Patrol Boats No. 34 and 35. In the *Jintsu* I sortied from the south channel and moved eastward to take command of the entire force.

My advance force of six destroyers encountered no enemy submarines as it steamed southward at 22 knots. The other ships followed along on a zigzag course at 8½ knots. A radio message from the Eighth Fleet on the seventeenth announced that Crudiv 6 would operate as an indirect escort and that Desdiv 24 would be added to my command. Accordingly, around noon of the following day, three more destroyers caught up with and joined the convoy.

Operating on schedule, the six advance destroyers avoided discovery by the enemy and arrived in the vicinity of Cape Taivu at 2000 on 18 August. There they unloaded nine hundred troops of the Ichiki Detachment within four hours. Desdiv 17 then returned directly to Rabaul, while the *Kagero* and two ships of Desdiv 4 (*Hagikaze, Yamakaze*) remained to guard the landing area.

Early in the morning of 19 August, although there were as yet no enemy planes operating from the field on Guadalcanal, the *Hagikaze* was hit by bombs from a B-17.[4] She was damaged enough that I ordered her to withdraw to Truk in escort of the *Yamakaze*, leaving the *Kagero* alone in the vicinity of the landing.

Since there was no Japanese reconnaissance of the waters

The author of this article, Raizo Tanaka. At the time this photo was taken he was a rear admiral. He became the principal figure in the "Tokyo Express" bringing troops and supplies to Guadalcanal. *Official U.S. Navy photograph*

south of Guadalcanal, we were totally unaware of what forces might be there. Early on the morning of the twentieth the *Kagero* was bombed by carrier-based planes. She was not damaged, but the appearance of these planes was clear evidence of an enemy striking force nearby. This was confirmed when one of our Shortland-based flying boats reported one carrier, two cruisers, and nine destroyers about 250 miles southeast of Guadalcanal.

The crack troops of the Ichiki Detachment, after making their bloodless landing on Guadalcanal, attempted a night assault on the enemy's defenses at midnight on 20 August to recapture the airfield. This reckless attack by infantrymen

163

without artillery support against an enemy division in fortified positions was like a housefly's attacking a giant tortoise.
The odds were all against it.

Most of our men met violent death assaulting the enemy
lines. The only survivors were some twenty men of the signal
unit who had remained near the landing point. They made a
radio report of the defeat, then managed to cross the island
through almost impenetrable jungle and join some of our
army forces, which landed later. Colonel Kiyonao Ichiki himself committed suicide after burning the regimental colors.
Thus our first landing operation ended in tragic failure.

I knew Colonel Ichiki from the Midway operation and was
well aware of his magnificent leadership and indomitable
fighting spirit. But this episode made it abundantly clear that
infantrymen armed with rifles and bayonets have no chance
against an enemy equipped with modern heavy arms. This
tragedy should have taught us the hopelessness of "bamboo
spear" tactics.

Upon receipt of the report that there was an enemy task
force southeast of Guadalcanal, Vice Admiral Nishizo Tsukahara, commander of the Southeast Area, ordered my slow
convoy to turn about immediately and come north. This order was followed shortly by one from the commander of the
Eighth Fleet directing that my ships turn to course 250 degrees, that is, twenty degrees south of west! Thus I had orders
from the area commander and from my own immediate superior, but they were contradictory! Considering the situation, I decided to change to course 320 degrees. Unfortunately, radio conditions went bad about that time and created
an additional problem in that I could not communicate with
either headquarters ashore. That afternoon, 20 August, I sent
the *Kawakaze* ahead to relieve the *Kagero* at Guadalcanal.

Around 1420 I got news that twenty enemy carrier planes
had landed on the field at Guadalcanal. This meant that they
had succeeded in capturing and completing the airfield in less

than two weeks, and it was now operational. This would make our landing all the more difficult.

It was welcome news, however, on the night of 21 August to learn from Eighth Fleet Headquarters that the Second Fleet (the advance force) and the Third Fleet (the carrier force) would move to the waters east of the Solomons on 23 August to support our operations and destroy the enemy task force. This message designated the position to be taken by our convoy at 1600 on the twenty-third, and our landing on Guadalcanal was postponed to the next night.

Highly encouraged by the prospect that we would finally be given support by the Combined Fleet's main body, we again steamed southward while I sent the four patrol boats to fuel at the Shortland Island anchorage. The enemy task force was sighted on 21 August by another of our reconnaissance planes. It was still in about the same position where it had been sighted the day before. Another scout plane reported two enemy transports and a light cruiser about 160 miles south of Guadalcanal. I sent the *Kawakaze* and *Yunagi* south to get this latter group, but the destroyers found nothing. The *Kawakaze* returned to the waters off Lunga on the twenty-second, where early in the morning she torpedoed and sank an enemy destroyer.[5] She then came under attack by carrier planes whose strafing injured some of her crew but did no damage to the ship.

My slow convoy advanced southward to within two hundred miles of Guadalcanal on 23 August. As expected, there were one or two U.S. "Consolidated" flying boats shadowing us continually in spite of a steady rain. We continued toward our designated point, anticipating that there would be fierce raids by carrier planes the next day.

An urgent dispatch came from the commander of the Eighth Fleet at about 0830 directing the convoy to turn northward and keep out of danger for the time being. We complied hastily, but knew that this would delay our landing until 25 August. Hence, we were startled at 1430 to receive the following order from the commander of the Eleventh Air Fleet: "The convoy will carry out the landing on the twenty-fourth." I replied that this would be impossible because some of our ships were so slow. Our uneasiness at the impending battle situation, the difficulties of our assignment, and this *second* set of conflicting orders was heightened by atmospheric disturbances which again disrupted our radio communications and greatly delayed the receipt and sending of vital messages.

On the twenty-fourth, too, enemy flying boats shadowed us from dawn to dusk. At 0800 we had a radio warning that thirty-six planes had taken off from the field at Guadalcanal. We continued to operate according to plan, expecting a mass attack, which never came.

At 1230 we spotted a heavy cruiser speeding southward on the eastern horizon, closely followed by an aircraft carrier. These were the *Tone* and *Ryujo*, who, with two destroyers, were serving as indirect escort to my reinforcement group. Also, the *Ryujo's* planes were to attack the airfield at Guadalcanal, and twenty-one of them were launched about this time. Two hours later we saw signs of an air attack on these warships to the southeast: diving enemy planes, smoke screens being laid, and, most fatefully, a gigantic pillar of smoke and flame that proved to be the funeral pyre of the *Ryujo*. She was fatally hit with bombs and torpedoes from enemy carrier-based planes and sank in the early evening.

The *Ryujo's* planes, returning from the Guadalcanal strike and finding no carrier to land on, patrolled briefly over my ships and then flew off to the northwest to land at Buka, on the northern tip of Bougainville. They reported success in having bombed the Guadalcanal airfield and shot down more than ten enemy planes.[6]

News of the *Ryujo's* sinking was not received in the various headquarters until 25 August. It seemed to us, in fact, that every time a battle situation became critical our radio communications would hit a snag, causing delay in important dispatches. This instance was typical, but it seemed to hold no lesson for us, since communications failures would continue to plague us throughout the war.

At about 1400 on 24 August, a radio message from Combined Fleet headquarters announced that the group of enemy ships located east of Malaita was steaming southeastward. This was a powerful force consisting of three aircraft carriers, a battleship, seven cruisers, and a number of destroyers.[7] Bomber squadrons from our carrier group (*Shokaku, Zuikaku*) attacked this force some twenty to thirty miles south of Stewart Island.[8] There they found the enemy split into two units, each centered on an aircraft carrier, and took them under attack, setting two ships on fire.[9] Our night fighter forces pursued, but the eastbound enemy had too much of a start in his withdrawal. The chase was abandoned as all Japanese ships reversed course and headed northward. Thus ended the second naval battle of the Solomon Islands, or the Battle of the Eastern Solomons.

My reinforcement convoy, meanwhile, had been ordered to withdraw temporarily to the northeast, but on hearing that two enemy carriers were on fire, we turned again toward Guadalcanal. Considering the battle situation and the movement of the enemy, I had grave doubts about this slow convoy's chances of reaching its goal, but it was my duty to make the attempt at any cost. I had a feeling that the next day would be fateful for my ships.

By 0600 on 25 August we were within 150 miles of the Guadalcanal airfield. Five of our destroyers, which had shelled enemy positions there during the night, had afterward raced north as planned to join my warships in direct escort of the transports. These additions were the aged *Mutsuki* and *Yayoi* of Desdiv 30, plus the *Kagero, Kawakaze,* and *Isokaze.* Upon their joinder, my signal order was issued concerning our movements, formations, and alert disposition for entering the anchorage that night. And just as my order was being sent, six carrier bombers broke out from the clouds and came at my flagship.

We were caught napping, and there was no chance to ready our guns for return fire. The dive-bombing was followed by strafing attacks. Bombs hit the forward sections of the flagship with terrific explosions while near misses raised huge columns of water. The last bomb struck the forecastle between guns No. 1 and 2 with a frightful blast, which scattered fire and splinters and spread havoc throughout the bridge. I was knocked unconscious, but came to happy to find myself uninjured. The smoke was so thick that it was impossible to keep one's eyes open. Severely shaken, I stumbled clear of the smoke and saw that the forecastle was badly damaged and afire. There were many dead and injured about. Strangely, however, the *Jintsu* did not list, and she seemed in no danger of sinking. Such emergency measures as flooding the forward magazine, fighting the fire, and caring for the injured were carried out in good order. Luckily the magazines did not explode, the watertight bulkheads held, and the engines remained in running condition. The cruiser was still seaworthy, but bow damage precluded her running at high speed, and so she was no longer fit to serve as the flagship.

The light cruiser *Jintsu*, Admiral Tanaka's flagship. *Official Imperial Japanese Navy photograph*

Meanwhile, the attacking enemy had not ignored the transports. The *Kinryu Maru*, the largest and carrying about one thousand troops of the Yokosuka Fifth Special Landing Force, was set afire by a bomb hit. Induced explosions of stored ammunition rendered her unable to navigate and left her near sinking. Seeing this, I ordered Desdiv 30 and two patrol boats to go alongside and take off her troops and crew. At the same time I sent the other ships northwestward at full speed to avoid further attacks.

Transferring my headquarters and flag to the destroyer *Kagero*, I ordered the *Jintsu* to return to Truk by herself[10] for repairs. She was still able to make twelve knots. Now enemy B-17s appeared and bombed the *Mutsuki* as she engaged in rescue work alongside the *Kinryu Maru*. With no headway, the destroyer took direct bomb hits and sank instantly. The consort *Yayoi* rescued her crew while the two patrol boats continued to rescue men from the *Kinryu Maru* just before she sank. I ordered all rescue ships to proceed at once to Rabaul.

My worst fears for this operation had been realized. Without the main combat unit, the Yokosuka Fifth Special Landing Force, it was clear that the remaining auxiliary unit of about three hundred men would be of no use even if it did reach Guadalcanal without further mishap. To complete the dismal picture, the flagship *Jintsu* had to be withdrawn because of heavy damage, the *Kinryu Maru* and *Mutsuki* were sunk, and three of my other escort ships had to withdraw with rescuees. It would be folly to land the remainder of this battered force on Guadalcanal. I reported my opinion to headquarters and began a northward withdrawal toward the Shortlands. My decision was affirmed by messages from the Combined Fleet and the Eighth Fleet, and the operation was suspended, ending in complete failure the effort of this convoy to reinforce our Guadalcanal garrisons.

Even as we headed for the Shortland Islands, however, I received an Eleventh Air Fleet order directing that the remaining three-hundred-odd troops be transported to Guadalcanal on the night of 27 August in fast warships. I could not help but feel that this was a hasty decision not based on careful planning. Nevertheless, I prepared the following operational order:

> *Umikaze, Yamakaze,* and *Isokaze* will take the 390 troops now loaded in the transport, together with four rapid-fire guns and provisions for 1,300 troops, and leave Shortland for Guadalcanal at 0500 under the commander of Desron 24. At 2100 they will arrive at Cape Taivu to land troops and supplies. During the night they will return from Guadalcanal.

As soon as we had entered Shortland anchorage on the night of the twenty-sixth, I summoned the army commander and advised him of my plans. The entire night was spent in transferring troops and munitions to the destroyers.

Early the next morning the three destroyers were on their way. They had been gone only a few hours when I received an Eighth Fleet dispatch saying that the landing operation at Guadalcanal should take place on the twenty-eighth! To my immediate reply that the destroyers had already departed, the Eighth Fleet responded, "Recall destroyers at once. Am sending Desdiv 20 to Shortland where it will be under Comdesron 2."

It was inconceivable that no liaison existed between the headquarters of the Eleventh Air Fleet and the Eighth Fleet, since both were located at Rabaul, and yet such seemed to be the case. I had again received contradictory and conflicting orders from the area commander and my immediate superior and was at a loss as to what to do. If such circumstances continue, I thought, how can we possibly win a battle? It occurred to me again that this operation gave no evidence of careful, deliberate study; everything seemed to be completely haphazard. I was the commander of the reinforcement force, and this put me in a very difficult position.

I was compelled to recall the destroyers immediately, and they returned that evening. While they refueled and took on supplies, I summoned the commanding officers and made arrangements for the operation to be conducted on 28 August.

The *Aoba* and *Furutaka* of Crudiv 6 arrived at Shortland around 1600, and I visited Rear Admiral Aritomo Goto in the flagship *Aoba* to brief him on the area situation. He had preceded me as Comdesron 2, and as we were good friends there was a frank exchange of views. We agreed to cooperate closely. Little did we know that this meeting would be our last. My friend Admiral Goto met a hero's death in the battle of Cape Esperance in October.

From successive dispatches I finally learned why four Desdiv 20 destroyers had been temporarily assigned to my command. It had been planned that they would load an advance force of the Kawaguchi Detachment from Borneo and bring it to Guadalcanal to be landed in the vicinity of Cape Taivu on the night of 28 August with the remaining troops of the Ichiki Detachment as second-wave reinforcements. When this became clear, I ordered Captain Yonosuke Murakami, Comdesdiv 24, to take his own destroyers together with the *Isokaze* and four ships of Desdiv 20 to make that landing on the night of the twenty-eighth.

A hitch in this plan developed, however, when I received word from Desdiv 20 that, because of a fuel shortage, it could not stop at Shortland but would go on south and, staying east of the Solomons, operate independently of the *Isokaze* and Desdiv 24. This further served to increase my pessimism about the success of the landing operation.

A subsequent urgent dispatch from Desdiv 20 confirmed my fears with a report that it had been bombed for two hours in the afternoon of the twenty-eighth by enemy planes at a point about eighty miles north of the Guadalcanal airfield. The division commander, Captain Yuzo Arita, was killed, the *Asagiri* sunk, the *Shirakumo* damaged badly, and the *Yugiri* damaged moderately. As a consequence, their advance on

Guadalcanal had to be abandoned and the surviving ships returned to Shortland. Another plan had come to nought.

This made it more obvious than ever what sheer recklessness it was to attempt a landing against strong resistance without preliminary neutralization of enemy air power. If the present plan for Guadalcanal was not altered, we were certain to suffer further humiliating and fruitless casualties.

We were in the midst of a midnight conference called to discuss the unfavorable situation when Desdiv 24 reported that it was also returning to Shortland. In this decision the commander acted independently, without orders, on grounds that the battle situation had taken an unfavorable turn. Such conduct was inexcusable. Yet, if I now ordered these destroyers to turn about and head for Guadalcanal, they could not make it before dawn and would then fall easy prey to enemy planes. Repressing my fury and disappointment, I had no choice but to concur with the decision of Comdesdiv 24, but he got a severe reprimand when he returned the next morning. And I, in turn, received strong messages from the Combined Fleet and the Eighth Fleet expressing their regret at our setback.

On the morning of 28 August, the *Kinugasa* of Crudiv 6 entered port, signaling that she came under Eighth Fleet orders to serve as flagship of the reinforcement force. Admiral Mikawa had made this move, realizing that the communication facilities of a destroyer are not adequate for a force flagship. I transferred at once from the *Kagero* and expressed my appreciation to Mikawa for his timely thoughtfulness.

Early on the twenty-ninth, the Eighth Fleet ordered, "Use destroyers to transport army troops." Thereupon I directed Desdiv 24 and the *Isokaze,* then at Shortland, to load troops and supplies and depart at 1000 so that landings could be carried out during the night. At the same time I ordered Patrol Boats No. 1 and 34 to embark the remaining 120 troops of the Ichiki Detachment for Guadalcanal, where they would be unloaded on the night of the thirtieth.

172

Meanwhile, the transport *Sado Maru* arrived at Shortland carrying the main force of an army detachment under Major General Kiyotake Kawaguchi, which had been selected to reinforce Guadalcanal. I invited General Kawaguchi and several of his senior officers to come on board the *Kinugasa* so that we could make plans and arrangements. The Kawaguchi Detachment had earlier achieved notable success in landing operations on the southwest coast of Borneo, after a passage of five hundred miles in large landing barges. It was disturbing to me, however, when General Kawaguchi insisted that his force should continue southward in the transport *Sado Maru* as far as Gizo Harbor, which was just beyond the range of the enemy's land-based planes at that time. From there they would proceed to Guadalcanal using all available landing barges. The general was supported by all the other army officers in rejecting my proposal to transport their troops by naval vessels.

This presented a serious handicap to the whole operation, and I was at a loss for a solution, since I had no knowledge of what orders the Kawaguchi force had been given about transportation. I reported the situation to my superiors at Rabaul and advised General Kawaguchi to inform the commander of the Seventeenth Army of what had come up and see if his intentions would be approved. The conference closed with our agreement to hold further meetings about the reinforcement operations.

With the present unfavorable war situation, it was the navy's hope that all reinforcements could be transported without a moment's delay, and we were willing to exert every effort for this purpose. Any delay was regrettable, and this one was even worse, since it was caused by a conflict of opinion between our own army and navy forces at the front. I was in an extremely difficult position.

On the night of 29 August Captain Murakami's four destroyers landed troops in the vicinity of Cape Taivu, as did three ships of Desdiv 11. A radio message from Guadalcanal during that day indicated that there was an enemy force of two transports, one cruiser, and two destroyers near Lunga Point. Accordingly, Admiral Mikawa, commander of the Eighth Fleet, sent an order direct to Comdesron 24 for Murakami to attack that enemy force as soon as the landing of troops had been completed. To my great astonishment Murakami ignored this order and, as soon as the troops had been landed, set course for Shortland. This was a flagrant violation of a direct order, and on his return I summoned Captain Murakami to demand an explanation of his action. He said he had not made the attack because the night was clear and lighted by a full moon, and many enemy planes had been seen overhead. So dumbfounding was this statement that I could not even think of words to reprove him. Blame attached to me, of course, for having such a man in my command, and I was conscience-stricken. He was transferred shortly to the homeland.

In the morning of 30 August the *Amagiri* and *Kagero* entered the anchorage at Shortland carrying the advance force of the Kawaguchi Detachment and towing the badly damaged *Shirakumo*. I ordered the undamaged *Amagiri*, *Kagero*, and *Yudachi* (the *Isokaze*'s replacement) to load the main force of the Kawaguchi Detachment and rush to Guadalcanal. The warships hastily completed all preparations for departure, but General Kawaguchi and his officers were still strongly opposed to warship transportation, since they had received no orders from the Seventeenth Army and they were not disposed to comply with our naval order. At 1000 I was compelled to have the remaining troops of the Ichiki Detachment depart in the *Yudachi* for Guadalcanal. I thereupon reported to the Eighth Fleet, requesting that Seventeenth Army Headquarters be consulted at once and asked to issue necessary instructions to General Kawaguchi. That night Mikawa's chief of staff sent a dispatch criticizing me bitterly because the *Amagiri* and *Kagero* had not also departed for Guadalcanal. It was lamentable, to be sure, but could hardly be attributed to anything but the narrowness of General Kawaguchi and his officers.

Patrol Boats No. 1 and 34, which had departed the previous day, were twice attacked by enemy planes but sustained no damage. They radioed asking instructions for their run-in to Guadalcanal, and I directed them to follow close behind the *Yudachi* when she dashed in to land reinforcements. I was greatly relieved and gratified when the report came in that all three had successfully landed their army troops before midnight, 30 August.

I negotiated with General Kawaguchi again on 30 August about the transportation of his troops, but he stubbornly refused my proposal on the ground that he had still received no instructions from his superiors. As commander of the reinforcement force, I could brook no further delay. Thereupon, I ordered eight destroyers—the *Kagero* and *Amagiri*, with Desdivs 11 and 24 each supplying three—to make preparations for departure early the next morning. Around 2000 a message came from the Eighth Fleet saying, "Under our agreement with the commander of the Seventeenth Army, the bulk of the Kawaguchi Detachment will be transported to Guadalcanal by destroyers, the remainder by large landing barges." I lost no time in resuming discussions with the general and his officers, but they were not easily convinced. Contending that the order was not directed to them, they held out until Kawaguchi himself finally gave way; the commander of the regiment never did agree. The ponderous task of getting the troops on board the destroyers was begun at once.

It was noon of 31 August when eight destroyers sortied for Guadalcanal carrying General Kawaguchi and some one thousand of his officers and men. All troops were landed successfully at midnight, and the ships returned without meeting any opposition. This was the third time that a complete army unit had been landed successfully from destroyers.

On 30 August I had received the following message from

175

the Eighth Fleet: "Comdesron 3 will depart Rabaul for Shortland early in the morning of the thirtieth. Upon the arrival of Comdesron 3, Comdesron 2 will relinquish his command and proceed to Truk on board the *Yugiri*."

My first reaction to this unexpected transfer order was a feeling of indignation because I had spared no effort to carry out this assignment successfully. On second thought, however, I realized that much had happened during my few short weeks in this command. I had lost many ships and men in difficult battle situations, one of my subordinate commanders had proven inadequate to his assignment, and there had been delay in one reinforcement operation because of my conflict with the stubborn army commander. I was not free of responsibility in these matters, but there were other considerations. I had had to change flagship three times in as many weeks and, with the exception of the *Kagero,* which had been with me since the start of the war, every unit of my command had been added by improvisation with no chance to train or practice together. All these factors contributed to my difficulties in achieving a unified command. To make matters worse, I was so exhausted—mentally and physically—that I could hardly keep going. Under these circumstances it was only proper that I be given relief from the strain of this command. I was especially gratified to learn that my close friend of Naval Academy days, Rear Admiral Shintaro Hashimoto, would be taking my place.

Early in the morning of 31 August, Admiral Hashimoto's Desron 3, consisting of the flagship *Sendai* and Desdiv 18, arrived at Shortland. My command was turned over to him in a brief ceremony. I then transferred from the *Kinugasa* to the damaged destroyer *Yugiri* and departed for Truk with a heavy heart, accompanied by members of my staff and headquarters.

We reached Truk the next day and again became a part of Vice Admiral Nobutake Kondo's Second Fleet. Now that I was back once more to my basic assignment as Comdesron

2, my energies could be concentrated on the reorganization and rebuilding of my squadron.

Rear Admiral S. E. Morison, Mr. Hanson Baldwin, and other American naval writers have acknowledged the excellent performance of Japan's *Fubuki*-class destroyers and powerful long-range torpedoes. The success of these ships and weapons was not the product of a moment nor of chance. It was the result of careful planning and training. The Sino-Japanese and Russo-Japanese wars indicated that torpedo-attack warfare seemed to agree with the character of Japanese sailors. A great deal of study was devoted to torpedo tactics. Especially after the Russo-Japanese War, tremendous expenditures and effort were put into the production and improvement of torpedoes and craft to use them. Special emphasis was also placed on the training of skilled crews for handling torpedoes on board the ships.

At the Washington Conference in 1921, the 3:5:5 ratio that was decided upon for fleet strengths of Japan–United States–Britain placed Japan in a position of numerical inferiority. To offset this the Japanese navy formulated a policy aimed at improving its night-combat strength, based largely on torpedo firepower. Warship construction consisted of *Furutaka*-class (7,700 tons) and *Nachi*-class (10,000 tons) cruisers and *Fubuki*-class (2,300 tons) destroyers. These ships were

The *Usugumo,* illustrative of the *Fubuki*-class destroyers, which played an important role in the Solomons.

177

equipped with four to nine torpedo tubes to handle our new 23-inch oxygen torpedoes (warhead charge of 770 pounds), whose effective range was 16,000 yards at 45 knots. With this kind of armament a single destroyer was capable of sinking a battleship. This torpedo power could be used to advantage in day as well as night actions, since these same weapons had an effective range of 32,500 yards with a speed of 30 knots. Thus great reliance was placed on the offensive power of such torpedoes.

An ideal torpedoman is full of aggressive spirit and has a strong sense of responsibility and pride in his work. If a commander, he must be skilled in shiphandling, be capable of absolute control over his men, and possess the determination and mental acuity so necessary in night combat. Such qualities are developed only after intensive and continuous training. Torpedo officers start their careers in small vessels and spend most of their time at sea acquiring the experience that must accompany the torpedoman spirit. There were many veterans of this field during the war, including such men as Admirals Kantaro Suzuki and Keisuke Okada (each later served as premier of Japan), and Admirals Chuichi Nagumo and Jisaburo Ozawa.

Most of Japan's torpedo craft at the outbreak of war were commanded by qualified experts. I believe it may be said with justifiable pride that at the beginning of the war our torpedo forces were the best night combat forces in the world. But once the United States, equipped with effective radar, began in late 1942 to conduct bombardments and torpedoings without having to use searchlights, then the advantage of Japan's fleet in night combat was drastically reduced.

My Desron 2 had been the navy's crack night combat force since before the war. My division commanders and skippers were brilliant torpedo experts, and from top to bottom the training and discipline of the crews was flawless. Operational orders could be conveyed by the simplest of signals, and they were never misunderstood. I knew that with such men under my command I could accomplish any mission, no matter how difficult it might be.

Since my assignment to bring reinforcements to Guadalcanal, however, most of my combat-tested ships, officers, and men had been diverted to other commands. Such replacements as I received had no chance for the training and drilling so essential to the success of closely coordinated operations. I say this not in self-justification but merely to tell of events as they occurred and facts as they existed.

On my arrival at Truk, I was pleased to find that additional destroyers had been made available to Squadron 2. There were three each from Desdivs 9 and 15, and four from Desdiv 2, bringing the squadron to its original strength of ten units. I chose the *Hayashio* as my flagship.

The general attack aimed at recapturing the Guadalcanal airfield was to be launched on 12 September. The three thousand or so men of the Kawaguchi Detachment who had been landed on Guadalcanal from destroyers and landing barges were to effect the recapture. To cooperate with this undertaking, the Second Fleet (Crudivs 4, 5, 8, with Desron 2 as direct escort) and Third Fleet (carrier task force) headed southward from Truk on 9 September with the object of destroying the enemy fleet. Everyone in this large fleet was optimistic as the ships sped on their way.

On Guadalcanal the army's scheduled attack took place on the night of 12 September, but it ended in failure because of inadequate liaison and cooperation between our various units. The main force of our fleet searched from a point 350 miles north of Tulagi southward as far as Ndeni on the thirteenth but failed to sight an enemy ship. Sailing northward the next day, our ships were about 350 miles northeast of Tulagi when we were attacked by ten B-17s, none of whose bombs hit. While refueling near the equator on 15 September, we learned that an enemy task force was operating about two hundred miles south of Guadalcanal and that the Japanese submarine *I-19* had sunk the carrier *Wasp*.[11] When fueling was completed on the seventeenth, our ships headed southward in search of the enemy but failed to find him. We circled back to the sea east of the Solomons, where, on the twentieth, we received orders to return to Truk. We reached port uneventfully on the twenty-third after thirteen days of what proved to be nothing more than a fuel-consuming operation.

Meanwhile, operations for reinforcing Guadalcanal were being pushed by Desrons 3 and 4 and the minelayers *Nisshin* and *Tsugaru,* and enemy planes were damaging our destroyers with painful regularity. Failure of the Kawaguchi Detachment to recapture the airfield convinced the high command that a larger force was needed for that task. Accordingly, studies were made of a plan for carrying out full-scale amphibious operations, and it was decided to transfer Lieutenant General Masai Maruyama's Second Division from Java to Shortland. Thence the main body of the division was to be carried to Guadalcanal in six high-speed transports escorted by the reinforcement force. The troops were to be disembarked at Guadalcanal on the night of 14 October, and a general attack would take place on the twenty-second.

In support of this reinforcement operation, the Second and Third Fleets sortied from Truk on 11 October. A few days before, the light cruiser *Isuzu* had been joined as flagship of Desron 2, and the newly organized Desdiv 31 (*Takanami, Makinami, Naganami*) had also been incorporated into the squadron, which was again at full strength, and everyone was in the best of spirits.

While Crudiv 6 (*Aoba, Kinugasa, Furutaka*) and two destroyers were moving south on the night of 11 October to bombard the Guadalcanal airfield, they encountered an American surface force of four cruisers and five destroyers to the north of Savo Island. In this Battle of Cape Esperance, as it has become known, an enemy cruiser and a destroyer were sunk and one cruiser was damaged.[12] Japanese losses were the cruiser *Furutaka* and the destroyer *Shirakumo* sunk, the flagship *Aoba* damaged, and the force commander, Vice Admiral Aritomo Goto, killed. The destroyer *Murakumo* was bombed the next day and heavily damaged while withdrawing. The destroyer *Natsugumo* of Desdiv 9 went to her rescue and was bombed and sunk. It was a crushing defeat for the Japanese navy. Enemy counteroffensives were becoming increasingly ferocious, his airpower was growing stronger, and no one could doubt that the next amphibious operation would be beset with formidable difficulties.

The first essential of a successful amphibious operation is to deprive the enemy of control of the surrounding air. At Guadalcanal this meant the destruction of planes on the enemy's airfield. But the enemy had more planes in the area than we did, and so some other means had to be used. In consequence, it was planned to use battleships in a heavy night bombardment of the field to destroy the enemy planes. A new bombardment shell had just arrived from the homeland—designated Type Zero, these had a firecrackerlike shrapnel burst—and there were enough for the battleships *Kongo* and *Haruna* to have five hundred rounds each for their thirty-six-centimeter guns. These two big ships were scheduled to make the bombardment on the night of 13 October. Vice Admiral Takeo Kurita (Combatdiv 3) commanded the force, which consisted of the light cruiser *Isuzu* and three ships of Desdiv 31 as a screen, a rear guard of four Desdiv 15 ships, and the two battleships with my Desron 2 as direct escort.

Advancing toward Guadalcanal at twenty-five knots, we reached a point west of Savo Island shortly before midnight, encountering neither enemy planes nor ships on the way. Speed was dropped to eighteen knots, and the sixteen big guns of the two battleships opened fire simultaneously at a range of 16,000 meters. The ensuing scene defied description as the fires and explosions from the thirty-six-centimeter shell hits on the airfield set off enemy planes, fuel dumps, and ammunition stores. The scene was topped off by flare bombs

181

from our observation planes flying over the field, the whole spectacle making the Ryogoku fireworks display seem like mere child's play. The night's pitch darkness was transformed by fire into the brightness of day. Spontaneous cries and shouts of excitement ran throughout our ships.

The attack seemed to take the enemy by complete surprise, and his radio could be heard sending emergency messages such as "Intensive bombardment by enemy ships. Damage tremendous." Enemy shore batteries at Tulagi and Lunga Point turned searchlights seaward, probing frantically and fruitlessly for our ships. Star shell and gunfire also fell short of our location. The *Isuzu* returned some fire against a coastal battery on Tulagi, but the main show was the battleships' bombardment, which continued for an hour and a half, after which all ships withdrew safely and on schedule to the east of Savo Island. At about this time several motor torpedo boats of the enemy came out to pursue our rear guard ships, but the destroyer *Naganami* drove them away. We anticipated attacks by enemy planes the next morning, but not a single plane appeared even to threaten us, testimony indeed to the effectiveness of the night's bombardment.

On the night of 14 October, the Eighth Fleet cruisers *Chokai* and *Kinugasa* unleashed a similar bombardment with their twenty-centimeter guns while six transports carrying General Maruyama's Second Division arrived off Guadalcanal to unload passengers and cargo in escort of Desron 4. The unloading was still going on early the next morning when enemy carrier planes from a task force to the south descended upon us. A few troops and weapons had been landed during the night, but three loaded transports had to be run aground when they were bombed and set afire. The other three transports got away, but this attempt to land a completely equipped army force ended in failure.

The *Myoko* and *Maya* of Crudiv 5 bombarded the airfield with their twenty-centimeter guns during the night of 15 October. Desron 2 again served as escort, divided between van and rear. We parted from the main force shortly after noon and headed for Guadalcanal at high speed. We arrived east of Savo Island at 2100, reduced speed to twenty knots, and commenced firing. Cruiser guns were not nearly so effective as the battleships', and only a few fires broke out at the airfield. Each cruiser fired some four hundred shells during the one-hour bombardment, and two destroyers sent about three hundred shells into the coastal battery, but there was no return fire. Their work done, all ships withdrew to the north.

Our aerial reconnaissance on 16 October spotted bomber planes being dispatched to Guadalcanal from carriers sixty miles southeast of the island, and a powerful enemy force that included four battleships was sighted to the south of San Cristobal Island. It seemed certain that the enemy must have a strong carrier force near the Solomons, but we could not find it. We conjectured that the enemy was planning to decoy our carriers toward his battleship force and himself conduct carrier-based raids from the southeast.

Our main force spent 17 and 18 October in refueling just north of the equator, and then headed southerly with the hope and object of engaging enemy carriers, since General Maruyama's troops on Guadalcanal were scheduled to launch a general attack on the night of the twenty-second. Hampered by the jungle, however, the advance of our land forces was unduly delayed, and the general attack had to be postponed to the twenty-fourth. Meanwhile, the submarine I-175[13] had torpedoed and destroyed an enemy warship southeast of Guadalcanal.[14]

It was our opinion that if we could recapture the airfield, the enemy would be forced to withdraw from Guadalcanal. In accordance with this notion a plan was mapped out whereby the Eighth Fleet would advance to a point 150 miles northwest of Guadalcanal and the Second Fleet take position a like distance to the northeast while Desron 4 (Rear Admiral Tamotsu Takama) rushed directly toward the island. Upon receipt of a message during the night of 24 October that our troops had occupied the field (it later proved to have been incorrect), Desron 4 advanced toward its destination as planned. The next morning the squadron was attacked by enemy planes. The light cruiser *Yura* was damaged so badly that she had to be sunk, and the flagship *Akizuki* was also damaged. The general attack launched by Maruyama's division had, in reality, failed. (This was the third time that a general attack had not succeeded.) Here again was a pitiful example of a lack of cooperation between the army and the navy.

On 26 October the Second and Third Fleets sent planes to the south on dawn reconnaissance. At 0530 a plane from the cruiser *Tone*, flying the easternmost search leg, sighted an enemy force two hundred miles north of Santa Cruz. This force was promptly reported as consisting of three carriers, two battleships, five cruisers, and twelve destroyers. Our carrier force, cruising some two hundred miles to the northwest, dispatched two groups of attack planes, which struck the *Enterprise* and *Hornet*, damaging both. The latter was abandoned by her crew and finally sunk early the next morning by torpedoes from the destroyers *Makigumo* and *Akigumo*. Our pilots claimed a third carrier set afire and the sinking of a battleship, two cruisers, and a destroyer, as well as the shooting down of a number of enemy planes.[15]

American planes also made successful attacks this day, scoring bomb hits on the carriers *Shokaku* and *Zuiho*, setting them afire, and rendering their flight decks unusable. Both ships were forced to withdraw without recovering their strike aircraft. A few of these planes were recovered by the *Zuikaku* and *Junyo*, but most of them were forced down at sea. The cruiser *Chikuma* was jumped by about twenty planes, which scored many near misses and enough direct hits to send her limping northward. The rest of our ships under Admiral Kondo sped toward the location where our carrier planes had scored such successes through their offensive initiative, seeking to engage the enemy fleet. They found only the burning carrier, which was dispatched by two of our destroyers. The rest of the enemy ships fled southeastward at high speed, pursued unsuccessfully by Desron 2. Search operations were continued through 27 October, but there was no further sign of the enemy. Admiral Yamamoto then recalled the fleet to Truk, and all ships reached there safely by the end of October.

As commander of one of the naval forces involved in Guadalcanal operations, I wish to present my own views of the general situation prevailing at the end of October 1942. Failure of the Ichiki and Kawaguchi detachments had led to the mounting of a full-scale amphibious operation, to be conducted jointly by the army and navy, in which high-speed transports carried Maruyama's Second Division, whose goal was to recapture the airfields at Guadalcanal. This effort was supported by all surface and air strength available in the Solomons, but it ended in failure. Many reasons may be cited for the failure, but primarily it is attributable to the enemy's aerial superiority. Our prelanding bombardments by surface ships had destroyed many planes on the ground. These losses were quickly replenished, however, thanks to the fantastic mass-production techniques of the United States. An auxiliary airfield was prepared in an amazingly short time, and the enemy's air strength could then be greatly increased. Enemy carriers kept station near Guadalcanal while our nearest plane bases were at Truk and Rabaul. Our movements were watched so closely that the enemy could unleash intercepting operations at a moment's notice. Although we sank or damaged his carriers in the Santa Cruz battle and elsewhere, the enemy was able to repair or replace his ships with speed that astonished us. Thus the United States not only maintained its aerial strength in the Pacific despite our successful assaults against it, but also managed to exceed by leaps and bounds our strenuous efforts to achieve superiority in the air.

Because surface ships are no match against strong aerial assault, it seemed to me imperative that Guadalcanal reinforcement operations be suspended while Rabaul was built up as a rear base, and an advanced base was established in the vicinity of Buin. In this way we could have built up fighting forces that might have been able to deal effectively with the enemy. To our regret, however, the Supreme Command stuck persistently to reinforcing Guadalcanal and never modified this goal until the time came when the island had to be abandoned. We could not help but doubt that this judgment was right. The success or failure of a military operation often hinges on whether the people at the fighting front have been consulted. If our views had been considered with an open mind, the way could have been paved for unity and coordination at all levels of command, which might have brought us success. But this was not done. Needless to say, although a war cannot be won without risk, there is a limit to adventure and recklessness. Men who direct military operations must always keep this under consideration.

While my Desron 2 was engaged with the fleet in the South Pacific, Desrons 3 and 4 continued to escort reinforcement convoys to Guadalcanal. Both of these squadrons sustained heavy losses as a result of aerial bombardments and surface engagements. Many of their ships had been sunk, most of the rest damaged, and the few that escaped actual injury were in no condition for further operational assignments.

Still the Supreme Command clung to the idea of seizing the Guadalcanal airfields, and the Seventeenth Army formulated a plan to achieve this end. After being reinforced by the Thirty-eighth Division, it would make a frontal attack against enemy positions. The decision was made to transport these troops in high-speed army vessels, although really serviceable ones were very scarce at this time, and Desron 2 was assigned as escort.

Immediately upon our return to Truk on 30 October, maintenance and replenishment of ships were undertaken with all possible speed. Accordingly my ships were able to sortie on 3

November. With the light cruiser *Isuzu* as flagship, my squadron consisted of eight destroyers of Divisions 15, 24, and 31. We were accompanied by Crudiv 7 (*Suzuya, Maya*) and two ships of Desdiv 10. Unlike some previous assignments, this mission would be successful, I believed, because the force was adequate and my subordinates were all experienced.

Two days out of Truk we arrived at Shortland. I called on Vice Admiral Mikawa, whose Eighth Fleet flagship *Chokai* had entered the anchorage just ahead of us. He informed me that Desron 2 would replace Squadrons 3 and 4 in reinforcement operations and that I would command the entire force.

The Shortland Islands were very important at this time, as they constituted a vital point in the reinforcement of Gua-

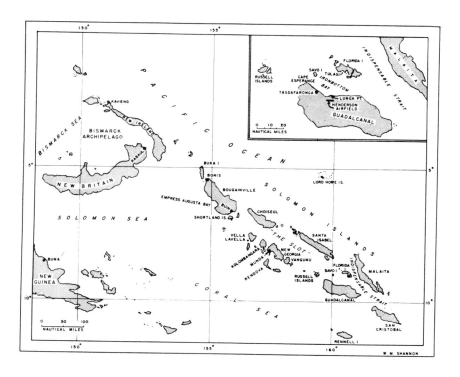

dalcanal; hence there was always considerable activity in the anchorage. Yet there were surprisingly few land-based fighters to fly cover for direct air defense and patrol over this territory. The only airstrip—seven hundred meters long and twenty-five wide—was located on the coast near Buin at the southern tip of Bougainville. There were some seaplanes based in the mouth of a bay on the eastern end of Bougainville. They patrolled the anchorage entrance and provided the only direct cover for vessels shuttling to Guadalcanal.

Soon after we had anchored, Admiral Mikawa directed that Desron 2 plus two ships of Desdiv 10 would escort a convoy of six Army transports to Guadalcanal on 7 November. I laid out details for the operation and summoned my ship captains for a briefing. The next day, however, the original plan was altered so that, instead of transports, destroyers were to be used to lift the troops. Furthermore, it was announced that on 13 November the main body of the Thirty-eighth Division would be carried in eleven high-speed army ships escorted by Desron 2. Indirect cover would be provided by the Eighth Fleet and the Second Fleet main body, operating to the east and west of the Solomons, respectively.

I had planned to take direct command of the destroyers leaving on 7 November, with my flag in the *Hayashio*, but was specifically ordered to remain in Shortland. Therefore I appointed Captain Torajiro Sato (Comdesdiv 15) to lead the eleven destroyers carrying the advance unit of 1,300 troops and directed him to take the northern route to Guadalcanal.

The ships departed on schedule on the morning of 7 November. In midafternoon they were attacked by about thirty ship-based bombers. Six escorting fighters that were providing air cover put up such a brave defense (in which all were destroyed) and the destroyers maneuvered so skillfully that they escaped without damage. The force arrived at Tassafaronga, west of Lunga Point, shortly after midnight and landed the troops without incident. We welcomed the safe return of the destroyers to Shortland in mid-morning of 8 November.

188

That same day army transports arrived carrying the main body of the Thirty-eighth Division. Two days later six hundred of these troops under Lieutenant General Tadayoshi Sano were embarked in the destroyers *Makinami, Suzukaze,* and three ships of Desdiv 10, and headed south by the central route. Some twenty enemy planes attacked in midafternoon with bombs and torpedoes, but the ships were not damaged. Near the debarkation point a nighttime attack by four torpedo boats was repulsed and the division commander and his troops were landed safely. The ships were back at Shortland on 11 November.

Our reconnaissance planes sighted an enemy carrier task force bearing 130 degrees and 180 miles from Tulagi on 11 November. That night several enemy planes raided Shortland and bombed shipping in the harbor but did no damage. It was evident that the enemy was aware of our plan and was making an all-out effort to disrupt it by concentrating his sea and air forces around Guadalcanal. Consequently, we had good reason to expect that the landing of the Thirty-eighth Division main body at Guadalcanal would be extremely difficult.

Enemy planes raided Shortland again at dawn on 12 November and tried to bomb the transports, but no damage was sustained. At 1800 the eleven army transports moved the anchorage southward, escorted by twelve destroyers. In the flagship *Hayashio* I led the formation and wondered how many of our ships would survive this operation.

That night the *Hiei* and *Kirishima,* of Vice Admiral Hiroaki Abe's Batdiv 11, escorted by Desrons 4 and 10, approached Guadalcanal to shell the airfield, as Batdiv 3 had done previously. But this time the enemy was aware of our plan and had made preparations to disrupt it. Contact was made with an enemy cruiser and destroyer force just as Abe's ships passed to the south of Savo Island on a southeasterly course, preparatory to making their bombardment. The flagship *Hiei* got off only two salvos in the ensuing battle before

189

being hit by shells from an enemy cruiser, with the result that both her steering rooms and her fire-control system were put out of service, and she cruised in circles quite out of control. The destroyers *Akatsuki* and *Yudachi* were sunk, and the *Amatsukaze* and *Ikazuchi* damaged. Suffering these heavy losses, the force was compelled to give up its intended shelling. In this night battle our ships claimed two heavy cruisers and several destroyers sunk,[16] and the fray was thought to be a draw.

Dawn of 13 November saw the start of a series of intensive attacks against the *Hiei* by enemy planes. As a result of successive direct hits, fires broke out in all sections of the battleship. When fire fighting proved useless, the order was given to abandon ship, and the crew was transferred to destroyers. Despite an order from the Combined Fleet directing the *Kirishima* to take the *Hiei* in tow, this effort was not made, and instead the flaming battleship was intentionally sunk. With surviving destroyers, the *Kirishima* cleared out of the arena and joined the main force of the Second Fleet in waters north of Guadalcanal.

My escort force and our charges had turned back to Shortland around midnight on 12 November after receiving a Combined Fleet order that our debarkation had been postponed until 14 November. We returned shortly after noon on 13 November and one hour later were on our way again toward Guadalcanal. I had a premonition that an ill fate was in store for us.

While we headed southward, the *Maya* and *Suzuya* of Crudiv 7 prepared the way by shelling the Guadalcanal airfield. The transports in my convoy sailed in a four-column formation at eleven knots. My flagship led the escorting destroyers, which were spread out in front and to either side. We were subjected to attack at dawn on 14 November by two B-17s and four carrier-based bombers, but they did no damage, and three of the latter were shot down by fighters that were serving as our combat air patrol. An hour later two more carrier bombers came at the convoy, but they were both shot down.

At this time we also sighted a large formation of enemy planes to the southwest. I ordered all destroyers to make smoke and each column of transports to take separate evasive action. Instead of attacking my ships, however, these planes struck some fifty miles to the west at warships of the Eighth Fleet, which were providing our indirect cover. The *Kinugasa* was sunk, and the *Isuzu* was damaged heavily and the *Chokai* and *Maya* lightly, with the result that the Eighth Fleet had to give up its indirect cover mission and return to Shortland.

Later in the morning we were attacked by a total of forty-one planes. There were eight each of B-17s, torpedo bombers, and fighters, and the rest carrier-based bombers. Under cover of a smoke screen the transports tried to withdraw on zigzag courses, but enemy torpedoes sank the *Canberra Maru* and *Nagara Maru* while the *Sado Maru* (carrying the army commander) was crippled by bombs. When the enemy planes had withdrawn, survivors from the transports were picked up, and the *Sado Maru* headed back toward Shortland escorted by the destroyers *Amagiri* and *Mochizuki*.

Less than two hours later we were again under air attack, this time by eight B-17s and two dozen carrier bombers. The *Brisbane Maru* was hit, set afire, and sunk. Her survivors were picked up by the destroyer *Kawakaze*.

The next attack was on us within an hour when eight B-17s and five carrier bombers bombed and sank the *Shinanogawa Maru* and *Arizona Maru*. Survivors were rescued by the destroyers *Naganami* and *Makinami*.

A respite of half an hour was broken by three carrier bombers which attacked assiduously but without success. Any conjecture on our part that our troubles for the day were over proved illusory, however, when twenty-one planes struck half an hour before sunset. Four were B-17s, the rest carrier bombers. The *Nako Maru* was their only victim, and she

191

burned brightly from bomb hits. The destroyer *Suzukaze* managed to come alongside and take off survivors before this 7,000-ton transport's fires were quenched in the ocean depths. And before the sun could set, three more carrier bombers came to plague our force, but all their bombs missed.

In six attacks this day on my immediate force, the enemy had sent more than one hundred planes. These had sunk six transports[17] with bombs and torpedoes, killing a total of about four hundred men. Amazingly, some five thousand men of the embarked troops and crews had been rescued by destroyers.

The toll on my force was extremely heavy. Steaming at high speed, the destroyers had laid smoke screens almost continuously and delivered a tremendous volume of antiaircraft fire. Crews were near exhaustion. The remaining transports had spent most of the day in evasive action, zigzagging at high speed, and were now scattered in all directions.

In detail the picture is now vague, but the general impression is indelible in my mind of bombs wobbling down from high-flying B-17s, of carrier bombers roaring toward targets as though to plunge full into the water, releasing bombs and pulling out barely in time; each miss sending up towering columns of mist and spray; every hit raising clouds of smoke and fire as transports burst into flame and took the sickening list that spells their doom. Attackers departed, smoke screens lifted and revealed the tragic scene of men jumping overboard from burning, sinking ships. Ships regrouped each time the enemy withdrew, but precious time was wasted and the advance delayed. But the four remaining transports,[18] escorted by the *Hayashio* and three ships of Desdiv 15, still steamed doggedly and boldly toward Guadalcanal.

These were a sorry remnant of the force that had sortied from Shortland. With seven transports sunk and as many destroyers withdrawn to rescue survivors, prospects looked poor for the operation. It was evident by evening, to make matters worse, that the transports could not possibly reach the unloading position at the appointed time. Even steaming at thirteen knots, they could not arrive until almost sunup of 15 November.

By midafternoon of 14 November a friendly search plane had reported the presence of four enemy cruisers and four destroyers steaming northward at high speed in the waters east of Guadalcanal. There was no doubt that they were after our transports. It was estimated that on their present course our transports would meet these warships off Cape Esperance. Our Eighth Fleet, which was supposed to have provided indirect escort, had now withdrawn to the north and was unavailable. Furthermore, it was unknown if the Second Fleet main body would be in a position to counterattack. It was difficult, therefore, to decide whether to risk the transports against the enemy now or withdraw to await a more favorable opportunity. My indecision was resolved by a late afternoon dispatch from the commander in chief of the Combined Fleet ordering that we continue directly toward Guadalcanal.

Unusually successful radio communications at this time provided information that the Second Fleet was advancing at full speed to attack the reported enemy fleet. This meant that the fleet flagship *Atago*, the battleship *Kirishima*, two ships of Crudiv 4, and several destroyers would be supporting our effort. Thus it was with a feeling of relief that I gave the order to proceed with the operation. By sunset I was further heartened by the sight of several of my rescue destroyers, filled to capacity with army troops, catching up with my depleted force. Shortly before midnight, with visibility at seven kilometers, we were greatly encouraged to sight our Second Fleet main body dead ahead. With these stalwart guardians leading the way, we continued the advance.

Approaching from east of Savo Island, our van destroyers were first to engage the enemy, opposing several heavy cruisers. Heavy gunfire ensued, and the entire vicinity was kindled by flare bombs. We could see individual ships set afire—

193

friend and foe alike. The *Atago's* searchlights soon played on enemy vessels, which we were surprised to find were not cruisers, but *Washington*-class battleships! This then was the first battleship night action of the war!

The *Atago, Takao,* and *Kirishima* loosed their guns in rapid succession, and the enemy opened return fire. I chose this moment to order a northward withdrawal of the transports, feeling that for them to continue into the battle area would only add to the confusion. At the same time I called for the three ships of Desdiv 15, under Captain Torajiro Sato, to advance and attack the enemy. As the three destroyers dashed forward a weather front closed in, reducing visibility to three kilometers. My earlier judgment was confirmed by the next radio message from the Combined Fleet, which now ordered a northward withdrawal of the transports. It was already in progress.

An hour past midnight this battle, which had started and ended in darkness, was over. It was believed that two enemy heavy cruisers and one destroyer had been sunk, and one heavy cruiser and one destroyer seriously damaged.[19] When my ships reached Guadalcanal, a burning enemy heavy cruiser was observed. We were of the opinion that two enemy

The heavy cruiser *Atago,* sunk by the USS *Darter* on 23 October 1944.

battleships were damaged by torpedoes from Desdiv 11 and the *Oyashio* of Desdiv 15. We suffered the loss of the battleship *Kirishima* (her crew was rescued by destroyers) and the destroyer *Ayanami* but felt that this Third Battle of the Solomons (or Naval Battle of Guadalcanal) had ended in our favor.

From a vantage point to the rear I anxiously watched the progress of this heroic night battle. My mission was still to get the transports unloaded and their troops ashore. Of my command, only the flagship *Hayashio* and the four transports remained. We headed at full speed for Tassafaronga. The plan had been for unloading to begin around midnight and be completed within two hours, allowing for safe withdrawal of the ships. Strenuous activities of the preceding day and night had so delayed our schedule, however, that unloading at the debarkation point could not possibly be commenced until after daybreak. There was no question that the usual method of landing the troops would subject the ships to fierce aerial attacks, as on the previous day. It would be more than tragic to lose so many men after coming so far through the perils of enemy attacks. I resolved, accordingly, to effect the unloading by running the transports aground. The concept of running aground four of our best transports was, to say the least, unprecedented, and I realized full well that their loss would be regrettable. But I could see no other solution. This recommendation was made to the commanders of the Eighth and Second Fleets and was met by flat rejection from the former. The commander of the Second Fleet was directly responsible for this operation, and his reply was, "Run aground and unload troops!"

This resolute approval was gratefully received. As we approached Tassafaronga by the early light of dawn, I gave the fateful order that sent the four transports hard aground almost simultaneously. Assembling my destroyers, I ordered immediate withdrawal northward, and we passed through the waters to the east of Savo Island.

Daylight brought the expected aerial assaults on our grounded transports, which were soon in flames from direct bomb hits. I learned later that all troops, light arms, ammunition, and part of the provisions were landed successfully.

The last large-scale effort to reinforce Guadalcanal had ended. My concern and trepidation about the entire venture had been proven well founded. As convoy commander I felt a heavy responsibility.

The superiority of Japan's prewar navy in night-battle tactics is, I believe, generally acknowledged. Long training and practice in this field paid off in early actions of the war such as the battles off Java and Surabaya when our ships scored heavily against enemy forces. But by the time of the battles of Cape Esperance and of Guadalcanal, the U.S. Navy was beginning to overcome our initial advantages, and these actions resulted in fairly equal losses to each side.

American progress in naval night actions is directly attributable to the installation of radar in warships, which in our opinion was begun in early June 1942—about the time of the Battle of Midway. At that time our radar program was still in the research stage and our warships were not generally radar-equipped until well into the following year. Radar permitted detection of targets in the dark of night and provided accurate control of gunfire. This worked an obvious and drastic change in nighttime operations. Flares were still used by both sides to illuminate targets, but radar-equipped ships of the U.S. Navy were able to fight night battles without the use of searchlights. The slight advantage accruing to the United States through the use of radar in the naval battles of mid-1942 became increasingly pronounced as the war continued.

An absolute prerequisite of victory is to know the enemy situation. American intelligence, radio communication (including radar and interception), and submarine search were far superior to Japan's efforts in these fields. Carelessness in our communications, and a corollary astuteness in that of the enemy, resulted in the untimely death of Admiral Isoroku Yamamoto, commander in chief of the Combined Fleet, and several members of his staff. The careful planning and execution of this accomplishment must stand as a tribute to the skill of the enemy.

Search operations in the front-line Solomons area were conducted mainly by planes. From Shortland to Guadalcanal there are three possible routes of surface transit running along the north or south, or through the center of these islands. Our ships moving to and from Guadalcanal had to follow one or another of these routes, hoping always to evade the enemy. But the enemy search net, without exception, always thwarted this hope, and his ships and attack planes were always alerted, fully prepared for interception. In these circumstances it is understandable that we were unable to achieve surprise attacks.

Even at Shortland our assembled vessels came to be attacked by big bombers such as the B-17s. Enemy planes attacked by day and by night, and when they were not attacking they were reconnoitering our situation. Our only counter to these attacks and searches was to keep our ships at Shortland on constant alert during the day and anchor them at various points along the coast during the night.

The end of the effort to reinforce Guadalcanal found more than ten thousand Japanese troops on the island, without any regular means of supply. None of the usual methods had been successful, and our losses in destroyers were proving prohibitive. Provisions and medical supplies were needed so desperately that daring expedients were called for to provide them. Supply by air would have been tried if we had had air superiority, but we could not even claim this.

The first novel method of supply to be tried was what may be called the drum method. Large metal cans or drums were sterilized and then filled with medical supplies or basic foodstuffs such as cereals, leaving enough air space to ensure buoyancy. Loaded on destroyers, these drums were linked together with strong rope during the passage to Guadalcanal. On arrival all drums were pushed overboard simultaneously while the destroyer continued on its way. A power boat would pick up the buoyed end of the rope and bring it to the beach, where troops would haul it and the drums ashore. By this means unloading time was cut to a minimum, and destroyers returned to base with practically no delay.

Transport was also attempted by submarines that would be loaded with supplies, be brought to the landing point, cruise there submerged during the day to avoid air attacks, and surface near the friendly base at night, when the supplies would be carried ashore by motor boats. Submarine transport, however, was not new, as it had been conducted by Germany during World War I.

Yet both of these were makeshift measures and, even when successful, resulted in the provision of only a few tons— enough for a day or two—of supplies. Almost daily came radio messages reporting the critical situation on the island and requesting immediate supplies. It was indicated that by the end of November the entire food supply would be gone, and by the latter part of the month we learned that all staple supplies had been consumed. The men were now down to eating wild plants and animals. Everyone was on the verge of starvation, sick lists increased, and even the healthy were exhausted. When we realized these circumstances, every effort was directed to relieve the situation.

On 27 November, two destroyers from each of Desdivs 15 and 24, which had been on transport duty to Buna, moved from Rabaul to Shortland loaded with drums of food and medical supplies. After conferences, preparations, and a trial run, the fleet commander issued orders for the first supply effort by the drum method to take place on 30 November. Of eight destroyers that were to take part, six were to be loaded with 200 to 240 drums. To accomplish this, reserve torpedoes were removed from these six ships, leaving in each only eight torpedoes—one for each tube—and cutting their fighting effectiveness in half. No drums were loaded on board the flagship *Naganami* nor the destroyer leader *Takanami*, which carried the commander of Desdiv 31.

Preparations were completed on 29 November, and I led the ships from Shortland that night. In an attempt to conceal our intentions from the enemy we sailed eastward during the next morning. Nevertheless, we were shadowed constantly by his alert search planes. Around noon we increased speed to twenty-four knots and shaped a southward course to Guadalcanal. Three hours later, in spite of heavy rain, speed was upped to thirty knots.

About this time we received word that a friendly reconnaissance plane had sighted "twelve enemy destroyers and nine transports." Immediate preparations were made for action. But our main mission was to deliver supplies and, with no reserve torpedoes, it would be impossible to win a decisive battle. Nevertheless I exhorted all ships under my command, "There is great possibility of an encounter with the enemy tonight. In such an event, utmost efforts will be made to destroy the enemy without regard for the unloading of supplies."

By sunset heavy rain began to fall, and it became very dark. This caused confusion in our formation and speed was temporarily reduced. But the rain did not last long, and with its passing, visibility improved. An hour before midnight we passed west of Savo Island and then swung southeastward in attack formation. Visibility was about seven kilometers.

Minutes later three enemy planes with lighted navigation lights were observed forward of our course circling at low altitude. Still we continued toward the designated unloading points off Tassafaronga (*Takanami* and three ships of Desdiv 15) and Segilau (*Naganami* and three ships of Desdiv 24). Since no aerial flares had been observed, and in view of the enemy practice of dropping them upon sighting our ships at night, we concluded that these planes were yet unaware of us. The tense silence was broken by a sudden radio blast from the lead ship *Takanami*, "Sighted what appear to be enemy ships, bearing 100 degrees." And this was followed immediately by "Seven enemy destroyers sighted."

My destroyers had already broken formation, and those carrying supplies were on the point of tossing the joined drums overboard. But hearing these reports, I abruptly ordered, "Stop unloading. Take battle stations." With this order each destroyer prepared for action and immediately increased speed, but with no time to assume battle formation, each had to take independent action.

Within minutes, the flagship *Naganami*'s lookouts sighted the enemy at bearing 90 degrees, eight kilometers distant, and raising my binoculars, I could easily distinguish individual enemy ships. In a moment it was clear that we had been recognized, for the circling search planes dropped dazzling flares. The minute these parachute flares burst into light, enemy ships opened fire on the nearest ship, which was the *Takanami*. The brilliance of the flares enabled the enemy to fire without even using his searchlights.

With all possible haste I issued a general order, "Close and attack!" Our destroyers opened fire, but numerous illuminating shells and parachute flares suddenly set off by the enemy brightened our vicinity so that it was extremely difficult to

Another view of the cruiser *Atago. Courtesy of Shizuo Fukui*

make out the formation of the enemy fleet. The *Takanami* scored a direct hit with her first salvo. After five more salvos she had set afire the second and third ships of the enemy formation and made recognition of enemy ships easier for our other destroyers.

Concentrated enemy fire, however, inflicted many casualties in the *Takanami*, including her skipper, Commander Masami Ogura; the ship was burning and crippled. The flagship *Naganami* now caught an enemy cruiser in her searchlight and opened fire. Because she was on an opposite course from her target, the *Naganami* turned hard to starboard and came about to run abreast of the enemy ship. Continuing her salvo firing, the *Naganami* approached the cruiser and launched eight torpedoes at a range of four kilometers, all the while a target herself of a tremendous concentration of enemy gunfire. There were deafening explosions as shells fell all around my flagship, sending up columns of water. The *Naganami* was showered by fragments from near misses but, miraculously, sustained no direct hits. I have always felt that our good luck was accountable to the high speed (thirty-five knots) at which the *Naganami* was traveling, and that enemy shells missed us because of deflection error.

The *Oyashio* and *Kuroshio* of Desdiv 15 fired ten torpedoes at cruisers, and the *Kawakaze* of Desdiv 24 fired eight after reversing course and coming abreast of the enemy line. Meanwhile, enemy torpedoes were not inactive. Two deadly tracks passed directly in front of the *Naganami*. The *Suzukaze,* the second ship of Desdiv 24, was so busy avoiding enemy torpedoes that she was unable to loose any of her own. Both sides exchanged gunfire as well as torpedoes, in the glare of parachute flares and illuminating shells, and there were countless explosions.

In the ensuing minutes, torpedoes from our destroyers were observed to hit a cruiser, setting it afire, and it was believed to sink immediately.[20] We shouted with joy to see another enemy cruiser set afire and on the point of sinking as a result of our attack. It seemed that the enemy force was thrown into complete confusion. During a sudden cessation in firing by both sides, we sighted what appeared to be two destroyers that had been set ablaze by the *Takanami's* gunfire.

The *Kuroshio* and *Kagero*, each still having four torpedoes, sent the last underwater-missile attack against the enemy. And the *Kagero*, using searchlights for spotting her targets, got off several rounds of gunfire. Thus more than thirty minutes of heavy naval night action came to an end as both fleets withdrew and the quiet of the night returned.

I was anxious to know what had happened to the damaged *Takanami*. When repeated calls brought no response, and after checking the location of each of my other ships, I ordered the *Oyashio* and *Kuroshio* back to find and help her. These ships, under Comdesdiv 15, Captain Torijiro Sato, found the *Takanami* southeast of Cape Esperance, crippled and unnavigable, and started rescue work. The *Oyashio* had lowered lifeboats and the *Kuroshio* was about to moor alongside the stricken ship when an enemy group of two cruisers and three destroyers appeared at such close range that neither side dared fire. Our two destroyers were forced to withdraw, leaving many *Takanami* survivors who made their way in cutters and rafts to friendly shore positions on Guadalcanal.

When the battle was over, my scattered ships were ordered to assemble near the flagship. Since all torpedoes had been expended, it was impossible to effect any further naval action. I decided to withdraw and return to Shortland by way of the central route, spelling an end to the night naval action of 30 November 1942, which is known in Japan as the Night Battle off Lunga, and in the United States as the Battle of Tassafaronga.

We did not know what losses the U.S. Navy had sustained in this battle but judged, on the basis of destroyer reports, that two cruisers and one destroyer had been sunk, and two destroyers heavily damaged.[21] Our loss of the *Takanami*, with a large number of men including the division commander,

Captain Toshio Shimizu, and her skipper, Commander Masami Ogura, was a matter of deep regret. On the other hand, it was amazing good fortune that all seven of my other destroyers had escaped damage in this close encounter against a numerically superior enemy, and it added to the glory of our squadron.[22]

The problem of getting supplies to starving troops on Guadalcanal remained. Returning to Shortland by noon on 1 December, I set to work at once on plans and preparations for another attempt to bring stores to that island. Three more ships were added to my command when Desdiv 4's *Arashi* and *Nowaki* arrived at Shortland the next day, and the *Yugure* of Desdiv 9 came in during the morning of 3 December.

Preparations were completed by early afternoon of 3 December, and I departed for Guadalcanal by the central route with ten destroyers. The *Makinami*, *Yugure*, and flagship *Naganami* served as escorts to the other seven ships, which were loaded with drums of supplies. When, soon after our departure, we were sighted by B-17s, speed was increased to thirty knots and the advance continued, though we expected that a large-scale air attack would soon be upon us. By late afternoon there came a formation of fourteen bombers, seven torpedo bombers, and nine fighters. Twelve Shortland-based Zero seaplanes, flying patrol for our force, bravely challenged the enemy. On board the destroyers we watched with fascination to observe a total of five planes—friendly and enemy—plunge flaming into the sea. The thought occurred to me, why should our fast destroyers with well-trained crews fall prey to air attack? Our antiaircraft fire was concentrated against carrier dive-bombers and low-flying torpedo planes, which came in at very close range as we avoided them by rapid and frequent turns to right and left. The only damage to us was caused by a near miss on the *Makinami*, the last destroyer in the formation, resulting in a few casualties, but this did not affect the squadron's advance.

Arriving southwest of Savo Island on schedule, we approached the coast near Tassafaronga and Segilau in formation to unload. This was accomplished soon after midnight, when all seven supply-laden destroyers dumped drums overboard, hauled rope ends to the shore, hoisted boats back on board, and pulled away. They were unmolested by the enemy, whose only action was with PT boats, which were easily repelled by the *Naganami, Makinami,* and *Yugure.* Knowing of our plan, it is strange that the enemy fleet did not oppose this transportation, but it was probably still recovering from damage sustained in our last night engagement.

After the unloading was completed, all destroyers assembled around the flagship *Naganami* and started back to base. Of 1,500 drums unloaded that night, it was most regrettable that only 310 were picked up by the following day. The loss of four fifths of this precious material was intolerable when it had been transported at such great risk and cost, and when it was so badly needed by the starving troops on the island. I ordered an immediate investigation into the causes of the failure. It was attributed to the lack of shore personnel to haul in the lines, the physical exhaustion of the men who were available, and the fact that many of the ropes parted when drums got stuck on obstacles in the water. Furthermore, any drums that were not picked up by the next morning were sunk by machine-gun fire from enemy fighter planes. Our troubles were still with us.

We returned to base on 4 December without further loss and began preparations at once for a third supply effort. That evening the Eighth Fleet flagship *Chokai* arrived at Shortland with the commander in chief on board. I called on Admiral Mikawa directly to report the battle situation and confer about future operations. I told him frankly that a continuation of these operations was hopeless and would only lead to further losses and complete demoralization and, since the situation was becoming steadily worse, strongly recommended that the starving troops be evacuated from Guadalcanal as soon as possible. It was my further suggestion that efforts be concentrated on building up a strong base in the vicinity of Shortland.

The next day my force was increased to thirteen ships with the arrival of the *Tanikaze* and *Urakaze* of Desdiv 17 and the *Ariake* of Desdiv 9, which were added to my command. Another welcome addition came with the arrival of the newly built *Teruzuki* on 7 December. She was 2,500 tons and capable of thirty-nine knots, and my flag was shifted to her.

Early in the afternoon of that day ten destroyers were dispatched on a third drum transportation effort led by Captain Torajiro Sato, Comdesdiv 15. At nightfall an urgent radio message from Captain Sato reported that his force had been attacked by fourteen carrier-based bombers and fighters. The planes had been driven off, but not before they had scored bomb hits on the *Nowaki*, making her unnavigable. She was on her way back to base under tow of the *Naganami* and escorted by the *Yamakaze* and *Ariake*. I started for the scene in my new flagship.

On the way I learned that the rest of the force that had continued toward Guadalcanal had fought off six torpedo boats west of Savo Island. It was prevented from unloading, however, by presence of enemy planes and more torpedo boats. Accordingly, it was on its way back to base without having made delivery. Under the circumstances I was forced to agree with its decision. Another attempt had failed.

All destroyers returned to base on 8 December, while endless plans and preparations went on for our next attempt. Eleven B-17s and six fighters raided the Shortland anchorage on 10 December and hit the tankers *Toa Maru* and *Fujisan Maru*. The latter was set afire by a bomb hit in its after section. The minelayer *Tsugaru* came alongside and was able to extinguish the flames with the help of all fire-fighting units in the port. Both tankers escaped sinking.

In the afternoon of 11 December, eleven destroyers departed for Guadalcanal on another transportation mission.

Led by the *Teruzuki,* the force consisted of three ships of Desdiv 15, two each from Desdivs 17 and 24, plus the *Arashi, Ariake,* and *Yugure.* We advanced without incident until sunset, when we were suddenly attacked by twenty-one bombers and six fighters. Our escort planes had already withdrawn, but we succeeded in downing two of the enemy with antiaircraft fire. We also managed to dodge their repeated dive-bombings and continued on our way without damage.

We rounded Savo Island shortly after midnight and sighted a group of torpedo boats immediately to the south. The *Kawakaze* and *Suzukaze,* protecting our flanks, engaged this enemy and sank three of these small boats. While this was going on, seven of our transport destroyers approached Cape Esperance, dropped some 1,200 drums of supplies, and started their withdrawal. Patrolling the inner harbor at twelve knots, my flagship sighted a few torpedo boats nearby. We took course to maneuver around them and attacked but took an unexpected torpedo hit on the port side aft, causing a heavy explosion. The ship caught fire and became unnavigable almost at once. Leaking fuel was set ablaze, turning the sea into a mass of flames. When fire reached the after powder magazine there was a huge explosion, and the ship began to sink.

Directing operations of my force on the bridge when the torpedo struck, I was thrown to the deck unconscious by the initial explosion. I regained consciousness to find that the *Naganami* had come alongside to take off survivors. With the help of my staff, the flag was transferred to this ship. I received treatment for shoulder and hip injuries and was ordered to rest. Most of the crew was rescued by the *Naganami* and *Arashi,* which had also come alongside, but both ships were forced to leave suddenly when torpedo boats came to make another attack. Lifeboats were dropped for the remaining survivors, most of whom managed to reach Guadalcanal.

The loss of my flagship, our newest and best destroyer, to such inferior enemy strength was a serious responsibility. I have often thought that it would have been easier for me to have been killed in that first explosion. Forced to remain in bed because of my injuries, I reported by radio the fact that the flag had been shifted to the *Naganami*. I withheld any mention of my being hurt for fear of the demoralizing effect it might have on the force.

On 12 November I returned to Shortland and received the fleet order "Guadalcanal reinforcements will be discontinued temporarily because of moonlit nights. The reinforcement unit will proceed to Rabaul and engage in transportation operations to Munda for the present."

I sent the damaged *Nowaki* to Truk under tow from the *Maikaze*, escorted by the *Arashi*. With my remaining eight destroyers I arrived at Rabaul on 14 December. The pain from my wounds made it extremely difficult for me to move about, but I continued in command of the force.

The New Georgia Group in the Central Solomons consists principally of the islands of Vella Lavella, Kolombangara, New Georgia itself, and Vangunu, stretching in that order from northwest to southeast. Munda is located under the southwestern tip of New Georgia, the largest of these four islands, and it was there that the high command decided to establish a stronghold. On 15 December I sailed for Munda in the flagship *Naganami* with six other destroyers (four of them carrying troops). The following evening our destination was reached, and troops began to debark. Frequent squalls made visibility so poor that several enemy planes that came searching for us had to fly extremely low to make their sightings. Spotting us, they came in to make persistent attacks. About the same time an enemy submarine crept up on us and fired four torpedoes, which did no damage. Our patrol boats counterattacked the submarine with depth charges whose effect was unknown. These attacks made it clear that the enemy was aware of our transportation intentions to Munda, and thereafter his attacks in this vicinity became increasingly intense.

Our force returned safely to Rabaul on 18 December. In the next seven days our group of ten destroyers, the minelayer *Tsugaru,* and a few transports completed five runs to New Georgia. One of these moves was accomplished by six destroyers carrying army personnel to construct a base at Wickham on the southwest coast of Vangunu.

On Christmas Day, during the last of these transportations to Munda, the transport *Nankai Maru* took a torpedo from an American submarine. The destroyer *Uzuki,* in trying to retaliate against the submarine, collided with the transport and became unnavigable when two firerooms were flooded. I proceeded at once with four destroyers to the rescue of the damaged ships. The crew of the *Nankai Maru* were taken on board our destroyers, and we returned to base with the *Uzuki* in tow.

On Guadalcanal more than fifteen thousand officers and men of the Imperial Japanese Army and Navy were on the point of starvation. Those who had not been tapped by hunger were suffering from malaria, so that their fighting power was practically gone. An unfortunate situation had become desperate. All efforts to bring in adequate supplies had failed. To leave these men on the island any longer meant only to lose them to death and capture. As this inevitability became obvious to the Supreme Command, the decision was finally made for a general withdrawal, and orders to this effect were issued to the local headquarters of both services. Joint conferences were held at Rabaul in utmost secrecy. Plans were discussed and adopted, and methods for carrying out the plans were worked out in fine detail. The evacuation operation was scheduled for early January 1943; the withdrawal point was to be Cape Esperance, on the northwest tip of Guadalcanal. It was further decided that, instead of transport ships, every available destroyer of the reinforcement unit would be used to conduct the evacuation. Tardy as it was, my staff and I, fully realizing and understanding the forlorn situation, were glad that the operation was finally going to be carried out.

Full plans and preparations for the evacuation of Guadalcanal had just been completed when I received orders of transfer to the Naval General Staff, effective 27 December. My successor, Rear Admiral Tomiji Koyanagi, chief of staff of the Second Fleet, arrived at Rabaul on 29 December. We discussed in detail his new assignment, and I turned over the command. There were sad farewells to my staff and friends, who had for so long shared, fought, and suffered the fates of war with me. In the late afternoon of that day, pained and weary, I boarded a plane and left Rabaul for the homeland.

A simple statement of the facts makes it clear that the Japanese attempt to reinforce Guadalcanal ended in failure. The causes of this failure, however, are probably as diverse as the people who may offer them. From my position as commander of the reinforcement force, I submit that our efforts were unsuccessful because of the following factors:

Command complications. At one and the same time I was subject to orders from the Combined Fleet, the Eleventh Air Fleet, and the Eighth Fleet. This was confusing at best; and when their orders were conflicting and incompatible, it was embarrassing at least, and utterly confounding at worst.

Force composition. In almost every instance the reinforcement of Guadalcanal was attempted by forces hastily thrown together, without specially trained crews, and without previous opportunity to practice or operate together. Various types of ships of widely varying capabilities were placed under my command one after the other, creating unimaginable difficulties and foreordaining the failure of their effort.

Inconsistent operation plans. There never was any consistent operation plan. Vessels, troops, and supplies were assembled piecemeal to suit the occasion of the moment without overall long-range plan or purpose. This was a frailty our army and navy should have recognized soon after the outbreak of the China Incident. It was a fatal Japanese weakness that continued through the attempts to reinforce Guadalcanal and even after.

Communication failures. Our communication system was seldom good, and during the fall and winter of 1942 it was almost consistently terrible. In wide theaters of operations and under difficult battle situations it is indispensable for a tactical commander to have perfect communication with his headquarters and with his subordinate units. The consequence of poor communications is failure.

Army-navy coordination. This situation was generally unendurable. It did little good for the army or the navy to work out their own plans independently, no matter how well founded, if they were not coordinated. Time and time again in these operations their coordination left much to be desired.

Underestimation of the enemy. Belittling the fighting power of the enemy was a basic cause of Japan's setback and defeat in every operation of the Pacific War. Enemy successes were deprecated and alibied in every instance. It was standard practice to inflate our own capabilities to the consequent underestimation of the enemy's. This was fine for the ego but poor for winning victories.

Inferiority in the air. Our ships, without strong air support, were employed in an attempt to recapture a tactical area where the enemy had aerial superiority. This recklessness resulted only in adding to our loss of ships and personnel.

The greatest pity was that every Japanese commander was aware of all these factors, yet no one seemed to do anything about any of them. Our first fruitless attempt to recapture Guadalcanal was made with a lightly equipped infantry regiment. The key points of the island had already been strongly fortified by the U.S. Marines under cover of a strong naval force. The next Japanese general offensive was made with one lightly equipped brigade against the same points, and it also failed. Meanwhile the enemy had increased and strengthened his defenses by bringing up more sea and land fighting units.

Japan's only response was to bring forward a full division in a direct landing operation. Ignoring the tremendous difference in air strength between ourselves and the enemy, this landing operation was attempted directly in front of the enemy-held airfield. As a result, officers and men were able to disembark, but there was no chance to unload our heavy guns and ammunition. We stumbled along from one error to another while the enemy grew wise, profited by his wisdom, and advanced until our efforts at Guadalcanal reached their unquestionable and inevitable end—in failure.

It was certainly regrettable that the Supreme Command did not profit or learn from repeated attempts to reinforce the island. In vain they expended valuable and scarce transports and the strength of at least one full division. I believe that Japan's operational and planning errors at Guadalcanal will stand forever as classic examples of how not to conduct a campaign.

Operations to reinforce Guadalcanal extended over a period of more than five months. They amounted to a losing war of attrition in which Japan suffered heavily in and around that island. The losses of our navy alone amounted to two battleships, three cruisers, twelve destroyers, sixteen transports, well over one hundred planes, thousands of officers and men, and prodigious amounts of munitions and supplies. There is no question that Japan's doom was sealed with the closing of the struggle for Guadalcanal. Just as it betokened the military character and strength of her opponent, so it presaged Japan's weakness and lack of planning that would spell her defeat.

7

The
Battle
of
Savo
Island

TOSHIKAZU
OHMAE

During the struggle for Guadalcanal, each side prevailed at certain points or in different dimensions of military activity. Early in the contest a Japanese force approached undetected at night and virtually destroyed an Allied cruiser concentration, giving the Japanese navy temporary control of the waters around Guadalcanal. Allied troops ashore, striving to consolidate their position and protect the airfield, were deprived of support from the sea.

The Battle of Savo Island was the most effective attack on the American forces during the vacillating course of this vicious land, sea, and air campaign, yet it had no direct bearing on the campaign's eventual outcome. The following article presents an inside account of the entire enterprise. Here the night-battle efficiency of the Japanese and their propensity for surprise are demonstrated. Also emphasized are shortcomings of interservice coordination, the competition between carrier- and land-based air units, and the assignment of responsibility for the defense of the Solomons to the navy alone. The Japanese miscalculation of American intentions—concluding that American air raids on Guadalcanal were merely diversionary—and their gross underestimation of the number of U.S. troops on the island provide further evidence of inadequate intelligence, both in the gathering and in the interpretation. Again, one is reminded of lost opportunities, although Admiral Mikawa presents a cogent defense of his decision not to attack the transports.

The Japanese momentum was blunted at the Coral Sea, thrust back at Midway, and terminated at Guadalcanal. Henceforth the Imperial Navy assumed a defensive role.

B Y APRIL 1942 the Japanese navy had accomplished all of its missions originally scheduled for the opening phase of the Pacific War. Since 7 December 1941 it had severely crippled the U.S. Fleet in Hawaii; supported landings, invasions, and seizures of southern areas rich in resources sorely needed by Japan; and gained control of the sea lanes of the central and western Pacific. And all of these objectives were achieved at far less cost than had been anticipated.

Japanese staff studies of second-phase operations were initiated as early as January 1942. By February, plans had been worked out and developed between the Navy Section of Imperial General Headquarters in Tokyo and the Combined Fleet. Members of both staffs were so enthusiastic over the early successes that they were now firmly in favor of going ahead with plans for further conquest, before the United States had a chance to recover.

In March the staff of the Combined Fleet proposed the capture of Midway in order to secure a foothold in the mid-Pacific and to bring about the greatly desired decisive battle with the U.S. Fleet. They insisted that Midway should be

213

captured and fortified before the wounds inflicted at Pearl Harbor had time to heal. It would be a stroke of especially good luck for the Combined Fleet, they believed, if a chance arose to engage the Americans in a decisive surface fleet action in connection with the Midway operation. Initially that entire undertaking was opposed by the Navy Section of Imperial General Headquarters for two reasons: 1) the difficulties involved in supplying such a distant base after it had been seized, and 2) the impossibility of bringing up reinforcements in the event of a sudden enemy attack. The two staffs were pitted against each other at a joint conference held in Tokyo on 2–5 April. Under strong pressure from the Combined Fleet, Admiral Osami Nagano, chief of the Naval General Staff, finally yielded, and the tentative plan to attack Midway was formally approved.

The plan for second-phase operations was accordingly revised by Imperial Navy Directive No. 86 on 16 April. The occupation of Port Moresby was set for early May, of Midway and the Aleutians for June, and of Fiji, Samoa, and New Caledonia for July. In the spring of 1942 the cherry blossoms, at their fullest bloom, seemed like a symbol of continuing victory for the Japanese navy; but Japan's wind of misfortune was making up and would soon begin to blow.

On 8 April came the Halsey-Doolittle raid on Tokyo. The Battle of the Coral Sea in May shattered Japan's sea road to Port Moresby. A month later in the Battle of Midway the Imperial Navy suffered its most bitter defeat. At Midway four first-line aircraft carriers of the Combined Fleet were lost at one blow, and with them went the fleet's mobility and strength. On 11 June, as a result of these reverses, the Fiji–Samoa–New Caledonia operations scheduled for July were postponed and later canceled.

Plans had been made to activate the Eighth Fleet as a local defense force for Fiji, Samoa, and New Caledonia after the occupation of those islands. The cancellation of these operations was a personal disappointment to me. As a prospective staff member of the Eighth Fleet, I had been studying and preparing for the exploitation of advantages that would accrue to Japan. One bright goal was the nickel and chrome mines of New Caledonia. Another was the chance to see Noumea as a submarine base from which to conduct raids against the lines of communication between the United States and Australia.

Since the balance of naval power in the Pacific inclined toward the United States after Midway, the Japanese concluded that the southeast Pacific offered the most probable arena for a decisive naval action. The Eighth Fleet was activated on 14 July, under command of Vice Admiral Gun'ichi Mikawa, with the assignment of defending the area south of the equator and east of 141°E longitude. The operational designation was the Outer South Seas Force.

Admiral Mikawa had been second in command to Vice Admiral Nagumo of the Pearl Harbor Striking Force, in which he himself had the Support Force, consisting of Battleship Division 3 (*Hiei, Kirishima*) and Cruiser Division 8 (*Tone, Chikuma*). In this command he continued to support the carrier task force as it proceeded with raids on Lae, Salamaua, and Ceylon. Following the Battle of Midway his command of Batdiv 3 passed to Vice Admiral Takeo Kurita on 12 July, and two days later Mikawa was placed in command of the Eighth Fleet. A gentle, soft-spoken man and an intelligent naval officer of broad experience, Admiral Mikawa was recognized for his judgment and courage.

On the very day of his appointment to command of the Eighth Fleet, I visited Admiral Mikawa at his modest home in Setagaya, an outlying ward of Tokyo. His first job for me was to "go out to the forward areas for a firsthand look at the war situation and survey local conditions at our bases." I left Yokohama by flying boat in the early morning of 16 July, staged through Saipan, and flew on to Truk. This base was

215

the headquarters for Vice Admiral Shigeyoshi Inoue's Fourth Fleet, which was then responsible for operations in the Outer South Seas, or southeast Pacific area.

Fourth Fleet staff members outlined to me the following operational plans:

> 1) The seizure of Port Moresby was to be carried out, this time by overland operation starting from Buna. The Nankai Detachment, as the first echelon, was scheduled to leave Rabaul on 20 July and land at Buna the following night. Additional forces would come after this initial contingent, which was to follow the Kokoda trail through and over the Owen Stanley mountains to Port Moresby. The Buna landing and its follow-up operations were considered to be the most urgently important of the Fourth Fleet's present plans.
>
> 2) As a result of lessons learned from the Coral Sea and Midway battles, efforts were being made to establish and strengthen air bases in the Solomons and Eastern New Guinea. A survey conducted in cooperation with the Eleventh Air Fleet had shown that there were favorable sites for an airfield at Buna, in Papua, and near Lunga Point on Guadalcanal, in the southern Solomons. Construction had been started on a landing field and a nearby dummy strip at Guadalcanal. But no suitable location for an airfield had yet been found in the central Solomons.
>
> 3) It was conceived that, after the occupation of Port Moresby, our air garrison there should be limited to fighter planes. Bombers would be sent there only as needed and, after their mission, would return to Rabaul to avoid the risk of losing them on the ground.

I asked for an estimate of the situation in the area and the enemy's capabilities. On these points the Fourth Fleet judged that:

> 1) For the time being, the United States was incapable of effecting large-scale counterattacks.
>
> 2) The U.S. Carrier Task Force attack on 20–21 February on Rabaul had been successfully repulsed. There were

no indications that a similar effort was being planned. There was little probability of such attacks in the near future.

3) We had a seaplane unit deployed at Tulagi, which had been there since early July. It was necessary to establish a land-based air garrison at Guadalcanal as soon as the airfield was ready, but the Eleventh Air Fleet saw difficulties in accomplishing this because of a scarcity of reserve planes.

Upon completion of these studies, I left Truk by flying boat at 0700 on 20 July and arrived at Maruki seaplane base in Simpson Harbor, Rabaul, shortly after noon. White smoke drifted lazily from the mouth of the nearby active volcano. At the pier was a half-submerged merchant ship, her red hulk a striking contrast to the sparkling blue sea. Transports and small naval vessels anchored in close order along the beach offered easy targets in the event of an enemy air raid. Upon landing I expressed this thought and was surprised at the lack of concern shown by the commander of the local defense.

This area's defense was the responsibility of the Eighth Base Force. Air operations were under the direction of the Twenty-fifth Air Flotilla, which was a part of the Eleventh Air Fleet. But the Eleventh Air Fleet Headquarters and its commander in chief were located at Tinian, in the Marianas. Although the Eighth Base Force and Twenty-fifth Air Flotilla were supposed to be acting in close cooperation, it was soon apparent to me that the local atmosphere was anything but cooperative. Observing this situation, I could understand the rumored ill feelings that had sprung up at the Battle of the Coral Sea between the carrier task force and the air forces based at Rabaul.

In conversation with staff officers of the Eighth Base Force, the situation in the Solomons was presented to me as follows:

1) On 2 May, Tulagi and Gavutu had been occupied by the Maruyama Company of the Kure Third Special Naval

217

Landing Force (about two hundred men) and an antiaircraft detachment of about fifty men from the Third Base Force. Starting on 4 May, some four hundred men—the Marumura and Yoshimoto companies—of the Kure Third Special Naval Landing Force conducted mopping-up operations in key areas of Savo, Florida, and Santa Isabel Islands, after which they rejoined the main body at Kavieng.

2) On 8 June, a section of the Tulagi garrison occupied the Lunga area of Guadalcanal. Eleven days later, an airfield survey group headed by officers from the Eleventh Air Fleet and Fourth Fleet was sent to Guadalcanal. As a result of this survey an airfield site was chosen, and 1,221 men of the Thirteenth Construction Unit (Lieutenant Commander T. Okamura) were brought in. They were joined on 6 June by 1,350 men of the Eleventh Construction Unit (Captain K. Monzen), and within ten days work had begun on an airfield. There were occasional small-scale air attacks by the enemy, but these inflicted little damage and did not interfere with the construction of the airfield.

3) The Eighty-fourth Garrison Unit (Lieutenant Commander Masaki Suzuki), reinforced by the First Company of the Eighty-first Garrison Unit, was organized locally to defend the area, pending the establishment of the air base at Guadalcanal. The total strength of this force was about four hundred men.

4) After the occupation of Tulagi, some four hundred officers and men—roughly two thirds of the strength of the Yokohama Air Group—commanded by Captain Miyazaki, proceeded to Tulagi. A detachment of 144 men from the Fourteenth Construction Unit under Lieutenant Iida had been working on the Tulagi seaplane base since 8 July.

5) The general situation in the Solomons was quiet. Efforts were being made, by aerial reconnaissance, to find a suitable airfield site somewhere between Rabaul and Guadalcanal, so far without success. But since early July the main part of the Fourteenth Construction Unit had been improving an emergency airfield at Buka, which would be adequate for medium bombers. When the bases

218

at Guadalcanal and Buka were finished, the air defense of the Solomons would be complete.

Thereafter the conversation changed to problems involved in the Port Moresby operation. I had the distinct feeling from these talks that a new higher command organization at Rabaul would be most unwelcome. It was clear to me that the present command felt that everything was going quite well. In fact, they showed their really negative attitude when it came to a discussion of housing for the headquarters of the Eighth Fleet. It was pointed out to me that there were no adequate accommodations on shore—although the present commands were certainly housed in comfortable quarters— and that any surface force commander would certainly prefer to keep his headquarters afloat in his flagship in order to cope with possible emergencies.

It so happened that Admiral Mikawa had informed me in advance of his wishes about the stationing of his ships. He was well aware that it would be unfavorable to have a division of heavy cruisers stationed where they would be exposed to enemy attack. He had determined that his ships should train in the safer rear areas such as Kavieng, Truk, or the Admiralties; but that local operations should be commanded from ashore at Rabaul. If the need arose, Admiral Mikawa could always move his headquarters to a ship and take command afloat. Accordingly, I requested that preparations be made ashore for the fleet headquarters, and this was done, but the accommodations offered were far inferior to those of the lesser headquarters of the Eighth Base Force.

I next paid my respects to the commander of the Twenty-fifth Air Flotilla and discussed the local situation with his staff. By early August the airfield at Guadalcanal would be completed, they informed me, and ready to accommodate about sixty planes, and by the end of the month it would be able to handle the entire flotilla. They also raised the doubt, as had the Eleventh Air Fleet, that there would be sufficient

219

reserve strength to divert an effective number of planes to Guadalcanal. It was my feeling that the Twenty-fifth Air Flotilla people were not really concerned about obtaining planes for the new base. The reason for their lack of interest arose from the fact that the Twenty-fifth Air Flotilla, which had long been engaged in the strenuous air battle against Port Moresby, was soon to be relieved by the Twenty-sixth Air Flotilla. Upon being relieved, the Twenty-fifth would withdraw to a rear area for refitting and replenishment, and thus be free from local responsibilities.

It was plain that the fighting spirit of the base force and of the air flotilla was sorely tried, but this was understandable, since they had both been involved in drawn-out, monotonous operations. After two days at Rabaul, I returned to Truk, where, on 23 July, Lieutenant General H. Hyakutake arrived with his Seventeenth Army Headquarters. I was invited to a dinner in their honor given by the Fourth Fleet commander, Admiral Inoue. At this gathering I learned that the interests and energies of the Seventeenth Army were to be devoted entirely to the Port Moresby invasion operations and that they had absolutely no concern with the Solomons. This information made me skeptical of the wisdom of the central army-navy agreement, which had placed responsibility for the defense of the Solomons upon the navy alone.

The Eighth Fleet flagship, the heavy cruiser *Chokai*, escorted by Destroyer Division 9, entered Truk harbor on 25 July and dropped anchor at noon. I reported to Admiral Mikawa at once, giving him a full account of what I had learned in the past eleven days. There was a conference this same day between the staffs of the Eighth and Fourth fleets. Mikawa's staff expressed concern at the possibility of a large-scale enemy attack against the Solomons or the eastern part of Papua. This concern was dismissed by the Fourth Fleet staff as the mere anxiety of a newcomer. The Eighth Fleet assumed command of the Outer South Seas Forces at midnight on 26 July, and the flagship *Chokai* sailed for Rabaul at 1500 the

The heavy cruiser *Chokai*, sunk by U.S. carrier aircraft in the Battle of Leyte Gulf, 25 October 1944. *Courtesy of Hajime Fukaya*

next day. It was a revival for me, after five years' absence from sea duty, to be under way in this fine cruiser. It brought back memories of the battle of Woosung Landing by the Third Army Division, five years before, when I had commanded the lead destroyer.

At 1000 on 30 July we entered Simpson Harbor, Rabaul. Vice Admiral Mikawa moved ashore that same day, and his flag was raised above a ramshackle building near the Second Air Group billet. The modest, indeed humble, quarters lacked even toilet facilities, but Admiral Mikawa was not discouraged. And he stood by his decision to hold the cruisers in the rear area at Kavieng.

In a planning room borrowed from the Eighth Base Force, we conferred on the last day of July with the Seventeenth Army regarding the Port Moresby operation. The advance contingent of the Nankai Detachment had already occupied Kokoda and was continuing its transmontane advance. The need was urgent for a coastal transport route to Port Moresby, because it would be impossible to bring daily supplies, let alone heavy weapons, through the Owen Stanley

221

range. We made plans for a seaborne invasion of Port Moresby by mid-August, after Samarai and Rabi, in Milne Bay, had been occupied. Meanwhile the Eighth Fleet was fully engaged in transporting Seventeenth Army troops to Buna, and by local army-navy agreement, preparations were under way for the invasion of Rabi.

At this time a steady stream of messages was coming from Lieutenant T. Okamura, commanding officer of the construction unit at Guadalcanal, requesting planes for that base. But the Eleventh Air Base Headquarters gave no sign of complying with this request. Enemy air attacks on Guadalcanal were increasing steadily. Single-plane raids every second or third day against Tulagi and Guadalcanal were giving way to almost daily raids by several enemy planes. There were seven B-17s on the last day of July, ten on 1 August, eleven on 2 August, two on 3 August, nine on 4 August, and on 5 August five planes attacked. Imperial General Headquarters Special Duty Group (Radio Intelligence) sent a dispatch on 5 August suggesting the possibility of active enemy operations in the South Seas Area, based on an increase in communications activity. The Eighth Fleet digested this information and concluded that the focus of this enemy endeavor would be in Papua, where the Owen Stanley thrust by our army troops was making a rapid advance along the Kokoda trail toward Port Moresby. It was logical that the enemy would move a carrier task force to disrupt our supply line to Buna. In addition to raids on Buna, it was likely that the enemy would repeat his carrier-borne attacks of 10 March on Lae and Salamaua. We concluded that the air raids on Guadalcanal must be diversionary.

On 31 July a convoy consisting of the minelayer *Tsugaru*, the transport *Nankai Maru*, and the subchaser *PC-28* was attacked by enemy planes and forced to abandon its plans to enter the anchorage at Buna. We believed that the enemy would make every effort to intercept our next big convoy to Buna, scheduled to arrive there on 8 August. This convoy, which carried the main body of the Nankai Detachment, consisted of three transports: the *Nankai Maru, Kinai Maru,* and *Ken'yo Maru,* escorted by the light cruiser *Tatsuta,* the destroyers *Uzuki* and *Yuzuki,* and by the *PC-23* and *PC-30.* The Eighth Fleet's principal mission at this point was the seizure of Port Moresby. It was planned, therefore, to stage an all-out air attack against Rabi in the early morning of 7 August because we were aware that the enemy had recently been building up the air base there.

On 6 August a message from Guadalcanal informed us that natives helping our construction forces to build the airfield had suddenly fled into the jungle the previous night. This provoked no concern at headquarters, since native laborers had been known to abandon work unexpectedly and without apparent reason. Our search planes reported no enemy activity south of Guadalcanal on 6 August, and the day passed without incident.

The calm of the following dawn was shattered with the arrival of an urgent dispatch at headquarters: "0430. Tulagi being heavily bombarded from air and sea. Enemy carrier task force sighted." It was soon evident that the strength of the enemy force was overwhelming, as successive messages indicated: "One battleship . . . two carriers . . . three cruisers . . . fifteen destroyers . . . and thirty to forty transports." [1] And by the time that the Eighth Fleet staff had been roused from sleep and had assembled at headquarters, the situation looked most discouraging. It appeared next that the enemy was effecting landings simultaneously at Tulagi and on Guadalcanal.

Contact with the forces on Guadalcanal was broken after a last word that they had "encountered American landing forces and are retreating into the jungle hills." The last news from our base at Gavutu was that our large flying boats were being burned to prevent their falling into enemy hands. And at 0605 came a fateful message from the Tulagi Garrison Unit: "The enemy force is overwhelming. We will defend our positions to the death."

It was plain that our forces of about 280 riflemen on Guadalcanal, and only some 180 at Tulagi, were no match for the enemy's well-equipped amphibious troops. The situation was serious.

We did not know at first whether this was a full-scale enemy invasion or merely a reconnaissance in force. But as the picture became clear of the size of the enemy forces involved, we soon had to recognize the enemy's intention to stay and seize these islands. With this awareness, it was immediately apparent how serious it would be for our position if the enemy succeeded in taking Guadalcanal with its nearly completed airfield. A plan of action was hastily worked out.

All available planes of the Twenty-fifth Air Flotilla, which stood ready for the morning's intended raid on Rabi, were at once diverted to attack Guadalcanal. A surface force of all available warships would proceed to the enemy anchorage at Guadalcanal and destroy the enemy fleet in night combat. At the same time ground reinforcements would be moved to Guadalcanal, to land immediately after the fleet engagement and drive off the invading enemy. All available submarines (there was a total of five, belonging to Submarine Squadron 7) were, of course, ordered to concentrate around Guadalcanal to attack American ships and keep in contact there with lookout posts. At 0800 Admiral Mikawa ordered all the heavy cruisers still in the Kavieng area to make best speed to Rabaul, thence to carry out an offensive penetration of the enemy forces at Guadalcanal.

The deployment of Japanese naval forces within the area of the command of the Eighth Fleet on 7 August was as follows:

Planes

Vunakanau	32 Bettys
Lakunai	34 Zekes
	16 Vals
	1 Type 98 recon.
Maruki seaplane base	5 Mavises

Warships
Kavieng   CA *Chokai,* Crudiv 6 *(Aoba,*
                                       Kinugasa, Kako, Furutaka)
Rabaul   CL *Tenryu, Yubari,* DD *Yunagi*

There were, in addition to these, the three destroyers (*Tatsuta, Uzuki, Yuzuki*) engaged in escort of the Buna convoy. The submarine *RO-33* was on lookout station off Port Moresby, and the *RO-34* was conducting a commerce-raiding mission off Townsville, Australia.

In planning this operation our most serious problem was how to deal with the American carriers, of which it was estimated that there were at least two—and possibly three. It had to be expected that the enemy would launch at least one carrier-based air attack against our assaulting ships. It would be ideal if the planes of the Twenty-fifth Air Flotilla could eliminate the enemy carrier threat, but complete destruction of these mighty ships solely by air attack could not fairly be expected. If, somehow, a thrust from the enemy carriers could be avoided, we felt assured of reasonable success against the other enemy ships because we had complete confidence in our night-battle capabilities. The time set for our penetration of the Guadalcanal anchorage was midnight.

Another vital element was the landing of infantry reinforcements for our small force on Guadalcanal. This had to be done speedily, before the enemy could establish a firm foothold on the island. In conference, the Seventeenth Army staff was confident that it would not be difficult to drive out whatever meager American forces might be delivered to Guadalcanal. In this judgment they sadly underestimated the capability of the enemy.[2] They also said that a decision for immediate diversion of the Nankai Detachment to Guadalcanal could not be made at Seventeenth Army level—which meant that no army forces were available to reinforce the island. Consequently, the Eighth Fleet hastily organized a reinforcement unit of 310 riflemen with several machine guns, and 100 men of the Fifth Sasebo Special Naval Landing Force and Eighty-first Garrison Unit, then at Rabaul. It was arranged for this small force, commanded by Lieutenant Endo, to board the 5,600-ton *Meiyo Maru* and head for Guadalcanal under escort of the supply vessel *Soya* and the minelayer *Tsugaru*. As details were being worked out, the *Chokai* was ordered into Rabaul to embark Admiral Mikawa's staff while Crudiv 6 headed for the rendezvous point in St. George Channel.

In the flurry of excitement at headquarters we were startled at 1030 by the sound of three shots of gunfire—the air-raid alert. Enemy daylight air attacks were a novelty at this time, and all of us at headquarters rushed outside to see what was happening. There were thirteen American B-17s flying eastward at about seven thousand meters. We decided that they were making a strike at the Vunakanau air base in support of the enemy's operation at Guadalcanal, and therefore we returned to the myriad urgent details of planning that screamed for our attention.

One prime difficulty of our planning was that the ships involved had never operated together as a fighting force. Except for Crudiv 6 ships, they had never so much as trained together in steaming in column formation. The speed standards of each ship had, therefore, not been adjusted, and we realized that great care would have to be exercised in making the frequent changes of speed required in the intricate formations of nighttime maneuvering. But the commander of each ship was a skilled veteran, and we felt sure that a maximum of effectiveness could be achieved in night battle by using a single-column formation.

Admiral Mikawa's greatest concern was about the imperfectly charted seas of this region and the danger to his ships of unknown underwater reefs. He told me just after the battle that he was confident of victory once our ships had passed safely through the danger of the unknown waters. It was decided that the fleet would proceed southward through the central channel ("the Slot") of the Solomons, on the advice

226

of the commander of the Eighth Base Force, who said that it was almost deep enough for the battleships.

Thus the Eighth Fleet plan was completed, and by noon of 7 August it had been sent to headquarters. Captain Sadamu Sanagi, then one of the chief planners of the Naval General Staff, is my source for the reaction when this plan reached Tokyo. Admiral Osami Nagano, chief of the Naval General Staff, considered the plan dangerous and reckless, and, at first, ordered that it be stopped immediately. Upon further consideration and after consultation with his staff, he decided to respect the local commander's plan.

The *Chokai* entered Rabaul Harbor at 1400, just before the second air-raid warning of the day was sounded. It was a relief to learn that this time it was a false alarm: the planes were our own bombers returning from their mission. We had sent out a total of twenty-seven Bettys and seventeen Zekes from Rabaul at 0730 to hit the enemy's transports. The weather was bad at the enemy anchorage area, and these planes had attacked cruisers at 1120 with poor results. Nine Vals had left Rabaul later in the morning and attacked enemy destroyers at 1300, claiming damage to two of them. None of our search planes had sighted aircraft carriers this day, and our air losses came to five Bettys, two Zekes, and five Vals.

Admiral Mikawa and his staff boarded the *Chokai* with all possible speed, and the flagship sortied from the harbor at 1430, accompanied by the light cruisers *Tenryu* and *Yubari* and the destroyer *Yunagi*. It was a fine clear day, the sea like a mirror. Our confidence of success in the coming night battle was manifest in the cheerful atmosphere on the bridge. Three hours out of Rabaul we rendezvoused with Crudiv 6, and thus our seven cruisers and one destroyer were assembled for the first time. "Alert cruising disposition" was ordered at a point fifteen miles west of Cape St. George. As darkness approached, an enemy submarine was detected to the south, and we altered course to the east to avoid it, which we did

227

successfully. It was probably this same submarine whose torpedoes shortly claimed the *Meiyo Maru,* which sank with the loss of crew and the 315 troops intended for Guadalcanal. This loss caused abandonment of our present plans to reinforce the island, and it was a bitter blow. The thought persisted then and later, however, that once the army was dispatched in force, there would be no difficulty in driving the enemy from the Solomons. We continued southward, confident and, considering the circumstances, secure.

At 0400 the next morning, five seaplanes were catapulted from our cruisers to reconnoiter Guadalcanal, Tulagi, and the surrounding waters. The *Aoba's* plane reported at 1000 that an enemy battleship, four cruisers, and seven destroyers had been sighted to the north of Guadalcanal at 0725, and fifteen transports at 0738. The same plane also reported the sighting of two enemy heavy cruisers, twelve destroyers, and three transports near Tulagi. The picture presented by this count of ships cast serious doubt on the results reported by our earlier air attacks, which had claimed two cruisers, a destroyer, and six transports sunk, plus three cruisers and two transports heavily damaged. It was concluded that most of the enemy's invasion strength was still in the Guadalcanal area, and that although no carriers had been reported, they too must still be in the area, but probably to the south or southeast. We judged that if the enemy carriers were not within one hundred miles of Guadalcanal, there would be little to fear of a carrier-based attack unless it came this morning, or unless we approached too close to the island before sunset. At any rate, the whereabouts of the enemy carriers was so important to our plan that Admiral Mikawa radioed to Rabaul for information about their location. We learned later that the Twenty-fifth Air Flotilla sent out reports of negative information on the enemy carriers, as the result of their morning reconnaissance flights, but this information did not reach us.

With the information at hand a signal was sent out to the effect that our force would proceed southward through Bou-

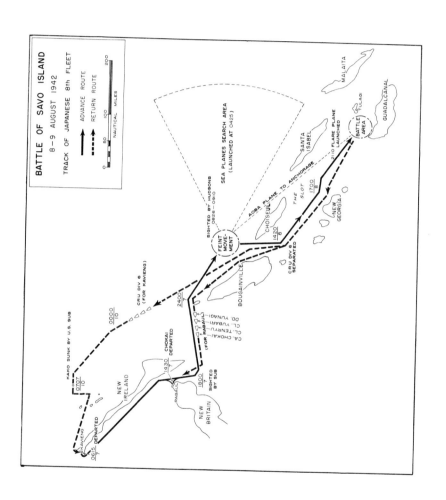

BATTLE OF SAVO ISLAND
8-9 AUGUST 1942
TRACK OF JAPANESE 8th FLEET

ADVANCE ROUTE
RETURN ROUTE

NAUTICAL MILES
0   50   100   150   200

SEA PLANES SEARCH AREA
(LAUNCHED AT 0425)

SIGHTED BY HUDSONS
0826-0910

FEINT
MOVE-
MENT

MALAITA

GUADALCANAL

TULAGI

BATTLE
AREA

2110 FLARE PLANE
LAUNCHED

AOBA PLANE TO ANCHORAGE

SANTA
ISABEL

CHOISEUL

THE
SLOT

1700
8

1420
8

NEW
GEORGIA

CRU DIV 6
SEPARATED

CRU DIV 6
(FOR KAVIENG)

BOUGAINVILLE

2400
7

0000
10

KAKO SUNK BY U.S. SUB

0707
10

NEW
IRELAND

CHOKAI
DEPARTED

1430
7

1800
7

SIGHTED
BY SUB

RABAUL

(FOR RABAUL)

C.A. CHOKAI
C.L. TENRYU
C.L. YUBARI
DD. YUNAGI

NEW
BRITAIN

KAVIENG DEPARTED

0615
7

gainville Strait, would recover float planes (at about 0900), and would then pass between Santa Isabel and New Georgia islands to approach Guadalcanal for a night assault against the enemy at about 2230.[3]

While pursuing a southeasterly course some thirty miles northeast of Kieta, we observed an enemy Hudson bomber shadowing us at 0825. We made ninety-degree turns to port to throw him off immediately after the sighting and headed back to the northwest. When the Hudson withdrew to the north, we reversed course at once and, at 0845, recovered the seaplanes. While they were being brought on board, we were spotted by another Hudson, flying quite low. Salvos from our eight-inch guns sent this observer on his way, and we resumed our course for Bougainville Strait.

These contacts naturally caused us to assume that our intentions had been perceived by the enemy, and that more search planes would appear, increasing the imminent possibility of air attack. An early approach to Guadalcanal became increasingly disadvantageous. The decision was made, accordingly, to decrease our speed of advance and delay our assault until 2330.

We were advancing down Bougainville Strait at 1145 and there sighted friendly planes returning toward Rabaul by twos and threes. The lack of formation indicated that they had encountered heavy fighting. We watched them with grateful eyes. We cleared the strait shortly after noon and increased speed to twenty-four knots. The sea was dead calm, and visibility was, if anything, too good.

At 1430 our battle plan was signaled to each of the other ships: "We will penetrate south of Savo Island and torpedo the enemy main force at Guadalcanal. Thence we will move toward the forward area at Tulagi and strike with torpedoes and gunfire, after which we will withdraw to the north of Savo Island." While drafting this order, I had the firm conviction that we would be successful.

There was a tense moment on the bridge at 1530, when a

mast was sighted at a distance of thirty thousand meters on our starboard bow. Friend or enemy? We were much relieved to discover that it was the seaplane tender *Akitsushima*, of the Eleventh Air Fleet. She was en route to establish a seaplane base at Gizo.

Meanwhile we were intercepting a great deal of enemy radio traffic. We heard, loud and clear, much talk of flight deck conditions as planes approached their landing pattern, such as "Green base" and "Red base." Happily, we could be fairly sure of no air attack from the enemy on 8 August, but it was made clear to our entire force that we could expect an all-out attack from their carriers on the following day. The very existence of the enemy flattops in the area was a major concern to Admiral Mikawa, and this dominated our later tactical concepts.

At 1630 every ship was ordered to jettison all deck-side flammables in preparation for battle. Ten minutes later the sun dissolved into the western horizon, and a message I had drafted for Admiral Mikawa was signaled to each ship in his name: "In the finest tradition of the Imperial Navy we shall engage the enemy in night battle. Every man is expected to do his best."

After 1600 there was no further radio indication of enemy carrier activity. With the end of daylight and still no carrier-based air attacks, the chances of success for our ships looked much brighter, and spirits brightened in the flagship. The morale of the whole fleet climbed when we heard the results of the morning attack by our planes. They, according to their reports, had hit two heavy and two light cruisers and one transport and had left them in flames.

Just before dark our ships had assumed night battle formation, following the flagship in a single column with 1,200-meter intervals between ships. At 2110 the cruiser planes were again catapulted for tactical reconnaissance and to light the target area. The pilots had had no experience in night catapulting, so this was a risky business, but the risk had to

231

be taken. A water takeoff would have necessitated our dispersing the formation, and then reforming, making for a delay the schedule would not allow. The planes were catapulted successfully.

We encountered sporadic squalls at 2130, but these did not interfere with our advance. Long white streamers were hoisted to fly from the signal yards of each ship for identification purposes, and at 2142 speed was upped to twenty-six knots.

The catapulted seaplanes reported that three enemy cruisers were patrolling the eastern entrance of the sound, south of Savo Island. All hands were ordered to battle stations at 2200, and the formation turned up to twenty-eight knots. All was ready for combat. Narrow though the seas were in the battle area, we intended to adhere to the original battle plan: pass counterclockwise on the Guadalcanal side to the south of Savo Island and then turn toward Tulagi.

At 2240 the unmistakable form of Savo Island appeared twenty degrees on the port bow, and the tension of approaching action was set three minutes later when a lookout shouted, "Ship approaching, thirty degrees starboard!"[4] On the flagship bridge all breathing seemed to stop while we awaited identification of this sighting.

It was a destroyer, at ten thousand meters, about to cross our bows from right to left.

An order was radioed: "Stand by for action!"

Should we attack this target? We might be steaming into an ambush. At this moment the all-important question was whether we should strike this target or evade it. Admiral Mikawa made his decision and ordered, "Left rudder. Slow to twenty-two knots." He had reasoned clearly that this was not the moment to alert the enemy to our presence, and at high speed our large ships kicked up a wake that would have been difficult to conceal. Breathing became more normal again as we watched the enemy destroyer's movements. From her deliberate, unconcerned progress it was plain that she was unaware of us—or of being watched—and of the fact that every gun in our force was trained directly on her. Seconds strained by while we waited for the inevitable moment when she must sight us—and then the enemy destroyer reversed course! With no change in speed she made a starboard turn and proceeded in the direction from which she had come, totally unaware of our approach.

In almost the same instant, and before we could fully appreciate our good fortune, another lookout reported, "Ship sighted, twenty degrees port."

A second destroyer![5] But she was showing her stern, steaming away from us.

Admiral Mikawa's reaction was almost automatic: "Right rudder. Steer course 150 degrees."

We passed between the two enemy destroyers, unseen, and they soon disappeared in the darkness. It was a narrow escape, but our emphasis on night battle practice and night lookout training had paid off. This advantage was later to be increased by the local situation in which the enemy's backdrop was brightened by the flames of burning ships, reflected from clouds, while we moved out of utter darkness.

But at the present moment the disadvantage to the enemy of lights and shadows gave rise to the further concern that once we had passed the line of the patrolling destroyers, the advantage of the lighting would be reversed against us. That this did not work against us in the next half hour must be attributed to plain good luck and the fact that the enemy was exhausted after many hours of alert during landing operations. We were fortunate, too, that apparently there had been no report of our approach by enemy search planes.

It was time now for positive action, and remembering the search-plane information that three enemy cruisers were patrolling south of Savo Island, we rushed in. The attack order was given at 2330. Battle was only moments away.

The speed of advance was pushed to thirty knots. The destroyer *Yunagi*, the rear of our formation, was ordered back

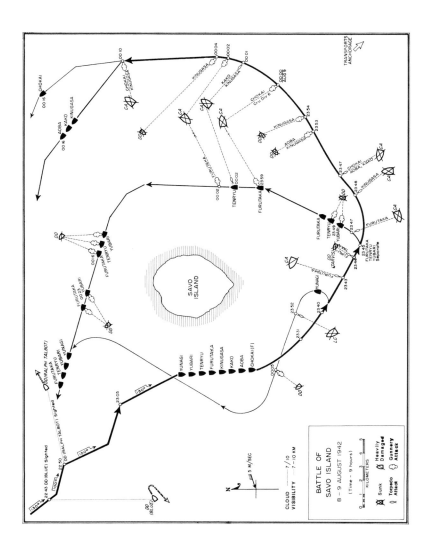

BATTLE OF
SAVO ISLAND
8 – 9 AUGUST 1942
(Time – 9 hours)

234

to attack the enemy destroyers we had just bypassed. This move was made because of the *Yunagi*'s inferior speed, which might have caused her to straggle from our attack formation, and also in the hope of securing our withdrawal route from disturbance by either of the two enemy destroyers patrolling north of Savo Island.

I stood beside Admiral Mikawa. Before me was a chart on which were plotted the locations of enemy ships. We peered into the darkness. The voice of a lookout shattered the tense silence: "Cruiser, seven degrees to port!"

The shape that appeared in that direction seemed small; it could be only a destroyer. It was still a long way off.

"Three cruisers, nine degrees to starboard, moving to the right!"

And then a parachute flare from one of our planes brought reality to the scene. There they were, three cruisers! Range, eight thousand meters.

The *Chokai*'s skipper, Captain Mikio Hayakawa, was ready. His powerful voice boomed throughout the bridge, "Torpedoes fire to starboard—Fire!"

It was 2337.

Almost immediately the deadly weapons were heard smacking the water one by one. While we waited for them to hit, the radio announced that our following cruisers had opened fire with guns and torpedoes.

Then it happened. There was a sudden explosion that had to be a torpedo. It had struck an enemy cruiser that was on our starboard beam.

Our course was now northeasterly. The *Chokai* launched a second set of torpedoes, and following the first great explosion, there seemed to be a chain reaction. Within ten minutes after the first torpedo explosion, there were explosions everywhere. Every torpedo and every round of gunfire seemed to be hitting a mark. Enemy ships seemed to be sinking on every hand!

Our course was now northeast, and we sighted another

group of enemy ships thirty degrees to port. The *Chokai*'s searchlights illuminated these targets, and fire was opened on an enemy cruiser at 2353.

The *Chokai*'s searchlights were used for the double purpose of spotting targets and also informing our own ships of the flagship's location. They were effective in both roles, fairly screaming to her colleagues, "Here is the *Chokai!* Fire on *that* target! . . . Now *that* target! . . . This is the *Chokai!* Hit *that* target!"

The initial firing range of seven thousand meters closed with amazing swiftness. Every other salvo caused another enemy ship to burst into flames.

For incredible minutes the turrets of enemy ships remained in their trained-in, secured positions, and we stood amazed, yet thankful while they did not bear on us. Strings of machine-gun tracers wafted back and forth between the enemy and ourselves, but such minor counterefforts merely made a colorful spectacle, and gave us no concern. Second by second, however, the range decreased, and now we could actually distinguish the shapes of individuals running along the decks of enemy ships. The fight was getting to close quarters.

From a group of three enemy ships the center one bore out and down on us as if intending to ram. Though her entire hull from midships aft was enveloped in flames, her forward guns were firing with great spirit. She was a brave ship, manned by brave men. But this ship immediately took a heavy list as our full firepower came to bear and struck her. It appears, from postwar accounts, that this was the U.S. heavy cruiser *Quincy,* and she certainly made an impression on the men of our force. At short range she fired an eight-inch shell which hit and exploded in the operations room of the *Chokai,* just abaft the bridge, and knocked out our No. 1 turret. We were all shocked and disconcerted momentarily, but returned at once to the heat of battle as the *Chokai* continued firing and directing fire at the many targets.

As the range closed to four thousand meters we saw that three enemy cruisers had been set afire by our guns. Enemy return fire had increased greatly in amount and accuracy, but we were still without serious damage. Then, almost abruptly, the volume of enemy gunfire tapered off, and it flashed in my mind that we had won the night.

There was an enemy cruiser burning brightly far astern of us as we ceased fire. I entered our operations room on the *Chokai* and found it peppered with holes from shell fragments. Had the eight-inch hit on the *Chokai* been five meters forward, it would have killed Admiral Mikawa and his entire staff.

We were still absorbed with details of the hard fight just finished and had lost all track of time. I was amazed to discover that it was just shortly after midnight, and that we were headed in a northerly direction. If we continued northward, we ran the risk of going ashore on Florida Island, so we made a gradual change in course to the left. I asked the lookout if there was any sign of pursuing ships. There was not.

While checking our position at the navigation chart desk, I heard someone say, "Gunfire, ahead to port!" I immediately went forward and stood beside Admiral Mikawa on the bridge.

The *Furutaka*, *Tenryu*, and *Yubari* had taken a sharper turn to the left than the flagship and the others when the first torpedoes had been fired, and had been pursuing a northward course, parallel to our own. We concluded that these three ships had cleared north of Savo Island and had again turned to the left, where they found additional targets; it was their gunfire we now observed. We warned them by signal light of our presence while the gunfire continued.

Meanwhile, Admiral Mikawa and his staff had been making a rapid study of the situation in order to determine our next move. They concluded that the force should withdraw immediately. This decision was reached on the basis of the following considerations:

1) The force was at 0030 divided into three groups, each acting individually, with the flagship in the rear. For them

237

The cruiser *Furutaka* as she appeared during trials in 1939. *Courtesy of Shizuo Fukui*

all to assemble and reform in the darkness it would be necessary to slow down considerably. From their position to the northwest of Savo Island it would take thirty minutes to slow down and assemble, a half hour more to regain formation, another half hour to regain battle speed, and then another hour to again reach the vicinity of the enemy anchorage. The two and a half hours required would thus place our reentry into the battle area at 0300, just one hour before sunrise.

2) Based on radio intelligence of the previous evening, we knew that there were enemy carriers about one hundred miles southeast of Guadalcanal. As a result of our night action these would be moving toward the island by this time, and to remain in the area by sunrise would mean that we would only meet the fate our carriers had suffered at Midway.

3) By withdrawing immediately we would probably still be pursued and attacked by the closing enemy carrier force, but by leaving at once we could get farther to the north before they struck. The enemy carriers might thus be lured within reach of our land-based air forces at Rabaul.

In making this decision we were influenced by the belief that a great victory had been achieved in the night action. We

238

were also influenced by the thought of the army's conviction that there would be no difficulty about driving the enemy forces out of Guadalcanal.

Admiral Mikawa received the opinion of his staff and, at 0023, gave the order, "All forces withdraw."

There was no questioning of this order on the bridge of the *Chokai*. The signal went out by blinker, "Force in line ahead, course 320 degrees, speed thirty knots."

The *Chokai* hoisted a speed light and withdrew. Shortly after the signal we sighted the *Furutaka*'s identification lamp in the distance, and the battle was over. Our estimated dawn position was radioed to Rabaul in hope that Eleventh Air Fleet planes might be able to strike any pursuing enemy carrier.

Detailed reports were soon coming in from each ship concerning results achieved, damage sustained, and munitions expended. I went to the wardroom to prepare the action report for the force. The detailed report of shell consumption and casualties is given on page 240.

Reported claims came to a total of one light and eight enemy heavy cruisers and five destroyers sunk, five heavy cruisers and four destroyers damaged. But upon close analysis of the claims, and based on our view of the action from the flagship bridge, we estimated finally that five enemy heavy cruisers and four destroyers had been sunk.[6] With Admiral Mikawa's approval, this report was radioed to headquarters.

When my immediate tasks were completed, I took a nap on the shelter deck. Shortly before 0400 I was awakened by the cry "Battle stations! All hands to battle stations!"

But the warning proved to be illusory. It was a fine morning. We continued northwest at full speed.

The hours passed, and no enemy planes were sighted. There was no indication at all of the enemy carriers whose transmissions we had heard so loud and clear on the previous afternoon. It was reassuring to know that we were not being followed, but our spirits were dampened by the thought that

Japanese Shell Consumption and Casualties

Ships	20-cm. Gun	14-cm. Gun	12-cm. Gun	8-cm. Gun	8-cm. AA Gun	25-cm. Gun	Torpedoes	Depth Charges	Casualties
Chokai	308		120			500	8		34 killed 48 wounded
Aoba	182		86			150	13	6	
Kako	192		130			149	8		
Kinugasa	185		224				8	6	1 killed 1 wounded
Furutaka	153				94	147	8	6	
Tenryu		80		23			6	6	2 wounded
Yubari		96					4	20	
Yunagi			32				6	1	
Total	1,020	176	592	23	94	946	61	39	35 killed 51 wounded

now there would be no chance for our planes to get at the enemy carriers.

Having witnessed the enemy air raid on Rabaul two days before, we considered it dangerous to have all our ships at one base. Accordingly, at 0800 Crudiv 6 was ordered to separate south of Bougainville and head for Kavieng. They encountered an enemy submarine on the way, and the cruiser *Kako* was sunk by its torpedoes at 0707 on 10 August. The three accompanying ships fought off the submarine and managed to rescue survivors from the stricken ship so that her total casualties were only thirty-four killed and forty-eight wounded. The *Aoba*, *Furutaka*, and *Kinugasa* entered Kavieng at 1611 on 10 November.

The activities of our Eighth Fleet submarines during this operation were uneventful. The *I-121* and *I-122* had sortied from Rabaul on 7 August, had reached Savo on 9 August and sighted no enemy ships, but had maintained station, keeping in touch with lookouts ashore. The *I-123* started from Truk on 7 August, did not get to Savo until 11 August, and sighted no enemy; neither did the *RO-33*, which came north from patrolling around Papua on 7 August and reached Savo on 10 August. The *RO-34* had proceeded northward from Australia and patrolled Indispensable Strait, but made no sightings.

Upon receiving our action report, the Combined Fleet sent an enthusiastic message to Admiral Mikawa complimenting him on his success in this notable action. The withdrawal of the Eighth Fleet without having destroyed the enemy transports has, since that time, come in for bitter criticism, especially after it was disclosed that the enemy carrier force was not within range to attack—and, most especially, after our army was unable to dislodge the enemy from Guadalcanal. But critics should remember that Admiral Mikawa initiated and carried out this penetration on his own, without specific orders or instructions from the Combined Fleet.

It is easy to say now that the enemy transports should have

been attacked at all cost. There is now little doubt that it would have been worthwhile for the *Chokai* to have turned back, even alone, ordering such of her scattered ships as could to follow her in an attack on the enemy transports. And if all had followed and all had been sacrificed in sinking the transports, it would have been well worth the price to effect the expulsion of the enemy from Guadalcanal. The validity of this assumption, however, is premised on the fact that the survival of those transports accounted entirely for our army's subsequent failure to expel the enemy from its foothold in the Solomons.

The reasons for our early retirement were based in part on the Japanese navy's "decisive battle" doctrine that destruction of the enemy fleet brings an automatic constriction of his command of the sea. The concept of air power (both sea-based and land-based), which invalidates this doctrine, was not fully appreciated by us at this time, nor were we fully convinced of it until the summer of 1944, and then it was too late.

Another reason behind our decision to withdraw was the lack of a unified command of our air and surface forces. Under the circumstances, we in the Eighth Fleet ships could simply not expect of our land-based planes the degree of co-operation required to cover us in a dawn retirement.

With the benefit of hindsight I can see two grievous mistakes of the Japanese navy at the time of the Guadalcanal campaign: the attempt to conduct major operations simultaneously at Milne Bay and in the Solomons, and the premature retirement from the Battle of Savo Island. I played a significant part in each of these errors. Both were a product of undue reliance on the unfounded assurances of our army and of a general contempt for the capabilities of the enemy.

Thus lay open the road to Tokyo.

[Since Admiral Mikawa had been in command of the Japanese forces engaged in the Battle of Savo Island, he was requested to read Captain Ohmae's article for accuracy. His comments follow:]

I have read Toshikazu Ohmae's article, "The Battle of Savo Island," and find it well written and complete. It covers all the important facts of the battle as I remember them. There are a few points, however, that I wish to emphasize.

Upon my arrival at Rabaul, in late July 1942, as commander in chief of the Eighth Fleet, there was no indication that the quiet Solomons were soon to be the scene of fierce battle. Nevertheless, I recognized the mobile capability of U.S. carrier task forces and, accordingly, ordered my heavy cruisers to the safer rear base at Kavieng rather than Rabaul.

It was a serious inconvenience and a shortcoming that my command extended only to sea and land operations in the area. Air operations were entirely outside of my responsibility and control. I found, for example, that there was no program or plan for providing planes to the new base at Guadalcanal, and there was nothing that I could do about it.

As soon as the U.S. landings at Guadalcanal were reported on 7 August, and the invasion strength was apparent, I determined to employ all the forces at my command to destroy the enemy ships. My choice of a night action to accomplish this purpose was made because I had no air support on which to rely—and reliable air support was vital to anything but a night action. On the other hand, I had complete confidence in my ships and knew that the Japanese navy's emphasis on night battle training and practice would ensure our chances of success in such an action, even without air support.

My two major concerns for this operation were that enemy carriers might repeat against my ships their successes of the Battle of Midway before we reached the battle area, and that our approach to Guadalcanal might be hindered by the poorly charted waters of the Solomons. But both of these worries were dispelled once we had passed the scouting lines of enemy destroyers to the west of Savo Island, and I was then sure of success in the night battle.

The element of surprise worked to our advantage and enabled us to destroy every target taken under fire. I was greatly impressed, however, by the courageous action of the northern group of U.S. cruisers. They fought back heroically despite heavy damage sustained before they were ready for battle. Had they had even a few minutes' warning of our approach, the results of the action would have been quite different.

Prior to action I had ordered the jettisoning of all shipboard flammables—such as aviation fuel and depth charges —to reduce the chance of fire from shell hits. While my ships sustained no fires, we observed that U.S. ships, immediately after they were hit, burst into flames that were soon uncontrollable.

The reasons given by the author for not attacking the transports are the reasons that influenced my decision at the time. Knowing now that the transports were vital to the American foothold on Guadalcanal, knowing now that our army would be unable to drive American forces out of the Solomons, and knowing now that the carrier task force was not in position to attack my ships, it is easy to say that some other decision would have been wiser. But I believe today, as then, that my decision, based on the information known to me, was not a wrong one.

[signed] G. MIKAWA

8

The
Withdrawal
from
Kiska

MASATAKA
CHIHAYA

The Japanese attack on the western Aleutians was a
part of the Midway operation intended to broaden their defense boundaries and to lure American forces north to facilitate the invasion of Midway. By the time the American fleet
had returned, the occupation would be completed and the
Japanese task force could concentrate on its second objective: namely, the destruction of the remaining enemy warships. In its initial stages the Aleutian campaign was successful, although Admiral Nimitz was not taken in by the ruse;
but the defeat at Midway placed the Aleutian operation in
great jeopardy and rendered impracticable its attempt to
neutralize the American base at Dutch Harbor.

Errors in the planning and execution of this abortive ploy
are indicated in the following article—errors that ranged
from the strategic blunder of fortifying Kiska more than
Attu to the lack of equipment for building an airfield. The
bulldozer, as Admiral William Halsey contended, was one
of the decisive instruments of the war.

The author describes the multiplicity of factors involved

in preparing for the evacuation, the allowances for American radar, the vital significance of appropriate weather, and the reliance on doing the unexpected. Emerging most clearly is the crucial role of the commander, for Admiral Kimura's steadfast determination to carry out the task, his anticipation of obstacles, and his sound judgment were essential to the success of the operation.

Nevertheless, the author concludes that even with all the Japanese skill in execution, the evacuation would have been impossible had it not been for the unwitting cooperation of American blockading forces.

AS RARE AS the perfect game in baseball is the "perfect operation" in battle—if there is any such event in the annals of warfare. Perfect means, of course, one-hundred-percent achievement of an objective in an assigned mission with negligible loss on the part of a military force.

The Japanese forces, the losers in World War II, strangely enough scored this rare case of the "perfect operation" twice—first, in the withdrawal operation from the shell-torn island of Guadalcanal in early 1943, and second, in their subsequent evacuation of their besieged garrison force from the doomed stronghold of Kiska Island, the latter evacuation conducted under the very noses of vastly superior Allied military forces.

From the hopeless trap of Kiska, the Japanese successfully shuttled 5,200 troops to safety without bloodshed. The only living things left behind were several puppies; otherwise the island was completely deserted.

So perfect was the evacuation that it was not until eighteen days later that the Allied Powers finally became aware of the sudden disappearance of the Japanese garrison—when the full-fledged landing was made on the uninhabited island. Nearly 35,000 Allied troops, spearheaded by a specially

246

trained and equipped commando force and backed by massive air-sea support, assaulted Kiska Island, only to find that "the bird had flown the coop"!

How could such a perfect operation have been carried out so successfully? Was it a trick or mere chance?

In retrospect, some may say that the developments that led to the Japanese success were nothing but the turn of events beyond the control of men. While this is in some respects true, it must not be overlooked that the fortunate turn of events for the Japanese was brought about only by the patient and unflinching will of the commanding officer of the Japanese evacuation force, a characteristic that is quite unusual for the average Japanese.

It is clear that without him the course of the entire operation would have been entirely different. Not only would his force have been doomed, but the Japanese defenders on the island would have suffered the utter devastation that was the fate of the defenders of Attu Island.

Ever since the Japanese forces had invaded the Aleutians in June 1942 in conjunction with their futile attempt to capture Midway, their expeditions had at all times been plagued by misconceptions and miscalculations. The Japanese aim was to occupy both Kiska and Attu islands, in order to frustrate and repel Allied counterattacks from these areas.

However, it was the Japanese intention to evacuate the two captured islands in the winter after destroying enemy installations there. This concept was based upon the assumption that it would be difficult to winter on these islands, while combat activities would necessarily be restricted. Also, airstrips could be built only under the most difficult of circumstances owing to the forbidding topography.

The Japanese were to pay dearly for these assumptions.

Contrary to previous judgment, not only was it possible to remain in the Aleutians in the winter, but even major operations were not impossible, as subsequent developments proved. Rough terrain was, as it turned out, an obstacle to

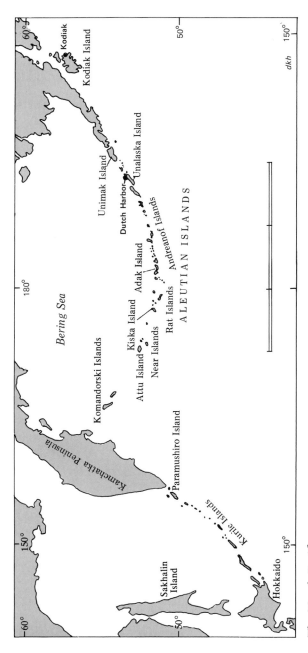

The North Pacific

248

the Japanese but not to the Allied forces. Soon after their invasion of both islands, the Japanese realized their misconceptions, or military blunders, and revised their original plans in the attempt to retain both captured strongholds during the winter.

Another surprising development was the unexpectedly quick and determined assaults by the Allies. Within a week of the capture by the Japanese of the two islands, Kiska was subjected to the first attack by Allied planes. By the middle of July, only five weeks after the Japanese invasion, a transport, three destroyers, and two sub-chasers had been sunk, and two destroyers suffered considerable damage from enemy action. The damage was wrought by either submarine or aircraft.

This was far from what the Japanese military strategists had anticipated. They had expected little in the way of determined enemy retaliation.

Immediately after the Japanese invasions, Kiska, Shemya, and Amchitka were found suitable for building airstrips, while Attu was ruled out. The initial garrison force at Attu was then moved to Kiska by sea, and this operation was completed by mid-September 1942. However, another change had to be made again in October. By this time the Japanese had learned a bitter lesson in the southwest Pacific: Allied techniques of building airstrips were so advanced that even such rugged terrain as on Attu could be leveled for airstrips.

Belatedly realizing this, Japanese army troops were sent in haste to the island of Attu, which they had abandoned.

The Japanese began work on airstrips on both Kiska and Attu in late October, although progress was lamentably slow. Poor equipment, consisting mainly of shovels, picks, and hand trucks, was like "sweeping the sea with a broom" against the rugged terrain. Intensified Allied air raids against transport caused construction to lag even further. It was a heartbreaking fact for the Japanese military that after six months of backbreaking toil no planes could land on either island.

249

The fact that not even a single air base was available virtually determined the outcome of what had already become a deteriorating situation.

Attempts to reinforce Kiska had to be made by high-speed naval vessels by December, and even this was fraught with great difficulties, which steadily increased. The pattern of severed communications, which had been bitter tea to the Japanese since the autumn of 1942 in the southwest Pacific, was repeated again in the Arctic.

The beginning of 1943 marked stepped-up activities by the Allies. On 13 January they landed on Amchitka, just ninety miles from Kiska! And even more alarming, they immediately began to build an airstrip there, although the Japanese did not become aware of the Amchitka landing until 24 January.

To the Japanese, the Allied landing on that island was tantamount to a dagger dangerously close to their heart. All they could do to ward off the impending crisis, however, was to launch air attacks on a small scale by Kiska-based seaplanes, and these were unsuccessful.

Imperial General Headquarters in Tokyo was disturbed by this turn of events, realizing the weakness of Attu, and decided to rush reinforcements to that vulnerable island. The initial reinforcement was successfully sped to the island by fast transports escorted by powerful naval units. But plans to send the second contingent of reinforcements in the same manner were frustrated when the escorting fleet ran into an Allied intercepting force some 180 miles west of their destination at dawn on 27 March.

The result was the sea battle off Komandorski Island. And although the Japanese fleet was superior in strength to the enemy, and it was also favored, by the turn of luck, in trapping the Allied fleet from the rear, the Japanese not only allowed the enemy to slip away but also gave up their operational mission of escorting the convoy to Attu.

Subsequently only two reinforcement attempts by destroyers were made. The first, on 3 April, was successful, but the second, on 10 April, failed due to poor visibility. Therefore, only half of the originally planned reinforcements reached Attu, and the Japanese fully realized that should the situation remain as it was, the tragedy of Guadalcanal would be repeated. However, there was little that the Japanese forces could now do in the way of reinforcing the threatened garrison on Attu.

Then the Allied forces attacked the island, and they threw a great scare into the Japanese forces by bypassing the key bastion on Kiska. Attu's doomed garrison numbered not more than 2,500, including those recently arrived. Few defense installations packing any power were ready. Attu was the softest spot in Japan's northernmost defense line.

Should Attu fall—an eventuality few doubted—Kiska, situated nearly 160 miles to the east, would be cut off and "wither on the vine." By now the Japanese were very conscious of the heavy toll they had had to pay for their initial blundering.

The initial reaction of the Japanese forces to the enemy invasion of Attu Island was quick and seemingly decisive. Immediately upon receipt of an urgent appeal from the besieged island, the Japanese high command in Tokyo planned to dispatch a powerful force to bolster the defenders.

It was decided at the same time that naval units based at the Kurile Islands should engage the enemy naval forces. Admiral Mineichi Koga, the commander in chief of the Combined Fleet, ordered the Twenty-fourth Air Flotilla, a land-based wing, together with destroyers and submarines of his own surface force, to come under the command of the Fifth Fleet, which was charged with the defense of the northern areas of Japan.

Koga left Truk anchorage on 17 May for Tokyo Bay, leading under his direct command the battleship *Musashi*, the Third Battleship Division of the *Kongo* and *Haruna*, and the Second Carrier Division of the *Hiyo*, the Eighth Cruiser Division of the *Tone* and *Chikuma*, and five destroyers. This was the first sortie by Admiral Koga since he had assumed command of the Combined Fleet after the death of Admiral Isoroku Yamamoto.

Meanwhile, developments happened quickly on hard-pressed Attu. Greatly outnumbered and poorly equipped, the Japanese garrison had little chance and few illusions of stemming the overwhelming tide of an Allied invasion. The outcome was obvious to the defenders even before there was any fighting.

All that the Japanese could do for the doomed garrison was to launch seven sorties by submarines and three by land-based medium bombers from Paramushiro Island, the second from the northernmost Kurile island.

The result was miserable: four subs and two medium bombers were lost, virtually for nothing. The Japanese fighting strength was waning badly.

The situation in the northern theater was now hopeless for the Japanese. The only possibility was to evacuate the garrison from doomed Kiska, a risky undertaking indeed. With Attu assaulted by superior Allied forces, the strategic strength of Kiska was gone forever. The evacuation was decided upon.

On 19 May, only a week after the Allied landing, the high command in Tokyo decided to abandon the Aleutian Islands. The high command ordered that "efforts be made to evacuate the garrison force on Kiska as soon as possible, by submarine."

Notably in this case, the order for the evacuation was given in the form of an Imperial General Headquarters directive. In the case of the withdrawal from Guadalcanal four months before, Imperial General Headquarters' decision had been given in the form of an order calling for an evacuation to be carried out by "all means." Moreover, that decision had been made in the presence of the emperor—an extraordinary procedure in the Japanese high command.

This meant that while the determination was to carry out the evacuation from Guadalcanal at all costs, the order for the removal of the Kiska garrison was halfhearted in comparison. As an added indication of Japanese military policy at this time, the evacuation of the cold, wet, stubborn defenders of Japan's remaining grip in the north was left to the discretion of the Fifth Fleet commander.

Evacuation by submarine of the garrison on Kiska was no picnic. When the island was cut off from the rear by the Attu debacle, the Japanese forces on Kiska consisted of approximately 2,600 army troops under the command of Major General Toichiro Mineki, the North Seas Garrison Force commander, and about 3,400 navy personnel led by Rear Admiral Katsuzo Akiyama, the Fifty-first Naval Base commander.

Not taking into account other factors, even simple mathematical calculation indicated that it would take at least several months to save the isolated troops with all the available submarines placed under the command of the Fifth Fleet. On top of this, when considering enemy air raids, now intensified with the fall of Attu, and an increased enemy surface blockade, there was not even a slim chance of succeeding in the evacuation.

The possible heavy loss of submarine strength in the evacuation worsened the situation. In the latter stage of the Guadalcanal campaign, a considerable number of submarines had been employed in supply missions to that hard-pressed island, and fifteen were lost due to enemy action. It was this toll that discouraged submarine crews from taking part in a similar mission—a lamentable omen from the standpoint of leadership.

Nevertheless, evacuation attempts by submarine had been made every other day with one submarine since 27 May 1943. These attempts had been successful up to the middle of June, when the interception by enemy patrol vessels around the besieged island became suddenly brisk. By 22

253

June, three submarines had either been sunk or had lost contact, and in two cases submarines had been surprised by the enemy through the white blanket of fog.

Underwater evacuation attempts were, therefore, abandoned on 23 June. The task was simply too great for submarines. By this time twelve attempts had been successful, and a total of 820 men had been removed from the island.

There was nothing left now but an attempt to evacuate the Kiska garrison by a surface force, taking advantage of the heavy fog prevailing in this area in summer. But even riskier than the costly underwater evacuation was an evacuation by a surface force. Indications had already pointed out that even this natural cover to hide a ship from the visual observer was being pierced by electronic eyes—radar.

Since the preceding autumn, the Japanese had been only too aware of the Allied forces' monopoly of this new "weapon." Previously it had been the enemy who was outmaneuvered by Japanese cruisers and destroyers in the dark. That was bitter tea now. Japanese submarines on the evacuation mission around Kiska were continuously attacked by an undetected enemy despite the shield of the fog. Most Japanese naval vessels operating in this district had not yet been equipped with radar.

The general plan of a surface evacuation was to have the force proceed to a point some five hundred miles southwest of the island, skirt outside the enemy aerial reconnaissance circles from Attu and Amchitka, and then reach Kiska while hidden by fog.

The surface force the Japanese were able to muster consisted of only three light cruisers and several destroyers—a poor match for the reportedly overwhelming enemy force, which included battleships and cruisers. And the Japanese could expect no air support.

The time necessary for the daredevil evacuation try was

estimated to be well over a week, all the time through dense fog and chilly seas. How to make so long a run through the fog with a formation of about a dozen vessels, and how also to make refueling operations with visibility extending only a few hundred yards, were big navigational problems. Never had the Japanese navy experienced anything like this before.

Success of the contemplated venture, if any, would lie entirely in whether the Japanese could sneak through a gap in the enemy ring under the cover of fog. It was more than a gamble, relying on what could not be counted upon. No one doubted that this evacuation operation would be one of the most difficult any commander had ever confronted.

The man to whom this extremely difficult operation was entrusted was Rear Admiral Masatomi Kimura, a veteran torpedo officer. After graduating from the naval academy in 1910, he had spent most of his naval career on board destroyers. In the early part of the war, he was the commanding officer of the heavy cruiser *Suzuya* and then the flag officer of the Third Destroyer Squadron. In the latter capacity, he participated in the Bismarck Sea Battle, in which most of his force and all of the escorting transports were virtually wiped out by a fierce air attack.

On 11 June 1943, he assumed command of the First Destroyer Squadron; in his new capacity he was to direct the hazardous operation of evacuating the garrison on Kiska.

The husky admiral sported an old-fashioned and luxurious mustache, which was not then common among Japanese naval officers. As he had not had the choicest posts during his career, he had been better known in Japanese naval circles for his flowing mustache than for his record as an able torpedoman.

In appearance, he reminded some of a "sea wolf" from older days, but he was a man possessing great patience coupled with firm determination and yet a flexibility of concept, as the developments of the evacuation so amply proved. Even when the situation appeared hopeless, he kept his head and never lost patience or judgment.

But the admiral was not chosen for the job of evacuating the Kiska garrison force because of his patience, judgment, and flexibility, even though, fatefully, no one else would have been more qualified.

Another of his assets was that the peculiar features of the northern sea were not entirely unfamiliar to him, as he had seen duty in patrolling the Kuriles and other northern regions as a young officer. And, fortunately, during the evacuation operation he was ably assisted by a very capable senior staff officer, Captain Rokuji Arichika, who had been in the north ever since the initial invasion of the Aleutians in June 1942.

Although the admiral was not the type to grumble over the difficulties of an assigned mission, he was not the least bit optimistic when the job was flung at him. Recently Admiral Kimura recalled that he thought at the time that his chances were slim, if not nil.

Upon taking charge of the operation, Rear Admiral Kimura was given discretion on every detail. The first step he took was to request an immediate reinforcement of at least four destroyers, including the *Shimakaze*, to his force. Only two light cruisers and four destroyers had been assigned to him. The *Shimakaze*, only recently commissioned, was an experimental ship of high speed and the sole destroyer in the Japanese navy at that time boasting radar. This was why Admiral Kimura so urgently requested, and succeeded in obtaining, the services of this ship.

Six destroyers, including the coveted radar-equipped *Shimakaze*, were then ordered by Admiral Koga, commander in chief of the Combined Fleet, to steam to the Paramushiro base, where preparations were to be made. They reached their destination around 22 June 1943.

Kimura and his staff were most concerned about whether they would be blessed with heavy fog, coming in time and lasting long enough to hide the evacuation. Meteorologists assigned to the Fifth Fleet and Kimura's force conducted an extensive statistical study of weather conditions in order to make a long-term, at least ten-day, forecast.

Kimura was not unduly worried about the problems of navigating in fog and of refueling, as he had great confidence in the veteran destroyer skippers who were going along. These men had shown their skill during the fierce struggle for Guadalcanal and were not found wanting.

However, a full dress rehearsal with all vessels participating was arranged to be made at sea prior to departing for the make-or-break evacuation attempt.

The embarkation plan was a big problem, too. Kimura and his staff planned to embark 1,200 men aboard the light cruiser *Abukuma*, 900 on the light cruiser *Kiso*, 500 each aboard four latest-type destroyers, and 400 men each aboard three older destroyers. Three other destroyers were to be reserved for protection.

This allocation of troops per vessel was considered somewhat too heavy, but the inconvenience had to be borne in order to take aboard all of the 5,200 to be evacuated at one time.

On the isolated island there still remained about ten landing craft, each of which was capable of carrying about 120 men. In order to carry all of the personnel to the naval vessels in two waves, ten would not be sufficient; twelve more were necessary. So six more landing craft were loaded aboard the light cruisers *Abukuma* and *Kiso* and one each on seven destroyers, making one extra for good measure.

Unloading the landing craft from the derrick-equipped light cruisers was no problem, but it was a different story from the aft deck of a destroyer. Here again Kimura's veteran destroyer skippers made the task possible.

The next major problem was to find an approach course to the island. The usual course to Kiska Harbor, which faced east, was from the south, going around the southern tip of the island upon arriving from a westerly direction. This was safer to navigate, and a much shorter distance. But it also involved the risk of being spotted by the enemy. On the other hand, the course passing west of the island to the north, then rounding its northern tip to the east side of the island, was regarded as hazardous to navigation as well as involving a much greater distance to be covered. Seldom did vessels take the latter route to enter Kiska Harbor.

Kimura chose the latter, however, for the reason that it offered less possibility of meeting the enemy en route to the bay.

Complete radio silence was maintained by the evacuation force throughout the operation. Ever since the plane carrying the late commander in chief of the Command Fleet, Admiral Yamamoto, had been ambushed from the air and shot down over Bougainville in April 1943, the horrible suspicion that its code had been broken had hung heavy over the Imperial Navy. It was imperative for the evacuation force to maintain complete radio silence throughout the operation, regardless of inconvenience, the Japanese planners decided.

Inconvenience during the operation was expected. Perhaps the greatest problem was how to inform the defenders of the complicated evacuation plan and its subsequent possible alterations without resorting to radio communication. Earlier, during the underwater evacuation attempt, however, army and navy staff officers had been removed from Kiska by submarine and taken back to Paramushiro, where they were briefed in detail on the plan. This thorough briefing included transmitting radio beacon signals from the island for the incoming force, using a searchlight at the northern entrance of Kiska Harbor for a navigation aid, and designating the anchoring position of a ship and the embarkation position on the beach plus an embarkation plan.

The big problem remaining was what time the Kiska garrison should be ready for an immediate embarkation, and how. The garrison should not reveal its withdrawal prematurely, and at the same time should begin the evacuation immediately after the rescue force had entered Kiska Harbor.

If everything went as planned, there would be no problem at all, even though complete radio silence was maintained. But nothing could be less sure than the operation timetable. This operation depended entirely on the occurrence of fog, which could never be forecast with certainty.

In case a change should be made in the schedule owing to unfavorable weather or other hitches, how could the island defenders change or adjust their embarkation preparations accordingly, when they were not to be informed of any such change?

The Japanese planners' solution to this problem, a grave one, was noteworthy indeed, especially in the sense of reflecting an unusual characteristic of the Japanese, which is seldom seen elsewhere. Their general idea was to have the evacuating troops assemble at the embarkation beach from 2100 (about half an hour before sunset) to midnight, both local time, every day after the designated day of evacuation, which was set for the fifth day after the departure of Kimura's force from the Paramushiro base.[1] This withdrawal to the beach was to be repeated until the actual evacuation, or until they were informed that an attempt had eventually failed, a telegram to such effect to be transmitted only after Kimura's force had returned to its Paramushiro base.

As it turned out, the troops had to repeat their withdrawal to the beach as many as eight times before they were able to make out with hungry eyes the daring rescue force entering the bay.

And withdrawing just to the beach was not exactly child's play. Aside from the keen disappointment incurred in the repetitious withdrawal to the beach from hill positions, it was an operation requiring extraordinary patience and arduous effort. Some troops had to hike five miles over wet and spongy

259

muskeg and through rugged mountain passes to the beach, and then, with hope failing a bit more every trip, drag themselves back to their positions in the foggy night.

Soon after the briefing, an army staff officer took a submarine to the isolated island to return to his original post. Incidentally, the sub had a duel with an American patrol vessel just before reaching its destination and was forced to ground on the island's southern coast. Refloated with the help of the Kiska garrison, the sub attempted an escape on 22 June, but in vain. She was the last sub to reach the trapped garrison.

It was good fortune for the Kiska garrison force to have the army staff officer who had been briefed thoroughly on the evacuation plan. To the troops and marines, hard-pressed and now besieged and cut off by the fall of Attu, he provided the only bright light in an otherwise dark and gloomy situation.

What Kimura stressed most in preparing for the adventure was to practice his evacuation plan as realistically as possible, since his small force was not familiar with the peculiar features of the northern sea. He deemed it imperative that a formation could be kept even under the worst conditions and under complete radio silence.

On 26 June 1943, Kimura led two light cruisers, ten destroyers, one other ship, and a tanker out of Paramushiro Bay and went through vigorous dress rehearsals in the prevailing fog. The training continued for eight hours, practicing refueling, gunnery, torpedo firing, sounding, and even unloading landing craft and taking on evacuees. Although conducted only once because of fuel restrictions, the rehearsal served to give Kimura and the skippers of his force some confidence about maneuvering as a team through the blanketing fog. The admiral, on the bridge of the cruiser *Abukuma,* was seen to give a satisfied tug at his large mustache.

Now that everything was ready, all that Kimura and his staff were concerned about was whether they would be fa-

vored by timely fog long enough to cover the actual operation.

As it turned out, they were not soon favored by suitable
weather. In fact, hoping for a heavy fog is entirely the reverse
of normal circumstances—fog, that enemy of mariners everywhere. The early part of July dragged by, and Kimura and his
staff were becoming more and more jittery. And they had
good reason for becoming increasingly nervous.

Time was running out for the trapped garrison. Since mid-
June enemy air raids on the island had been intensified, and
then naval bombardment commenced. An enemy invasion
seemed imminent—and it was. The defenders were suffering
from an acute shortage of food and ammunition. On top of
this, the rescue party was warned that after August there
would be less fog, its only ally now. Then there were the fuel
restrictions, another major concern.

In the early afternoon of 7 July a weary weatherman, after
a long and painstaking study of conditions, came to Kimura
and reported that a favorable fog would settle down over the
operational area in a couple of days. Kimura decided to act,
and the signal order of "weigh anchor at 1600" was flashed
out in the bay. At the designated time, two light cruisers, ten
destroyers, and a tanker headed into the northern Pacific
waters through a fog that was incidentally fading and threatening to lift altogether. As the force set a course of almost
south out of the bay, however, the fog decided to cooperate,
and a good blanket of it settled in, concealing the vessels.

After an uneventful two days of sailing in the southerly
and then the easterly directions, the force reached its standby
point about five hundred miles southwest of the steel-ringed
island stronghold. But when the force altered its course toward Kiska as scheduled, Kimura found the weather not so
cooperative. He made an "about face" accordingly. Then,
after refueling from the tanker, the admiral noted prospects
of the fog thickening and again headed for Kiska on 12 July.

The following morning, however, Kimura found himself in a predicament. With daylight, the fog started fading once more, and by shortly before noon, local time, the ceiling had lifted to five hundred yards, with a clear horizon in sight. A weather report from Kiska brought little hope. In addition, there were indications that enemy patrol planes were around.

But Kimura could not give up the evacuation attempt so soon. He had fuel for one more try, but no more. Moreover, weather conditions were not entirely hopeless—there still might be a chance of the fog closing in again. Low clouds overhead were moving swiftly, and it was anybody's guess what the weather would do. Should he go ahead, Kimura puzzled, or should he give up his evacuation attempt altogether at that time? An able staff officer advised him to give it up. Reluctantly, he decided: "Well, let's give it up, as there may be another chance. If we fail, there will be no chance at all."

To the non-Japanese, his reasoning may not have seemed strange, but it was peculiar and unique from the standpoint of the character of the Japanese, who are apt to lose their temper and flexibility when excited or grimly determined. This trend is especially conspicuous when the Japanese is in despair or cornered.

Meanwhile, there were restless days back on Kiska, with the fog settling in and rising. The defenders daily repeated their fruitless withdrawals to the beach. Kimura and his frustrated evacuation team steamed back to Paramushiro. Two days later the single-code-word telegram was sent from Paramushiro to end the withdrawals to the beach of the lonely island. The troops had made five rugged trips to the beach. Now the darkness of despair settled again on the island.

What awaited Rear Admiral Kimura upon his return to the base was severe criticism, but behind his back. Most of this came from "armchair strategists" with the staff of the Fifth Fleet. Even the fleet chief of staff, who should have understood and been sympathetic, was critical. "They should have disregarded the damned enemy patrol planes," the staff lamented. "Our shortage of fuel should have been strongly impressed on the evacuation force!"

Yes, everybody was displeased with Kimura's actions. Nevertheless, they had no other choice but to allow him to make a new attempt—even if it meant scraping the bottoms of the tankers.

To a Japanese fighting man, nothing could be more insulting than to be called "coward." Under such circumstances many would have been grimly determined to go through with an attempt now, at any cost. They would prefer reckless action to one that smacked of cowardice. Kimura, however, whether conscious or unknowing of the barbs, remained cool and calm. Even under such circumstances, he was sometimes seen playing *go,* a checkers-like game, with his able staff officer.

Admiral Kimura's staff officer was smarting. He advised the admiral to have a briefing conference with his men, which was held on 19 July. The attendance of the senior staff officer of the Fifth Fleet was especially requested. When Kimura's staff officer reviewed the abortive operation and commented that the suspension of the evacuation had been justified, other commanders and destroyer skippers of the evacuation force unanimously agreed. Kimura's obvious intention in holding the briefing was to prove to the fleet staff officer that the evacuation officers had indeed not been "cowards."

Then the admiral allowed his senior staff officer to make an extraordinary request. "If permissible," he said, "we would like very much to see our commander in chief accompany us on our next trip to Kiska Island."

Kimura's aim was to have his boss go along for the ride in order really to appreciate the circumstances under which Kimura would have to make up his mind to head for the island or withdraw. Kimura could also have had in mind that, if his skeptical boss didn't like the way he was handling the evacuation operation, then his boss himself could make a try.

At any rate, preparations were rushed for another sortie, and by the evening of 20 July everything was set. And this time the light cruiser *Tama* flew atop her mast the flag of Vice Admiral S. Kawase, commander in chief of the Fifth Fleet. He was going along too, but not to command the operation. His aim was to encourage Kimura's force, or, more realistically, to judge Kimura's actions.

On the calm dawn of 21 July 1943 Japan's northernmost bay lay entirely shrouded by cream-thick fog. Neighboring vessels were hardly visible at a few hundred yards. When weathermen predicted the next morning that the prevailing heavy fog would last, Kimura decided to leave the bay toward evening of that day.

The Japanese seadogs were jubilant with the "favorable" turn of the weather. However, there was one thing they hadn't reckoned on—now there was too much fog! The problem now was how to get through the narrow channel out of the bay with a formation of fifteen vessels. But Kimura decided to go through with it, regardless of the extremely thick fog.

The light cruiser *Abukuma*, Kimura's flagship, was the first to raise anchor. Kawase's *Tama* sailed next. Following were another light cruiser, ten destroyers, one escort vessel, and a tanker. Darkness was quickly approaching, to add to the dimness of the fog, through which the navigation and speed lamps of only one or two vessels were dimly seen.

Contrary to previous apprehension, the passage through the narrow channel of Paramushiro Bay was uneventful. The force, completely blacked out except for a dimly lit stern lamp, set a southerly course at ten knots.

The foggy night ushered in a foggy day no less thick than the previous one. Everything went along well until midafternoon, when the force altered its course to due east. While making a sharp turn following the white wake of a towing spar towed by the preceding ship, an escort vessel and a tanker, both sailing at the rear, fell out of the formation.

Contact with the tanker was regained through interservice phone and her course was altered correctly, but the other vessel, with an inexperienced skipper, could not be brought back into the formation.

A radio signal was too risky, and a vessel nearby sailing "wild" in the fog could mean a collision, which was what later happened. Two light cruisers and a destroyer had radar, but not good enough to be used under the circumstances. And aside from their lost escort vessel, getting the tanker in line again posed a headache, even though contact was maintained with her. Without refueling, a long sailing with so many short-haul destroyers was out of the question.

Finally Kimura hit upon an idea: firing three rounds from army ack-ack guns temporarily installed on the after deck of his flagship (Japanese light cruisers at this time were very poorly equipped with antiaircraft weapons).

This primitive method, when belatedly attempted the next morning, worked well. Hearing the shots, the tanker slowly showed up dimly through the fog and joined the rear of the formation, which continued on an easterly course.

By midafternoon on 25 July the force had reached the designated standby point, some five hundred miles southwest of Kiska, and had the first refueling from the tanker. The force was to cruise near the standby point while refueling, until Kimura saw the time was ripe to go ahead.

Rear Admiral Kimura was indeed patient. He had shown extraordinary patience in his first ill-fated attempt, and this time, too, he was to exhibit uncommon patience waiting for the very best time to come, without thought of criticism. As it turned out, his unusual patience was to have much to do with his subsequent good fortune.

Refueling was repeated on the morning of 26 July, this time on a northwesterly course. On the evening of that day the missing ship suddenly loomed out of the fog and closed to the starboard side of the cruiser *Abukuma,* then the second vessel in the formation. The cruiser was struck on her starboard side by the wandering escort vessel before she could get out of the way.

An immediate "emergency turn" was ordered by interservice phone to avoid further danger, but not fast enough to prevent a chain reaction in the long single column. Visibility extended no farther than the preceding vessel from the one right behind it.

Thanks to the seamanship of the veteran skippers, all the vessels down to the twelfth in line managed to avoid colliding, but the thirteenth banged her bow into the stern of the ship ahead.

This was a serious setback. Although the light cruiser *Abukuma* and the destroyer *Naganami* were able to continue despite slight stern damage to the destroyer, the destroyer *Wakaba*, with her nose stove in, and the escort vessel were unable to follow the other vessels. The escort ship was ordered to head back to the base alone, while the injured destroyer was reassigned to escort the tanker.

The admiral appeared almost unperturbed by the disaster. "Don't worry," he told his crestfallen staff. "This setback will not prevent us from accomplishing our task. More important is how to cope with the future. I rather think that this fog, as it is, will give us more help than harm."

By 27 July the force was steadily under way on an easterly course. Kimura intended to head for Kiska Island that day after dark, if there were no unexpected developments.

In midafternoon, however, the fog suddenly began to thin, and the sun could be dimly seen. It was a completely unexpected and extremely unwelcome development for the admiral and his staff. They were now bewildered.

However, after five days of dead reckoning in heavy fog the thankful navigators lost no time in fixing the position of the force with the help of the sun. Even a single position line could be precious for those who had so long sailed the northern Pacific with tricky currents and with no celestial fixes. It was this position line that had much to do with the force heading correctly to the island. By evening the fog was back, thick as ever. Apparently the navigators thought they were blessed. Weather charts suggested that dense fog would hover over the northern Pacific for some time to come.

"Now the time is ripe," Kimura said and gave orders for his force to set a course of 25 degrees for their destination.

On the morning of 28 July the final refueling was made from the tanker, and then she was ordered back to Paramushiro under the protection of the limping destroyer *Wakaba*. Kimura's force steamed for Kiska at nearly twelve knots.

The admiral must have been asking himself these questions: Was his decision a good one? Could he slip through the Allied ring around the isolated island? Did he know what the enemy's besieging force was up to? These questions were not easy ones to answer at that juncture. It was strictly a gamble. And it would continue to be.

But the die had been cast.

Life hadn't been pleasant for the garrison force on Kiska, either. The news of the suspension of the evacuation attempt on 15 July had been very bitter tea indeed.

To all of them on the island it was evident that an enemy invasion was imminent, as the island was being pounded daily by planes and even enemy blockading vessels were seen from time to time. They had all but resigned themselves to the fate of their comrades on Attu. So one can indeed imagine their feelings upon receipt of another single coded word informing them that another attempt had got under way on 22 July.

On 23 July the island was subjected to the most furious bombardment the defenders had yet experienced. Pounding the island was a flotilla that included two battleships, five cruisers, and nine destroyers. However, the troops were well holed-up, and damage was slight. The bombardment drove the point home, though, that the enemy was growing impatient and the sands of time were running out to a trickle.

Now the greatest concern of the defenders was not only

267

whether their evacuation force could sneak through the tight enemy siege lines, but whether it had time for this desperate move.

Since 25 July a strange situation had appeared to be developing around the island. On that day there wasn't a cloud in the sky, and fine weather continued on the following day. After 2200 on that day, the Japanese garrison was puzzled to note points of light gleaming over the horizon toward the southwest of the island and hear what appeared to be gunfire. A night battle at sea? It sounded like it.

Yet what was puzzling was that the besieged men knew Kimura's force could not be that close to the island. Neither were there any known Japanese subs operating in those waters. Rear Admiral Akiyama, commander of the naval garrison force on the island, felt that it must have been a battle between the Allied ships themselves, as there were no vessels in sight the next day from the island. This information was immediately sent to Kimura.

No less eager than Kimura, the naval commander on the island had been studying various conditions that would cause fog to settle thickly. On the night of 27 July he concluded that despite clear weather during the previous three days, a thick fog would show up on 29 July.

So confident of this was he that not only did he send a recommendation to that effect to Kimura, but he also advised the latter to advance the time of arrival at Kiska Harbor from the originally set 2100 to 1500, both local time. Akiyama believed that daylight was preferable in carrying out an evacuation operation.

The withdrawal movements to the shore for evacuation had been resumed since the evening of 27 July with renewed expectations. The assembly time at the beach was advanced by six hours from 29 July in compliance with Akiyama's recommendation to Kimura.

To the southwest of the island Rear Admiral Kimura's force was now stealthily approaching its destination in dense fog, after long and seemingly vacillating movements. Its course was adjusted from time to time from a radio beacon on the island.

Except for a couple of hours on the afternoon of 27 July, the force had at all times been screened by a favorable perpetual fog, which had in fact been moving to the northeast with the force. Kimura had received Akiyama's information on the "strange" enemy activities on the night of 26 July and also the following morning, but that was only a minor factor in helping him to make up his mind. However, Akiyama's advice to advance the arrival time was accepted fully. His plan of getting into the bay was accordingly adjusted.

After the parting with the tanker and destroyer on 28 July, the day passed without event. Even when the force was within one hundred miles of Kiska and extreme alert was maintained, time slowly ticked on. The night was uneventful.

By early morning of 29 July the force had passed through an area where an enemy encounter was most anticipated. Visibility was roughly one thousand yards. The weather report from Kiska showed that Akiyama had been right about the weather. Ideal circumstances were prevailing. Kimura was delighted.

"Now it is time to let the *Tama* go," Kimura told his senior staff officer, with confidence reflected on his sea-burnt face.

A message of thanks to Vice Admiral Kawase for his support was flashed out with a signal lamp. The cruiser immediately answered with a "good luck" and soon disappeared into the fog, heading back to base at Paramushiro.

Kimura's next concern was how to spot Cape St. Stephen, the southwestern tip of Kiska, so that the northerly course might be altered at that point to northeast along the northern coast of the island. After two hours' sailing with the use of sounding and careful navigation, the cape was dimly seen through the fog almost abeam of Kimura's flagship. Though the sighting lasted only a few seconds, it was long enough for navigators to make sure of their position. After nearly a week of dead reckoning, their luck had still held.

What remained after the change of course was an approx-

Evacuated Japanese forces leave the dreary island of Kiska. *Courtesy of Masataka Chihaya*

imately twenty-mile run to Sirius Point, the northern end of the island. This was through a hazardous sea noted for treacherous currents and uncharted rocks. Hydrographic data advised ships not to take this route, and it was for this very reason that Kimura had chosen it—to avoid an enemy encounter.

A light purple sea surface was far from reassuring. Within the small world visible in the oppressing fog blanket here and there could be seen creases and eddies, large and small. Except for occasional reporting by lookouts and soundings, everybody was silent as the rescue force felt its way through unknown waters.

At about 1530, local time, about an hour and a half behind the new timetable, Kimura skirted the northern end of the island in a great circle, and finally set course almost southwest, direct to Kiska Harbor. The radio beacon guided them.

Soon after the force had slowed its speed in the last stretch, an unexpected development shook everybody. With a report of "what seems to be an enemy cruiser in sight," the flagship executed a hurried emergency turn and fired four torpedoes at the target—which turned out to be Little Kiska Island. It had been a tense moment.

While the force was recovering from its scare, a faint searchlight flicker could be seen toward the west through the fog. It was a signal from the North Head embracing the bay from the north to guide the force into the bay. They had arrived safely! The enemy trap supposed tightly clamped around the island had been wide open for some unknown reason or reasons.

As the naval garrison commander had predicted, an ideal fog blanket had covered the island since 28 July. Only the Kiska Harbor area remained open, like a small hole cut in a great white blanket.

By the scheduled assembly time of 1500 on 29 July, shortly before Kimura's force reached Sirius Point, all of the defenders except for a limited number of watch, radar, communications, and command personnel had assembled on the beach. Most of them came on foot, crossing barren land indented by bomb and shell craters. Others came by truck. Those few still remaining were to come to the beach only after the rescue party entered the bay and an order for destroying installations was given.

Troops were weary from being holed up under fierce air raids, naval shelling, and short rations. Many were bearded. Clad in odds and ends of uniforms, they were a far cry from the way they had first appeared. Personal belongings, even rifles, had been ordered abandoned. The men waited patiently to be evacuated; they sat at several assembly areas marked on the beach with colored flags.

There was very little jubilation, as this had become an old story. For seven previous sessions they had waited on the beach, shivering in the cold air of the Arctic summer night, in vain. That was enough to dim all hope.

On that fateful day, 29 July, they had already waited one hour and a half for the rescue force. As time went by, their despair was growing.

But now, lo and behold! There came in the dead calm bay

271

the dim silhouette of a light cruiser, making her way slowly but steadily out from the fog wall. Obviously it was not an illusion, since it was followed by another ship. Their rescue force had arrived to save them from certain annihilation. Other vessels appeared. Some of the men, after staring in disbelief, wept with joy; some jumped with excitement and happiness, while others hugged one another gleefully.

About ten landing craft readied along the beach started their engines, while personnel who had remained at their posts hurried to the beach after setting fuses to demolish installations. The embarkation began.

Kimura and his men also rejoiced as their vessels dropped anchor in the cold waters of Kiska Harbor. "Thank God for our luck," the admiral said with a smile. They had succeeded in doing what had been considered impossible.

Two destroyers stood by outside the bay, while another sped to Little Kiska Island to evacuate a detachment stationed there. The embarkation went off without a hitch. Landing craft were lowered from the ships and headed for the beach, while those waiting at the beach came out filled with evacuees.

"Thank you for saving us" was an often-heard expression from the grateful troops and marines. "Many thanks for your great troubles," replied those of the rescue party with Oriental politeness. There wasn't enough time to carry on much of a conversation. Ashes of dead comrades were allowed to be brought on board. Some of the personnel were extremely reluctant to leave their rifles. They had long been indoctrinated never to abandon their rifles under any circumstances.

Last to come aboard was the naval garrison commander, Rear Admiral Akiyama. The landing craft were scuttled to destroy any trace of the evacuation. In no time, an order of "weigh anchor" was given, this time by a flag signal from the light cruiser *Abukuma*. It was 1735 on 29 July, only fifty-five minutes after the cruiser *Abukuma* had dropped anchor in the bay. In that short period the incredible number of 5,183 men had been evacuated.

Few evacuation operations have been more orderly or more swiftly carried out than that of the Japanese garrison from Kiska Island.

Out of Kiska Harbor there was again the world of fog. The men had escaped from a dreadful trap, and their longing to be home now became irresistible.

After formation was made at sea, Kimura steamed up to twenty-one knots and then to twenty-six knots as the force rounded Sirius Point and moved southwest. Though the fog was not as thick as before, it was a difficult and risky task to retain control of a formation at such a high speed with limited visibility of about one thousand yards. Only the previous painstaking experience in the perpetual fog made it possible.

While the force was racing down along the northern coast of the deserted island, something happened that made the blood run cold and created a mystery that is to this day yet unsolved. To their starboard, almost abeam, a submarine was seen to surface almost at the limit of visibility. She was seemingly not ready for combat. Immediately the course was altered to prevent closer contact with the unknown sub.

Was it really an American submarine? That is a mystery, although Kimura and others have been unanimous on reports of sighting the vessel. If she was an American sub, how did she miss Kimura? Nothing known to date has been published on this sub in American accounts of the Aleutian campaign.[2]

After hurrying through the "danger zone" around the island, the force reduced its speed. The rest of the homeward sailing was uneventful, as the force took nearly the same route as when coming up. By 1 August the force split into three groups and returned safely to Paramushiro base, where green mountains and hills under a bright sky greeted the evacuees. They could now take a deep breath of the sweet air of their homeland.

Thus the tragedy of the futile Japanese invasion of the Aleutians, which had been fought since June 1942 virtually for nothing, came to an end. The only consolation, if any, was

The Evacuation Route of Kimura's Forces: Attu had been recaptured by American forces before the Japanese decided to attempt the withdrawal of their Kiska force. At first submarines were employed, but it soon became apparent that a surface force would have to make the run from Paramushiro to the fog-shrouded Aleutians if the garrison was to be saved from annihilation in the impending American invasion.

274

the safe and complete evacuation of the Kiska garrison force from the brink of sure death.

The Japanese naturally accepted this successful evacuation as a helping hand of divine providence, and it surely deserved to be so considered. Only because of an unbelievable succession of errors on the part of the U.S. blockading force were the steel jaws of the trap opened for Kimura.

What the Japanese on Kiska saw and heard on the night of 26 July was actually gunfire from the U.S. blockading force, but not an accidental battle between its own ships, as Rear Admiral Akiyama thought. Surprisingly, the force was, as a matter of fact, firing on a "phantom fleet"—the illusion of a Japanese sea force.

The first fallacy occurred on 24 July, when a Catalina patrol plane reported radar contact with seven vessels two hundred miles southwest of Attu Island. Kimura's force at the time was some five hundred miles from Attu.

Believing this report to be a reinforcement convoy for Kiska, the U.S. North Pacific Force Command alerted its Kiska blockading force covering the approaches to the doomed island. Two destroyers on the direct watch of the island were then pulled away from their stations to join the intercepting fleet, thus leaving open the close approaches to the island.

Such an error alone would not seem uncommon and could happen in any operation. But what followed was all but fantastic.[3] The most serious part came on 28 July, the next day, when Admiral Kinkaid, commander in chief of the North Pacific Force, ordered the victors of the phantom battle to fuel at a point 105 miles south-southeast of Kiska. They made the rendezvous on the morning of 29 July.

This refueling movement resulted in leaving the approach to Kiska from the southwest wide open at least from the evening of 28 July up through the next day. Kimura unknowingly passed through the vicinity of the phantom battle on the night of 28 July and reached Cape St. Stephen on the following morning. What wise timing indeed! Just one day earlier or later, Kimura would have certainly been intercepted by the radar-equipped U.S. blockading force.

We cannot help feeling that only a high perception attained through his complete disregard of honor, criticism, and even his own life enabled him to make such superhuman judgment. It was not mere chance nor a cheap trick.

Kimura's good fortune lasted further, when his force closed in on Kiska Harbor. In place of the two Allied destroyers pulled off direct guard of the island, two others had been ordered to reestablish the Kiska blockade, but one of them had to refuel too, and so missed Kimura's force. Another one was patrolling independently in an area north of Kiska and Segula Island, some thirteen miles off the former, when Kimura got into the bay.

The god of destiny sometimes plays a funny prank, and it was as another instance of such that the epilogue of this mysterious withdrawal from Kiska was written.

Even after the Japanese garrison force entirely deserted the fateful island, it continued to exert an influence on the minds of the invaders for another eighteen days or so. A full-fledged landing was necessary to discover its absence.

After customary minesweeping and bombarding, the landing party hit the beach midway on the western side of the island early on the morning of 16 August. No enemy resistance was met at all, of course.

The bewilderment of the landing troops by the sight of no defenders on the island was described by a member of the special units as follows:

> Once ashore there was no sign of the enemy. We lost no time in proceeding with the next step of the operation, climbing the heights of a very steep mountainous ridge, where we were to dig in along the crest. After the beach was secured with the landing of the main force, we then moved from the ridge and searched for the Japanese, who

had puzzlingly failed to show up. By that time the initial delight of having succeeded in making a surprise landing had turned into bewilderment. Where were they?

In deserted dugouts we saw clothes hung on walls and even bits of food in plates on the tables, food that hadn't yet begun to mildew and looked as though it hadn't been set out for many hours. It was all very mysterious, and the mystery was not cleared any by the ghostly fog, which at times almost completely blanketed the area. In a small world of extremely limited visibility, suspicion raised dark monsters, and several shooting incidents occurred.[4]

As a matter of fact, the casualties caused by confused troops cost the invasion force some twenty-five killed and thirty-one wounded. Moreover, there were more casualties at sea: seventy dead or missing and forty-seven wounded when a patrol vessel struck a drifting mine at night.

It was not until two days after the landing that the invasion force found the island was completely deserted. The only creatures the Japanese had left behind were several puppies, and this reportedly caused one flier to lament, "We dropped 100,000 propaganda leaflets on Kiska, but those dogs couldn't read."[5]

The prank played by the god of destiny seemed indeed to have gone a little bit too far, but all this fuss might be attributed to the fact that Admiral Kimura played his evacuation role so magnificently.

9

Ozawa in the Pacific: A Junior Officer's Experience

MINORU NOMURA

In 1942 and early 1943 the Japanese continued to focus their efforts in the southwest Pacific. They bitterly contested U.S. efforts to take Guadalcanal, and after evacuating that island in February 1943 they still launched furious and costly air assaults against the Americans in the area. Their efforts were in a sense well directed, for General Douglas MacArthur intended to make the Solomons–New Guinea–Philippines route the American path to Tokyo. But in 1943 Admirals King and Nimitz proposed a second invasion route, through the central Pacific. Capture of key points in this region would protect MacArthur's flank and provide bases from which to bomb the Japanese home islands. The Joint Chiefs of Staff accepted their proposal, and the invasion of Tarawa in the Gilberts followed in November. Nimitz bypassed important Japanese bases in the Marshalls to capture Kwajalein and Eniwetok in early 1944. These actions set the stage for a thousand-mile leap forward to the Marianas. A powerful U.S. armada under Admiral Raymond Spruance invaded Saipan on 15 June. Admiral

Marc Mitscher's Task Group 58, composed of many carriers and a battle line of heavy surface vessels, provided cover for the landing forces.

Commander in Chief of the Combined Fleet Soemu Toyoda was caught off balance by this American thrust. He had not believed that the Americans could continue their energetic offensive in the southwest Pacific, as indeed they were with MacArthur's push on Biak at this very time, and still mount a major assault in the central Pacific. When he learned of the Saipan landings he immediately ordered all major naval forces toward Saipan, activating Operation A, which aimed at the long-awaited decisive battle with the Americans. Japanese airmen hoped for spectacular victories against U.S. carriers, something on the order of a Midway in reverse. Japanese battleships would then rush upon the American landing craft at Saipan.

The Japanese force was inferior to the American in both carriers and aircraft. The Combined Fleet planned to overcome this deficiency by using land-based aircraft from Tinian, Rota, and Guam. The proposition of many Japanese naval air advocates that land-based planes could turn the tide would again be tested.

The Battle of the Philippine Sea, or, as the Japanese call it, the Battle of the Marianas, began on 19 June 1944. Japanese carrier groups launched their aircraft at extreme range in the early morning. But American radar detected them well in advance, and Mitscher's fighters destroyed many of them before they could attack. Some Japanese aircraft got through, only to be shot down by the formidable antiaircraft fire of the American battle line. Japanese planes from Tinian, Rota, and Guam scarcely came into action at all, as Mitscher had sent air strikes against bases on these islands early that day and many Japanese planes were destroyed on the ground. Some attack waves from the Japanese carriers missed the Americans. They made for Guam or other bases and were shot down while trying to land. Not only were

Japanese air strikes ineffectual; two of the Imperial Navy's greatest carriers, the veteran *Shokaku* and the spanking new *Taiho*, were torpedoed by American submarines. Late the next day, Mitscher launched attacks against the Japanese fleet, which was refueling to the west, and sank the carrier *Hiyo*. Both sides then retired.

The battle was a disaster for the Japanese. They wanted a decisive battle and they got it. The carrier force alone lost over three hundred aircraft. After the battle the navy could never again muster a proper offensive, as its air power was tethered to the island bases of the Pacific. Perhaps the hundreds of Japanese airmen who went resolutely to their deaths on 19 June deserve better than the derisive American title for the action of that day, "the Marianas Turkey Shoot." But the title evokes the futility of the Japanese effort in the face of the extraordinary organization, technical excellence, and material superiority of the American forces.

Surprisingly, historians have been more critical of the victor, Admiral Spruance, than of the Japanese leadership. Spruance was supposedly too cautious in not going after the Japanese carriers on 19 June, but it is generally accepted that he did right by holding back and protecting the Saipan landings. On the Japanese side, the major command difficulty was insufficient or misleading information. The carrier forces did not know of the debacle that was occurring on the airfields of Guam and the other islands.

The subject of the following article is the Japanese commander at the battle, Vice Admiral Jisaburo Ozawa. We are afforded a more human portrait than we usually get of the Japanese naval leadership. Also, we are given glimpses of the Japanese carrier navy in the comparatively calm year of 1943 as it went about its business of refitting and training. The events of that year are, however, clearly pictured as a prelude to the great carrier battle in the Philippine Sea in 1944. To the Western observer it is remarkable that Ozawa did not dwell on material factors in accounting for the outcome of the battle. Instead he singled out deficiencies in the training of his pilots, though this training was rigorous and approximated battle conditions. Perhaps Ozawa is exhibiting a common trait of Japanese military men by stressing training. Training is a function of will, and will of moral quality. These, according to advocates of the Japanese "military spirit," are the ingredients of victory. Whether or not Ozawa felt this way, it is clear that he was a leader of great stature.

O N 14 JULY 1942 Vice Admiral Jisaburo Ozawa left his post as commander of the Southern Expeditionary Fleet to take up duties with the Naval General Staff. He had been singled out early to succeed Vice Admiral Chuichi Nagumo as commander of the carrier fleet. Well before Pearl Harbor, the staff chief of the Combined Fleet, Rear Admiral Matome Ugaki, had written in his diary, *Sensoroku*, that Ozawa should assume that position. Ozawa's duty on the staff was of course a necessary preparation for the job as commander. The Navy Ministry's Personnel Bureau chief, Rear Admiral Yoshimasa Nakahara, put forth the actual proposal that Ozawa be made the navy's carrier commander. Admiral Shigetaro Shimada, the navy minister, gave his consent, and soon the ministry approved the posting, to take effect after a short period of leave for Ozawa. Isoroku Yamamoto, commander in chief of the Combined Fleet, certainly approved of Ozawa. It is even possible that the Personnel Bureau acted with his wishes in mind.

After Midway, the navy's carrier force, the First Fleet, was designated the Third Fleet. Nagumo continued to command it until after the Battle of the Santa Cruz Islands on 26 October. He was only then relieved of his command, ostensibly

Vice Admiral Jisaburo Ozawa, the premier carrier commander of the Japanese navy.

on the grounds of his responsibility for the defeat at Midway. Ozawa received the emperor's personal appointment to command the Third Fleet on 11 November.

Ozawa made the fleet carrier *Zuikaku* his flagship. She had returned to the Inland Sea for the rebuilding of her air groups, which had been mauled at the Santa Cruz Islands. Ozawa raised his flag on her at Kure on 14 November. She was an old campaigner with a long record that started at Pearl Harbor. Her heroic figure, blackened by many battles, was an object of reverence for us. I was a midshipman on the *Musashi* then, and I can recall those times as though they were yesterday. We would conduct air exercises in the western end of the Inland Sea, with the *Zuikaku,* flying Ozawa's flag, in the center and many battleships of the First Fleet forming a circular screen around her.

The forces of the Third Fleet under Ozawa's command

The carrier *Zuikaku*, on which the author served under Admiral Ozawa in 1943.

varied from time to time, but on 1 April 1943 they were as listed below:

> First Carrier Division: CVs *Zuikaku, Shokaku;* CVL *Zuiho*
> Second Carrier Division: CVs *Junyo, Hiyo*
> Third Battle Division: BBs *Kongo, Haruna*
> Seventh Battle Division: CAs *Kumano, Suzuya*
> Eighth Battle Division: CAs *Tone, Chikuma*
> Tenth Battle Division: CA *Agano;* Fourth Destroyer Squadron (Destroyer Divisions 10, 16, 17, and 61)
> Fiftieth Carrier Division: CVLs *Hosho, Ryuho;* DD *Yukaze;* Kanoya Naval Air Group; Tsuiki Naval Air Group
> Auxiliary: CL *Oyodo*

On 18 January 1943 Ozawa ordered his forces, from the refitted *Zuikaku* on down, to get under way from Iwakuni. Our destination was Truk, the forward base of the fleet. I had received orders to the *Zuikaku* just two days before and had hurriedly reported aboard. I was to serve in the navigation department under Commander Bunkichi Otomo; the ship's commanding officer was Captain Tameteru Nomoto.

The war was being fought mostly in the Solomons at the time. Priority was being given to the quick dispatch of supplies and army forces to the area. When we left home waters

283

the *Zuikaku, Musashi,* and the other ships carried many supplies and soldiers. Although we were headed for the forward area in the east and not the Solomons, we felt we had to cooperate in the transportation effort.

Soon after we got to sea I laid eyes on Ozawa for the first time. I had met flag officers occasionally, but never one like him. His visage was not that of a refined gentleman of cosmopolitan experience and grace. He looked like a rustic samurai, a rough soldier of fortune. I had heard his nickname. It was "the gargoyle."

This commander with the frightening face spoke to me one day as we were about to enter the harbor at Truk. I was on the flag deck at the rear of the bridge carrying on a relaxed conversation with some signalmen. Ozawa asked, "Junior navigation officer! What is glass made of?" I am afraid his question stupefied me. I had no idea what he had in mind. Why did the fleet commander need to know a thing like that? He did not seem to be teasing me, the newly arrived midshipman, but there was a smile on his face. I answered something like, "Silicon and quartz are the main constituents," and then added, "I will find out the exact details." In the next few days I rushed about putting questions to friends and looking in reference works; then I memorized my findings. But no matter how much I thought about it, I could not guess why Ozawa wanted to know the composition of glass. The next time I met him I gave him all of the information I had memorized. He responded, "The surface of glass cannot be made perfectly flat, then. Light rays passing through it will be bent ever so slightly. And that means it is not good for the lookouts to use the telescopes with the windows up." With these words I finally understood what his concern was. There were large telescopes on both sides of the bridge. The best lookouts were stationed there at the beck and call of the duty officers and the captain. They had been using the telescopes with the windows in place on the bridge, and it was Ozawa's intention to end this practice. I made sure that this new rule was strictly

The *Musashi* (foreground) and *Yamato* at Truk as photographed by Commander Kanda. *Courtesy of the Japan Defense Agency, National Institute for Defense Studies*

observed, of course, keeping a close watch on its enforcement through the responsible petty officers and in my own right.

This little incident showed me Ozawa's discretion and prudence. Being a master of night fighting, he would not tolerate what the lookouts were doing. But if he had cautioned the ship's commanding officer or navigation officer, they might have taken it as a loss of face. In going through a person like me, it was a minor matter. By asking me the question he undoubtedly sought to both educate me as a navigation officer and serve his own purposes. The commanding officer and the navigation officer never found out about the incident, to my knowledge.

We reached Truk on 23 January. There at anchor was the *Yamato* flying Commander in Chief Yamamoto's flag. With Ozawa's arrival the atoll had a full lineup of major commanders; Second Fleet Commander Nobutake Kondo was also there on the *Atago*. (Kondo was a vice admiral on our arrival but became a full admiral on 2 April.) Yamamoto transferred his command to the *Musashi* on 11 February. An often-reprinted photograph from this time shows the *Yamato* and *Musashi* together, with the *Musashi* probably closest to the camera. Commander Takeo Kanda, a destroyer captain, took this picture from the destroyer anchorage at Summer Island. Incidentally, within the lagoon at Truk there were four main islands in the east and seven in the west. Accordingly,

285

the eastern ones were named after seasons of the year and the western ones after days of the week. The fleet anchorage was ringed by Spring, Summer, and Fall islands.

We had nicknames for the two big battleships at Truk. They were "the *Yamato* school" and "the *Musashi* gymnasium." Captain Chiaki Matsuda, commanding officer of the *Yamato,* was always giving lectures on strategy and tactics to his junior officers, while Rear Admiral Kaoru Arima, commanding officer of the *Musashi,* was constantly promoting calisthenics, boxing, and judo for his officers.

The period from our arrival until Operation I in early April was, it seems, the quietest for Ozawa. The only action was far to the south around Rabaul. For us at that time Truk was a kind of South Sea island paradise.

Within the atoll there were, however, no appropriate recreation facilities for the crews. Considering long periods of shipboard life unhealthy, Ozawa approved two- and three-hour rest periods ashore to allow the men to stretch their legs. Ozawa himself would often go ashore for hikes with members of his staff. They would go to Monday Island in the western end of the lagoon; it was off limits to other personnel. Since on the *Zuikaku* it was the practice for a navigation officer to command the admiral's barge, I would ferry them over. I recall that one member of the admiral's staff always carried a hunting rifle. According to Commander Masao Suekuni, an administrative staff officer, Ozawa would borrow this rifle from Matome Ugaki, the Combined Fleet chief of staff. I never saw Ozawa bring back any large game. He hunted for birds like the Micronesian starling, dusky thrush, and heron. Monday Island had a large church and a population of natives. On it the supply section of the Fourth Fleet had planted vegetable gardens.

In February 1943 some of the Third Fleet's fighter planes flew to Buin on Bougainville to take part in Operation KE for the evacuation of Guadalcanal. Then Yamamoto put into ef-

286

fect a plan conceived earlier to blunt the U.S. counteroffensive. He initiated a fierce air assault in the southeast area using Ozawa's planes together with those of the Eleventh Air Fleet under Vice Admiral Jin'ichi Kusaka's Southeast Area Fleet.

On 2 April Ozawa left Truk in a medium bomber bound for Rabaul.

Large forces were committed to Operation I: 195 planes from the Third Fleet (excepting those from the *Shokaku*) and 224 planes from the Eleventh Air Fleet for a total of 419 planes. The operation produced impressive results. According to the summary report of the staff of the Combined Fleet to Imperial General Headquarters, the enemy lost 1 cruiser, 2 large destroyers, 6 large transports, 9 middle-sized transports, 3 small transports, and 133 aircraft.[1] Our side lost 18 fighters, 16 fighter bombers, and 9 land-based torpedo bombers for a total of 43 aircraft.

In the midst of this operation, on 13 April, Yamamoto, Kusaka, Ozawa, and others attended an emotional reunion of naval academy graduates. The story has been told in many books; it need not be related here.[2]

On 18 April Yamamoto flew south toward Buin to raise the morale of front-line forces; Ozawa flew north to rejoin the fleet at Truk. I was waiting at the pier on Spring Island to receive him in my capacity as the admiral's barge officer. Administrative staff officer Suekuni relates that Ozawa and his party were uneasy during the flight because they had received no message confirming Yamamoto's arrival at Buin. In the barge on the way back to the *Zuikaku*, he says, the staff officers fussed about this and that. Only after arriving on board did Ozawa learn what had happened to Yamamoto.[3] The ashes of the commander in chief were quietly returned to the *Musashi* at Truk on 23 April.[4] His trip to Rabaul had been known only to the highest officers on the ship, and his death was kept strictly secret for some time. My fellows and

Admiral Mineichi Koga, commander in chief of the Combined Fleet from May 1943 to March 1944. *Official U.S. Navy photograph*

I, therefore, knew nothing about it or the arrival of Mineichi Koga on the *Musashi* to take over command of the Combined Fleet on 25 April. We found out about Yamamoto's death when we heard that Lieutenant Commander Chikataka Nakajima, the staff communications officer, had cautioned fleet command personnel to be on the lookout for a change in U.S. transmissions because there would be a casualty report involving a commander in chief. The public announcement of Yamamoto's death came later, on 21 May. Looking back, I understood why there had been such an odd atmosphere on the bridge of the *Zuikaku* during the preceding weeks.

Ozawa weighed anchor at Truk for home waters on 3 May, taking the First Carrier Division and subordinate units back to the western end of the Inland Sea. There, air groups that had suffered losses in Operation I would receive replacements and be brought back to full readiness. We reached our destination on 8 May.

Soon after, on 12 May, U.S. forces landed on Attu in the Aleutians. Commander in Chief Koga could not ignore this. He returned to Yokosuka with the main fleet units, principally the Second Carrier Division, the Seventh Battle Division, and the Eighth Battle Division. The *Yamato* and ships of the Fifth Battle Division led the way, with the *Musashi* carrying Yamamoto's remains.

For a while Imperial General Headquarters and the Command of the Combined Fleet worked on a plan for decisive battle with the Americans in the Aleutian area. The Third Fleet and other forces made hasty preparations for a sortie into the North Pacific. It was decided that Ozawa should sail his nearly refitted fleet up to Tokyo Bay. Accordingly, we got under way on 15 May, leaving as usual by the eastern track of the Bungo Channel. When entering the channel from the Inland Sea, we would sight Cape Sada to port and, at the channel entrance, Hayasui Strait, alter course hard to port. As the main body of the fleet, the First Carrier Division, approached the turning point on this occasion, we were suddenly enveloped in a thick fog. From the *Zuikaku* we immediately lost sight of the next ship in line, the *Shokaku;* soon we could not even see our own bows. When we looked down from the bridge we could discern no more than the dim flight deck directly below us.

This was the first experience of such thick fog for us junior officers. Signalmen ran to the stern and began sounding a bugle in the direction of the *Shokaku* with all their might. There had been no time to stream fog buoys. Moment by moment we came closer to the turning point. The staff chief, Rear Admiral Shigeyoshi Yamada; the staff navigation officer, Lieutenant Commander Tetsuo Azuma; the ship's commanding officer; and the navigation officer could scarcely conceal their impatience. But Ozawa kept silent and just stared ahead.

Were we to alter course as scheduled or stay on course? If we continued to hold our course we would have little margin for error because the shore at Saganoseki was close by. I was figuring our position from our speed and elapsed time. When I saw by my calculations that we had reached the turning point, I announced it in a loud voice to everyone on the bridge. The *Shokaku* was still not visible behind us. The agitated staff navigation officer, apparently making up his mind when he heard my voice, faced Ozawa and exclaimed, "Commander, we are going to turn!" Ozawa had one severe word in reply: "No!"

After the war Ozawa told some of us in the War History Office of the Defense Agency, "He who does nothing more than accept the proposals of his staff cannot be called a commander." He was speaking mainly of operations plans, drafts, preparations, and execution, of course, and not necessarily the kind of minor technical nagivation problem just described. It is indispensable, nevertheless, for the commander to express his will clearly when a decision is needed.

Ozawa said no because, based on long experience, he believed it was safer to steam beyond the turning point when entering the Bungo Channel no matter what the *Shokaku* might do. Following his order, the *Zuikaku* continued on its course. The shore was near. The navigation officer and I desperately stuck at our post by the depth gauge. Luckily the fog began to thin out. The *Shokaku* reappeared and the first Carrier Division passed through the Bungo Channel without incident.

On arrival in Tokyo Bay, Ozawa's fleet anchored off Kisarazu. We spent busy days getting ready for the operation in the north. Each day I practiced with the air bubble sextant taking sights of our ship's position in the fog. But confirmation soon came that Attu had fallen. Despite a heroic fight to the last man, the end came on 30 May. A bit earlier, on 21 May, Imperial General Headquarters had ordered the evacuation of Kiska. The bad weather in the north Pacific would in any case have made the employment of air groups a doubtful proposition, and the whole operation was canceled just prior to sortie. Submarine units that had already left port were hurriedly recalled.

Ozawa returned with his forces to the Inland Sea, reaching Kure on 2 June. Once there, however, he got under way for Truk again immediately, commanding a force composed mainly of the First Carrier Division, the Eighth Battle Division, the Tenth Battle Division, the heavy cruiser *Mogami*, and the light cruiser *Oyodo*. We reached Truk on 15 July. A detachment consisting mainly of the Second Carrier Division, the Third Battle Division, and the Seventh Battle Division preceded us from Yokosuka.

I occasionally ferried Ozawa over to Monday Island and back, as before. But this time I was very busy coming and going between the ship and Maple Island, located in the center of the atoll. We had started construction on an airfield there using crews of the fleet in rotation. The sailors actually enjoyed the work because it allowed them to go ashore.

After the war I learned that Ozawa had petitioned his superiors to build the airstrip. Originally there were airfields on Spring and Bamboo Islands. But when Ozawa returned to Truk this second time, he was surprised to find them unimproved and exactly as they had been before. To employ land-based air forces efficiently, more large airfields were necessary. Ozawa warned the command of the Combined Fleet about this, but officers there answered that they were too busy to attend to the matter. Ozawa pushed hard for this project, saying to Commander in Chief Koga, "We have to build an airfield, even if it means using the labor of the fleet." And so construction began using shipboard personnel even though this would normally have been a job for the specialists of the construction corps.

The building of the strip on Maple Island and enlarging of the field on Spring Island were the main accomplishments of our stay at Truk. A staff operations officer told me that the

291

aviation staff officer, Commander Takeshi Naito, often spoke of the urgent need for a field on Maple Island for the fighter aircraft of the Third Fleet. Ozawa said that in war it was necessary to "anticipate the future and prepare for it." He stated emphatically that both the ability and the industry needed to "anticipate the future" were lacking on the Japanese side in the Pacific War.

Admiral Kondo, commander of the Second Fleet, was of course senior to Ozawa. Based on lessons learned from the Battles of the Eastern Solomons and the Santa Cruz Islands, the concept had arisen that the Third Fleet (carrier) commander should be senior to the Second Fleet (surface force) commander. But at this time and until the formation of the First Mobile Fleet in March 1944, thinking on this issue was still in transition. On 9 August 1943 Vice Admiral Takeo Kurita arrived to take over command of Kondo's Second Fleet. Kurita, junior to Ozawa, got the post because Navy Minister Shimada requested him and Commander in Chief Koga strongly backed him. This change meant that, with the exception of the First Battle Division under Koga (with the *Musashi* and *Yamato*), it could happen that all the fighting forces of the surface fleet would come under Ozawa's command.

At this time the Combined Fleet was planning Operations Y and Z. If an Anglo-American force attacked from the Indian Ocean area, the fleet would move westward and engage it in a decisive battle; this was the Y plan. If American forces attacked from the Marshalls area, the entire fleet, with Ozawa's carrier force as its mainstay, would sortie eastward to meet them and fight a decisive battle; this was the Z plan.

The fleet undertook two sorties toward the Marshalls in September and October 1943. The first began on 18 September, with the fleet returning to Truk on 25 September. The second lasted from 17 to 26 October. The purpose of the first was to engage in exercises and respond to the movement of U.S. forces. The second was in dead earnest; its purpose was to fight a decisive battle in waters near Wake. There seemed to be good prospects for such a clash in light of our estimate of U.S. intentions, which was based on communications intelligence. If all went well and we discovered the American mobile force, Operation Z would go into effect.

Ozawa commanded the first sortie; Koga himself took over the second. Both used Eniwetok Atoll as a transit base, the first sortie anchoring there for four days (20–23 September) and the second for five (19–23 October).

On the second expedition we put out from Eniwetok in the direction of Wake, dispatching search planes ahead. We experienced our tensest moments at that time. From Ozawa on down, all personnel wore white battle dress and were eager for action. But we did not discover the U.S. Fleet.

On the second day of this expedition we continued our reconnaissance around Wake. That day there was trouble. A search plane failed to return. Search aircraft had sometimes been late in getting back to the ship. They would lose track of their positions and miss the carrier. On these occasions Ozawa unhesitatingly ordered destroyers of the screen to make intermittent smoke. The overdue planes would spot the smoke and find their way back. At night we would also use searchlights to attract the planes.

But this time, in waters off Wake, the situation was different. The enemy was near. We guarded against submarines, as on previous sorties. This time we also had to be ready for the enemy's main strike force, which we had every reason to believe lay before us. But Ozawa was not deterred; that night our searchlights went on and lit up the sky.

The plane's time limit was reached, however, and still it had not returned. This aircraft, a carrier-based Type 97 attack plane (a Kate), carried a crew of three. What had become of it? We wondered what Ozawa would do and kept an eye on how the command was handling this emergency. Members of plane crews were especially sensitive to the measures taken, thinking of the missing men and saying to themselves, "Tomorrow it could be me."

The command had reached a decision. The next morning

carriers launched reconnaissance planes to search for the three men, who presumably had ditched. Several cruisers were sent out in line formation to search waters where the plane might have gone down.

The three men had in fact made an emergency landing on the water and climbed into their life raft. They spent the night drifting in the middle of the immense Pacific Ocean, not knowing whether friendly forces would attempt to rescue them or not.

The desperate search of the reconnaissance crews for their comrades yielded results. The raft was spotted from one of the planes. A cheer went up on the bridge of the *Zuikaku* when the report came in. I distinctly saw tears streaming from the eyes of the ship's commanding officer, Tomozo Kikuchi. (He had replaced Nomoto on 20 June.) Ozawa seldom smiled on the bridge, but this time a broad grin spread across his face. We soon received a report that the *Oyodo,* which had rushed to the scene of the sighting, had rescued the three men.

As soon as the fleet returned to Truk, its air groups once again flew to Rabaul for an offensive. The Combined Fleet Command apparently decided on this course of action somewhat impulsively, on the ground that U.S. forces had not come to the Marshalls. Ozawa left Truk with the air groups on 1 November. Thus began Operation RO, in which several air battles developed near Bougainville. Commander in Chief Koga received an imperial commendation for the success of this operation on 11 November. He had remained at Truk while Kusaka and Ozawa had gone to the scene of action to pool their efforts in battle.

In this operation, however, our air groups suffered heavy losses. By this time the Americans had developed the VT fuse, called the "radio-wave activated proximity fuse" in Japanese. This device, the existence of which we were not aware of until after the war, had been under development in England since 1939. It was handed over to the Americans for further work and perfected in 1942. After that it was put into mass production. It contained a small radar transmitter, which caused the shell to explode if it came within a certain distance of the target. Even without a direct hit, therefore, a shell fitted with it could bring down an airplane. Needless to say, the VT fuse brought about a revolutionary improvement in antiaircraft fire. Many of our planes were victims of this device.

Ozawa returned to Truk with the air groups on 13 November. As usual I went over with the admiral's barge to meet him on Spring Island. I was astonished by the small number of planes that had returned. There were hardly any fighters to be seen. But it was worse with torpedo planes and fighter bombers. None of them had come back. After tying up the barge at the pier, I approached the airfield as closely as I could. On the field Ozawa was giving the commander's speech of instruction that customarily followed an operation. Afterward I heard from some fliers about the speech. Ozawa had climbed the platform to address them and, being overcome with dismay at how few of his men had survived, was unable to utter a word. He stood there on the platform in silence for a very long time, weeping bitterly.

Fliers easily became critical of superior officers who did not themselves have a background in aviation. Ozawa was not an aviator. But as far as I know, the fliers who served under him had unbounded veneration for him. They felt deeply that he took the utmost care to preserve their lives.

With Operation RO over, the First Carrier Division returned to home waters once again to rebuild its air groups. The *Zuikaku* reached Kure on 12 December without Ozawa, who had shifted his flag to the *Oyodo* on 6 December and remained behind at Truk to continue his duties as fleet commander. Soon the *Shokaku* became his flagship, and so my days of shipboard service with him were over.

In 1943 Ozawa had operated out of Truk, from the Solomons in the south to the Marshalls in the east. As 1944 began, all of this changed. The Naval General Staff and the Command of the Combined Fleet shifted the forward base of the fleet westward from Truk to the Palau Islands and the Singapore area. The main reasons for the move were the contraction of Japan's defense perimeter and the shortage of fuel oil.

Early in the morning of 6 February 1944, Ozawa ordered the *Shokaku* and *Zuikaku* of the First Carrier Division to weigh anchor for Singapore. Leaving the Sumoto anchorage off Awaji Island, the ships headed south through the Kii Channel accompanied by the heavy cruiser *Chikuma,* the light cruiser *Yahagi,* and Destroyer Divisions 10 and 61.

The carriers were in top condition by this time, having been refitted since their withdrawal from Truk. The *Shokaku* had gone into dock at Yokosuka, the *Zuikaku* at Kure. Usually when carriers sortied they left their air groups behind and recovered planes in the western end of the Inland Sea. But this time both ships had taken on planes from lighters along with base supplies at Iwakuni. The First Carrier Division had lost so many aircraft in the Solomons that the air groups it embarked were newly constituted ones. Their pilots had not completed training in carrier landings, and consequently flying the planes out to the carriers was impossible. Some of the air groups were delayed and had to fly out later, staging via bases along the way.

By this time I was radar officer on the *Zuikaku.* A large air search radar was installed on the highest point above the bridge and another somewhat smaller retractable one on the port side of the flight deck amidships. I was responsible for the maintenance of these two installations and for training in their use; in battle they were under my control. On carriers, radar belonged to the navigation department. The commanding officer of our ship was Captain Takeo Kaizuka; the navigation officer was Commander Fusao Yano. Since Ozawa had transferred his flag to the *Shokaku,* I rarely saw him.

By leaving through the Kii Channel that February morning, Ozawa sought to avoid enemy submarines that lurked along the normal sortie route, the Bungo Channel. East of the Lu-

The *Shokaku,* Admiral Ozawa's flagship as carrier commander in early 1944. The submarine *Cavalla* sank her in the Battle of the Philippine Sea.

zon Strait he again adopted a tactic of deception, taking a course to the south and making it appear his destination was the Philippines or Palau. Then in the middle of the night he swung more than ninety degrees to starboard, slipping through the Balintang Channel. Some of us navigation officers felt that the fleet command was being abnormally cautious about submarines. Once in the South China Sea we negotiated a mineswept channel inside the shallows of the Spratlys, eyeing one another intently over the charts. Ozawa was doubtless intimately acquainted with these waters from his offensive operations there at the start of the war. But for us this was a new experience, a novelty and a diversion after our cruises in the open spaces of the central and south Pacific. Ozawa's ships reached Singapore on 13 February. The *Shokaku* and *Zuikaku* rested at the Seletar naval anchorage.

The air groups attached to the First Carrier Division used the airfields on Singapore Island—that is, the Seletar base in the northeast near the naval anchorage, the Sembawang base in the north, and the Tengah base in the northwest. There was also the Kalang Airport in Singapore, but it was reserved for army and civilian use.

On 20 February the *Zuikaku,* accompanied by an escort of three destroyers of a single destroyer division, left Singapore for the home islands. After arrival at Kure on 27 February, it took on aircraft at Iwakuni for its own air groups and those of the Southwestern Area Fleet. We left the Sumoto anchorage once again on 8 March, arriving at Singapore on 15 March. While this movement was taking place, the Naval General Staff on 1 March organized the First Mobile Fleet with Ozawa as commander. Since the end of 1943 he had strongly urged Commander in Chief Koga to create such a fleet as a seaborne strike force for decisive battle against the possible advance of U.S. naval forces. The organization of the First Mobile Fleet as of 1 April 1944 is given below:

First Mobile Fleet (Vice Admiral Ozawa)

Second Fleet (Vice Admiral Kurita)

First Battle Division: BBs *Yamato, Musashi, Nagato*
Third Battle Division: BBs *Kongo, Haruna*
Fourth Battle Division: CAs *Atago, Takao, Maya, Chokai*
Fifth Battle Division: CAs *Myoko, Haguro*
Seventh Battle Division: CAs *Kumano, Suzuya, Tone, Chikuma*
Second Torpedo Division: CL *Noshiro*, Destroyer Divisions 27, 31, 32, and DD *Shimakaze*

Third Fleet (Vice Admiral Ozawa, also commander of First Mobile Fleet)

First Carrier Division: CVs *Taiho, Zuikaku, Shokaku*
Second Carrier Division: CVs *Junyo, Hiyo;* CVL *Ryuho;* 652nd Naval Air Group
Third Carrier Division: CVLs *Chitose, Chiyoda, Zuiho;* 653rd Naval Air Group
Tenth Battle Division: CL *Yahagi;* Destroyer Divisions 4, 10, 17, 61
Auxiliary: CA *Mogami;* 601st Naval Air Group

When the Naval General Staff organized the new air units, it introduced a system of separate land-based command to the carrier forces. Until this time, air units had taken orders from the commanding officers of their carriers, but now a new air group was established for each carrier division and had its own commanding officer ashore. That is, only when an air group was embarked on a carrier did it come under the authority of the ship's commanding officer. The 601st Air Group attached to the Third Fleet in a supposedly auxiliary capacity actually belonged to the First Carrier Division.

On 1 March Ozawa moved his command from the *Shokaku* to the Seletar air base. Fleet units were widely dispersed, with the Second and Third Carrier Divisions undergoing training and maintenance in the western portion of the bay. I and my fellow officers from the *Zuikaku* made frequent tours of Singapore Island and the Malayan Peninsula to view battle sites. We also visited each airfield to observe the state of training of the various air units. Every now and then I caught sight of Ozawa, sitting in the command tent at one of these fields, intently watching the performance of his airmen.

The *Zuikaku* left Seletar on 20 March for Lingga Roads, about one hundred miles to the south. The *Shokaku* had preceded her there, along with the *Nagato*, ships of the Third and Seventh Battle Divisions, and several destroyers. Lingga Roads, near the Palembang oil fields of Sumatra, is formed by the large mass of Sumatra on the east and by Lingga Island and many smaller islands on the west and south. By blockading the channels into it, we could deny entrance to enemy submarines. It was large enough, however, that carriers could practice launch and recovery of aircraft without leaving it. Entire carrier divisions, moreover, could conduct maneuvers there. Ozawa gave the order to begin training in aircraft operations as soon as we arrived. This training was a fearsome thing.

Previously the First Carrier Division had carried Zero fighters, Val dive bombers, and Kate torpedo planes. As a flagship, the *Zuikaku* had carried in addition two Judy Type 2 reconnaissance planes. In the case of most planes, when we heard the report "Aircraft coming in for a landing," we thought, "We'll take it on safely." But it was different with the Type 2. To take off, it had to begin its run from the farthest point aft. Its landing speed was much higher than that of the other planes. When one of these was coming in for a landing, our feeling was that it was "plunging in," and our next thought would be, "Can we snare it?" When we were retrieving Type 2s, there was always great tension on the bridge. We had special respect for the crews of these planes.

As a result of the reorganization of air units, we had the Judy (*Suisei* or "Comet" dive-bomber) as replacement for the old Val, and for the Kate, the Jill (*Tenzan* or "Heavenly Mountain" torpedo plane). The engine and fuselage of the Judy were of course basically the same as those of the Type 2 reconnaissance plane. The Jill was much larger and faster than the Kate.

The air groups would fly out from their airfields at Singapore for launch and recovery exercises, conduct their training on the *Shokaku* and *Zuikaku,* and when finished fly back to Singapore. Because of the switch to the newer, faster aircraft types, we came to experience at all times the unease and uncanny tension we had felt earlier when Type 2s engaged in flight operations. We had one aircraft accident after another. I witnessed perhaps ten of them myself. In many instances, planes would lose speed and go down at the "fourth turning point" on the landing approach, that is, just after having lined up with the stern of the carrier. They would come in at low speed and, without time to regain proper attitude, would crash into the water. Zero fighters were particularly prone to this.

Planes coming in for landing with tail hooks down usually were caught by arresting wires strung across the rear of the flight deck. Planes missing the wires would have to gun their engines immediately and take to the air again. Once a Judy landed too far forward and its hook did not catch. It did not have enough runway to gun its engine and take off again. Everyone held his breath and watched what seemed like a slow-motion shot in a movie. The plane reached the end of the flight deck and lazily tumbled over onto the machine-gun

The Judy or *Suisei*, a carrier-borne bomber that replaced the Val in 1943.

A Jill (*Tenzan*) as it takes off from the *Zuikaku* during training in the Inland Sea around September 1944. *Courtesy of Konnichi No Wadaisha*

301

deck on the bow below. Another time a Jill missed the landing approach and ran into the island, wounding personnel in the area and spreading destruction everywhere. On still another occasion, a flight of Jills was forming up above us for the return to Singapore, its training completed. At the lookout's cry we turned our eyes skyward to see a Jill that had collided with another explode in a great mass of flames.

On 25 March Ozawa came to Lingga Roads on a destroyer and hoisted his flag on the *Shokaku* once more. There is no question that he was heartsick over the many casualties he witnessed in consequence of these fearsome training operations. At some point the rumor circulated that Ozawa had said, "We don't need any more launch and recovery training. All we need is to get the planes in the air; that way we can launch a first attack from the carriers and stage them through our land bases for a second attack. I cannot bear to lose the lives of any more of my men in these accidents."

On 30 and 31 March, Palau came under air attack from a U.S. fast carrier task force. Admiral Koga was on the scene and, having learned of the approach of the American force several days in advance, ordered Ozawa on 30 March to move the air group of the First Carrier Division (601st Naval Air Group) forward to Davao and to prepare all fleet units at Lingga Roads for an advance into the southern Philippines. The *Shokaku* and *Zuikaku* were exempted from this movement because their air units would of necessity operate from land bases in meeting the American attack.

On 31 March Ozawa returned with the *Shokaku* to the Seletar anchorage. On 2 April he flew to Surabaya (Soerabaja) in an advance party of aircraft. It was just at this time that Admiral Koga was lost on a flight between Palau and Davao. The command of the Combined Fleet went to Admiral Shiro Takasu, commander of the Southwestern Area Fleet, who was at Surabaya. Ozawa, opposing the interruption of his airmen's training, persuaded Takasu to cancel their deployment to Davao.

Ozawa returned to the Seletar base on 3 April and, after raising his flag on the *Shokaku* the next day, came down to Lingga Roads, where we lay at anchor. Soon after, the new heavy carrier *Taiho* arrived at the Roads. Its construction had been completed on 7 March and after training exercises in the Inland Sea had proceeded to Singapore, reaching there on 5 April. Whenever the opportunity presented itself, we went aboard to inspect her. We estimated the thickness of the heavily armored flight deck and stood on her distinctive bridge, debating her strong and weak points in comparison to the *Zuikaku*. As for the officer complement on the *Taiho*, it seemed to us that all of our key officers of the *Zuikaku* had been transferred in a body to her. The *Zuikaku*'s commanding officer, Captain Tomozo Kikuchi, became the *Taiho*'s chief. Our gunnery officer, Commander Saneo Miyamoto, took up the same duties on the new ship. And our navigation officer, Commander Bunkichi Otomo, moved up to executive officer on the *Taiho*. When we came to call on our former superiors we visited them in their quarters. We were struck by how cramped their cabins were, even the commanding officer's suite. On the *Zuikaku*, now without the fleet staff, the quarters we junior officers occupied were more spacious than Captain Kikuchi's on the *Taiho*. These features lent the *Taiho* the atmosphere of a fierce man-o'-war. The carrier somehow reminded us of a huge, heavily armored insect. But we were disappointed that it had only one hangar deck to the two on the *Shokaku* and *Zuikaku* and could not carry many aircraft.

The *Taiho* was one of the vessels that had her origin in the Fourth Naval Expansion Plan of April 1939. When she was built she was supposed to be a staging point for air groups from carriers steaming well to the rear of the enemy. She was to operate close to the enemy because it was believed that her heavily armored flight deck would allow her to survive enemy bomb attacks.

On 15 April Ozawa shifted his flag from the *Shokaku* to

The *Taiho* at Tawitawi, May 1944. *Courtesy of the Japan Defense Agency, National Institute for Defense Studies*

the *Taiho*. We considered it only natural that he would exercise command from this newest crack ship of the fleet. The reason he chose her, however, probably had little to do with the original conception of her operational role. The flagship *Akagi* at Midway and the flagship *Shokaku* at the Santa Cruz Islands had both been hit at the outset of the battle. On those occasions the fleet was without command and in utter confusion for a time. The lesson Ozawa learned was that he should be on the *Taiho* because her heavy armor would allow him to exercise secure command from her throughout the battle.

Once we finished launch and recovery operations, our main training was in flight operations involving the entire fleet and all air groups. Our ships would get under way from Lingga Roads with destroyers, cruisers, and battleships surrounding carriers of the First Carrier Division, making three separate circular screens, one for each carrier. The *Nagato* escorted the *Taiho*, the *Kongo* escorted the *Shokaku*, and the *Haruna* escorted the *Zuikaku*. Air groups would take off from Singapore and stage mock attacks on the fleet.

Our air search radar on the *Zuikaku* was displaying considerable effectiveness at the time. A year or more earlier, this kind of radar in good repair could pick up large flights of aircraft over one hundred kilometers out, but the apparatus was liable to break down. Now its components had been improved and the men operating it were more thoroughly trained. Its effectiveness and reliability had rapidly improved. During these air operations, we of the *Zuikaku* radar department were able to locate air units accurately and with time to spare.

First our radar would detect flights after takeoff from Singapore, normally almost an hour before they would reach our carriers for their bombing and torpedo runs. At some point the commanders of these flights would give the command "Assume attack formation." Our lookouts would search the sky in the direction indicated by radar and sing out loudly upon sighting them. The bombers would approach from high above. Shortly afterward the Judys would dive in one after another. If we looked out to sea just above the horizon, we could spot Jill torpedo planes coming in from all directions. They would conduct torpedo attacks at different altitudes against our beam, crisscrossing over us after completing their run-ins. Such was the normal pattern for fleet air exercises at that time.

We soon found out the basic operational plan Ozawa would adopt in the coming decisive battle. First, air units of the new aircraft types would attack the American carrier groups beyond the range of the American planes. This was the "outranging tactic." Our attacks would deprive the enemy of its ability to launch and recover aircraft. Immediately thereafter the entire Japanese fleet would close on the enemy, destroying its fleet down to the last vessel. All of us in the *Zuikaku*'s gunroom (the junior officers' mess) had faith in this plan.

When air training was about finished, map exercises were held on the *Taiho*. I attended the sessions as an observer with our commanding officer and navigation officer. In the crowded conference room I would see Ozawa at the head of the table, intently taking in the declarations of the participants without saying a word.

The air-bombing target ship *Hakatsu* had been at the Roads since the end of the previous year, and the Naval Gen-

305

eral Staff had assigned it to the Combined Fleet. Bomber groups practiced dive-bombing at it, dropping real bombs. Torpedo groups used the carriers as targets, releasing torpedoes equipped with special water-expulsion heads. These heads replaced the high explosive in the normal torpedo. They were filled with water and the torpedo was adjusted to run deep enough to pass under the keel of the carrier. At the end of the torpedo's run, water would be expelled from the head. The torpedo would become buoyant and rise to the surface. Thus it became possible to recover our precious torpedoes for future use.

One day during maneuvers the *Zuikaku* was attacked by ten or more Jills. The captain ordered frantic turns to port and starboard to evade them, but to no avail. Several torpedoes definitely passed under the *Zuikaku*, their electrically lit crimson tips clearly visible. We felt certain that had this been a real battle, we would have gone to the bottom instantly. I was on the battle bridge, directing the radar as usual. Then a terrible accident occurred. Even now it remains vivid in my memory. A Jill approached our starboard bow on its torpedo run. It passed the release point without dropping its torpedo. We held our breath to see if the pilot would release late; if he did, there was a danger that the torpedo would punch through our hull rather than pass under us. But the plane just cleared the bows, roaring over us to port, and we heaved a sigh of relief as we gazed after it. Perhaps thinking he would double back for another pass, the pilot began to bank for a right turn. At that instant his right wingtip made contact with the water. Plane and crew disintegrated instantly. It was over in a moment. A large light-green wave ring remained on the blue surface of the sea, but that was all. Soon a plane appeared from somewhere and began to circle mournfully above this pretty circle of green. The pilot was probably the officer directing the attack exercise.

At about this time there was talk that a propeller bearing on the *Zuikaku* needed repair. We soon returned to Singapore; the *Zuikaku* went into dry dock at the Seletar naval base on 29 April. She was fitted with a new lignum vitae bearing and out of dock on 5 May.

Since the introduction of the new system of separate land-based command for air units, relations between the *Zuikaku*'s regular officers and the airmen had become even cooler than before. Already there were strong indications that we were about to proceed to forward areas for battle. Someone made the suggestion that we take the opportunity offered by our stay at Seletar to cultivate friendships with the air officers who would shortly be serving with us on board. One evening we gathered at a small Japanese restaurant in Johore Bharu, across the causeway made famous during the capture of Singapore. When the appointed time came, none of the fliers appeared. We waited with growing uneasiness. Then word came that a Judy had crashed upon landing at the airfield and its crew members had been killed. As I remember it, hardly any of the airmen finally came. All of us ship's officers from the captain on down finished our meals in a gloomy mood and returned to the ship without delay.

The *Zuikaku* left Seletar and reached Lingga Roads again on 7 May. There the feeling was stronger than ever that battle was imminent. In our absence the *Yamato* had arrived and anchored at the Roads. Seeing her imposing figure again after so long a time dispelled our gloominess.

Just after we returned to Lingga Roads I unexpectedly received orders for transfer. My new assignment was to the Tokyo Communications Station and concurrently to the Naval General Staff. I knew nothing about this position. I could not figure out the purpose of my posting, nor could anyone on board. The navigation officer more or less cross-examined me, asking, "Did you ever put in a request for communications?" I promptly denied this. At the time I had on record in my file a request for the billet of navigation officer on a destroyer. Several of my classmates from the academy had already gotten such assignments. The executive officer, Captain

Yujiro Murota, said with an air of dissatisfaction, "The Bureau of Personnel certainly does not make assignments with the operational needs of the fleet in mind." I was upset over these orders myself. I was leading a very busy life just then. In addition to my responsibilities as radar officer, I had the collateral duty of captain of the gunroom (head of the junior officers' mess). I felt a special obligation to provide leadership to the many midshipmen and ensigns of the mess in my charge. Also, I had the pride so typical of youth. I put in a request that I be allowed to remain where I was for the coming deployment. Yet my successor, an academy classmate from the *Taiho,* had arrived on board to take up my post. By this time Ozawa had transferred all air command functions to the carriers from the Singapore airfields. Each carrier had embarked its air units and was in full readiness for action. The last packet destroyer had weighed anchor for Singapore. The fleet had severed all sea communications with the outside world. To all appearances my request to remain on board had been granted.

But the fleet was delayed in getting under way for two days. A small wooden victualing boat remained at the Roads. The executive officer insisted that if I remained on board for the deployment, there would be no telling when I would be able to proceed to my new duty station. I would have to leave the ship. I felt somewhat disgraced by his order but gradually became convinced it was correct, considering what the position of my successor would be if I did not leave.

On the evening of 10 May there was a party on the *Zuikaku* to celebrate the deployment. I went over about halfway through. Everyone came around to say good-bye to me. The executive officer and all of those who had been close to the navigation department left the party to see me off. A pilot from the academy class before mine joked, "Give my regards to the chief of the Naval General Staff!" The two of us, of course, never met again.

Standing on the boat that had been sent over for me, I

waved my hat to my friends in farewell. When I stepped into the cabin of the boat, my eyes were suddenly overflowing with tears. The master of the victualing boat was kind to me. He offered me his cabin, the only place on board where one could sleep comfortably. When I awoke on the morning of 11 May, the boat was already under way. Looking out over the Roads, I saw that Ozawa's fleet, which until the day before had dominated these waters, had largely disappeared. The First, Third, Fourth, and Seventh Battle Divisions under Kurita's command and the Second Torpedo Division had sortied in the moonlight the night before. The First Carrier Division and the Fifth and Tenth Battle Divisions, which were under Ozawa's command, were still there but would follow shortly. The whole fleet would head for its forward base at Tawitawi, located halfway between Borneo and the Philippines on the edge of the Celebes Sea.

At dusk that evening I finally went ashore at a pier at Singapore's commercial port on the southern coast. I saw two German submarines mooring in the harbor.

When in March 1944 the staff of the Combined Fleet Command had been disbanded following Admiral Koga's death, the Military Affairs Bureau of the Navy Ministry considered merging the Combined Fleet Command with the Naval General Staff instead of rebuilding it. But this proposal was not adopted after all, and on 3 May a new Combined Fleet Command was created under Admiral Soemu Toyoda.

Throughout April the Naval General Staff and a nucleus of officers scheduled for the new Combined Fleet Command had been at work putting the finishing touches on plans for Operation A. Then on 3 May the Naval General Staff announced the aims of this operation (Navy Directive No. 373). It involved Ozawa's First Mobile Fleet, which since the end of the previous year had been patiently husbanding, training, and reequipping its forces, and Vice Admiral Kakuji Kakuta's First Air Fleet (land-based). These two would be thrown at the enemy in a single raging wave. The object was to destroy completely the main forces of our old opponent, the American fleet.

Navy staff chief Shigetaro Shimada issued a directive to Admiral Toyoda regarding the main points of the decisive battle. It went as follows:

> 1) The First Mobile Fleet and the First Air Fleet will complete preparations for action by the latter part of May. The First Mobile Fleet will be held in alert status in the central and southern Philippines area. The First Air Fleet will be deployed in the central Pacific, the Philippines, and the New Guinea–Solomons areas. They will be held in readiness for a decisive battle. If a favorable opportunity presents itself, the full strength of the two above-mentioned fleets will be committed to battle with due regard for their proper employment. The main force of the enemy will be intercepted and destroyed.
>
> 2) The decisive battle will be fought as close as possible to the forward base of our mobile fleet.

At this time the Naval General Staff regarded the area below the western Carolines as the most likely location for the decisive battle. Given the lack of navy tankers to accompany the fleet, Ozawa could not be ordered as far as the waters off the Marianas. The Naval General Staff was silent regarding Ozawa's outranging tactic.

On 3 May the Combined Fleet Command also issued an order regarding the plan of Operation A (Secret Fleet Operations Order No. 76). It designated waters off the Palaus as one area for the decisive battle, the seas off the western Carolines as a second. Under this plan, the enemy was expected to invade the islands of the western Carolines. As for the Marianas, only carrier-based air attacks were anticipated; no invasion was foreseen. This plan also explicitly prescribed Ozawa's outranging tactic: "It is considered most important that daylight air attacks be carried out with large forces beyond the range of enemy carrier-borne attack aircraft."

310

After the promulgation of the Naval General Staff's operational objectives and the Combined Fleet Command's operational plan, a liaison conference of 6 March between the government and the high command approved the drafting of 60,000 additional tons of tankers for navy use. This decision made it possible for Ozawa to operate as far as the Marianas. But the Combined Fleet's Operation A outline was adopted essentially without revisions regarding the role of Ozawa's fleet. It may be said that a basic flaw in our navy's A plan was its failure to anticipate the U.S. invasion of the Marianas.

Having been left behind at Singapore by Ozawa's fleet, I hastened to my new duty station. But I found it rather difficult to get a seat on an outbound flight. My rank of lieutenant junior grade and the mysterious nature of my new assignment with the Naval General Staff combined to make my travel priority rather low. In response to my many persistent requests for a seat, the staff officers there retorted, "We never clear anyone for transport to the Tokyo Communications Station or the Naval General Staff!" I finally got a seat on a plane out of Kalang Airport; I flew to Taipei via Saigon and Hoihow (Hainan Island). At Taipei I also had a terrible time getting a flight. I finally reached Tokyo's Haneda Airport after stopovers at Oroku on Okinawa and Gannosu at Fukuoka. I reported to the Tokyo Communications Station on 1 June.

At my new post my living arrangements were taken care of by the Communications Station. My real work, however, consisted of assisting officers of the Operations Room of the First Section of the Naval General Staff. My primary responsibility ordinarily was to produce clear war situation reports. The chief of the general staff used these as drafts for reports to the throne. According to Rear Admiral Iwao Kawai, chief of the First Section of the Personnel Bureau at the time, the Army General Staff had quite a number of junior officer assistants in its operations section. Navy staff officers of the First Section noticed this and, being overburdened with work

311

themselves, urgently requested some junior line officers to lighten their load. The result was that an academy classmate and I received orders to the First Section.

When I arrived at my new post, Ozawa's fleet was concentrating at Tawitawi. The forces from Lingga Roads were being augmented by the Second and Third Carrier Divisions and the battleship *Musashi* from the home islands. At that time the so-called Operation KON was going forward in response to American attacks against Biak Island. I recall arriving early at the Naval General Staff building, taking maps of Biak from the chart shelves in the corridor, and poring over them until late at night to gain a clear picture of the land battles in progress there.

The Operations Room was put on the alert by the discovery of an American fast carrier force at Majuro Atoll in the Marshalls. Also detected were large convoys of U.S. transports coming and going in the Admiralties. The movements of the U.S. and Japanese fleets displayed on the chart of the Operations Room increased our eagerness for a showdown.

On 20 May Admiral Toyoda issued the order to "Commence Operation A" and left the waters off Kisarazu in Tokyo Bay with his flag on the light cruiser *Oyodo*. He arrived at the Hashirajima anchorage in the western Inland Sea on 23 May. He directed all navy operations from there.

On 11 June U.S. carrier planes hit the Marianas. Judging from the nature of the attacks, it was clear that they had come from the American fast carrier force that had been at Majuro. Our problem was to decide whether these were simple air attacks or the prelude to an invasion of the Marianas. On 13 June U.S. naval forces shelled Saipan and Tinian, while destroyers began sweeping for mines in the waters west of Saipan. But we failed to discover the enemy's invasion armada in time, and reports were still coming in of large convoys of transports in the Admiralties. Even after the report of minesweeping off Saipan, a staff officer declared in the Operations Room, "This well may be a feint by the U.S. Forces."

Earlier Ozawa had moved the fleet from Tawitawi to an anchorage at Guimaras, in the central Philippines, between the islands of Negros and Panay. His purpose was to train his air units. Regarding the U.S. actions against Saipan on 13 June, he later wrote in a detailed battle report,

> Though we conceded that the enemy's true intent might be to invade, we felt there was good reason for moving the fleet to Guimaras. Our pilots needed training and we had to take on replacement aircraft at Davao. In addition, Guimaras was a good location from which to respond should American operations in the Marianas be expanded into an invasion. Therefore the Mobile Fleet left Tawitawi at 0900 on 13 June, as scheduled, for Guimaras. Only later in the day came news that the enemy had started shelling coastal defenses and gun batteries and that enemy destroyers had begun minesweeping. We saw strong indications that landings on Saipan were next.

On the evening of 13 June, Admiral Toyoda gave the order to "prepare for the decisive battle of Operation A." Upon receiving confirmation of enemy landings on Saipan, he finally radioed, "Set Operation A in motion for the decisive battle."

Ozawa arrived at Guimaras on the evening of 14 June. He spent the night taking on 1,800 tons of fuel and got under way immediately. He reached the San Bernardino Strait by 1730 on 15 June and headed east toward the enemy. At the time he made an estimate of enemy intentions:

> The objectives of their strategy are one or more of the following, with a strong likelihood that all three will be attempted.
> 1) Invasion of the main bases of the Marianas.
> 2) Simultaneously with the above, strengthening their advance in western New Guinea or attacking strategic points in the Carolines.
> 3) Luring our mobile fleet forces into a decisive battle.

When he passed through the San Bernardino Strait, Ozawa defined operations of the mobile fleet: "The aim of the present operation is to defeat enemy mobile forces in the vicinity of the Marianas on the nineteenth. Thereafter, in accordance with the principles of Operation A, we will pursue remaining enemy forces until they are annihilated."

The Battle of the Marianas was in essence a decisive clash of aircraft. Consequently, a reckoning of the carrier and air units involved is essential.

On 11 June, the day of the U.S. air attacks, a Japanese unit on the scene captured a crewman of a downed American plane. He had a list of call signs, which he was not supposed to have carried on the aircraft. Vice Admiral Chuichi Nagumo, commander of the Central Pacific Area Fleet, radioed this information regarding the organization of U.S. carrier groups to the proper commands that evening. It correctly specified the organization and ships of the carrier task force, which was under the overall command of Admiral Spruance and the tactical control of Vice Admiral Mitscher. Here is the order of battle as it was known to us then. I have appended the numbers and types of aircraft carried, drawing on postwar sources.

Task Group 58.1
  CV *Hornet*
    Fighters: 36 F6F Hellcats, 4 F6F-3N night fighters
    Bombers: 33 SB2C Helldivers
    Torpedo planes: 4 TBF Avengers, 15 TBM Avengers
  CV *Yorktown*
    Fighters: 42 F6Fs, 4 F6F-3Ns
    Bombers: 40 SB2Cs, 4 SBD Dauntlesses
    Torpedo planes: 1 TBF, 16 TBMs
  CVL *Belleau Wood*
    Fighters: 26 F6Fs
    Torpedo planes: 3 TBFs, 6 TBMs
  CVL *Bataan*
    Fighters: 24 F6Fs

Torpedo planes: 9 TBMs

Task Group 58.2 (Rear Admiral Montgomery)
CV *Bunker Hill*
Fighters: 38 F6Fs, 4 F6F-3Ns
Bombers: 33 SB2Cs
Torpedo planes: 13 TBFs, 5 TBMs
CV *Wasp*
Fighters: 35 F6Fs, 4 F6F-3Ns
Bombers: 32 SB2Cs
Torpedo planes: 18 TBFs
CVL *Monterey*
Fighters: 21 F6Fs
Torpedo planes: 8 TBMs
CVL *Cabot*
Fighters: 24 F6Fs
Torpedo planes: 1 TBF, 8 TBMs

Task Group 58.3 (Rear Admiral Reeves)
CV *Enterprise*
Fighters: 31 F6Fs, 3 F4U Corsair night fighters
Bombers: 21 SBDs
Torpedo planes: 9 TBFs, 5 TBMs
CV *Lexington*
Fighters: 38 F6Fs, 4 F6F-3Ns
Bombers: 34 SBDs
Torpedo planes: 17 TBFs, 1 TBM
CVL *San Jacinto*
Fighters: 24 F6Fs
Torpedo planes: 6 TBFs, 2 TBMs
CVL *Princeton*
Fighters: 24 F6Fs
Torpedo planes: 9 TBMs

Task Group 58.4 (Rear Admiral Harrill)
CV *Essex*
Fighters: 39 F6Fs, 4 F6F-3Ns
Bombers: 36 SB2Cs
Torpedo planes: 15 TBFs, 5 TBMs
CVL *Langley*
Fighters: 23 F6Fs
Torpedo planes: 7 TBFs, 2 TBMs

CVL *Cowpens*
    Fighters: 23 F6Fs
    Torpedo planes: 3 TBFs, 6 TBMs

Vice Admiral Mitscher had his flag on the *Lexington* of Task Group 3. The supreme commander, Admiral Spruance, had his on the heavy cruiser *Indianapolis,* which was operating as a ship of the defensive screen of Task Group 3.

The American fast carrier task force embarked 902 planes in all, 475 of them fighters. The fact that fighters comprised over half of the carrier aircraft decisively affected the outcome of the Marianas battle.

In addition to the task groups commanded by Mitscher, American forces under Spruance included the Joint Expeditionary Force commanded by Vice Admiral Turner with two task groups having a total of seven escort carriers with FMs (Wildcat fighters), TBMs, and TBFs, for a total of 169 planes, 98 of them fighters.

Ozawa's forces had the following aircraft. The figures are those that were on hand at the Naval General Staff at the time.

First Carrier Division (Ozawa)
    11 Zero Model 21 fighter-bombers
    80 Zero Model 52 fighters
     9 Val bombers
    70 Judy Model 21 bombers
    44 Jill torpedo planes
       Total 214
Second Carrier Division (Rear Admiral Takaji Joshima)
    27 Zero Model 21s
    53 Zero Model 52s
    29 Vals
    11 Judy Model 21s
    15 Jills
       Total 135
Third Carrier Division (Rear Admiral Sueo Obayashi)
    45 Zero Model 21s

18 Zero Model 52s
9 Jills
18 Kates
    Total 90

All carrier aircraft totaled 439, although the complement of the mobile fleet was originally 450. Ozawa had in addition 36 Jake Type 0 reconnaissance seaplanes on battleships and cruisers.

Vice Admiral Kakuta's First Air Fleet had an official complement of 1,750 planes, a very large force. The aircraft that the central naval authorities were able to allot to his bases and actually deliver to the scene, however, amounted to less than half of that figure. As U.S. air strikes against the Marianas began on 11 June, Kakuta's force was thought to number 435 aircraft. The attacks whittled down his air fleet day by day as Ozawa steamed toward the battle area. According to reports received by the Naval General Staff on 18 June, Kakuta had only 156 planes to commit to the decisive battle.

Another complication was the U.S. employment of seaplanes. A report of them was received at the Operations Room on the afternoon of 17 June. We had intercepted a transmission stating that four or five PBYs had arrived in waters west of Saipan. Rear Admiral Tasuku Nakazawa, chief of the First Section, expressed grave concern. He pointed out that U.S. contact might now be made with Ozawa at extreme ranges.

When Ozawa was about to exit the San Bernardino Strait on 15 June, he noticed ominous signal fires on the peaks of the coast to the south. After his fleet left the strait, the U.S. submarine *Flying Fish* sighted it. Another U.S. submarine, the *Seahorse*, observed Vice Admiral Matome Ugaki's force, composed of the *Yamato, Musashi,* and other ships, as it made its way northward to rendezvous with Ozawa's main body. The *Seahorse* sighted Ugaki in seas east of Mindanao on the evening of 15 June only a short time after Ozawa was discovered.

317

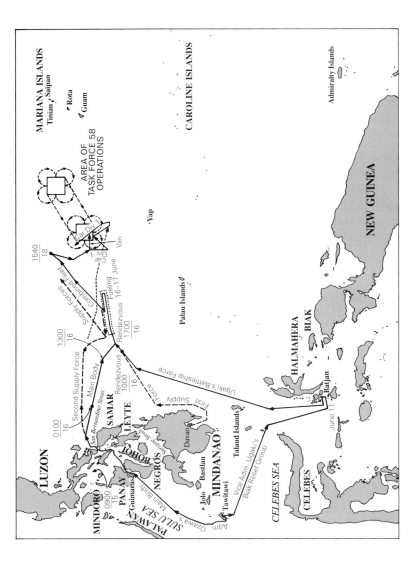

Battle of the Philippine Sea

Receiving reports of these two sightings, Admiral Spruance ordered seaplanes equipped with radar that were based at Eniwetok Atoll to proceed speedily to Saipan. These seaplanes, actually PBMs, were the ones that detected Ozawa at 0115 on 19 June, having most probably made contact with the van under Vice Admiral Kurita. Further, large land-based PB4Ys under MacArthur's command patrolled wide areas from their base in the Admiralties. At the Operations Room we had discounted searches from this quarter because of the great distances involved.

U.S. submarine forces displayed unusual activity as they deployed in the western Pacific and particularly around the Philippines in the period preceding U.S. operations in the Marianas. These U.S. submarines, under the command of Vice Admiral Lockwood at Hawaii, were transmitting frequently, and when they did, our naval communications stations at various locations got bearings on them. The central Naval Communications Station at Owada in Saitama Prefecture would determine their positions and analyze how these transmissions were being handled within the U.S. communications net. By comparing this information with activities of our own units, we were able to infer with considerable accuracy the nature and content of the transmissions. The Special Duty Section of the Naval General Staff would send out intelligence on these submarines to the entire navy at a set time every day through the Tokyo Communications Station.[5] When the occasion demanded, special intelligence was sent out immediately to the proper units.

Our communications stations had of course intercepted the transmissions of the two submarines that sighted our forces on 15 June. Noting that these transmissions were picked up by Hawaii and all other networks, we believed it likely that our forces had been discovered. The chief of the Combined Fleet staff, Ryunosuke Kusaka, sent out a warning to that effect (Dispatch No. 1850 of 16 June).

I think it was when the morning situation report of 18 June was being given in the Operations Room that Captain Hidenari Morikawa appeared. He was commander of the Owada Communications Station and concurrently a member of the Special Duty Section of the staff. Following reports by officers of the First Section, he gave a communications intelligence briefing. Obviously tense, he declared in a powerful voice that Ozawa was being shadowed by a U.S. submarine. He explained that the submarine would surface at night and, maintaining contact with Ozawa's force, transmit reports on its location. At Owada they had oscilloscopes that allowed them to compare wave forms of different transmissions. The wave forms in this case matched, confirming they were from the same vessel.

After hearing Captain Morikawa's report, officers of the First Section were of the opinion that Ozawa should be sent a warning. I do not know if such a warning was ever sent or what it contained. Since the war I have searched through many relevant documents and to the present day have found nothing to substantiate its existence. According to American sources, Ozawa's shadow was the *Cavalla*, which first discovered tankers of the supply force at 0510 on 17 June and made contact with Ozawa's main force at 2115 the same day. It maintained contact until 0630 on 18 June. Captain Morikawa's assertion that a U.S. submarine was surfacing at night and tailing Ozawa turned out to be correct. It was the *Cavalla*, of course, that torpedoed and sank the *Shokaku* on the day of the decisive battle, 19 June.

On the afternoon of 18 June, Ozawa got the drop on the Americans by discovering their carrier groups. The Third Fleet (Rear Admiral Obayashi) launched attack aircraft right away. But Ozawa called off the strike. At the time, back in the Operations Room in Tokyo, I had in my mind's eye the air groups launching. I could almost see the planes heavily loaded with bombs and torpedoes as they took off. I prayed for their safety.

When the chief of the First Section, Nakazawa, saw Ozawa's order canceling the attack, he groaned, "The Command of the Mobile Fleet has certainly not lost its composure."

It was becoming ever more apparent that the decisive battle was going to take place on 19 June. On the evening of 18 June the atmosphere in the Operations Room was one of suffocating anxiety. Several days earlier the Tokyo Communications Station and related commands required that all hands remain on the premises. Thus a wave of tension spread outward from the Operations Room to engulf other navy offices at the capital.

Ozawa later related the following about the measures taken on the evening of 18 June.

> The attack of 18 June was canceled because its execution was impossible without staging through land bases. The decision was made to attack with all forces on the 19th, the day of the decisive battle. An attempt would be made first to annihilate the fleet carrier groups of the enemy as they steamed out from the western side of the [Marianas] archipelago. For this purpose we planned as follows: We would come up from the south at the outset of the attack, keeping at a distance of three hundred nautical miles from the advancing enemy carrier groups. We would be 580 nautical miles from the archipelago, so that if the carrier groups did not materialize we would be able to attack the vicinity of the archipelago the same day. Further, should a night reconnaissance make contact with the enemy mobile force, a search strike would be carried out. In accordance with the above, the van was detached and dispositions made for air combat.[6]

Ozawa's intention, therefore, was to advance more or less parallel to the line of the Marianas, which extended from Guam in a north-northeasterly direction to Rota and Tinian and Saipan. He would sweep in on the enemy fleet and destroy it.

After an anxious night in the Operations Room, we dis-

321

covered that aircraft of Vice Admiral Kakuta's base air force did not do as well as expected in keeping contact with the enemy. A medium attack bomber from Yap sighted carrier groups that appeared to be the enemy's main force but soon lost contact, as it was a very dark night.

On the morning of 19 June Ozawa discovered the U.S. carrier groups and launched the long-awaited strikes. In the Operations Room the staff officers marveled at his calm resolve, evident in the way he waited until search planes had reached the limit of their range before giving the order to attack.

I waited expectantly for the transmissions from aircraft indicating that the assaults on the American fleet had begun. I expected first to hear *to-tsu-re,* which was code for the order from the flight commanders to their planes, *totsugeki jumbi taikei tsukure* ("assume attack formation") and then, *to,* which stood for *zengun totsugeki seyo* ("all forces attack"). But time passed and no transmissions came in. The messages delivered to the Operations Room were largely those from Ozawa on the *Taiho,* Kurita on the *Atago,* and Obayashi on the *Chitose;* mixed in with them were some from bases on Yap, Tinian, and Guam. They concerned movements of their own units or else consisted of orders, intelligence information, and queries beamed to air groups aloft. I thought it over. Transmissions from the aircraft could probably not be received by the Tokyo Communications Station because of their different frequencies and weak radio sets. Our carriers surely already knew the situation of the air units and were themselves transmitting only urgent messages to them.

I boldly voiced my opinion on this matter. Vice Chief of Staff Seiichi Ito shot back, "At the time of the Pearl Harbor attack we picked up aircraft transmissions clearly here. It was the same with Midway and the Santa Cruz Islands." He was unconvinced. But I knew that transmission frequencies often had to be changed. I still felt that we were receiving nothing from air groups because their transmissions could not travel

A VF-1 "Top Hatter" F6F-3 is launched from the *Yorktown* to intercept Japanese planes, 19 June 1944. A crewman (just under the propeller) is holding the target information board. *Courtesy of the National Archives*

long distances. The impatience and tension in the Operations Room continued for several more hours. Commander Minoru Genda made the solitary remark, "It must be as young Nomura says; it must be."

The first bad news on 19 June came in the afternoon from the base on Guam. One of Ozawa's air groups was trying to land there, and the planes obviously still carried their bombs and torpedoes. They had not found their target. This base had been under observation and the sky above it dominated by enemy fighters since morning. Considerable numbers of enemy transports and warships, including escort carriers, were visible from the Marianas Islands. Therefore, the base commander at Guam requested that the approaching planes from Ozawa's force attack these vessels rather than land. Per-

323

haps the planes did not hear the request; perhaps they did not notice the enemy fighters. They tried to land and were shot down one after another. (I regretted our doctrine that planes were to attack only fleet carriers; I felt that they should be allowed targets of opportunity.) Before long we learned that this air group that had suffered such heavy losses was the Second Carrier Division's second strike force.

Then came the message "Planes of the First Carrier Division, land on the *Zuikaku*." We had no indication whatever that Ozawa's ships had come under attack. What then had happened to the *Taiho* and *Shokaku*? When a carrier was delayed in recovering aircraft from a first strike, it sometimes had to go off course far to windward. Upon the return of planes of the second strike the carrier would be far from the scheduled point of retrieval. Had this happened to the First Carrier Division, and was the *Zuikaku* operating independently?

The mood of uneasiness in the Operations Room gradually spread. Our apprehensions were confirmed by Ozawa's next two transmissions.

> *No. 191640.* As of 1600 will exercise command from *Haguro*.
> *No. 191710.* All forces set course northward.

It was now obvious that something had happened to the *Taiho* and the operation was not proceeding according to plan. It did not seem that Ozawa had been attacked by aircraft from a U.S. carrier group. But Commander Genda hypothesized that such a force might be operating undetected to the south of Ozawa and attacking his flank; U.S. planes could thus avoid the defensive fire of the van and directly assault the main fleet units.

In the evening a message from Ozawa arrived.

> *No. 191840.* At 0700 tomorrow, 20 June, take up station in number eight protective cruising formation. "A" Force position to be FHH00, course 90 degrees, speed 16 knots.[7]

I immediately looked on the grid chart for the concentration point Ozawa had ordered for the next morning. I was convinced that it would be just to the west of the Marianas. Surprisingly, the order had not specified a battle formation. I recalled that at Lingga Roads maneuvers the entire fleet would make a rush for the enemy right after the first strike. If the fleet steamed at high speed toward Saipan during the night, it would be very near it by morning. And there, unquestionably, the enemy fleet and transport convoys were to be found. At dawn, I said to myself, a grand melee would occur. If worst came to worst, Ozawa's fleet might be wiped out. I did not think beyond that point.

When I located the rendezvous on the map, it was surprisingly far to the west of the Marianas. Any person experienced in the use of position codes knew to ignore the first character and use the other four for a faster fix. Not believing my eyes, I looked at the first letter to confirm the position. When I searched the chart using all five, I found that indeed the point was about halfway between the Marianas and the Philippines. For a while I thought there must have been some error in transmission. But as I received messages later from Ozawa's fleet and the supply forces, I was forced to conclude that this position well to the rear was the true point of concentration.

Ozawa's resolve for the attack of the second day, 20 June, was as follows.

> If the results of the first day's attacks are considerable, we will close on the archipelago at dawn and, renewing our air attacks, will defeat the large part of the enemy carrier group while sending a raiding group forward to annihilate the enemy. If it is judged that the results of the attacks are slight, the mobile fleet will temporarily withdraw to the west for replenishment and repair; thereafter a second decisive battle is to be expected.

As it turned out, Ozawa chose the latter course of action. By 21 June evidence of our defeat was conclusive. On that day, I heard later, Ozawa told his staff in his cabin that if he had been the commander in chief of the Combined Fleet on the scene during the night of 19 June, he probably would have advanced with all units to engage the enemy in a night attack.

In the Operations Room we still had no idea what had become of the *Taiho* and *Shokaku*. I think it was in the middle of the night on the nineteenth that we got our answer. A messenger from the Navy Ministry's Telecommunications Section handed a telegram in an envelope to the staff officer on duty. Somehow I and my fellow officers understood that this was a message of the highest security classification. I still remember it clearly. The duty officer was Commander Yasuo Fujimori. I knew intuitively that the telegram in the envelope was a message of great importance from Ozawa and that it contained bad news. All eyes in the Operations Room were on the face of Fujimori as he read the telegram. The text was rather long. I think that Vice Chief Ito, First Department head Nakazawa, First Section head Chikao Yamamoto, and all the other important officers were present. Fujimori read. It was so quiet that wringing one's hands would have made an explosive noise. Fujimori's face twisted in agony, and I knew that my intuition had been correct. The telegram was Ozawa's confidential message to Naval Staff Chief Shimada and Combined Fleet Commander in Chief Toyoda reporting the sinking of the carriers *Taiho* and *Shokaku*. The atmosphere in the Operations Room, which up to then had been a mixture of uncertainty and anxiety, began to change to genuine despair.

Our remaining hope was that the Yawata Air Attack Group could be speedily dispatched from Iwo Jima, allowing Ozawa to regroup his forces and renew the attack.

On the afternoon of 20 June it was extremely difficult for us to form a clear picture of the battle situation. Messages from the scene of action came flying in wildly, adding to the confusion of the previous day's dispatches. A large number of messages suggested, however, that the U.S. carrier groups had gone over to the offensive. In the actions of 19 June a large number of planes had not returned to their carriers. We could only pray that these planes had achieved as yet unreported victories. But the fact that enemy carrier groups had steamed halfway to the Philippines, when earlier they had stayed close to the Marianas, indicated to us that Spruance had confidence in victory. The gloom in the Operations Room was at its deepest.

We were temporarily cheered by news that arrived later. The Fourth Naval Communications Station on Truk had intercepted some U.S. messages in the clear. Truk reported, "Survivors of the *Rebiru* are being rescued." *Rebiru* was our designation for the fleet carrier *Bunker Hill*. In the morning of 22 June Captain Morikawa reported on the interceptions and said there was a strong probability that the *Bunker Hill* had been sunk by Ozawa's attacks. This ray of hope continued to brighten the Operations Room for a time.

Ozawa returned directly to Japan, arriving at Nakagusuku Bay, Okinawa, on 22 June and Hashirajima on 24 June. Then we received confirmation that our air groups had failed to locate the enemy on 20 June and that we had launched no attack the next day. Our hopes for a sunken U.S. carrier were dashed. Pilots from the *Bunker Hill* had been unable to return to the ship because of the long range at which their attack had been carried out. They had ditched, and it was they who were being rescued on 21 June. We had assumed that the messages referred to survivors of the ship's crew.

The emperor was displeased to learn that the *Taiho* and *Shokaku* had been sunk by submarines. Later, on 30 April 1945, he questioned Navy Minister Mitsumasa Yonai. "During Operation A they knew that enemy submarines would be in the area, yet they pressed on and suffered a calamity. Did the commander in chief of the Combined Fleet order it, or did the Mobile Fleet commander himself decide it?"

At the time of the operation, the chief of staff did not report such details to the throne as the movements of enemy submarines. But aides-de-camp to the emperor were always com-

A Japanese plane is shot down over the *San Jacinto* or *Princeton*, 19 June 1944. Note the formidable concentration of 40-mm. flak bursts above the carrier. *Courtesy of the National Archives*

ing and going at the Operations Room, and through them he got a fairly detailed picture of the war situation. It may be said that because of the constraints on Ozawa, mainly the shortage of fuel and the narrow time frame, it would have been extremely difficult for him to carry out the operation while at the same time evading enemy submarines.

It had been some time since Japanese and American carrier forces had been pitted against each other. The Coral Sea, Midway, the Eastern Solomons, and the Santa Cruz Islands had been carrier battles in which the side first detecting the other and launching planes had the advantage. Carriers were strong on offense and weak on defense. But the defensive strength of the U.S. fast carrier forces, made up principally of *Essex*-class carriers built since the start of the war, greatly exceeded our expectations. There were several reasons for their defensive power.

First, the air search radar aboard U.S. ships was highly effective. Also important was the voice radio contact between planes aloft and their ships through the combat information center, or CIC. The large number of fighters on the American side was another critical factor. Finally, the VT fuses fitted on U.S. antiaircraft shells had a devastating effect.

Enemy radar would detect our search planes before their pilots had gained sight of the enemy. They would be attacked, often by surprise, by enemy fighters vectored to them by shipborne voice radio. Further, our attack aircraft would be assaulted by enemy fighters several tens of miles ahead of the first enemy ships, before the order "assume attack formation" could be given. Aircraft that managed to shake off enemy fighters would have to plunge through the enemy's protective screen. This circular formation of vessels threw up concentrated antiaircraft fire with VT shells. Only if our planes succeeded in passing through this curtain of fire could they reach their target, the enemy carriers. The widely held view that carriers were vulnerable became obsolete as soon as the U.S. fast carrier forces appeared in the Pacific.

In his detailed combat report, Ozawa wrote the following under the heading of "Factors Influencing the Operation":

> The Mobile Fleet concentrated at Tawitawi on 16 May. During the month spent at that anchorage until the sortie on 13 June, carrier air groups, not to mention surface units, were largely unable to engage in training. That is, when the air groups were supposed to be maintaining maximum readiness and peak form, they had no suitable air base nearby. Their alert status and the consequent need to be ready for sortie at any time meant that exercises could not be scheduled. Also, because neighboring waters were swarming with enemy submarines, carriers were able to put to sea for launch and recovery operations only once. Surface units could not put to sea because of fuel shortages and the submarine threat. It is believed that the above-related insufficiencies of training, particularly those of the

329

air groups, exercised a great influence on the outcome of the air battles.

Of the five separate air strikes launched during the battle, only two sighted their objective. This fact shows that the aircraft did not sufficiently correct for compass deviation and made large errors in navigation. This is especially true of search aircraft. The outranging tactic magnified these errors.

As noted earlier, the outranging tactic had become commonly accepted by all of us at Lingga Roads and was stressed in Toyoda's plan for Operation A. It gave me an odd feeling when I took up my duties with the Naval General Staff to learn that the staff did not share this appreciation of the tactic. Commander Fujimori told me that when Ozawa had launched planes on 19 June, Vice Chief Ito had groaned, putting his whole body into it, "It's so far! It's so far!" On 21 June I myself saw Commander Genda flare up violently against First Section chief Yamamoto. He hotly denied that the Mobile Fleet's strategy was like *kendo*. "It's more like Western fencing," he insisted.[8]

We had expectations that Ozawa's fleet would crush Mitscher's carrier groups. We hoped that Kurita's battleships would rout the U.S. vessels that crowded around Saipan and relieve the Japanese soldiers fighting desperately on the island. Now our dreams were shattered. Navy headquarters boiled over with disputes.

The view rapidly came to the fore that the navy should commit all of its strength to another advance on Saipan and pour in new army forces to recapture the island. Besides the surviving elements of Ozawa's fleet, forces that could be thrown into the operation were the Fifth Fleet of Vice Admiral Kiyohide Shima, which had hurriedly been ordered to Yokosuka from Ominato, and the escort carriers *Kaiyo*, *Shinyo*, and *Taiyo*. It was hoped that naval air training groups and army fighter groups in Japan could replace Ozawa's severely depleted air units. On 21 June the Naval General Staff drew up a proposal for the recapture of Saipan. The operation was to proceed as follows:

> 1 July—A convoy of transports totaling 80,000 tons with one army division aboard to get under way from home ports.
>
> 2 July—A convoy built around the Fifth Fleet and carrying one army regiment to put out from Yokosuka.
>
> 3 July—Two tankers for fleet replenishment to leave home waters.
>
> 4 July—A carrier force made up of the *Zuikaku,* Ozawa's other remaining carriers, and the escort carriers to weigh anchor. Embarked aircraft to be serviceable planes from naval air training groups and army fighters that needed only to be capable of taking off from carrier decks. No thought of shipboard aircraft recovery to be entertained. The Second Fleet also to leave home waters.
>
> 7 July—All aircraft, with fighters as the main force, to be thrown into battle in the Marianas area, recovering control of the air in the region. The full strength of remaining land-based air units to be committed, from Iwo Jima in the north and Yap in the south. Carrier-based aircraft to be launched to the west of the Marianas as our carriers approached. After initial battles for control of the air, all aircraft to land at our secure bases on Guam, Tinian, and Rota, and following this, to renew their attacks from these bases. Further, bases on the northern coast of Saipan not yet occupied by the enemy to be utilized. Approximately three hundred aircraft from our combat forces and the Marianas bases to participate in the battle for the air.
>
> 8 July—The Second Fleet to close on Saipan and crush the enemy fleet there. The Fifth Fleet's convoy to arrive at Saipan subsequently, as the first reinforcement. Air, navy, and army offensive forces to concentrate on Saipan.

331

> 9 July—The transport convoy to arrive at Saipan as the second reinforcement.

In the Battle of the Marianas, Ozawa's main goal was to destroy the U.S. fast carrier groups. But in this operation he would try to dodge the U.S. carriers and take advantage of their distance from the Marianas to retake Saipan.

Naturally the Naval General Staff had many misgivings. For example, the likelihood was great that U.S. seaplanes at Saipan would spot our approaching forces early. It might be possible to wrest control of the air from the enemy temporarily, but could it be held for long? Could army fighters really manage to take off from the carriers? Would the two reinforcements of Saipan be enough to win the ground battle for the island?

The Combined Fleet Command was not enthusiastic about this plan. Nevertheless, on 22 June Toyoda ordered Ozawa, who had just arrived at Nakagusuku Bay, to proceed with the entire fleet to the western end of the Inland Sea, where preparations could be made for the Saipan recapture operation. Up until this time the Second Fleet had orders to Guimaras in the Philippines; now it was to stay with the rest of the mobile fleet.

The Army General Staff opposed the navy plan. The army argued that prospects for success were slight and that no army aircraft could be spared for the operation. A new attack on Saipan without army forces made no sense. Thus the Saipan recapture operation died after a mere three days.

On 24 June the staff chiefs of the two services, General Hideki Tojo and Admiral Shimada, reported to the throne the cancellation of the Saipan recapture operation.[9] On this same day Ozawa anchored at Hashirajima. The following day a conference of fleet admirals and field marshals in the imperial palace formally approved the abandonment of the recapture operation.

.   .   .

In November 1944 Ozawa became vice chief of the Naval General Staff and reported for duty in Tokyo. He remembered me as one of his former navigation officers. By then I had been promoted to lieutenant. One morning, just after finishing a report on the war situation, I looked up from my work to see Ozawa in the nearly deserted Operations Room. He had apparently been watching me as I placed markers on the operations plot. When I raised my head, our eyes met. Ozawa patted his vice admiral's collar insignia and said, "Here you've gone and picked up three stars and I haven't gained a single one!"[10] Then he laughed.

If Ozawa had wanted another star, he could have gotten it. Navy Minister Yonai urged Ozawa to accept full admiral's rank and the post of commander in chief of the Combined Fleet. But Ozawa firmly declined the promotion.[11] I heard this directly from Admiral Shigeyoshi Inoue, an academy classmate of Ozawa's and at the time vice minister of the navy.

The Ozawa I knew was just that sort of man.

10

The
Air
Battle
off
Taiwan

SHIGERU
FUKUDOME

 In the summer of 1944 the American high command faced a basic decision over the next major step on the road to Tokyo. Navy leaders preferred to bypass the Philippines and invade Taiwan, while the army favored liberating the islands and using Luzon as a platform from which to storm the Japanese homeland. A conference at Pearl Harbor between President Roosevelt, General MacArthur, and Admiral Nimitz resolved the issue, and preparations began for a massive assault on the Philippines.

 Because of the virtual annihilation of the Japanese carrier-based air power in the Battle of the Philippine Sea, the Allied planners correctly anticipated that the major Japanese offensive against the invading forces would be mounted from Taiwan; heavy raids on airfields and installations to neutralize this expected resistance preceded the amphibious operation against the Philippines. The following article reveals the overall Japanese defense plan and the role Taiwan was to play in its implementation. Severely hampered by a shortage of experienced pilots and compelled to use army units not trained or equipped for combat at sea, the newly created Second Air Fleet resorted to unconventional tactics, including the exploitation of bad weather as a weapon. Among the factors worth noting in this account is the influence of a prospective war with Russia on the development of Japanese military aviation.

A FTER THE LOSS of the Marianas, Imperial Japanese General Headquarters revised its overall plan for the conduct of the war in order to meet the grave situation that had developed. The new policy was set forth in the *Sho* Operation Plan, which made the island chain of the Japanese homeland, the Ryukyu Islands, Taiwan, and the Philippines the last-ditch line of defense. The operation was further broken down into four regional divisions:

1) The *Sho-Ichi-Go* Operation for the defense of the Philippine Islands.

2) The *Sho-Ni-Go* Operation for the defense of Taiwan and the Nanseishoto Islands (Ryukyu Islands).

3) The *Sho-San-Go* Operation for the defense of the Japanese homeland.

4) The *Sho-Yon-Go* Operation for the defense of Hokkaido and the Kuriles.

These Japanese titles may be translated as Victory No. 1 Operation, Victory No. 2 Operation, Victory No. 3 Operation, and Victory No. 4 Operation.

According to the early estimate of the situation by Imperial General Headquarters, the enemy was most likely to direct his major invasion after the capture of the Marianas to the Taiwan-Ryukyu area—the region for the *Sho-Ni-Go* Operation.

In the Battle of the Philippine Sea, the carrier-borne air strength of the Japanese navy had virtually been annihilated. Although the surface units survived the battle almost intact,

335

the Japanese seagoing forces, deprived of carrier-borne air squadrons, were no longer capable of roaming the vast ocean at will. With their loss of mobility, the Japanese surface fleet had lost most of its value as a fighting force. Consequently, in the *Sho* Operation Plan the core of the fighting strength was built around land-based air forces.

In preparation for the *Sho* Operation, the Japanese navy regrouped its available land-based air power. Thus the Second Air Fleet came into existence, and I was assigned as its commanding admiral. The fleet was composed of the major portion of the then-existing naval land-based air units and deployed along the Taiwan–Ryukyu Islands–southern Kyushu line to carry out its defense assignment under the *Sho-Ni-Go* Operation.

Responsible for *Sho-Ichi-Go* was the First Air Fleet, which had been assigned to take care of the Philippine region. To prepare for *Sho-San-Go*, the Third Air Fleet had been organized in the homeland area. This air fleet was to continue its daily training and education of airmen as well as to prepare for an emergency in case the worst came prematurely. Also, in spite of the foregoing division of the regional assignments, all available strength was to be concentrated at once in any region where the enemy's main invasion might fall.

When the *Sho* Operation Plan was drawn up, the Second Air Fleet was officially allocated 510 land-based planes. The First Air Fleet was assigned 350 planes, and the Third Air Fleet 300 planes. Although the official number of planes allocated to the three air fleets totalled 1,160, about one third were actually not available. With Japanese aircraft production severely reduced, it was impossible for the air forces to make up for the attrition of war with new equipment. To make matters worse, few experienced, capable aviators were available. Inadequately trained pilots reduced even further the military potential of the aircraft assigned to the air fleets.

In addition to the land-based naval air power, the Japanese navy possessed slightly over one hundred planes belonging to the carrier division of the Third Fleet under the command of

Vice Admiral Jisaburo Ozawa. The remnant of the forces defeated at the Battle of the Philippine Sea on 19–20 June 1944, these carrier-borne air squadrons had lost much of their effectiveness as a fighting force. There were also the Twelfth Air Fleet under Vice Admiral Michitaro Tozuka in the Hokkaido and Kurile district, and the Thirteenth Air Fleet under Vice Admiral Shiro Takasu in the Malay and Dutch Indies area. Although the two air fleets were to reinforce the *Sho* operational forces in case of emergency, the planes they possessed numbered less than one hundred each.

The Japanese army air forces allocated about six hundred planes to the *Sho* Operation: about two hundred planes each from the Fourth Air Army stationed in the Philippines, from the Taiwan Army, and from the army training forces scattered in the homeland. As with the naval air forces, the actual combat ability of the army air forces had seriously deteriorated.

Unification of command was achieved during the battle off Taiwan, fought for five consecutive days beginning 12 October 1944, by placing all available aircraft under my immediate command. These forces aggregated 720 planes and included army air forces stationed in Taiwan, all the naval air units stationed in or reinforcing Taiwan, including the naval training air group in Taiwan, and the carrier squadrons from the Third Fleet. The total number also included my own Second Air Fleet deployed along the Taiwan-Kyushu line.

Having been appointed the commander of the Second Air Fleet on 15 June 1944, I established my headquarters at the Katori Air Base in Chiba Prefecture near Tokyo. Activated on the same date, the air fleet was composed of various flying units scattered all over Japan. By the first part of July, I ordered all these widely dispersed forces to concentrate in Kyushu, and moved my headquarters to the Kanoya Air Base on the southern tip of Kyushu on 10 July.

Our first essential task was to accelerate advanced training, since our units had been hurriedly formed by collecting green flyers fresh from elementary training and remnants of squadrons then somehow available. I personally directed the train-

337

ing at the Kyushu air bases for about three months, placing emphasis on two points.

The first point was related to the size of the flying formation to be employed in attacking enemy carrier task forces. I knew we had to deal with well-trained and powerful enemy carrier task forces as our foremost antagonist, but we did not have sufficient time to convert our green flyers into highly qualified combat aviators. The only solution to our problem was, I believed, to approach the target with a large number of torpedo planes and bombers under the strongest possible escort of our fighter planes and to resort to a simultaneous attack with that large formation. To my disappointment, however, most of the flyers had not yet completed basic individual training. To begin training these green flyers in a large formation flight was itself impossible until almost the end of our training period. Only three times, immediately before the Battle off Taiwan began, could we conduct attack training in large formation. Finally we had to content ourselves with the hope that we had somehow cast a mold for a large formation attack.

The second point on which my emphasis was placed concerned a special flying group called the T Attack Force. The *T* signified the initial letter of the word *typhoon*. This force was to be used in total darkness or in very bad weather in which enemy planes were considered inadequately trained to fight—such as in a typhoon. The force was composed of torpedo attack planes, which we intended to use against the enemy carrier task forces. The commanding officer of the group was Captain Shuzo Kuno, one of the few surviving first-rate veterans among the senior naval aviators. Crew members were selected from among veteran flyers then available. Organized in March 1944, the T Attack Force was first attached directly to Imperial General Headquarters, but on 15 June 1944 it was transferred to my command.

At this juncture I should like to explain the background of our military concept that gave birth to the T Attack Force. The story goes back to 1909, when the Japanese government

An American pilot photographed the carrier *Zuiho* during the Battle of Leyte Gulf in October 1944. The ship is camouflaged to resemble a battleship. *Official U.S. Navy photograph*

and high command, in order to cope with a new international situation after the Russo-Japanese War, formulated a new national defense policy and made the U.S. Navy the most probable enemy of the Japanese navy. Ever since then, the Japanese navy had felt it necessary to develop a tactical method to destroy, with its numerically inferior strength, a superior enemy. All naval training was devoted to attaining this objective. It was out of the question for the numerically inferior Japanese navy to conduct a costly expedition to American waters to seek out and fight the superior American fleet there. Instead, the Japanese naval plan was inevitably based on the so-called offensive-defensive strategy. According to this plan, the Japanese navy expected that the American fleet would steam across the Pacific. We anticipated that the American fleet would have maintenance troubles during the long trans-Pacific cruise, whereas we could conserve our strength while awaiting the enemy approach. Since we expected to fight a decisive fleet action in our home waters, we could take full advantage of superior geographic and local intelligence. From the foregoing basic policy of fighting a superior fleet with numerically inferior strength came realization of the need to emphasize night action. It was believed that the Japanese fleet, a smaller force, could more advantageously meet the American fleet, the larger force, in darkness than in broad daylight.

A similar line of thought applied to the deployment of submarines. The Japanese navy planned that its submarines should keep in touch with and continually attack the American fleet on its way across the Pacific, thereby achieving a diminution in American superiority. In brief, through a "war of attrition" the Japanese navy expected to attain a material reduction in the strength of the U.S. Fleet before battle was joined in Japanese waters.

In addition to the advantages of distance and the harassment of submarines, a third advantage could be gained, it was believed, through special training for bad weather conditions. In 1934 the Japanese Combined Fleet under Admiral Nobumasa Suetsugu placed emphasis on conducting training and exercises on rough seas under adverse conditions. In Japanese waters we have about eight times as many stormy days as in American waters. Even on ordinary days, the sea in the vicinity of Japan is seldom calm. Further, we in the Japanese navy believed that the U.S. Navy trained under easy natural conditions in the cool climate of Seattle and Halifax in summer, and in the warm breezes of lower California and Cuba in winter.

Though fighting efficiency is lowered on rough seas, we believed that the Japanese navy, constantly trained under adverse conditions, would be able to retain greater fighting efficiency than the American fleet, with its pleasant-weather training. In order to meet the requirement of rough-water training, the Japanese navy, first of all, generally built her warships bigger than each equivalent type of warship in other navies of the world.

Under Admiral Suetsugu I had been senior operations officer of his Combined Fleet. And the following year I was transferred to the Naval General Staff to head the operations section. There, under the chief of the Naval General Staff, Fleet Admiral Prince Fushimi, I planned a naval maneuver to be held with emphasis on rough-sea training. I planned to hold a grand maneuver in the latter part of October, the season when the northeast monsoon begins to blow hard in the sea near Japan. For this maneuver I chose an area to the northeast of the homeland where the sea is generally very high. Coincidentally, the naval maneuver planned that year met with a severe typhoon. With many ships having been damaged because of the typhoon, we were forced to abandon the exercise halfway. After this bitter pill and because of my resignation and that of Admiral Suetsugu, the two most ardent advocates of stormy-weather training, enthusiasm for the practice died down, though its importance was still recognized.

After the outbreak of the Pacific War, lessons obtained through wartime experiences made us feel that we had to revive the idea of rough-weather training, particularly in the field of aviation. The result was the organization of the T Attack Force. I, once a foremost promoter of rough-weather surface training, became particularly interested in the training of the TAF. I placed my greatest reliance for victory upon this unit.

Concerning the TAF, there is one thing to be particularly noted—the fact that half of the TAF was composed of army elements. The following circumstances led to the inclusion of the army planes.

For many years the Japanese army had built up its armament with a view to fighting the Russian Army in Manchuria

341

and had organized and trained all its forces along that line. Army planes had been exclusively assigned to the duty of cooperating with ground combat forces. The army's policy in building up aviation armament had been to maintain as many short-range tactical aircraft as possible. A change in policy came, however, with the experience gained through the military adventure in China, beginning in 1937. In China, naval aircraft could easily carry out a shuttle-bombing covering about a six-hundred-mile span between the bases in Kyushu and the targets in central China. But no army plane could carry war to the Chinese mainland from the nearest base in Taiwan, though the intervening distance was less than 120 miles. Later, as the Chinese war continued, the Japanese army found it necessary to launch strategic bombers against targets in the interior of the continent. Thereupon, the army began to manufacture a heavy bomber, called Type Ki-81 after the model of the navy's then-middle-sized torpedo bomber.[1] This new army bomber, if equipped with auxiliary fuel tanks, could carry out a shuttle-bombing with a radius of eight hundred miles.

Although the army bombers of this type had become available for actual battle missions by the middle of the Pacific War, the Army refused to use them for the defense of the Marianas. It was obvious to all of us that the loss of these strategic islands would result in fatal exposure of the Japanese lifeline to relentless enemy attack. It was also obvious that the defense of the Marianas depended mainly upon the use of land-based planes, the army's as well as the navy's. But the army, deeply committed to its activities on the continent, did not divert even a single plane for use in the defense of the Marianas, whereas the navy threw into the Marianas all the first-line air power then available.

After the fall of the Marianas, however, the army changed its policy. In the light of rapid changes in the war, the army realized that even army planes had to be diverted to operations on the ocean frontiers. The army authorities began thinking of training for oceanic missions with the Type Ki-81s, which were the only army planes capable of participating effectively in the new mission. At first, thirty planes of this type with their entire crews composing one flight squadron were experimentally placed under the command of Captain Kuno of the TAF, exclusively for training purposes. In the middle of the training, however, this squadron was ordered to become an organic part of the TAF. Later on, another squadron of the same type, numbering about thirty planes, was added to the TAF.

Of the foregoing two army heavy bomber squadrons, the one that was first incorporated into the TAF had completed about six months of hard sea training at the time of the Battle off Taiwan. As far as appearances were concerned, it was capable of joining a night attack as well as a daylight one. The other squadron, however, had completed only two months of sea training by the middle of October.

By the standard of those days, it was generally considered that before a green flyer could attain sufficient skill to carry out a night attack on ships at sea, he should have undergone at least three years of training, even if he had been trained from the first as a naval aviator. Army flyers, whose basic training was naturally different from that of the navy flyers, required much lengthier training for over-water assignments. But in the specific instance under discussion, the army flyers were given only two to six months of training for their sea mission. By our naval standards, therefore, we could not consider that the army flyers in the TAF had completed their initiation course for night attack training. Especially deplorable was their ability in recognition. Without exaggeration, I have to confess that there was virtually no one among the army flyers who could tell exactly which ship was of what type.

In this respect the navy aviators were not much better than the army flyers. By 1944, the status of the Japanese Fleet strength had so seriously deteriorated that it had become impossible for land-based aviators to train in cooperation with the surface units. When I inspected the TAF, I personally asked each aviator whether or not he had ever seen a submarine and found out there were many who never had.

In the Battle off Taiwan, almost every attack on enemy surface units was made by the TAF planes. The results achieved in these attacks were tremendously magnified in the reports. It seems to me that the cause of this fabulous exaggeration was chiefly that we had resorted to a night attack by those aviators who lacked recognition ability.

Immediately after the fall of Saipan, Imperial General Headquarters first estimated that the next enemy invasion would fall on Okinawa. Watching developments, however, we began to feel it was more probable that the enemy would strike the southern Philippines, with the western Carolines and Morotai as stepping-stones. On 10 September, with the foregoing estimate in mind, I moved my headquarters from the Kanoya Air Base in South Kyushu to the Takao Air Base in South Taiwan. Strenuous efforts were made to put every air base in Taiwan in good operational condition. At the same time I started to transfer my air units, one by one, to that island.

In planning the transfer of the air units, I had a bitter war lesson in mind. In February 1944 the First Air Fleet under Vice Admiral Kakuji Kakuta moved its torpedo bomber units from the homeland to the Marianas in advance of fighter units. On 22–23 February American task forces launched air raids on the Marianas, and Kakuta's torpedo-bombers, just transferred from the homeland, suffered disastrous damage tantamount to total annihilation. In my plan for the Taiwan transfer, I directed that as far as possible well-trained fighters move first. I also directed the transfer, parallel to the fighter migration, of some of the large flying boats to be used for long-range patrol duty.

By 12 October, when Taiwan was attacked by the American carrier task forces, I had transferred only about one hundred fighters, to be stationed in Takao and Shinchiku, and about ten flying boats, to be assigned to Toko Sea Plane Base. The remaining units composing the major portion of the Second Air Fleet units had not been readied for the transfer.

With my move to Taiwan, Imperial General Headquarters placed under my tactical command army air forces then stationed in Taiwan. Under the command of Major General Yamamoto, and belonging to the administrative chain of command of the commander of the Taiwan Army, General Rikichi Ando, the army air forces were composed of about two hundred planes in all, including about a hundred fighters. They were based in the main at an airfield near Taihoku and at the Heito airfield east of Takao. As for their military skill, I must admit that it was very low by our standards.

In addition to the above, I was ordered to assume tactical command of the naval training air units stationed on Taiwan. Among the planes of the training group, only about thirty at the Tainan Air Base could be considered ready for combat missions when handled by training instructors.

Including both the Second Air Fleet planes moved to Taiwan and the above-mentioned army and navy planes temporarily placed under my tactical command, all the air strength I could muster at the time of the Battle off Taiwan was actually 330 planes. As I have already explained, I had under my command about 350 planes of the TAF and other units of the Second Air Fleet, but these were still based in Kyushu. After the Battle off Taiwan began, about one hundred planes originally attached to the Third Fleet, then anchored in the Inland Sea, were placed under my command.

Immediately prior to the Battle off Taiwan, we had an air raid by American carrier forces on Okinawa on 10 October. On the previous day one of our long-range patrol planes dispatched from the Kanoya Air Base in South Kyushu had disappeared far to the east of Okinawa. Except for that incident, we did not have a single indication of the enemy's approach. The attack on Okinawa was, therefore, a complete surprise. To make matters worse, we had stationed no planes on Okinawa at the time. We had not been fully prepared for launching counterattacks from Kyushu either. Consequently, we could not help sitting by as spectators to what was going on in the Ryukyu Islands.

Judging from the circumstances of the Okinawa air raid, we believed that the enemy would soon attack Taiwan. At 0930 on 10 October, the commander in chief of the Combined Fleet, Admiral Toyoda, expecting that an enemy invasion was imminent, issued an order to alert his fleet for the *Sho-Ni-Go* Operation. At noon on the same day, he sent out another order to have his fleet alerted for the *Sho-Ichi-Go* Operation too. On 11 October, for the first time, our scouting planes were successful in discovering the enemy carrier groups. Convinced that a major enemy air raid would be launched upon Taiwan early on the morning of 12 October, I ordered my forces to complete all the following measures during 11 October, thus to be made ready for the impending battle:

1) Except for fighters and reconnaissance planes, all small aircraft stationed in Taiwan should be closely concealed under cover. Planes of larger types should seek refuge in Kyushu.

2) The 230 fighter planes presently stationed in Taiwan should be divided into two groups of equal strength: One group should be assigned for counterattacking incoming enemy air forces in the air above Takao, and the other group in the air above Taihoku.

3) The TAF, with its base in Kyushu, should launch repeated night attacks against the enemy carrier groups at sea. Other air forces stationed in Kyushu should execute a formation attack in full force against the carrier groups, with the Ryukyu Islands as refueling bases.

The twelfth dawned quietly, but at 0810 a radar station on the east coast of Taiwan detected a great formation of enemy planes. This was the first wave of the enemy attack. All of our fighters took off from their bases at once; one group circled above Takao and the other above Taihoku to wait for and

346

counterattack the enemy. By this time Imperial General Head-quarters in Tokyo had issued orders activating the two major operations, *Sho-Ichi-Go* and *Sho-Ni-Go*.

Although I was thoroughly aware of the manifest inferiority of our airmen's military skill as compared with that of the enemy flyers, I was confident that, as far as the defensive fighting in the air over Taiwan was concerned, the odds would be in our favor at a 6:4 ratio. My confidence was based on two facts: first, we were able to use simultaneously as many as 230 fighters, a number that would, in all probability, exceed the number of planes the enemy carrier task force could dispatch at one time; and second, we were able to take advantage of our defensive position for counterattacking the invaders on our home ground. I expected that the foregoing two points would surely work in our favor, and that, therefore, no matter how superior the enemy flyers might be to our own men in military skill, there was no fear of our losing the fight.

What actually happened, however, was utterly contrary to what I had expected. As I watched from my command post, a terrific aerial combat began directly above my head. Our interceptors swooped down in great force at the invading enemy planes. Our planes appeared to do so well that I thought I could desire no better performance. In a matter of moments, one after the other, planes were seen falling down, enveloped in flames. "Well done! Well done! A tremendous success!" I clapped my hands. Alas! to my sudden disappointment, a closer look revealed that all those shot down were *our* fighters, and all those proudly circling above our heads were enemy planes! Our fighters were nothing but so many eggs thrown at the stone wall of the indomitable enemy formation. In a brief one-sided encounter, the combat terminated in our total defeat. Looking up at the enemy planes that continued their perfect formation intact throughout the combat, I could not help heaving a deep sigh. It was a total surprise to me to see that, while our planes caught fire the instant they were hit, enemy planes, though momentarily

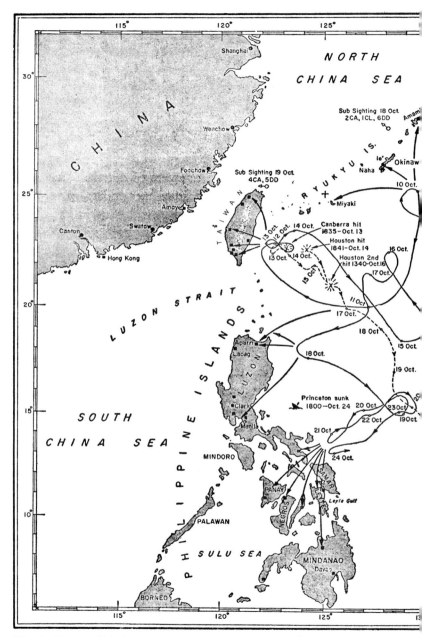

Track Chart of Task Force 38 Showing U.S. Attacks on Taiwan

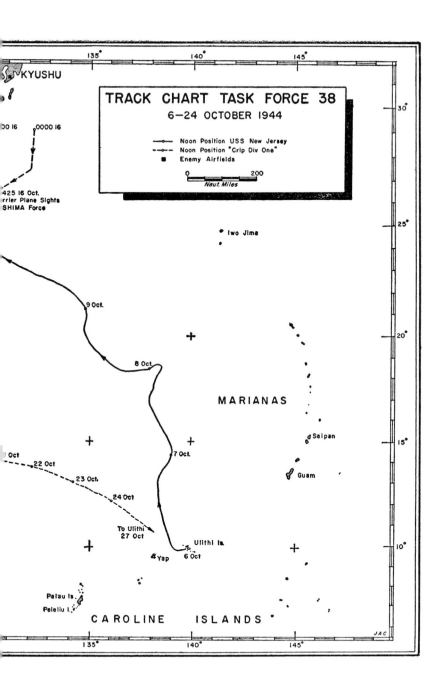

KYUSHU

00 16   0000 16

425 16 Oct.
rrier Plane Sights
SHIMA Force

TRACK CHART TASK FORCE 38
6–24 OCTOBER 1944

⊸— Noon Position USS New Jersey
–•– Noon Position "Crip Div One"
■ Enemy Airfields

0 _____ 200
Naut. Miles

• Iwo Jima

9 Oct.

+

8 Oct.

MARIANAS

Oct

22 Oct

23 Oct.

24 Oct

+

7 Oct.

+

⊘ Saipan

+

∅ Guam

To Ulithi
27 Oct

+

Ulithi Is.
6 Oct

⊘ Yap

+

Palau Is.
Peleliu I.

C A R O L I N E   I S L A N D S

JAC

349

smoking, did not catch fire, presumably because of their perfected fire-preventing devices.

Since our interceptors could not put up any real resistance, the enemy went on ravaging to his heart's content and inflicted terrific damage to our ground installations through strafing and bombing. Early on the morning of 12 October, a little before the attack by the enemy, my chief of staff, Rear Admiral Shie Sugimoto, recommended that, with a view to boosting the morale of the officers and men, I should remain in the exposed administrative office building instead of moving to the protected command post. But I thought otherwise and moved to the command post, which had just been completed in a cave in the middle of a hill about four thousand yards away from the administration building. About an hour later, in the first wave of the enemy attack, a bomb hit my office in the administration building and destroyed it completely. Seeing the destruction, the chief of staff said, "It is very fortunate that we moved to the command post as the admiral decided. If we had stayed in the administration office, all of us—the admiral and all other headquarters personnel—would have been finished." Looking into each other's faces, we could not help laughing ironically.

Though the number of fighters we lost in the first waves of the enemy attack was only about one third of our strength, the real effect was much more severe than the mere number suggests, since among those lost were many of the leader planes. Consequently, when the second wave of the enemy assault came, as few as between sixty to seventy of our fighters in the aggregate throughout Taiwan took to the air to meet the enemy. Worse still, none of them could offer resistance of any value. Finally, when the third wave came, none of our fighters could take to the air. True, the remnants of our fighters put up a scattered resistance to B-29s that invaded Taiwan from Chinese bases, but in that resistance, too, we could produce no appreciable result.

In the meantime, our forces based in Kyushu unleashed a

daring offensive against the enemy at sea. The offensive was launched on 12 October by 101 planes of the Second Air Fleet, utilizing Okinawa as a relay base. The sortie was made in a large formation in broad daylight and claimed, though dubiously, that two enemy carriers had been hit by bombs, with some damage. With reinforcement from the Third Fleet carrier squadrons, we repeated daylight formation sorties with about four hundred planes on 14 October and with about 170 planes on 15 October. But the last two-day sortie claimed no perceivable result, with most of the planes having failed to sight the target.

It was the TAF alone that was credited with giving an appreciable blow to enemy surface forces. Beginning with the night attack on 13 October, the typhoon-trained air unit conducted sneak attacks on three successive nights until the night of 15 October. Each night about thirty planes were used. Immediately after the Battle off Taiwan, Imperial General Headquarters announced that twelve enemy ships—cruisers and above—had been sunk and another twenty-three enemy ships had been otherwise destroyed. Most of this was credited to the TAF. Delighted by the victory, the commander in chief of the Combined Fleet, Admiral Toyoda, was determined not to miss this opportunity. On the morning of 15 October he ordered his entire fleet to make an all-out pursuit. Even the surface units then anchored in the Inland Sea were designated to join the pursuit. Needless to say, this pursuit ended in a fiasco.

In connection with the Battle off Taiwan, the forces of B-29s based on the Chinese mainland attacked Taiwan for three consecutive days, beginning on 14 October, and heavily bombed many important military installations, thus adding to the damage done by the carrier task groups.

As we have seen, the announced result of the Battle off Taiwan originated from the report by the TAF, which, under the command of Captain Kuno, was then based in Kyushu, away from my personal direction, though, as the Second Air Fleet commander, I was officially responsible for it.

After the war ended in 1945, I was told that of the ships in the U.S. Fleet only two cruisers had sustained serious damage. Why on earth had such an exorbitant exaggeration been made in our report? Having been informed of the real damage, I was startled indeed at the great discrepancy. We cannot shrink from the responsibility for having made such a report.

The losses on our part were really great. Against the surface units of the enemy carrier task forces, we made 761 sorties in all, and lost 179 planes in these sorties. In addition, we lost about 150 planes in the air and on the ground in Taiwan. The damage to the military installations was also very severe. An important aircraft arsenal that the Japanese navy had built at the Takao Air Base was reduced to mere debris in a brief severe bombing. My original confidence in our ability to fight out the battle with 6:4 odds in our favor was shattered. The battle was fought with 9:1 odds in favor of the enemy.

The results achieved by air forces were always exaggerated by airmen. This was particularly true in the case of a night assault. The basic reason for the exaggeration is that it is exceedingly difficult for the aviator to evaluate his success. As soon as the airmen came back to the base from their sortie, the commander closely interrogated each of them. The results of the interrogation were then submitted to superior commanders. Airmen, aspiring to fame, were likely to exaggerate their achievements. When they had attacked a destroyer, they believed it was a cruiser; a cruiser was often seen as a battleship; and a battleship was sometimes mistaken for an aircraft carrier. Night attacks resulted in universal exaggeration.

When two or more planes shared the same target, a single target was often claimed as several different targets. In a night action, the flare of a bomb-burst was not easily interpreted. Sometimes the flame of enemy gunfire was mistaken for direct hits. It seems to me that the airmen of the TAF repeatedly concentrated their attack on the same target, which was reported as a number of targets. Since we added these claims together, the result was an exorbitant exaggeration.

It is not very difficult to understand that such mistakes are likely to be committed. I, too, through statistical study, had determined that aviators were likely to magnify their battle achievements. When our flyers reported to us what they had actually witnessed, and then supported their reports with various evidence, we could not help accepting their claim. We had no concrete ground on which to deny it, except where we could clearly ascertain that there was a duplication or error. As the senior commanding officer stationed in Kyushu, Captain Kuno radioed his report directly to the commander in chief of the Combined Fleet and to Imperial General Headquarters, parallel to his reporting to me, the Second Air Fleet commander. Looking into his report, I realized instantly that it was undoubtedly exaggerated. Based upon my statistical study I thought the real result was about one third of what had been reported. As I have explained elsewhere, the TAF was the cream of my fleet strength and had been trained for night attack. I was convinced that such a trained unit could achieve one third of what it claimed.

As a matter of fact, however, the real result was less than one tenth of what it claimed. It seems to me that this is attributable to the fact that the daylight formation attacks were all fruitless, with the night attacks by the TAF alone being effective; and that the military skill of the TAF men who took part in the night attack was much inferior to what we had estimated. The exaggerated report caused Imperial General Headquarters to commit, though temporarily, a mistake in its estimate of the war situation. It made the nation indulge in a false celebration and created the illusion that the empire could turn the tide of the war.

For my part, I ascertained through the reconnaissance

planes' report on 16 October that the damage done to the enemy was slight, and I was convinced that a major invasion of the Philippines would soon be launched. As soon as the Battle off Taiwan was over, I made all haste with preparations for our move to the Philippine theater.

11

The Battle of Leyte Gulf

TOMIJI
KOYANAGI

The American liberation of the Philippines began with landings on Leyte Island protected by two fleets—the U.S. Seventh Fleet, with Vice Admiral Thomas Kinkaid under General MacArthur's operational control, and the U.S. Third Fleet, commanded by offensive-minded Admiral Halsey, who had orders to cover the Leyte operation and, if the opportunity arose, to attack the enemy fleet.

The Japanese command, anticipating an assault on the Philippines, decided to commit their remaining naval strength in an effort to disrupt the amphibious assault and, if possible, to destroy major components of the American fleet. This dual mission was to prove as confusing to the Japanese as was that assigned to Admiral Halsey, and it tends to explain some of the otherwise baffling developments during this complex series of engagements.

Actually, there were four major naval actions during the Battle of Leyte Gulf. Vice Admiral Kurita's Center Force was engaged in the Battle of the Sibuyan Sea, as well as in the Battle off Samar; Vice Admiral Nishimura's Southern Force was decisively defeated in the night action of the Battle of

Surigao Strait; and Vice Admiral Ozawa's Northern Force, successful in its attempt to decoy Admiral Halsey's Third Fleet away from Leyte Gulf, was badly mauled in the Battle off Cape Engaño.

Many of the factors that can affect the implementation and outcome of a campaign are revealed in the following article. The absence of a Japanese contingency plan to allow for possible adversity; the unavoidable reliance on surface forces to defend the Philippines; the hasty preparations necessitated by a two-month acceleration of the American timetable; the errors of judgment that stemmed in part from inadequate information and communications—all these combined with other circumstances to influence the multiple encounters.

Certainly there was enough blame on both sides to go around; as Samuel Eliot Morison has observed, "anything might have happened." But in retrospect it seems clear that Admiral Kurita did sacrifice an opportunity to inflict substantial damage on the American light carriers and auxiliary vessels supporting the Leyte landings.

IN 1944 I was chief of staff to Vice Admiral Takeo Kurita, commander in chief of the Second Fleet of the Japanese navy. Built around powerful battleships and cruisers, this fleet constituted the First Striking Force (sometimes translated First Diversionary Attack Force), which was the main attack force in the Battle of Leyte Gulf. Many critical accounts of this battle have been written, and I do not mean to challenge them. I wish only to recall and review the course of events and describe the battle as I saw it. Although wounded twice within two days, I was with Admiral Kurita throughout the battle, always in a good position to see what transpired. It is my hope that this essay may be of some value in clarifying the Battle of Leyte Gulf.

356

In June 1944 the Japanese navy suffered a devastating defeat in the fateful Battle of the Philippine Sea. We had to give up our hoped-for decisive battle and withdraw to Okinawa for fuel before returning to Kure. There the operations staff was called to Tokyo to report on the battle and confer regarding future operations. We had counted so heavily on a great victory to swing the tide of war in our favor that no plans had been prepared for the next move. Now the Combined Fleet and Imperial General Headquarters were both at a loss as to what to do. It was certain, however, that the Second Fleet must go to Lingga Anchorage because fuel necessary for training was not available in Japan.

At Lingga Anchorage, on the eastern coast of central Sumatra, we had trained in early 1944, only to lose three aircraft carriers and most of our carrier planes in the June battle. Now what remained of that fleet was at Kure, where all ships were being prepared to depart from the homeland—all, that is, except Vice Admiral Jisaburo Ozawa's Mobile Fleet, whose carriers were useless for offense until planes and trained pilots became available. Meanwhile, the fall of the Marianas was imminent, as American attacks were increasing in intensity. It was estimated that the next big enemy offensive would come within three or four months, and there was no hope that our carriers could be restored to fighting strength in that time.

Under these circumstances, only our Second Fleet and land-based air forces would be available for the next operation. But considering the low combat efficiency and reduced strength of our air force and the difficulty of cooperation between it and the fleet, it was clear that the latter would have to bear most of the burden. It also appeared that our next sea battle was likely to be our last.

We spent two busy weeks at Kure before starting for Lingga. For the first time, radar was installed in all battleships and cruisers. Antiaircraft guns were mounted on every avail-

357

able deck space. The work was carried out in grim determination with the knowledge that there would be no friendly air patrol for the next battle.

The First Striking Force arrived at Lingga in mid-July. On 10 August the operations officer and I flew to Manila for a conference. A member of the Naval General Staff predicted, in a situation estimate, that the next big enemy operation would be in the Philippines in late October. The senior staff officer of Combined Fleet Headquarters presented the *Sho* [Victory] Operation order, which was, in outline, as follows:

> Make every effort to discover enemy invasion forces at maximum distance (approximately seven hundred miles) by means of land-based air searches, and determine the enemy's landing place and time as early as possible so as to permit our forces to get into position for battle. The First Striking Force should be moved up to Brunei, North Borneo, in sufficient time to rush forward and destroy the enemy transports on the water before they disembark their troops. If this fails and the transports begin landing operations, the attack force will engage and destroy the enemy in their anchorage within at least two days of the landing, thus crippling the invasion effort.
>
> The First and Second Air Fleets will first make a surprise attack on the enemy carriers with a view to reducing their strength; then, two days before the arrival of our surface force, will launch all-out attacks on the carriers and transports and thus open the way for the First Striking Force to approach and engage the enemy.

Questions, answers, deliberations, and discussions followed. Disturbed at the idea of hurling our attack force in wherever the enemy attempted to land, instead of using it in a decisive engagement, I asked: "According to this order the primary targets of the First Striking Force are enemy transports, but if by chance carriers come within range of our force, may we, in cooperation with shore-based air, engage the carriers and then return to annihilate the transports?"

This question was answered affirmatively by Combined Fleet Headquarters.

Once the plans were clear, fleet training began at Lingga, with emphasis on the following points:

> 1) Antiaircraft action. Enemy air attacks must be repelled solely by our shipboard firepower. Every weapon, down to and including rifles, must be used at maximum efficiency for this purpose.
>
> 2) Evasive maneuvers against air attack. We practiced fleet ring formations and mass maneuvering as well as individual ship movements to evade bombs and torpedoes.
>
> 3) Night battle training was stressed as a possible opening to a decisive fleet engagement. Special emphasis was placed on night firing of main batteries with effective use of star shell and radar. Aggressive torpedo attacks were also worked out and tested.
>
> 4) Battle within the enemy anchorage. There were many problems to be worked out on this point, such as how to break into the anchorage where enemy shipping would be massed; how to destroy the enemy screening force; and how to attack the transports.

During our three months' stay at Lingga, the training progressed most satisfactorily. We were fortunate in having unlimited fuel available from Palembang, Sumatra. Our radar sets were the best available. And thanks to the guidance and assistance of electronics experts from the homeland, who worked night and day in training radar operators, the sets were dependable and accurate in locating targets, and valuable in increasing the accuracy of our heavy-caliber gunfire.

While training continued, high-ranking officers made studies of various locales and tactics. There were three likely landing points in the Philippines: Lamon Bay in the north, Leyte Gulf in the middle, and Davao Gulf in the south. Passages and pertinent topographical data were carefully analyzed. Fleet instructions and methods of approaching these areas were diligently studied and deliberated, and there were frequent conferences.

Such large-scale penetration tactics as confronted us had never been practiced in peacetime. As the studies progressed, the difficulties of our task became more apparent. But training gave us confidence that we would be able to withstand enemy air attack, and the idea developed that we could put up a good fight. We felt sure that the problem of penetrating the anchorage could be solved.

The Combined Fleet policy that our force should destroy enemy transports at anchor, and not engage his carrier task force in decisive battle, was opposed by all of our officers. The U.S. Fleet, built around powerful carrier forces, had won battle after battle ever since attacking the Gilbert Islands. Our one big goal was to strike the U.S. Fleet and destroy it. Kurita's staff felt that the primary objective of our force should be the annihilation of the enemy carrier force and that the destruction of enemy convoys should be but a side issue. Even though all enemy convoys in the theater should be destroyed, if the powerful enemy carrier striking force was left intact, other landings would be attempted, and in the long run our bloodshed would achieve only a delay in the enemy's advance. On the other hand, a severe blow to the enemy carriers would cut off their advance toward Tokyo and might be a turning point in the war. If the Kurita force was to be expended, it should be for enemy carriers. At least that would be an adornment for the record of our surface fleet, and a source of pride to every man.

Our greatest fear was that our planes might not locate the enemy at maximum search radius, in which case our force would be unable to reach the transports before they began unloading. If our attack should be delayed until several days after the enemy invasion, then judging from past experience, his transports would be emptied by the time of our arrival. It would be foolish to sink emptied transports at the cost of our great surface force!

While we tried to break into the anchorage, the enemy carrier forces would rain incessant air attacks upon us, and probably force us to a decisive engagement before we could even reach the transports. Thus top priority should be given to engaging the carrier striking force of the enemy.

Our officers were of the opinion that the commander in chief of the Combined Fleet should come from the homeland and personally command his fleet at this crucial phase of the war. Many officers also complained about the Combined Fleet's basic policy and expressed the hope that the operation order would be modified. But since it was an order, there could be no talk of changing it, and we had to comply without hesitation or question. Outwardly I rejected all complaints of this nature, but inwardly I understood and sometimes even agreed with my officers.

In short, our understanding was that we were to make every effort to break into the enemy's anchorage, but if the enemy striking force came within range, then we would carry on a fleet engagement.

I still believe that the Combined Fleet understood this to be our operational policy, because it had been fully explained in Manila and was later submitted in writing. But our whole force was uneasy, and this feeling was reflected in our leadership during the battle.

In the early morning of 21 October 1944, we received a Combined Fleet order to break into Tacloban Anchorage at dawn on 25 October and there destroy enemy ships. There were three routes from Brunei to Leyte Gulf:

1) Through Balabac Strait, east into the Sulu Sea, and into Tacloban Anchorage through Surigao Strait.

2) North through the Sulu Sea, transit San Bernardino Strait, turn south along the east coast of Samar, and approach Tacloban from the east.

3) North through Palawan Passage, into the Sibuyan Sea, pass through San Bernardino Strait, and head south along Samar to Tacloban.

361

A Japanese battleship, either the *Fuso* or the *Yamashiro*, under U.S. air attack as she heads toward Surigao Strait—and destruction— in October 1944. *Official U.S. Navy photograph*

Analyzing these, we found that number one was the shortest course to our objective, but it was within range of Morotai-based enemy search planes and would expose us to attack for the longest time. Number three was beyond enemy searchplane range and offered less chance of encountering carrier air patrols, but it was the longest route and it passed through the narrow Palawan Passage, a favorite hangout of enemy submarines. Number two was a compromise between one and three.

The Combined Fleet suggested that we approach in two groups, from the north and south, and it was accordingly decided that Admiral Kurita would take most of the ships via the third route, while a detachment of two old battleships and four destroyers under Vice Admiral Nishimura took route number one. These groups were both to reach Leyte Gulf at dawn on 25 October, a difficult achievement in itself considering the treacherous currents in narrow straits that each had to navigate. Timing was complicated by the great distances between the routes. And then there were the dangers of lurking enemy submarines and powerful enemy surface fleets. If concerted action was impossible, each force would carry out its attack alone.

The Kurita force sortied from Brunei on 22 October and was attacked at the next dawn in Palawan Passage by two submarines, with the result that the cruisers *Atago* and *Maya* were sunk and the *Takao* was seriously damaged.

The submarine hazard in Palawan Passage had been expected, and our force was keeping a strict alert and zigzagging at eighteen knots. But this submarine attack was a complete surprise, for we had sighted neither torpedo wake nor periscope and had no chance to evade. The main causes of our failure here were that a shortage of fuel restricted our speed and that we had no planes for antisubmarine patrol. All ship-based seaplanes had been transferred to San Jose, Mindoro, because the submarine threat had made it impossible to plan on recovering them. We tended to deprecate American submarines and torpedoes during the early part of the war, but by late 1944 they were our greatest menace, and our antisubmarine measures were totally inadequate.

When the flagship *Atago* was sunk, Kurita's staff transferred to a destroyer. Nine hours passed before we cleared submarine-infested waters and could transfer to the *Yamato*, flagship of the First Battleship Division. During this time Vice Admiral Ugaki in the *Yamato* had assumed temporary command of the entire force.

363

The cruiser *Takao* on her first speed run in 1932. The ship was damaged by submarine attack in the Sulu Sea on 23 October 1944. *Courtesy of Hajime Fukaya*

We had thought from the beginning that a *Yamato*-class battleship, the most powerful in the world, should have been flagship for the *Sho* Operation. The Combined Fleet, expecting a night action, rejected this idea because the commanding officer should always be in a heavy cruiser, the key ship of night actions. The Combined Fleet had never given up this traditional principle of fleet engagements, but the sacrifice of the *Atago* proved them wrong.

On 24 October Kurita's force in the Sibuyan Sea was the target of fierce raids by carrier-based planes from 1030 until 1530. The *Yamato*-class battleship *Musashi* was sunk, a heavy cruiser had to drop out of formation, and other ships were damaged. We had expected air attacks, but this day's were almost enough to discourage us.

Nothing was heard from Ozawa's mobile fleet, which was supposed to be maneuvering northeast of Luzon. We estimated that the enemy carrier force was just east of Lamon Bay, Luzon, but we had no indication that our air forces had been attacking it. Like a magnet, Kurita's force seemed to be drawing all of the enemy's air attacks as we approached San

364

Bernardino Strait. If we pushed on into the narrow strait and the air raids continued, our force would be wiped out.

We reversed course at 1530 to remain in the Sibuyan Sea, where we could maneuver until our situation improved, and at 1600 dispatched a summary report to the Combined Fleet; it concluded with our opinion that

> Were we to have forced our way through as scheduled under these circumstances, we would merely make of ourselves meat for the enemy, with very little chance of success to us. It was therefore concluded that our best course was to retire temporarily beyond range of hostile planes until friendly planes could strike a decisive blow against the enemy force.

At the same time we sent a message urging land-based air forces to attack the enemy. When, by 1715, the enemy air raids had ceased, we turned east again, without waiting for the Combined Fleet's reply, and headed for San Bernardino Strait. We had expected the air attacks to be maintained at least until sundown, but the enemy must have wanted to recover his planes before dark. By continuing aerial contact with us, he would have known that our retreat was only temporary. Then the enemy carrier force commander could have ignored Ozawa's mobile fleet and concentrated his ships outside San Bernardino Strait to ambush us. If he had done so, a night engagement against our exhausted force would undoubtedly have been disastrous for us.

Thus the enemy missed an opportunity to annihilate the Japanese fleet through his failure to maintain contact in the evening of 24 October. On the Japanese side, of course, Admiral Kurita should have notified Nishimura of our temporary retreat and ordered him to slow his advance. At 1915, a message was received from Commander in Chief Toyoda, which read: "With confidence in heavenly guidance, all forces will attack!"

Another message received from his chief of staff said:

Admiral Soemu Toyoda, commander in chief of the Combined Fleet, aboard his flagship *Oyodo*, about September 1944. *Official U.S. Navy photograph*

"Since the start of this operation, all forces have performed in remarkable coordination, but the First Striking Force's change in schedule could mean failure for the whole operation. It is ardently desired that this force continue its action as prearranged."

These messages clarified the decision of the Combined Fleet, so we responded: "Braving any loss and damage we may suffer, the First Striking Force will break into Leyte Gulf and fight to the last man." And another message was sent to air bases requesting attacks coordinated with the surface fleet.

Six hours behind schedule, we finally passed through San Bernardino Strait at midnight on 24 October and turned southward, hugging the east coast of Samar and planning to reach Leyte Gulf around 1000.

In the afternoon of 24 October, enemy search planes to the north located Ozawa's ships and judged them to be the main Japanese force, and a threat to the amphibious operation in Leyte Gulf. Erroneously thinking that Kurita had withdrawn in the Sibuyan Sea, the enemy left his position at San Bernardino Strait during the night and proceeded northward to strike Ozawa's fleet, making this the one part of our plan that worked perfectly.

I still cannot understand how the enemy, with his highly developed intelligence system, so badly overestimated Ozawa's force of two old battleships, one regular carrier, three light carriers, three light cruisers, and ten destroyers.

Just as day broke at 0640 on 25 October and we were changing from night search disposition to antiaircraft alert cruising disposition (ring formation), enemy carriers were sighted on the horizon. Several masts came in sight about thirty kilometers to the southeast, and presently we could see planes being launched.

This was indeed a miracle. Think of a surface fleet coming up on an enemy carrier group! We moved to take advantage of this heaven-sent opportunity. The *Yamato* increased speed instantly and opened fire at a range of thirty-one kilometers. The enemy was estimated to be four or five fast carriers guarded by one or two battleships and at least ten heavy cruisers. Nothing is more vulnerable than an aircraft carrier in a surface engagement, so the enemy lost no time in retiring.

In a pursuit the only essential is to close the gap as rapidly as possible and concentrate fire upon the enemy. Admiral Kurita did not therefore adopt the usual deployment procedures but instantly ordered, "General attack." Destroyer squadrons were ordered to follow the main body. The enemy withdrew, first to the east, next to the south, and then to the southwest,

367

on an arc-like track. In retreat he darted into the cover of local squalls and destroyer smoke screens, while attacking us continuously with destroyer torpedoes and attack planes.

Our fast cruisers, in the van, were followed by the battleships, and little heed was paid to coordination. Because of the enemy's efficient use of squalls and smoke screens for cover, his ships were visible to us in the *Yamato* only at short intervals. The enemy destroyers were multifunneled, with high freeboard. Their appearance and torpedo-firing method convinced us that they were cruisers. We pursued them at top speed for over two hours but could not close the gap; in fact it actually appeared to be lengthening. We estimated that the enemy's speed was nearly thirty knots, that his carriers were of the regular large type, that pursuit would be an endless seesaw, and that we would be unable to strike a decisive blow. And running at top speed, we were consuming fuel at an alarming rate. Admiral Kurita accordingly suspended the pursuit at 0910 and ordered all units to close. After the war I was astonished to learn that our quarry had been only six escort carriers, three destroyers, and four destroyer escorts, and that the maximum speed of these carriers was only eighteen knots.

Giving up pursuit when we did amounted to losing a prize already in hand. If we had known the types and number of enemy ships, and their speed, Admiral Kurita would never have suspended the pursuit, and we would have annihilated the enemy. Lacking this vital information, we concluded that the enemy had already made good his escape. In the light of circumstances I still believe that there was no alternative to what we did. Reports from our ships indicated that we had sunk two carriers, two heavy cruisers, and several destroyers. (We learned later that these statistics were exaggerated.) Our only damage was that three heavy cruisers had to drop out of formation.

Our task had been to proceed south, regardless of opposition encountered or damage sustained on the way, and break into Leyte Gulf. But for our unexpected encounter with the enemy carrier group, it would have been simple. We estimated that the enemy carrier task force that was east of San Bernardino Strait on 24 October had steamed south during the night and taken new dispositions the next day, separating into at least three groups so as to surround us, and that we had encountered the southernmost group.

We did not know on the morning of 25 October that Ozawa's mobile fleet had succeeded in luring the main enemy carrier task force northward. Admiral Kurita's main force consisted of four battleships, two heavy cruisers, two light cruisers, and seven destroyers. Our only report of enemy strength (transports and escorts) in Leyte Gulf was from Admiral Nishimura, who had the report of a *Mogami* seaplane reconnaissance at dawn on 24 October. We had to estimate that there would be a change in the enemy situation as a result of intervening events. We waited eagerly, but in vain, for reconnaissance reports from our shore-based air force.

The enemy situation was confused. Intercepted fragments of plain-text radio messages indicated that a hastily constructed air strip on Leyte was ready to launch planes in an attack on us, that Admiral Kinkaid was requesting the early dispatch of a powerful striking unit, and that the U.S. Seventh Fleet was operating nearby. At the same time we heard from Southwest Area Fleet Headquarters that a "U.S. carrier striking task force was located in position bearing 5 degrees distant 130 miles from Suluan light at 0945." (This report was later found groundless.)

Under these circumstances, it was presumed that if our force did succeed in entering Leyte Gulf, we would find that the transports had already withdrawn under escort of the Seventh Fleet. And even if they still remained, they would have completed unloading in the five days since making port, and any success we might achieve would be very minor at best. On the other hand, if we proceeded into the narrow gulf, we would be the target of attacks by the enemy's carrier-

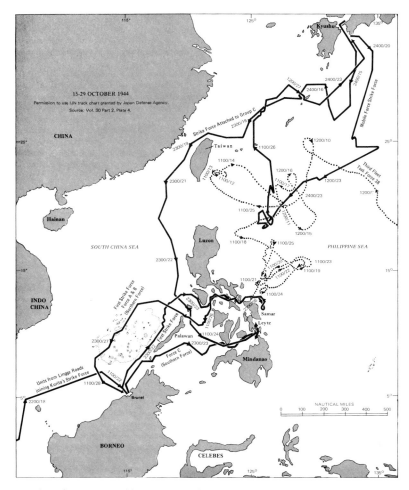

Battle of Leyte Gulf—Approach and Retirement, 15–29 October 1944

and Leyte-based planes. We were prepared to fight to the last man, but we wanted to die gloriously.

We were convinced that several enemy carrier groups were disposed nearby and that we were surrounded. Our shore-based air force had been rather inactive, but now the two air fleets would surely fight all-out in coordination with the First Striking Force. If they could only strike a successful blow, we might still achieve a decisive fleet engagement, and even if we were destroyed in such a battle, death would be glorious.

It was these considerations that made us abandon our plan to break into Leyte Gulf. We proceeded northward in search of the enemy carrier groups.

Looking back today, when all events have been made clear, we should have continued to Leyte Gulf. And even under the circumstances and with our estimate of the enemy situation at that time, we should have gone into the gulf.

Kurita and his staff had intended to take the enemy task force as the primary objective if a choice of targets developed. Naturally, our encounter with the enemy off Leyte on 25 October was judged to be the occasion for such choice.

On the other hand, there was considerable risk in changing our primary objective when we did not know the location of the other enemy task forces or how effective our land-based air forces would be. We should have chosen the single, definite objective, stuck to it, and pushed on. Leyte Gulf lay close at hand and could not run away.

Enemy air raids of 24 October had been fierce, and the next morning three of our heavy cruisers were damaged by air attacks. That afternoon we were pounded by carrier planes with no fatal damage, but near misses caused most of our ships to trail oil. On the morning of the third day we were again attacked from the air, and the light cruiser *Noshiro* was sunk. Around 1100, the flagship *Yamato* was the target of about thirty B-24s. The flagship suffered no direct bomb hits, but near misses around her bow raised gigantic columns of water. In this raid I was wounded in the waist by splinters from a bomb blast.

In three consecutive days the enemy sent some one thousand aerial sorties against us. Never was a fleet so heavily pounded by air attack.

To a surface fleet there is no engagement so disadvantageous and ineffective as an antiaircraft action. It does not pay off. We had no air cover to repel the enemy, for whom it was a pure offensive.

The *Yamato,* being the largest ship and flying an admiral's flag, was a constant target of attack. It was only through the maneuvering skill of her captain that she came out of the action virtually unscathed.

During these three long days of one-sided air poundings, our consorts were being sunk or damaged all around, but the men never faltered. They remained full of fighting spirit and did their very best. Their gallant attitude made them worthy of praise as the last elite of the Japanese Combined Fleet.

The enemy's high-speed battleships and carriers had headed south again upon learning that the situation at Leyte had become serious and that Ozawa had suddenly turned northward in the morning of 25 October. If the enemy carrier task force had seen that Ozawa's fleet was merely a decoy and had started south a few hours earlier, it could have caught Kurita.

In fact, after suspending our southward drive in pursuit of the enemy off Samar Island on the morning of 25 October, we fully expected to encounter the Americans before we could reach San Bernardino Strait. We were still ready for a last decisive battle under any condition.

Early in the morning of 24 October, the Americans had sighted Kurita's main force in the Sibuyan Sea as well as the Nishimura detachment to the south of Los Negros Island. Both forces could have been tracked thereafter to show our movements and destination. We had anticipated that, and we expected the Americans to take every measure to intercept us.

Our most serious problem on 24 October was getting through and out of San Bernardino Strait. Just the navigation of the strait was difficult enough with its eight-knot current, and transiting it by day with a single ship required considerable skill; one can imagine the increased difficulty of doing so with a large formation of ships at night.

372

In the strait we had to maneuver in a single column that extended over ten miles; once through, our formation had to be changed to a night-search disposition, which spread over a score of miles. At the time we were shifting formation, our force was extremely vulnerable to attack.

We anticipated enemy submarines at the exit of the strait to intercept us, and a concentration of surface craft to force a night engagement upon us. We were, therefore, greatly surprised when neither of these situations materialized.

We passed through the strait safely and headed southward, sure that the Americans were well aware of our movements. We also thought that the enemy's excellent radar must be tracking our force and plotting its every move. Thus we certainly never expected to encounter enemy carriers, as we did so suddenly at daybreak on 25 October. I still wonder why those carriers came so unguardedly within range of our ships' gunfire.

On land or sea, retirement is the most difficult of all tactics to execute successfully. But the retiring tactics of the American carriers in the Battle off Samar in the morning of 25 October were valiant and skillful. The enemy destroyers coordinated perfectly to cover the low speed of the escort carriers, bravely launched torpedoes to intercept us, and embarrassed us with their dense smoke screens. Several of them closed our force at 0750 and launched some ten torpedoes. The battleships *Yamato* and *Nagato* sighted them in time to evade but had to comb their tracks for five miles or more before resuming pursuit of the enemy.

The escort carriers maneuvered in tight combination. They made good their escape on interior lines, causing us to think that they were regular high-speed carriers. I must admit admiration for the skill of their commanders.

On 26 October the air raids against Kurita's force ended around 1100. As on the day before, we expected to be attacked all day long. We had not the least expectation that the enemy would suspend his raids an hour before noon. Perhaps

A salvo of shells from a Japanese cruiser (marked by the circle) falls around the ill-fated escort carrier *Gambier Bay* in the Battle of Leyte Gulf. *Official U.S. Navy photograph*

it was because we had pulled out of combat range of the enemy carrier task force.

Our greatest concern was that the enemy, following up his successes, might pursue us westward through San Bernardino Strait into the Sibuyan or Sulu seas and launch annihilating air strikes. If this threat had materialized, the American victory would have been complete.

374

Some may say that this would have been risky for the Americans. But what Japanese strength could have opposed U.S. carriers in pursuit of Kurita's retreating force?

Our shore-based air force, judging from its inactivity, must have been pretty well knocked out, and Ozawa's battered fleet had almost been destroyed. We might have inflicted some damage, but there was no Japanese force strong enough to give serious opposition.

American reluctance to give all-out pursuit is perhaps justified by some strategic concept that advocates prudence and step-by-step procedure; but from the Japanese point of view, the Americans gave up pursuit all too soon and missed chances of inflicting much greater losses upon us.

Analyzing the whole course of events of this battle, we see that chance played a definite role in each part of the action and thus influenced the whole.

As in all things, so in the field of battle, none can tell when or where the breaks will come. Thus events and their consequences are often determined by some hairbreadth chance in which the human factor has no control at all. Chance can make the victor of one moment into the vanquished of the next.

The Japanese navy's total of combatant vessels in this great battle theater was nine battleships, four aircraft carriers, thirteen heavy cruisers, six light cruisers, and thirty-one destroyers. Of these we lost three battleships, all four carriers, six heavy cruisers, four light cruisers, and seven destroyers. These losses, most of which were caused by air attacks, spelled the collapse of our navy as an effective fighting machine.

I would hardly say, however, that our losses were greater than we anticipated. Nor do I feel that the Japanese lost because their strategy and tactics were wrong, or that the Americans won because their strategy and tactics were particularly good.

The physical fighting strengths of both parties were too greatly divergent. On logical analysis, the *Sho* Operation plan

The escort carrier *White Plains* under fire of Japanese battleships at Leyte Gulf. This photograph was taken from the bridge of the *Kitkun Bay*. *Official U.S. Navy photograph*

formulated by Combined Fleet Headquarters was unreasonable. Both carrier- and land-based air forces had been weakened to a point where they could not be effectively coordinated with the surface fleet, which was thus subjected to concentrated enemy attack without any air protection.

In modern sea warfare, the main striking force should be a carrier group, with other warships as auxiliaries. Only when the carrier force has collapsed should the surface ships become the main striking force. However majestic a fleet may look, without a carrier force it is no more than a fleet of tin.

A decisive fleet engagement determines conclusively which contending party shall have sea and air supremacy. By October 1944 the Japanese fleet no longer actually had enough strength to carry on a decisive engagement. Its strength and ability had been so reduced that it had to resort to the makeshift plan of attacking transports.

Just think of sending a great mass of surface craft, without air cover, nearly 1,000 miles, exposed to enemy submarines and air forces, with a mission of breaking into a hostile anchorage to engage. This was a completely desperate, reckless, and unprecedented plan that ignored the basic concepts of war. I still cannot but interpret it as a suicide order for Kurita's fleet.

When Kurita suspended chase of the escort carriers off Samar on 25 October we had four battleships, two heavy cruisers, two light cruisers, and seven destroyers. Let us suppose that he had continued south, broken into Leyte Gulf as scheduled, destroyed all the transports and their escorts, and succeeded in withdrawing unscathed. Our initial operational objective would have been attained, but two facts remained. First, it was five days since the enemy convoy had started unloading. Hence, the transports would have discharged most of their cargo, making them practically worthless as strategic targets. Second, the convoy escorts were old ships and their destruction would have only slightly impaired the overall fighting efficiency of the enemy. If any of our ships had actually remained afloat after such an attack, they would still have been without carrier support, a tin fleet, existing only to be destroyed by the enemy. Their existence or nonexistence could not have affected the tide of war, and Japan was waning toward her final defeat. It is clear that our *Sho* Operation could not have influenced the outcome of the war.

During the Pacific War there were two decisive naval battles in which the whole outcome of the war hung in the balance. First was the Battle of Midway in early June 1942. At that time the fighting power of the Japanese Navy was at its zenith, and everyone in the Combined Fleet was firmly

377

The *Yamashiro* and the heavy cruiser *Mogami* under air attack in the Sulu Sea. The *Yamashiro* was sunk by surface ships, and the *Mogami* went down the next day. *Official U.S. Navy photograph*

convinced of victory. But our defeat in the carrier duel at the outset of the battle canceled our hope for a decisive engagement, and we had to withdraw.

The second was in mid-June 1944, the Battle of the Philippine Sea. There were many defects still to be remedied in our carrier striking force, but the Combined Fleet was able to engage in battle with a fair degree of self-confidence. Once again we suffered an aerial defeat in the opening phase of the battle, which drove us to a general retreat.

Until the battle for Leyte, our battleship force was relatively immune from loss or damage and did maintain its fight-

378

ing efficiency. To the uninitiated these ships must have appeared to be great floating forts, the key by which Japan might recover from her hopeless situation. But a fleet of superdreadnoughts alone, however powerful their guns, could no longer qualify as the main striking force in a decisive fleet engagement.

I have nothing but respect and praise for the excellence of weapons, thoroughness of training, tactical skill, and bravery of the enemy in this battle.

There is an old maxim: "Battle is a series of blunders and errors. The side that makes the least will win and the side that makes the most will lose."

The truth of this maxim was never more apparent than in the Battle of Leyte Gulf. Anyone who has experienced combat knows that errors in judgment made under fire are not always culpable. The ever-changing tide of battle subjects us to fate and chance, which are beyond our control.

ADDENDUM: INTERVIEW WITH THE AUTHOR

Captain Toshikazu Ohmae has been kind enough to translate my essay on the Battle of Leyte Gulf. After completing the task, he asked me two questions concerning the action which, because they may also occur to American readers of this article, I have tried to answer as fully as possible. The questions and my answers, which have been reviewed and approved by Admiral Kurita, follow:

Q. You [Vice Admiral Koyanagi] believe that the First Striking Force should have been committed to decisive battle with the enemy task force and should not have been expended on the enemy convoy. How did you estimate that the First Striking Force might have deployed to encounter and destroy the enemy task force?

A. It was obvious that without air support we had no chance of defeating the elite enemy task force of crack battleships and high-speed regular aircraft carriers. It was indispensable that we have the cooperation of friendly air forces.

379

The cruiser *Oyodo* alongside the damaged and listing *Zuikaku* off Cape Engano as Admiral Ozawa prepares to transfer his flag to her. The *Zuikaku* sank several hours later. *Official U.S. Navy photograph*

Analyzing Japanese air strength, however, we could see that with Ozawa's mobile fleet still recovering from its losses in the Battle of the Philippine Sea, there remained only our land-based air forces—the First and Second Air Fleets.

As it turned out, these two air fleets achieved practically nothing during the battle, whereas in planning the *Sho* Operation we had counted heavily on them. They should have conducted all-out attacks on the enemy fleet to support our surface force in this battle. If they had damaged enemy battleships and carriers, the First Striking Force could have carried out a decisive sea engagement.

We knew full well that the combat effectiveness of our air force was limited and should not be overestimated. It was the surface fleet that would have to bear the brunt of battle.

Despite all this, we were of the opinion that the First Striking Force should be committed to the destruction of the enemy task force, his strongest fighting unit, because this would be our last chance against it. This was the desire of all our senior officers, and we were happy with our assignment.

Q. You have said that the message giving the position of the enemy task force at 0945 was one of the main reasons for suspending our penetration into Leyte Gulf. This dispatch is not recorded in any document, but granting its existence, it pertained to the enemy task force approximately three hours before, and nothing had been reported since.[1] Hence our chances of catching this enemy were slim, while the stationary ships in Leyte Gulf could be hit with almost one hundred percent certainty.

I assume, then, that the First Striking Force gave up entering the gulf to seek the new enemy task force because of its belief that it should have been committed to the destruction of the task force in the first place. But the target of your attack was changed three times. Pursuit of the escort carrier group was abandoned after two hours' chase, and forces were concentrated for breaking into Leyte Gulf, but this objective was soon given up, and you proceeded northward in search of the newly reported task force. What caused you to change targets so often, and how did you plan to contact this enemy to the north?

A. Though I have already written about giving up the pursuit of the enemy escort carriers in the morning of 25 October, I can easily imagine that everybody wonders why we did not continue the pursuit of the vulnerable escort carriers and attempt their complete annihilation.

But as a matter of fact, we had concluded that these were regular carriers. (It was only after the surrender that I learned it was an escort carrier group, when I was interrogated by members of the United States Strategic Bombing Survey in Tokyo.)[2]

We judged that the enemy carrier group was steaming at a speed equal to or greater than ours because we did not close the distance to the enemy in two hours' pursuit. We could not observe the enemy situation because of local squalls and enemy smoke screens. Our intrafleet communication was so congested that we received no information of the enemy from our van cruisers, and we concluded that the cruisers had also lost contact with the enemy.

Another factor was that we could not be indifferent toward our fuel situation. Endless pursuit would mean fruitless consumption of valuable fuel, and the consumption of fuel in two hours' top-speed pursuits could not be overlooked. Our decision was to give up pursuit of the enemy carrier group.

The reason we then chose a northerly heading was that we wanted to separate from the enemy as much as possible. Critics may say that a southwesterly course would have quickened our regrouping, but there were local squalls to the southwest, and remnants of the enemy smoke screen still limited visibility. Moreover, we had to consider the offensive possibilities of the group we had just been chasing. Proceeding southward, we would be exposed to possible counterattacks by the enemy task group, which was thought to include high-speed battleships and large cruisers.

It was 1100 before we had regrouped, and by then not an enemy ship was in sight. Since the enemy force had been driven away, we determined to return to the initial strategic objective, breaking into Leyte Gulf, the operation set forth by the commander in chief of the Combined Fleet, and we accordingly changed our course toward the gulf.

Since our surprise encounter with the enemy task group early that morning, we had been so busily engaged in combat that there had been no time for cool analysis. Now that we were not engaged, the staff met for discussions of our next move. All available information was gathered and analyzed. It was concluded that the First Striking Force should give up the scheduled plan of breaking into Leyte Gulf and try for decisive battle with the enemy task force in the open sea. Admiral Kurita gave his consent to this new plan. The circumstances that led to this decision have been noted in detail in my essay.

It was certainly not a powerful enemy force in Leyte Gulf that repelled us from the gulf. In fact, we believed the force in Leyte Gulf to be rather weak. We seem to have been obsessed with the idea of the task force being our most important target.

After the war Admiral Kurita recalled:

> My force was attacked by an enemy bomber group that disrupted our formation as each ship evaded independently. I do not remember the exact time of that attack, but it was just after we altered course toward Leyte Gulf. It was at a point where many men from a sunken enemy carrier were floating. Unlike the sporadic attacks we had experienced that morning, this bombing was of a far larger scale and appeared to be more systematic. I concluded that fresh enemy carrier task groups had commenced all-out attacks upon us. Shortly before that we had known through enemy radio interception that the force in Leyte Gulf was requesting reinforcements and that it would be two hours before they could reach Leyte Gulf. From Manila had come a message giving us the 0945 position of an enemy task force. On the basis of these pieces of information we concluded that the powerful enemy task force was approaching. As it would be disadvantageous for us to be subjected to severe air raids in narrow Leyte Gulf, I thought we should seek battle in the open sea, if possible, where maneuvering room would be unlimited. The systematic air raid came just after I had reached this decision, so I immediately consented to the suggestion of my staff that we should seek the enemy task force instead of going after the ships in Leyte Gulf.

We had estimated that the enemy would not be far away, but we had not been able to confirm his exact position. We had no search planes, but we still believed that the Philippines-based air forces would conduct all-out attacks in the afternoon, delivering a serious blow to the enemy task force and revealing its position to us. We would then have a chance for a decisive sea engagement either by day or by night.

We anticipated no difficulty in making contact with the enemy task force, because we estimated that the enemy with all his power was already pursuing Kurita's force and would contact and challenge us by sunset at the latest.

12

Why Japan's Antisubmarine Warfare Failed

ATSUSHI
OI

Previous articles in this book have dealt with individual military actions. Although often dramatic and absorbing, accounts of particular battles tend to obscure the basic character of the war. It was not just a war of battles, of course, but also of production, supply, and communications. The industrial muscle Japan had developed since the turn of the century gave her great power but also new vulnerabilities. As a nation almost completely lacking in the natural resources needed for a modern economy, she had to protect her merchant shipping if she was to fight a long war. Yet most Japanese navy leaders thought in terms of the quick and decisive victories of the Sino- and Russo-Japanese Wars. Further, they had an anticommercial bias inherited from millennia-old Confucianism that made them ill-suited for cooperation with the merchant marine.

In this article a distinguished staff officer sketches out the background of Japan's economic war and the navy's lack of attention to antisubmarine warfare. The article's even tone of criticism and statistical demonstration of Japan's grim

385

losses in the war of attrition in the Pacific give it impressive authority, as does its broad reach: it covers the entire war, goes back to the prewar period, and even looks to the future. The author notes at the end that too little attention has been given to the problems of antisubmarine warfare. Yet since the oil crisis of 1973, something of a national debate has been going on in Japan about sea-lane defense. The subject has new relevance for the Japan of today, which is one of the world's greatest traders and importers of raw materials.

R ECENTLY I had an opportunity to read some American writings on the antisubmarine warfare (ASW) that the Japanese navy waged during the Pacific War. Among them are some chapters in *United States Submarine Operations in World War II* by Theodore Roscoe and *The War Against Japanese Transportation, 1941–1945* by the Transportation Division of the United States Strategic Bombing Survey.[1] As a staff officer of the Japanese Grand Escort Command Headquarters from its creation to its disbandment, i.e., from November 1943 through August 1945, I feel it my duty to explain what I know about the subject, so that the record may be made more complete. I take up this task particularly because the Pacific War records thus far compiled by the Japanese have said very little on the subject.

In a nutshell, Japan failed in ASW largely because her navy disregarded the importance of the problem.

Being at first a disciple of the British navy, the Japanese navy should have been very conscious of the importance of shipping protection. But by the beginning of this century she had established her own traditions on the basis of the proud lessons learned in the Sino-Japanese War of 1894–1895 and the Russo-Japanese War of 1904–1905. In the tradition-making era Japan was an agricultural state with little population pressure. Her sea-borne trade was not vital. Most of the naval lessons were learnt from the Battle of the Yalu, the Battle of Tsushima, and the other fleet-versus-fleet actions. True, there were some incidents where a troop ship was attacked and sunk. But the reflection of such incidents was overshadowed by the brilliant successes of many fleet actions.

World War I did little to add to the traditions of the Japanese navy. During the war, Japan became industrialized and depended more and more upon the sea-borne trade. She sent many destroyers to European waters to help the British navy in the fight against U-boats. But in studying the war, Japanese naval students, already imbued with the tradition of the Battle of Tsushima, liked to discuss the fleet engagements off Coronel, the Falkland Islands, and Jutland. Though some historians at the Naval War College lectured on the ASW of the British navy, they failed to arouse the interest of their pupils. Outside the Naval War College, the study of commerce protection carried little weight.

Maybe, at the bottom of our naval tradition, there was a problem of racial temperament. Compared with the Europeans, the Japanese are generally said to be more impetuous and less tenacious. They preferred colorful and offensive fighting to monotonous and defensive warfare. It was only natural that convoy-escorting and ASW were not jobs welcomed by Japanese naval men.

The more immediate reason for the neglect of the trade protection problem can be traced to naval policy, or rather national policy. As soon as the Russo-Japanese War of 1904–1905 was over, Japanese-American relations underwent an abrupt turn toward bitterness. In 1909 the Imperial Defense Policy of Japan was formulated. Up to that time Japan had thought, traditionally, that China and Russia were her most probable enemies. This time the United States was added to the long-standing list of probable enemies. Japanese leaders predicted that it was destined that the Japanese position in the Far East would collide with the westward expansion of the United States. Again, in 1922, as a result of the Washington Naval Armament Treaty and the Nine-Power Treaty, the Imperial Defense Policy was revised. Needless to say, Japan came to place more and more emphasis upon the United States as the probable enemy.

But Japan's national resources were miserably inferior to those of the United States. Moreover, since Russia and China were still considered probable enemies, Japan appropriated a large amount of money for the army, too, thus limiting the budget of the navy, which had to bear the main burden of dealing with the United States. With small means, the navy could not help concentrating its armament on one purpose, i.e., building and maintaining a first-line fleet strong enough to meet the American antagonist who was expected to come across the Pacific. Our navy also estimated that the U.S. Navy had no intention of waging any extensive warfare against merchant marines. The Japanese navy took it for granted that the role to be played by American submarines would be the same as that of Japan's own submarine forces, and slighted their role as raiders of commercial shipping. Those were probably the primary reasons why the Japanese navy neglected preparations for ASW.

In the 1930s the naval building race was resumed. While building a first-line fleet to compete with the mighty United States, the Japanese navy found it more and more difficult to divert its poor resources to the building of antisubmarine forces. Moreover, from its observation of the American naval building program, the Japanese navy became fairly well convinced that the American navy would seek a decisive fleet action as soon as possible. Meanwhile, the progress of the economic exploitation in Manchuria and North China begot a deceptive notion that the island empire was becoming a continental power with less dependence on sea-borne trade. The Soviet Union's buildup of a large underwater fleet was not taken seriously, probably because Japan already maintained a sufficient army in Manchuria with major logistic support there.

After the latter part of the 1930s the British Commonwealth was added to the probable-enemy list, side by side with the United States. Bewitched by Hitler's successive victories in Europe, the pro-Nazi expansionists clamored for seizure of the oil-rich southern resources area. Strangely enough, however, the problem of sea communications between the southern resources area and Japan was treated rather carelessly.

Japan's failure in ASW during the Pacific War had certainly been long destined. Further, I dare to assert that their singular underestimation of the submarine menace helped the Japanese leaders to cross the Rubicon. What underestimation was made in the decision of war or peace?

According to Vice Admiral Shigeru Fukudome's memoir, entitled *Kaigun no hansei* (Reflections on the navy), the Naval General Staff, of which the admiral was the operational division chief in 1941 and 1942, estimated in its pre–Pacific War study that the shipping losses in the contemplated war would be: for the first year of the war, between 800,000 and 1,100,000 gross tons; for the second year, between 700,000 and 800,000 gross tons; and for the third year, the same as the second year. The estimate was based on a study of World War I. First-year losses were predicted to exceed those in later years because the initial invasion operations involved great risk and because antisubmarine measures could not be adequate at the start of the war.

On 30 October 1941 the president of the Economic Planning Board (Lieutenant General Teiichi Suzuki) reported to the liaison conference between the government and the high command (the supreme policy-making conference) that:

1) If 3,000,000 gross tons of shipping bottoms were to be constantly secured for the use of economic purposes under civil control, the wartime mobilization plan would be effectively prosecuted; and

2) On the basis of estimates of the annual shipping losses at between 1,000,000 and 800,000 gross tons, and of annual shipping construction at about 600,000 gross tons, it was

389

expected that the shipping bottoms of 3,000,000 gross tons would be constantly secured under civil control.

If the estimate of the losses was low, the preparations for the prevention of the losses were more alarmingly neglected. All strategic policies and operational organization of the navy at the top level were decided in the operations division of the Naval General Staff. The operations division was divided into two sections: the first section of about ten officers, all chiefly dealing with the Combined Fleet operations; and the second section of three or four members, each separately in charge of miscellaneous duties including naval regulations, training, and near-line defense. The duty of shipping protection and ASW was included within the category of the rear-line defense of the second section. Before the fall of 1941, only one officer in the section was assigned for the entire duty of rear-line defense. With war imminent, the rear-line defense duty came under the care of two officers: one for mining and anti-aircraft defense and the other for protection of shipping. This allocation reflects the comparative weight the Naval General Staff gave to shipping protection warfare versus the Combined Fleet operations.

In the operational forces, too, this duty was relegated to an obscure position. The forces to take charge of shipping protection were the major and minor naval stations: the Yokosuka, Kure, Sasebo, and Maizuru Naval Stations and the Ominato, Osaka, Chinkai, Ryojun (Port Arthur, soon to be abolished), and Bako (later to be transferred to Takao) Minor Naval Stations. In these naval stations, from high-ranking admirals down to a green seaman, a notion was firmly seated that the major duty of the stations was to offer every possible service and accommodation to the Combined Fleet. The importance these stations attached to the protection of shipping may well be judged by the fact that the duty was attended rather halfheartedly in the station headquarters. For instance, in the headquarters of the Yokosuka Naval Station, whose area of responsibility included the sea lanes along almost the entire eastern and southern coast of Honshu (six hundred miles) and that from Tokyo Bay down to Iwo Jima (seven hundred miles), there was only one officer who dealt with shipping protection. This officer was called the staff officer for education, as he was mainly designated to administer various educational institutions. The remaining staff officers, numbering more than five, were largely indifferent to shipping protection. The same was true with the other naval stations.

As of 8 December 1941 there was no unit that had as its exclusive mission the protection of merchant ships. Such a mission was concurrently carried out by the forces engaging in sea patrol. As to troop transports, the escort was provided by units of the Combined Fleet as the occasion demanded. No convoy was organized in the case of nonmilitary shipping. Civil-controlled ships were encouraged to sail independently in order to secure the highest possible shipping circulation. Some regulations prepared for an emergency were laid down to control the sailing of merchant ships. Issued by each local naval commander, these regulations varied from one area to another, resulting in great confusion to ships' masters. It was not until the fall of 1942 that these regulations were unified in the form of a directive by the Naval General Staff, entitled "Doctrines Concerning the Protection of Sea Communications during the Greater East Asia War."

As we have seen, in calculating probable wartime shipping losses, the Naval General Staff consulted the record of World War I. As for the practical measures, however, little effort was made to follow the example admirably displayed by the Allied antisubmarine forces in 1917. Such an indifference on the part of the top strategists would produce a far-reaching effect. And the American navy men who are close students of Mahan may have doubts whether the Japanese strategists gave a moment's consideration to Mahan's lesson that only the nation that can both trade and fight will win a major war. The doubts are deepened more and more as we study the strategy the Japanese Naval General Staff followed during the whole course of the war.

As of 8 December 1941, the Japanese merchant vessels were distributed as follows:

Army use	519 ships	2,160,500 gross tons
Navy use	482 ships	1,740,200 gross tons
Civil use	1,528 ships	2,436,300 gross tons
Total	2,529 ships	6,337,000 gross tons

The figures shown above come from the history of the Maritime Commission of Japan compiled in Japanese by the commission in June 1947. Figures concerning wartime merchant shipping tonnage vary according to the source consulted. The figures shown above, however, are thought to be reliable. I will refer to Maritime Commission figures whenever possible in this article. I will also liberally refer to the U.S. Strategic Bombing Survey Report, *The War Against Japanese Transportation, 1941–1945,* since I believe its statistics are accurate enough for the purpose of the present study.

As has already been explained, the president of the Economic Planning Board demanded that at least 3,000,000 gross tons would have to be retained constantly for civil use. This was impossible at the outset of the war because of the extra shipping demand by the army and navy. In acquiescing to the military demand, the government obtained the high command's pledge that, of the military tonnage, 1,100,000 gross tons would be returned to civil control after April 1942, the expected date of the completion of the "first stage" of the war. The first stage was the period in which the Southern Resource Area, including the Dutch East Indies, Malaya, the Philippines, and Hong Kong, would be occupied. It was also expected that New Britain, as well as Wake Island and Guam, would be taken during this stage.

The invasion objectives aimed at for the first stage were

392

achieved much more easily than expected except for the hitch at Bataan. The army high command had a plan to return as many troops as possible to the homeland and Manchuria as soon as the first stage of the war was over. The army intended to attack Russia whenever a good opportunity was created by German military success in the west. The army also wanted to exert more military pressure against Chungking. The navy, on the other hand, was firmly convinced that Japan had to concentrate all her efforts on the enemies on the Pacific front, diverting no more forces to the continent. The navy thought that it would be suicidal to pursue a new war with Russia at a time when Japan's hands were more than full. It seems the difference of opinion on this most fundamental question between the army and the navy was left completely unresolved well into the middle period of the Pacific War.

For the present, however, elated with an easy success in the first stage, the military, with the navy taking the lead, improvised a more aggressive plan to extend the area of occupation. As soon as the sweep of the Indian Ocean was over in April 1942, the carrier task forces were ordered to prepare in haste for the next offensives. In May carefree operations were launched with a view to occupying Port Moresby in the south and capturing the Aleutians and Midway in the north, almost at the same time. The high command seems to have paid little heed that many more shipping bottoms had to be diverted from civilian use and the expanded line of communications would be exposed more and more dangerously to enemy attacks, inviting greater losses of tonnage.

It seems almost ridiculous from our postwar perspective, but a far more aggressive program than was actually put into execution was placed on the council table of the high command in the spring and summer of 1942. First of all, the navy proposed that the Hawaiian Islands be captured. With a shortage of troops as their reason, the army opposed the plan. Instead, the army considered occupying the Aleutians, the islands of Fiji, Samoa, and New Caledonia, eastern New

Guinea, the Cocos Islands, the eastern part of India, and Ceylon. Then the navy insisted on the occupation of the continent of Australia, which was also turned down by the army because of the logistic difficulties as well as the shortage of troops. Hot discussions ensued. It was finally agreed that the new areas to be occupied would include New Caledonia, Fiji, Samoa, the Aleutians, and Papua (including Port Moresby). If all of these far-flung occupations had been attempted, the deterioration of the Japanese shipping situation would have been incalculably faster and greater than actually occurred.

The reason the navy was more aggressive than the army in the plan of extensive occupation is two-fold. First of all, navy men had less trouble in the maintenance of the logistic support of their own forces, because the naval vessels could carry on board enough provisions and ammunition for many weeks. Thus they could maneuver independent of supply lines. Moreover, in case of adversity they could retreat as they saw fit. In the second place, the navy strategists foresaw from the very first that the war would be lost if prolonged. It was only natural that they were anxious to seek a decisive battle as soon as possible. To do so they had to create such opportunity even at some risk. Under the circumstances then prevailing, the American fleet would not come out if the Japanese fleet just assumed a wait-and-see attitude. To the above two reasons, one may add another: the navy wanted to draw the army's attention more to the Pacific lest the army should commit itself to the continent of Asia.

Earlier than calculated from the Pearl Harbor success, the second-stage aggressions in the Pacific were met by strong enemy counterattacks. In addition to the great adversities at Midway and on the Coral Sea, the airfield construction on Guadalcanal by a small naval unit gave birth to a disaster of the first magnitude. A bloody half-year struggle started for control of the strategic island. This proved to be the first instance where Japan incurred a major shipping sacrifice. Before this scramble started, some portion of these bottoms were gradually being returned to civil use by the military. As the result of the Guadalcanal struggle, however, many first-rate merchant vessels had to be again diverted for military use. As of the beginning of August 1942, the distribution of the shipping bottoms was as follows:

Under army control	1,382,900 gross tons
Under navy control	1,771,500 gross tons
Under civil control	3,112,400 gross tons
Total	6,266,800 gross tons

That was nearly the best situation of civil-controlled shipping in the entire course of the war. But the Guadalcanal operation had a high cost to the military bottoms, which had to sail in the waters not very far from hostile submarine bases as well as close to enemy air bases. As a result, by the beginning of January 1943 the shipping distribution had changed:

Under army control	1,623,400 gross tons
Under navy control	1,814,000 gross tons
Under civil control	2,629,300 gross tons
Total	6,066,700 gross tons

The prewar plan to secure 3,000,000 gross tons for civil use was thus shattered, not to be revived for the duration of the war.

In the meantime the interior regions were left almost entirely undefended. In some instances, what little had been installed for the defense of interior regions was dismantled to be transferred to fortify newly occupied frontier positions. Equipment that should have been used for antisubmarine purposes in rear lines (e.g., mines) was not excepted. In shipbuilding a similar development took place, and the construction of antisubmarine craft was deferred. In peacetime no antisubmarine craft were built, in the expectation that they could be easily and quickly built after a war was actually declared. In 1941, when the construction of four frigates was first approved, these craft were intended to be used not for escorting but for coastal defense or fishery protection. They were therefore called *kaibokan* (coast defense ships). Though frigates were later used almost exclusively as oceangoing escorts in face of the acute antisubmarine problem, it was not until June 1943 that the building of forty ships of this type was approved. And this belated approval does not seem to have been a willing one, judging from the fact that the antisubmarine branch requested 360 of them. Meanwhile, building priority was given to aircraft carriers, submarines, and high-speed navy transports.

Until 10 April 1942 the Japanese navy had no unit whose duty it was to escort merchant vessels. On that date, two escort groups were activated. The First Escort Group consisted of ten old destroyers, two torpedo boats, and five converted gunboats to escort merchant vessels sailing the 2,500-mile sea lanes between Singapore and the Japanese homeland (usually Moji). The Second Escort Group consisted of four old destroyers, two torpedo boats, and one converted gunboat to take care of military supply lines between Yokosuka and Truk. One glance indicates that these forces were far from adequate.

Even the belated birth of the two escort groups was made possible only with grudging consent. The officer at the Naval General Staff who insisted on the matter was temporarily transferred to the headquarters of the new First Escort Group, leaving his post in Tokyo vacant for about six months. As for the headquarters of the Second Escort Group, the personnel of the Fourth Base Force (with headquarters at Truk) were concurrently posted. During the entire Pacific War, the weakest point in naval preparedness lay in the scarcity of personnel whose experience was deemed to qualify them for staff duties. In other words, the Japanese navy was miserably lacking in naval academy graduates with the ranks of commander and lieutenant commander.

Luckily for the Japanese merchant vessels, however, some

of the American torpedoes proved to be ineffective. Frequently ships' masters saw premature explosion of enemy torpedoes. Some merchant vessels entered port with unexploded American torpedoes thrust into their hulls. A saying became fairly widespread that a tanker would not sink if torpedoed. Such being the case, the masters of merchant vessels preferred not to be bothered with convoy sailing. The shipping authorities wanted their ships to be allowed to sail independently, because sailing in convoy would mean a reduction of the efficiency of shipping circulation.

Postwar wisdom tells us that Japan should have reformed and strengthened her antisubmarine setup during these comparatively quiet months. Taking advantage of the God-given quietude, she ought to have made up for prewar negligence in antisubmarine preparedness. But this long period of quietude seems to have ultimately worked against Japan. The Americans built more submarines, trained submarine crews, and of course did everything to rectify the torpedo situation. Japan was lured to extend her lines of operation, exposing more and more of her precious shipping to enemy attacks. And nothing drastic was done to remedy antisubmarine unpreparedness. Besides the changes already mentioned, the only appreciable improvement in this direction was the creation on 10 October 1942 of an independent division within the Naval General Staff to take charge of shipping protection and other rear-line defense. The new division was named the Twelfth Division of the First Bureau. A captain headed the division, with three members as direct subordinates: one, a commander, took charge of homeland defense; another, a young lieutenant commander, convoy and routing, as well as antisubmarine activities in general; and the third, also a young lieutenant commander, the armament and signal equipment of merchant vessels.

If I remember right, it was about 20 August 1943 that we first realized that some innovation had come to the American torpedoes. The sinking rate of our torpedoed ships suddenly began to increase. Furthermore, since the previous spring our shipping losses in general had reached a higher level than ever before—far exceeding the level of 70,000 gross tons a month that the navy strategists had predicted in their prewar calculations. In the last days of August 1943 it also happened that the military at last began to doubt Japan's ability to check the predicted Allied onslaught in the Rabaul area, where, after the withdrawal from Guadalcanal, the army and navy had built up a fortified zone with a plan to stage a decisive resistance. The army had always been more willing than the navy to contract the Pacific front. This time, too, it was the army that first proposed to pull back the first line of defense to the area linking the Marianas, the Carolines, and western New Guinea.

Since July of that year I had been on the Naval General Staff as a member whose duty it was to assist the vice chief of staff in coordinating naval strategy with the overall national war policy. One bright September afternoon I happened to be sitting in a room where the navy vice chief of staff, Vice Admiral Seiichi Ito, was in a heated discussion with the army's vice chief of staff, Lieutenant General Hikosaburo Hata. The navy vice chief was at first reluctant to contract the defense line for the reason that more than ninety percent of naval defense materials had already been thrown into the Rabaul area, thus leaving very little, if any, to be used for the new proposed line of defense. To this the army vice chief retorted that the shipping situation was so much deteriorated that Japan would be unable to sustain the present Rabaul area for long. Finally the navy vice chief agreed to the army proposal. As of 1 September 1943, the Japanese merchant tonnage on hand was broken down as follows:

Under army control	1,179,400 gross tons
Under navy control	1,687,900 gross tons
Under civil control	2,692,500 gross tons
Total	5,559,800 gross tons

398

In connection with the program of retreating to the defense line of the Marianas–Carolines–western New Guinea area, two problems were raised: 1) Since a large portion of the military tonnage had been lost, additional bottoms were required to carry troops and materials to the projected new defense area; and 2) since the success or failure of the military operations became more and more dependent upon the air strength, there must be a very strong buildup of the air forces in the new defense area.

The high command requested of the government: 1) that a large amount of civil-controlled tonnage (at least 300,000 gross tons if this writer remembers correctly) be additionally transferred to army and navy control, and 2) that the production rate of aircraft be boosted to the level of 55,000 planes a year. The government could not swallow these requests. The shortage of civil-controlled shipping had been having a telling effect upon the economy of the nation, both in the field of munitions production and in the sustenance of people's lives. In order to raise the aircraft production to the mark of 55,000 a year (the best previous record was 1,470 a month in September 1943), the first essential was to have sufficient shipping bottoms for the importation of raw materials, such as bauxite ore from Bintan. Heated discussion was exchanged between the government and the high command, with the shipping problem as the center of argument. At last a compromise was reached: 1) that 250,000 gross tons of bottoms were to be diverted from civil control to the military, and 2) that the government would do its best to boost aircraft production to the mark of forty thousand planes a year.

The above compromise was based on the following understandings:

1) The high command would do its best to reduce the total of disabled merchant tonnage (through sinking and damage) below 1,000,000 gross tons a year (1944).

2) The high command would do its best, also, so that the efficiency of shipping circulation would be improved (mainly

through having escort forces more readily available, thus making it possible to reduce the time spent for convoy formation).

Both the military and governmental leaders felt that they were now faced with the gravest change in their war-making policy. The nation was also confronted with a great change in the world situation as Italy quit the alliance and Germany's fate in the war was open to question. On 30 September 1943, a conference was convened before the emperor between the leaders of the high command and the government. This was the most important imperial conference held since 1 December 1941. The salient points of the agenda were as stated above, with the addition of a diplomatic policy that the tie with Germany would be continued and that an effort would be made to mediate peace between Germany and Russia. This stage of the war also marked the inception of peace moves among elder statesmen, with Admiral Keisuke Okada taking the lead.

Despite this solemnized decision, the high command was very slow to act. No immediate effort was made to strengthen the defense of the Marianas–Carolines–western New Guinea zone, probably owing to the shortage of ships and defense materials. Instead, the Combined Fleet continued to commit itself, more deeply than ever before, to the death struggle in the Rabaul-Solomons area. The same apathetic attitude was maintained regarding shipping protection. The shipping losses in September soared to the highest record thus far of 172,083 gross tons, calling for urgent remedial measures. But no such measures were taken during October.

As we have seen, the fundamental weakness of the antisubmarine machinery lay in the fact that it lacked strong representation at navy headquarters, or the "Red Bricks." (The Navy Ministry and Naval General Staff were colloquially called the Red Bricks by navy men because of the red brick building in Tokyo in which they were housed.) Every nook and cranny in the Red Bricks was dominated by the influence of the Combined Fleet. Since almost the entire resources of the navy had been allocated to the Combined Fleet, no drastic improvement in antisubmarine measures was feasible without sacrificing the fleet strength in one way or another. Under such circumstances, it was evident that the first requirement in strengthening ASW was to have its voice resoundingly echoed in the Red Bricks. It was thus finally decided that a strong headquarters capable of competing with the Combined Fleet Command be established.

When I was asked for my opinion, I expressed my view that the Naval General Staff itself should be reorganized after the pattern of the British Admiralty of World War I, which was reformed on 31 May 1917, with Rear Admiral A. L. Duff appointed as the assistant chief of the naval staff directly under Admiral Jellicoe. I was of the opinion that unless the Naval General Staff itself was ready to shoulder all the responsibility, it would be impossible for anyone to counterbalance the unbridled influence of the Combined Fleet.

On 15 November 1943 the Grand Escort Command Headquarters (GEHQ) was created to exercise supervision and operational command over all the major and minor naval stations in the matter of shipping protection. The First and Second Escort Groups were placed under the direct command of the new GEHQ. Thus, every sea area except those outside the jurisdictions of the Combined Fleet and the China Seas Fleet became the area of responsibility of the GEHQ. In other words, only such local routes as those running between Truk and the Marshalls, south of Truk, south of Palau, south of the Philippines, in the Dutch East Indies, west of Singapore, and between Chinese ports were outside the responsibility of the GEHQ. Admiral Koshiro Oikawa was appointed commander in chief of the GEHQ. He was a former navy minister and was senior to all admirals in the operational field. And seniority was worth something in the Japanese navy.

Certainly the creation of the GEHQ was a great stride forward. The unified control of convoy routing and other antisubmarine activities became a reality. But a closer analysis revealed many shortcomings. To man the headquarters to its full complement took much time.

Admiral Oikawa was no happier with the strength of the escort ships. As of 15 November 1943 he had under his command fewer than fifty ships of eight hundred tons and above, including four converted gunboats and several destroyers so obsolete as to be incapable of ocean sailing. The best of the escort ships consisted of some fifteen destroyers built between 1920 and 1925. Of them, only four composed a destroyer group. When I recently read Samuel Eliot Morison's *The Battle of the Atlantic, September 1939–May 1943,* I was shocked by the striking contrast between American antisubmarine strength and that of the Japanese.[2]

In the list of Admiral Oikawa's forces as of 15 November 1943, we can see four escort carriers (CVEs) and the 901st Air Group. But all four CVEs had to undergo a great amount of repairs at navy yards. It was not until July 1944 that the first of them joined a convoy. One of them never joined. None could join more than twice, and most of them only once. The use of these CVEs was only experimental, perhaps doing more harm than good. To use the CVEs, it was necessary for the GEHQ to teach green fliers how to take off and land on a carrier. These fliers were forced to join a convoy mission before having been sufficiently trained. The result was numerous accidents to aircraft. And as soon as the fliers finished the first convoy trip, most of them were transferred to Combined Fleet carriers. We at the GEHQ felt very sorry to see the CVEs used not for ASW but rather as if they were training carriers. No wonder the convoys escorted by the CVEs met no luckier fate than others, the CVEs themselves falling victim to enemy submarines.

As for the 901st Naval Air Group, its initial condition was equally deplorable. In Japan no airmen had been specially trained for ASW. The group was the first air unit created for the exclusive purpose of ASW. Nor had there been established antisubmarine air doctrines. The group by itself had to develop the tactical doctrines from the start. It was necessary, therefore, for the group to be allowed much time for initial training and tactical study. But the shipping situation had deteriorated so wretchedly, with the monthly loss reaching as much as 265,068 gross tons in November, that the group was pressed to assume its mission about the middle of January 1944. In addition to the greenness of the airmen's skill, there was difficulty in communication between the air and the surface. Even the escort vessels, not to say merchant ships, had no facilities for direct communication with the air. Thanks to extraordinarily painstaking effort by the officers and men of the 901st Naval Air Group, the progress of their skill was rapid and tactical doctrines were developed by and by. But the air-and-surface cooperation was very slow to develop until the end of the war.

Certainly one of the softest spots in Japanese ASW existed in communications. At the time when the GEHQ was created in November 1943, the communications officer of the headquarters was surprised to find out that the system of communications varied according to each escort-of-convoy area because of the utter lack of unified control. While almost all convoys had to sail through two or more areas, it was impossible to secure good cooperation between neighboring commanders and between through-way escorts and local patrol forces.

Within a convoy itself, the situation was not much better. As we have seen, only four destroyers were organized into a destroyer group. All other oceangoing escorts were administratively independent of one another. There was neither unified tactical doctrine nor unified communication training between these individual escorts, which were temporarily assembled and composed to form an escort group as they were available and as occasion demanded. The overwhelming majority of these oceangoing escorts were "captained" by graduates from merchant marine academies. No matter how experienced they were in navigation and seamanship, merchant marine academy graduates proved, after all, to be inadequately qualified to unify and command a group of escorts. And they generally lacked interest in tactical matters. Because of the serious shortage of naval academy graduates, the Navy Ministry adhered to the policy of appointing graduates from merchant marine academies as commanding officers of the frigate-class ships. To formulate a permanent group of escorts would require an appointment of a competent naval academy graduate as the group commander. Despite persistent solicitations by the GEHQ, the Navy Ministry continued to turn a deaf ear.

In communication equipment and personnel, escort vessels were poorly treated. Obsolete equipment and personnel with inferior records were appropriated to these ships, since the navy always gave priority to equipping and manning the battleships, cruisers, carriers, etc., of the Combined Fleet. The communication division of a frigate consisted of six radiomen and one cryptographer, including at least one person whose skill was considered average or above by the standard of the navy. The condition of merchant ships was hopeless indeed. The army relentlessly exercised its authority to conscript men of military age. Naturally, the majority of merchant marine radiomen had been taken away to the armed forces. It was only after the shipping situation became irretrievably grave that the military authorities came to be more considerate in the matter. The GEHQ's efforts to introduce TBY (the intraconvoy radio telephone system) met a belated partial success in the case of escort vessels but ended in complete failure in the case of merchant ships.

One of the most pressing needs felt by the GEHQ was the use of radar in ASW. By the fall of 1943 both antiair and antisurface radars had generally been installed on first-line combat vessels of the Combined Fleet. As soon as the GEHQ was inaugurated, we made a strong plea for quick installation of the devices on escort vessels and antisubmarine planes.

Beginning in the spring of 1944, some of the escort vessels were experimentally equipped with radar. But it was not until late in the year that the electronic weapons were generally used by most of the oceangoing escorts.

There was no question that the best way to prevent the mounting shipping losses was to adopt a convoy system in full measure. As we have seen, however, in the fall of 1943 the cry was still loud for a faster circulation of shipping. On the other hand, there was no hope of an early remedy for the extreme shortage of escort vessels. The GEHQ, caught in this dilemma, hit upon the idea that faster shipping circulation would not necessarily be unfeasible if the best use of geographic advantage could be made. The idea occurred first to Admiral Oikawa. He himself penciled the plan, the heart of which was as follows:

1) The sea area linking the East China Sea, the Taiwan Strait, and the South China Sea was to be made safe from submarine intrusion, so that within this sea area merchant ships would be able to sail independently, without forming a convoy, and thus secure the highest possible efficiency of shipping circulation. For this purpose, the island chain comprising the Ryukyus, Taiwan, the Philippines, and Borneo was to be connected with mine barriers. As for places where mine-laying was not feasible, land-based radars and sonars as well as patrol planes and patrol vessels would guard the sea gaps.

2) The sea belt along the Nampo Shoto (including the Bonin and Volcano islands) and the Mariana Islands was to be guarded by radar stations that would be installed on these islands, as well as by patrol planes and ships, so that enemy submarines would find it difficult to invade the sea belt. Convoys would sail within the belt.

3) The sea lanes along the southern coast of Honshu (between Yokohama and Kobe) and along the eastern coast (between Yokohama and the ports of Hokkaido) would be guarded with shore-based radars, patrol planes, and patrol ships, so that ships would be free to sail safe from the sub-

405

marine menace. In those days the Sea of Japan and the Yellow Sea were not infested with submarines.

The idea was very enthusiastically received in government circles, although the Naval General Staff gave half-hearted support. The people of the Naval General Staff first insisted that all mines then on hand had to be reserved against the probable emergency of Russian entry into the war. Though this obstacle was at last surmounted, and though the government consented to appropriate necessary materials(especially steel) for the production of a sufficient number of mines, only four minelayers were made available. The minelaying took so much time that only the East China Sea and the Taiwan Strait had been partly mined before the air supremacy over the projected sea area had been wrested from Japan's hand. As for shore-based radars, the blueprint was completed in no time, but only one or two stations were actually installed before Okinawa was taken.

In the meantime the GEHQ delayed the adoption of a full-fledged convoy system. As late as mid-February 1944 the government was very much averse to the adoption of the convoy system. The more tonnage lost, the speedier circulation of shipping was needed in order to make up for the loss of shipping capacity. Admiral Oikawa's safety-zone plan was an honest reflection of the atmosphere. With no reasonable hope of success, the GEHQ attempted to set up such safe navigation zones in accordance with Oikawa's program. Indeed, the GEHQ was pressed by those concerned with shipping activities to have more ships freed from convoys, though convoys then formed were very small, consisting of between two and five ships in general.

In the GEHQ, I was in charge of arranging and routing convoys. Before that, in 1938–1939, I had studied British affairs in the Intelligence Bureau of the Naval General Staff. I knew better than the average Japanese about the convoy system the British navy had adopted in 1939. Late in 1939 some British naval bulletins describing escort-of-convoy activities were captured from an airmail bag dropped into the sea by a British plane. Of course I had drawn various lessons from the World War I British experience. But I had lacked firsthand experience. It took some time before I became confident in my opinion that a full-fledged convoy system must be adopted at any cost.

On 3 February 1944 an important oil-tanker convoy consisting of the *Goyo Maru* and the *Ariake Maru* was annihilated by a submarine in the middle of the East China Sea. The convoy was escorted by a frigate of the best type (displacement, 1020 tons), named the *Sado*. One escort per two ships was, of course, the best possible protection the GEHQ could afford to provide. This incident convinced me that one escort lacking cooperation with other escorts was of little use. If I remember correctly, the *Sado* acted merely as a rescue ship, unable to fight the enemy submarine.

On 19 February a more serious incident occurred, this time in the middle of the South China Sea. As is vividly described in Theodore Roscoe's book, five middle-size tankers, filled with as much oil as they could hold, hurried home under escort by a frigate named the *Shimushu*, the same type as the *Sado*.[3] This convoy was deemed an unusually important one, and its safe passage was anxiously awaited in oil-thirsty Japan. Then a report came that all of the five tankers had been sunk, which caused a great shock. Of course I, the operations officer of the GEHQ, was especially sorry.

I at once proposed that the system of convoy be reformed so that at least three escorts would be attached to each convoy plying between Moji and Singapore. Since in those days a convoy had been composed of from two to five ships with an escort, the proposal meant that each convoy should include about fifteen ships. To the Americans and Britishers who used to run a convoy of as many as seventy ships in the Atlantic, the operation of a fifteen-ship convoy is mere child's play. As we have seen, however, the Japanese preferred as small a convoy as possible. Escort commanders were also

407

afraid to include a large number of ships in a convoy. Formation of a convoy in more than three columns abreast was thought to cause confusion and collisions. Ships' masters were not trained for such complicated formations, and intra-convoy signals were extremely poor. Such being the case, when I made the proposal, I rather expected it would meet considerable opposition.

It happened that February 1944 saw the Japanese idle dreams shattered in quick succession. Early in the month the Marshalls fell. The Combined Fleet, which had long planned to fight a decisive fleet-versus-fleet engagement at the first opportunity, did nothing to challenge the invading U.S. Fleet to the cherished battle. Instead, it retreated to the homeland and to Palau. Having thrown ashore all its carrier-borne flying units to fight a war of attrition in the Rabaul area contrary to the supreme decision at the 30 September 1943 imperial conference, it was only natural that the Combined Fleet was unable to meet the U.S. Fleet at this time. Then, suddenly, on February 17–18, the U.S. carrier task forces raided Truk, which had long been used as the major base of the main body of the Combined Fleet. Though the fighting groups of the fleet had evacuated, many tankers and cargo ships of the fleet trains still remained in the harbor. In the two-day raid, a colossal total of nearly 200,000 gross tons of shipping was sunk or otherwise disabled. When the news reached Tokyo, the shock was beyond description.

In addition to the above disasters, there was another factor that worsened the shipping situation. To the utter neglect of the 30 September decision, the high command had used and spent a great amount of tonnage by continuing the struggle in the Rabaul-Solomons area. The projected fortification of the Marianas–Carolines–western New Guinea zone had thus been neglected. Now this vital zone was defenseless from an impending attack by the U.S. Fleet. Immediate fortification was needed, but there was no shipping available unless appropriated from the civil pool. No matter how wretchedly depleted the civil tonnage itself was, the civil authorities could not help responding to the S.O.S. by the military. A new transfer of 300,000 gross tons was agreed. But this was not all. The shipping losses caused by submarine attacks, too, were surprisingly great in both January and February, amounting to 240,840 and 256,797 gross tons respectively.

Though the exact reason was not clear at the time, it was probably due to the above situation that the proposal of a full-fledged convoy system was agreed to even by those who had thus far been strongly opposed. In other words, it seems the sudden and drastic reduction of tonnage caused everybody to admit that the preservation of tonnage was more essential than a higher efficiency of shipping circulation.

We called the new system a large convoy system. By the standards of the Americans and Britishers, it is certainly a misnomer, since the new system envisaged a convoy formation of only ten to twenty ships. But we were quite sincere in calling it that, and the system became operative at the beginning of March.

An extensive transport of troops and materials was started to the Marianas and the Carolines in March and to the Moluccas in April. The Naval General Staff and Navy Ministry, which were so far reluctant to appoint naval academy graduates to ASW posts, created a command set-up called the Escort-of-Convoy Headquarters, to ensure the safest possible passage of the transport of mid-Pacific fortifications. Since the adoption of a large convoy system required an efficient command organization, this was a very welcome coincidence.

The composition of the Escort-of-Convoy Headquarters had a fundamental weakness. The key personnel were a commander and a staff officer. The appointment of the commander was fortunate because he was a rear admiral with a good sea record. But the choice of the staff officer was very unfortunate, because he was appointed (from among members of the Naval General Staff, the GEHQ, or some naval schools) only temporarily and just before the sailing of each convoy. Such a temporarily appointed officer was unable to have time enough to prepare for the sailing. Such an impromptu relationship made it, also, difficult for him and his commander to understand each other's ability and personality. At any rate, many of the headquarters with a temporarily appointed staff officer perished during their convoy trip. Later the practice was gradually abandoned, to be replaced by the permanent appointment of the staff officer.

People in the Red Bricks used to say that escort-of-convoy was *common sense to a navy officer*. As a matter of fact, common Japanese naval officers had little knowledge or experience in this branch of warfare. Even destroyer men disliked this duty. Once I talked with a destroyer group commander on an escort mission. He said, "We are not trained to accompany merchant vessels but to fight a fleet action." In May–June 1944, the Japanese Mobile Fleet, staying at Tawi-tawi in preparation for the impending Battle of the Philippine Sea, wanted to send carriers to sea to give training to fliers. Since submarines infested the sea, destroyers were sent to hunt them. But four of the destroyers were sunk in quick succession, thus resulting in the abandonment of the training plan. The long break in the aviators' training immediately preceding the Battle of the Philippine Sea cost very dearly. Moreover, soon after the battle began, the two best carriers were sunk by submarines. It can be said that Japan lost the Battle of the Philippine Sea through her neglect of ASW training. At any rate, the attitude of the destroyer group commander was common among Japanese navy men.

Overall shipping losses in March were still very high because of air attacks at Palau. The Combined Fleet was at Palau in March with a plan quickly to intercept a prospective enemy invasion in the Marianas-Carolines zone. But the carrier strength of the Combined Fleet was away at Singapore. Late in March, when the U.S. fast carrier task force appeared off Palau, the Combined Fleet units then present were no match. Though the *Musashi* and other warships took refuge, no timely action was taken to protect the fleet trains. Some 87,000 gross tons of shipping were lost in the air raid.

410

Losses inflicted by submarines were nevertheless conspicuously reduced in March and April. The reduction was generally considered to be the result of the adoption of the new convoy system. But the lull was short-lived. Beginning in the last part of April, the submarine toll again began to rise. Soon it became known that the enemy had initiated wolf-pack tactics.

To meet these new tactics, the GEHQ felt it necessary to have frigates organized in groups on a permanent footing under each able group commander. The temporarily assembled escort vessels could not cooperate efficiently. But to secure the appointment of able group commanders for frigates, it was necessary to have these officers transferred from the Combined Fleet, in which almost all qualified officers were then in service. The Escort-of-Convoy Headquarters was unfitted for the task because it was activated only immediately before the sailing of each convoy, and was deactivated as soon as each convoy trip ended. It could not train escort forces prior to getting into its mission.

Though it was out of the question to get the above requirement met at the time when the Combined Fleet was in hot preparation for the Battle of the Philippine Sea (Operation A), I thought that with the loss of the fleet duel the navy would give more weight than ever before to the GEHQ's plea. In that battle almost all carrier-based flying units perished. It occurred to me that, being deprived of carrier forces, the First Mobile Fleet (the backbone of the Combined Fleet surface strength) was like an eagle without wings. It would no longer be possible for her to fight a modern sea battle. The cost of maintaining the crippled fleet could never be repaid. All remaining manpower and material of the navy had better be utilized in boosting shore-based air strength and in supplementing escort-of-convoy forces. At any rate, the import of such materials as oil, rubber, and bauxite from the south had to be sped up with more efficient protection. For this purpose, manning the escort forces with more and better personnel, both officers and men, was urgently needed. The only source

411

from which these personnel could come was the First Mobile Fleet.

Convinced of this, I first sounded out the opinion of the Red Brick authorities on 26 June 1944. But they were still gripped by the ideas of "battleship admirals." There was an outcry for the recapture of the Marianas with battleship forces while fighting was still going on there on land. After the fall of the Marianas had been made definite, the Naval General Staff held a map wargame from 24 through 27 July to study future strategy. I joined this war game, representing the GEHQ. Through this war game I found out that the Naval General Staff was planning to maintain the First Mobile Fleet en bloc and to have it execute a surprise attack at the enemy's next major landing point, which was expected to fall either in Halmahera or in the southern part of the Philippines.

On the last day of the war game, at the discussion conference, I officially expressed my view before the navy minister, the Naval General Staff, etc., that the First Mobile Fleet should be disbanded so that its personnel and equipment as well as destroyers could be used by the shore-based air forces and the escort forces. But my suggestion proved to have been in vain. In the meantime, only one frigate group consisting of four ships was organized in July with a captain as the commanding officer. This was the only answer to our persistent plea for many months.

On 3 August 1944 Admiral Oikawa was made chief of the Naval General Staff, and Admiral Naokuni Nomura was appointed commander in chief of the GEHQ. At the same time, the GEHQ was subordinated to the Combined Fleet Command in case of a major battle along the Kurile-Japan-Taiwan-Philippine line. Thus, the short-lived system in which the Combined Fleet Command and the GEHQ were juxtaposed came to an end. This new command relationship was destined to produce a disastrous effect upon the sinews of ASW in a few months.

In the middle of October (the twelfth through the fourteenth), the American fast carrier task force raided the Ryukyus, Taiwan, and Luzon. The Combined Fleet directed the GEHQ's 901st Air Group to act as a reconnoitering force. Thanks to strenuous effort and the ingenuity of its officers and men, the air group had become capable of using its radar fairly efficiently against submarines since about the end of July. The GEHQ had hoped that as the wider use of radar by the air group became feasible, ASW would be improved to a considerable extent. But now that the directive was given by the Combined Fleet, the GEHQ had but to comply. According to what was said by the Combined Fleet in connection with the directive, the 901st Air Group was the best qualified in the whole navy as a reconnoitering force because of its ability to detect such a small target as a submarine. Since any daylight attack was impossible because of the great air superiority of the enemy, night attack was necessary with the aid of radar reconnoitering by the 901st. But the battle was disastrous. All of the radar units of the 901st Air Group were destroyed in a strong enemy counterattack. Though the Japanese people as a whole, with the Naval General Staff taking the lead, were jubilant over the self-proclaimed "victory of the Air Battle off Taiwan," the GEHQ was very sad. The source of its hope for the future improvement of ASW was gone. Moreover, through a scrupulous examination of preliminary combat dispatches reaching the headquarters from moment to moment, we entertained grave doubts about the results claimed by the Naval General Staff.

It can be said, however, that as far as ASW was concerned, the decisive phase was over by the fall of 1944. With the enemy's air supremacy extended well up to the shores of China and the Japanese homeland, his submarine offensive against Japanese shipping was considered to have been relegated to secondary importance. From this time on, Japanese shipping protection warfare was fought chiefly against the menace of aircraft and air-strewn mines. The story at this stage enters a different subject. True, ASW efforts were continued until the very end of the war. Belated exertions were made to improve training and equipment in the ASW field.

But by the fall of 1944, Japanese ASW had irrevocably failed.

The military critic Fielding Eliot asserted that a sure way to lose a war was "the single military concept, the freezing of thought and effort by adopting one chosen means of maintaining the national security to the exclusion of others." He also pointed out that "the Japanese army and navy were separate forces of equal standing and authority."[4]

In the realm of the Japanese navy, the single concept was born long before the war began—the concept that the Combined Fleet was the sole embodiment of the navy. The Combined Fleet, in its turn, was gripped by a single concept that the fleet-versus-fleet action was the only warfare it must aim at. The task of protecting sea-borne trade was miserably slighted. The navy sold the concept to the nation. The nation expected the navy to win in fleet actions, overlooking the outcome of trade protection. If a fleet action was lost, the navy's popularity would be undermined. On the other hand, failure in ASW could be left unobserved. It was only natural the navy was more eager to win a fleet action than to succeed in ASW.

At the end of the war, economic hardship was keenly felt. The effect of the sea blockade was visible everywhere. The government reported to the Diet, which was convened immediately following the surrender, that the greatest cause of defeat was the loss of shipping. But it is problematical whether this lesson will be long remembered in future. The picture of a fleet action is colorful, while that of ASW is monotonous and unattractive. Though the result of a fleet action is obvious to everybody's eye, the effect of shipping losses is insidious even to a keen economic observer until it becomes irretrievably acute. At any rate, stories of fleet actions are emphatically told by numerous writers in the Japanese postwar publications, while little has been told about antisubmarine activities.

13

The Kamikaze Attack Corps

RIKIHEI
INOGUCHI
and
TADASHI
NAKAJIMA

There have been few instances in history where a
new weapon has altered the course of a war. But a nation
faced with the prospect of defeat and its deplorable after-
math may understandably grasp for any means that might
conceivably rectify the military situation. Japan, reeling
from a series of reverses, her defense perimeters contracting,
and her naval surface and air power shattered, resorted to
the manned bomb or suicide plane in an effort to halt the
American onslaught. The difficulty of this decision, the ago-
nizing choice faced by the responsible commanders, and the
means of implementing the program are revealed in the following article. A moving ceremony preceded the initial sortie, but the ultimate question involved not the strategic or
tactical legitimacy of the weapon but the moral propriety of
employing pilots in a sure-death mission.

Launched for the first time during the Battle of Leyte
Gulf, the kamikaze attacks caught the U.S. Navy unprepared, inflicted considerable damage on American vessels,
and proved substantially more effective than conventional

415

tactics. Although not decisive in any battle, the earlier utilization of kamikaze attacks might well have affected the direction, if not the outcome, of the war. Whether the kamikaze was a "diabolical tactic," as claimed by the authors, is a philosophical problem within the larger framework of the ethics of armed combat.

THE SETTING SUN cast lengthening shadows on a scene of wild disorder at Mabalacat Field. The two airstrips at this base had been raided by enemy planes in the morning, as had Banban Field across the river, the three Clark Field strips just beyond Mabalacat Town, and the two Marcot strips south of Clark. Each of these Luzon airfields, located midway between Lingayen Gulf and Manila, had been thoroughly bombed and shot up. All hands worked desperately to clear debris so that planes could be readied for an early-morning takeoff. The frantic atmosphere was understandable.

Two mornings earlier, on 17 October 1944, a lookout station on the tiny island of Suluan, at the entrance to Leyte Gulf, had radioed, "Enemy force sighted!" This electrifying message was followed shortly by another, final one that said, "The enemy has commenced landing. We are burning confidential documents. We will fight unto death. Long live the emperor!"

That day more than one hundred carrier planes swarmed over Manila, Legaspi, and Clark fields in determined attacks, which were extended the next day to include targets in Mindanao, the Visayas, and even northern Luzon. The enemy's intention to recapture the Philippines was abundantly clear, even before any large-scale landings were begun.

Upon the invasion of Suluan, Admiral Soemu Toyoda, commander in chief of the Combined Fleet, alerted all combat naval forces for the ironically named *Sho* (Victory) Opera-

Extremely youthful kamikaze pilots wore an ancient symbol, the white scarf (*hachimaki*) donned by samurai to indicate courage and prebattle composure.

tion. On 18 October came the order from Imperial General Headquarters in Tokyo to launch a decisive battle against the enemy at this outer perimeter of the crumbling empire.

This onslaught by the Allied Powers came as no real surprise. After the fall of Biak Island, in western New Guinea, followed by the seizure of the Marianas, Japanese planners well knew that the Philippines could be next. If they were, it had been decided that all available forces, army and navy, would be committed to their defense in the hope of turning the adverse tide of war.

417

The odds were tremendous against Japan. Her early supremacy, especially at sea, where the greatest successes had been achieved, had long since waned. Four months earlier, in the Battle of the Philippine Sea, the Japanese fleet had suffered such an overwhelming defeat that it was no longer capable of challenging the enemy in an ordinary naval engagement. Japan's only offensive resources were her land-based air fleets, whose pilots were pitifully inexperienced, and the firepower of her surface ships, which lacked the support of carrier planes.

The *Sho* Operation strategy relied most heavily on the planes of the army and navy, which were all concentrated at land bases for the first time in this war. They were to launch decisive attacks as enemy invasion forces approached the defensive barrier that extended from Okinawa to the Philippines. Our wingless surface ships were to drive down from the homeland and up from Malay bases to oppose the invasion.

Tremendous efforts were made in this extraordinary attempt to defend the vast area of the Philippine Islands, but it was too late. The ever-quickening tempo of Allied offensives allowed no time for the defenders to make preparations. Relentless air raids on Mindanao prevented the buildup of Japanese air power there, and even forced its withdrawal to the central and northern Philippines. The enemy's carrier planes even made strikes at Okinawa and Taiwan bases, further destroying fighting power that could have been available for the defense of the Philippines.

The rapid enemy offensives had also not allowed time in which to train fliers for Admiral Ozawa's carriers, which were to come down from the north as Kurita's ships approached from the west and south; but then there was not even an opportunity for a briefing between these two commands, so relentless was the drive of the enemy. Reinforcement convoys bound for the Philippines were subjected to endless submarine attacks before reaching their destination. Despite every

418

effort, little actual progress had been made toward achievement of our goal for the *Sho* Operation.

Allied landings at Leyte, coming a little sooner than expected, had caught the defender's naval air strength at a pitifully low ebb. Four months earlier Japan had committed the cream of her veteran naval aviators in a futile attempt to thwart the enemy invasion of the Marianas. As a result, Japanese air strength in the entire Philippines area on 18 October consisted of about seventy army and thirty-five navy planes. Reinforcements were expected from Formosa and the homeland to the extent of about 230 planes and pilots, but most of the latter, while eager for battle, were seriously deficient in training.

The sands of time were rapidly running out on a grave situation. Everyone was aware that it would take a miracle to save the empire from disaster. But indoctrination had given us assurance that our country could count on divine blessing to deliver us from such a crisis. It was becoming apparent, however, that neither surface, carrier, bomber, nor submarine forces could work the necessary miracle. It would have to be won, if at all, by fighter planes.

Japanese planes were so outnumbered and outclassed that the bombers could no longer operate by daylight with any chance of success. Their activities had to be confined to small-scale sneak attacks made at night or under cover of foul weather. Zero fighters, which early in the war had been so superior to all other planes, were the only type left that could in any respect cope with enemy interceptors.

The planes based at Mabalacat belonged to the 201st Air Group. This unit of the First Air Fleet had been moved up from Cebu after being caught there unawares on 12 September in an attack by enemy carrier planes.

In the attempt to rebuild depleted air forces, the greatest emphasis had been placed on increasing fighter strength, and fighter pilots were even drilled in skip-bombing techniques so that they could be employed as fighter-bombers. These pilots

419

A Japanese suicide plane maneuvering for a dive on the carrier escort *Natoma Bay*, 5 January 1945. *Official U.S. Navy photograph*

understood and appreciated the importance of their responsibility, and their morale was very high.

As dusk settled over the field, a black sedan drew up and stopped in front of the command post. A small yellow flag fluttering from the front of the car indicated that its passenger was of flag rank, but there had been no advance notice of a distinguished visitor. Speculation ended as to who it might be when the rear door was opened and Vice Admiral Takijiro Ohnishi stepped out of the car. Though his arrival was un-

420

announced, it was well known that he had been designated to assume command of the First Air Fleet. Since the death of Admiral Isoroku Yamamoto in April 1943, Ohnishi had been regarded as the foremost exponent of aerial warfare. He had arrived in the Philippine theater only two days before to succeed Admiral Kimpei Teraoka, and so his sudden appearance at this advance base was a surprise to everyone.

The executive officer of the 201st Air Corps who received the admiral was immediately advised to summon a conference of staff officers for consultation. The headquarters building was a two-story, seven-room Western-style house. Since all furniture had been removed from the first floor to make room for canvas cots, which now filled the downstairs, the meeting was held on the second floor.

When the staff officers had assembled, Admiral Ohnishi was introduced and addressed them. "The situation is so grave that the fate of the empire depends on the outcome of the *Sho* Operation. Missions have been assigned. A naval force under Admiral Kurita is to penetrate Leyte Gulf and there annihilate enemy surface units. The First Air Fleet has been designated to support that mission by rendering enemy carriers ineffective for at least one week. In my opinion this can be accomplished only by crash-diving on the carrier flight decks with Zero fighters carrying 250-kilogram bombs."

This idea had been discussed in recent days by flying officers, and so it was not new, but the already tense atmosphere was electrified by the admiral's words as his sharp eyes surveyed the occupants of the crowded room. It was now apparent that the purpose of his visit was to inspire these suicide tactics, which he believed to be the only effective means of countering the enemy offensive. Having this difficult task assigned to him at the crucial moment of an Allied invasion must have greatly increased his torment in arriving at this doleful solution.

The circumstances leading to this decision are described in

421

Admiral Teraoka's personal diary, under an entry of 18 October, where he recorded his meeting with Admiral Ohnishi in Manila to discuss the use of "special attacks" against the enemy:

> We can no longer win the war by adhering to conventional methods of warfare. . . . Instead, we must steel ourselves against weakness. . . . If fighter pilots set an example by volunteering for special attack missions, other units will follow suit. These examples will, in turn, inspire surface forces and army forces. . . .
>
> We conclude that the enemy can be stopped and our country saved only by crash-dive attacks on their ships. Admiral Ohnishi and I are in agreement that he should assume complete charge and responsibility for the formation of a special attack corps.

Within hours after this meeting, orders were received at headquarters of the 201st Air Group summoning the commanding officer and his air officer to First Air Fleet Headquarters the next day. They were late in arriving, causing some concern in Manila that their car might have been ambushed by guerrillas. This risk had to be taken, however, because it was no longer possible to fly our planes during the hours when U.S. carrier planes were about. That explains why even such an air-minded officer as Ohnishi had come to Mabalacat by automobile.

When Admiral Ohnishi had finished explaining the situation, Commander Tamai, the executive officer, asked permission for a short recess so that he might consult with the squadron leaders. In the absence of the commanding officer, Tamai was in charge, but he wanted to confer with his subordinates before giving an answer on a matter as grave as that proposed by the admiral. After confirming his colleagues' assent to the proposal, the conference was quickly resumed and he reported with proud determination that his force was ready to cooperate. Tamai concluded his statement with a prayer that organization of this special attack corps be left to

422

A Type 1 (Betty) bomber with a *Baka* (piloted bomb) loaded under the fuselage.

the group itself. Admiral Ohnishi was greatly moved as he listened to this report, and as it ended his face presented a vivid picture of agonized relief.

In this command were twenty-three pilots who had served under Commander Tamai in the Marianas campaign, which they had been lucky to survive. He was confident enough of their fervent loyalty to believe that most of them would dedicate themselves as human missiles when they heard of the plan. He afterward described their reaction: "They said little, but their eyes spoke eloquently of a willingness to die for their country." All but two men of this group volunteered, and they were both found to be in ill health.

The next step in this important mission was the selection of a leader. He must be a man of outstanding character and ability, since so much would depend on the success of this unit. It was considered desirable that the man chosen for this task be a graduate of the naval academy at Etajima, and

423

this served further to limit the list of those eligible. So many naval academy flying officers had been killed in action that there was seldom more than one or two of squadron commander rank in each air group, and such was the case in the 201st. The selection did not take long to make.

When Lieutenant Yukio Seki entered the room it was shortly after midnight. He was addressed by Commander Tamai, who said, "Admiral Ohnishi has brought to our base the idea of loading Zero fighters with a 250-kilogram bomb and having the pilots crash-dive on enemy warships. I have recommended you as a proper man to lead such a special attack."

Seated at the table, Lieutenant Seki leaned forward, supporting his head in his hands, elbows resting on the table, head inclined downward, and his eyes closed. This capable young officer had been married just before leaving the homeland. For several seconds he sat motionless except for the tightening of his clenched fists. Raising his head, he smoothed back his hair and spoke in a clear, quiet voice. "Please do appoint me to the post." The tenseness of the room was suddenly dispelled, like moonlight bursting through a break in clouded skies.

Shortly after sunrise Admiral Ohnishi summoned the newly appointed special attack pilots to the small garden adjoining his headquarters. There stood twenty-four men, six to a row, the morning sunlight shining on their youthful faces as the admiral spoke. His visage was unusually pallid and his voice shook with emotion. "Japan now faces a terrible crisis. The salvation of our country is beyond the power of ministers, the general staff, and lowly unit commanders like myself. It is now up to spirited young men such as you." At this point tears came to his eyes as he concluded, "On behalf of your hundred million countrymen, I ask you to do your utmost and wish you success."

It is hard to imagine a more poignant and tragic message. This was no mere exhortation to inspire men's fighting spirit.

424

Admiral Takijiro Ohnishi (*left*) inspects kamikaze pilots at a base in Manila.

It was an appeal for the extreme sacrifice with no chance of repeal. Never in history had a group of men been asked to carry out such an assignment by their commanding officer.

Admiral Ohnishi's feelings at having to make this request surpass comprehension. A few days after the kamikaze (divine wind) attacks had begun, he confided in his senior staff officer: "Several months ago, when Captain Eiichiro Jo kept insisting on this kind of attack, I was loath to accept his idea. But when I came to the Philippines and saw the actual state of affairs, it was clear that these tactics would have to be adopted. The situation here evidenced how poorly our strategy had been developed. We have been forced into these extreme measures although they are a complete heterodoxy of all the lessons of strategy and tactics."

425

Ohnishi foresaw some of the criticisms that would be heaped on the extraordinary procedures he had originated. He was known to have lamented to his adjutant on several occasions, "People do not understand my actions today, and a hundred years from now people will still misunderstand the course I am forced to follow."

The one-way character of these tactics made it imperative in Ohnishi's mind that the kamikaze attacks be employed only when success was fairly well assured. He rightfully felt that such an expenditure of the cream of Japan's youth must not be made if there was any chance that the mission might fail. At the same time he believed sincerely that this method of attack carried out by inspired young pilots was bound to be successful. He later told his staff, "On my return to Manila after organizing the first special attack corps, I went to Southwest Area Fleet Headquarters to request that the sortie of Kurita's force be postponed until after the enemy had been subjected to strikes by our special attack corps. On arrival I learned that the order for sortie had been issued just two hours earlier, so I withheld the request lest it merely add confusion to the situation."

While these events were taking place at Mabalacat, similar recruiting of pilots for kamikaze attacks was taking place at other air bases. At Cebu, the nearest base to the allied landings at Leyte, all hands were assembled in the evening of 20 October. The commanding officer addressed them as follows: "I have just returned from Manila carrying an order to organize a kamikaze attack corps at this base. You are to prepare a sealed envelope by nine o'clock this evening. Volunteers for the kamikaze attack corps will write their name and rank on a piece of paper and insert it in the envelope; enclose a blank paper if you do not wish to volunteer. You have three hours in which to give the matter serious consideration. There are good reasons for not volunteering. I request that you make independent decisions and not be influenced by your colleagues."

426

The commanding officer retired to his quarters, where he was shortly visited by a young reservist sublieutenant. His taut face and blazing eyes reinforced the firm determination of his voice. "May I be sure, Commander, that my name will be included in those chosen from among the volunteers?"

This particular man's action had not been unexpected. A university graduate, he was soft-spoken, mild-mannered, and a man of few words; but his superior had long before recognized his intense spirit. The air officer smiled, and there was an understanding look in his eyes. "You may rest assured, young man, because one of the special attack planes brought from Mabalacat is reserved for you." These words brought a smile of obvious relief to the flier's face, and he withdrew after bowing to his commander.

When the humble evening meal was finished, one of the fliers as usual began to play the piano that stood in a corner of the mess hall. Tonight's pianist had volunteered to die for his country, and the music was heavy with his emotion. There were few listeners who remained dry-eyed.

At nine o'clock sharp the senior petty officer pilot came to the commander's quarters, silently delivered an envelope, and departed. It was several minutes before the envelope was hesitatingly opened, for there was no way of knowing how many men would offer themselves for this suicide mission. Inside were more than twenty signed pieces of paper; only two were blank.

It was getting close to midnight when a reserve ensign appeared at headquarters. He had married upon graduation from St. Paul University in Tokyo, and it was a happy day for the whole unit when word came that his wife had borne him a son and heir. He now appeared fidgety and nervous, asked a few trivial questions, and retired. The next night he returned and his continued strange attitude caused the commander to become suspicious. When the ensign appeared the third successive night, with no apparent purpose, the commanding officer confronted him. "Is your presence here for the past three nights in some way connected with the special attack mission?" So direct a question startled the young officer, who admitted that he wanted to volunteer and continued, "But I am such a poor flier compared with the other pilots at this base that I am afraid that you will not accept me for the mission."

He was greatly consoled when the commander assured him that he qualified and would have a place in the mission. When the time eventually came for this young man to take off on his last flight, he left behind a most touching letter to his wife and the infant child he had never seen.

In the meantime great land and air battles centered on the island of Leyte, but Japanese counterattacks were limited in strength and terribly ineffective. The *Sho* Operation plans of the Combined Fleet called for reinforcement of the greatly reduced First Air Fleet by the transfer of planes from Taiwan on 23 October. These land-based planes were then to make an all-out air attack on 24 October. This was to be followed at dawn the next day with a driving thrust into Leyte Gulf by Admiral Kurita's surface forces.

Allied forces had begun landing on Leyte on 20 October and Japanese retaliation was limited to small-scale air attacks upon ships in the gulf—with very little success. There were no other air raids throughout the Philippines on this day when Admiral Ohnishi became commander in chief of the First Air Fleet.

During this period the "special attack" pilots awaited their chance to turn back the enemy advance by hurling themselves at his ships. In the afternoon of 21 October came the long-awaited flash: "Enemy task force built around six carriers sighted sixty miles east of Suluan Island." Six Zero fighters were ordered to take off immediately from the Cebu base.

Preparations were begun immediately and the planes were hauled up to the air strip from their hidden revetments, five hundred meters down the hillside. As they were lined up for takeoff, a flight of enemy Grumman fighters suddenly came in to attack and all six Zeros burst into flames. Within ten minutes after this raid, two more "special attack" fighters and one fighter escort plane were manhandled up to the strip and they roared into the air above the smoldering base. This flight was led by the piano player of the previous evening. His plane became separated from the other two, who returned to base when they failed to sight enemy targets, but he did not come back. It was thus this plane that led off the strikes of special attack missions—the first of the organized kamikazes.

A more dramatic ceremony attended the first sortie of kamikaze planes from the Mabalacat base. When the order was received, Lieutenant Seki was named to lead the first special attack unit. Six young pilots stood in a row and, passing a canteen-lid cup among them, took their last drink of water. Their fellow pilots, standing by to see them off, took up the ancient song of the warrior, "*Umi Yukaba*" (When Going Away to Sea). The doleful but stirring melody wafted out on the morning air:

> *Umi yukaba*
> *Mizuku kabane*
> *Yama yukaba*
> *Kusa musu kabane*
> *Ogimi no he ni koso*
> *Nodo niwa shinaji*

> *If I go away to sea,*
> *I shall return a corpse awash;*
> *If duty calls me to the mountain,*
> *A verdant sward will be my pall;*
> *Thus for the sake of the emperor*
> *I will not die peacefully at home.*

But these brave volunteers were not smiled upon by the God of War this day. They failed to sight any enemy force and had to return to their base. Four successive days they sortied, each time in vain; and when they returned to the field

Val dive-bombers readying for a kamikaze mission from an airfield near Manila.

they never expected to see again, Lieutenant Seki would tear-fully apologize to the commander for his failure to ·find his opportunity to die. Surprisingly enough, these pilots did not become nervous or desperate but were as composed as if they had just returned from a routine attack mission.

Meanwhile, Japan's war machine, which had long been geared toward facing the Allied Powers in a decisive battle, was moving inexorably toward its fate. The main naval strik-ing force, led by Admiral Kurita, had left Brunei on 22 Oc-tober to sail north along the Palawan Island chain and through San Bernardino Strait into the Pacific toward Leyte. Under Admiral Nishimura, one fleet element was headed through the Sulu Sea to transit Surigao Strait for a southern approach to Leyte Gulf. In concert with these two forces, Admiral Ozawa's decoy force, built around carriers practically devoid of planes, was coming from the homeland to lure the enemy task force northward. The Second Air Fleet, consisting of about 350 land-based planes, was to launch an all-out attack upon the invader on 24 October so as to facilitate the penetration into Leyte Gulf by the Kurita and Nishimura forces.

Any illusions Japan might have entertained about defeating the enemy in a decisive naval engagement were decisively shattered by the events of three days beginning on 23 October. Early that morning the Kurita force was caught and attacked in Palawan Passage by U.S. submarines. Two heavy cruisers were sunk and another was damaged so that it had to drop out of formation. Reaching the Sibuyan Sea the next day, Kurita's ships, with no protective cover of fighter planes, were subjected throughout the day to unrelenting attacks by carrier planes. This air-sea contest resulted in the sinking of the battleship *Musashi,* whose powerful eighteen-inch guns had been counted as such a great asset for surface engagements. Japanese retaliation that day in the form of an air attack by 226 planes—all that could be mobilized—succeeded in sinking only one light carrier and inflicting some damage on several other ships.

At daybreak on 25 October Kurita's force found itself in the unexpected, unbelievably happy situation of being within sight of an enemy surface force. Coupled with this good fortune was the fact that Ozawa's decoy force was serving its purpose and had succeeded in luring the enemy carrier task force to the north as planned. It was on this day that the battleship *Yamato,* the giant of Kurita's force, first fired her eighteen-inch guns against enemy ships.

The first successful kamikaze unit attack was carried out on this day by six planes, which took off at dawn from Davao in southern Mindanao. They scored hits on enemy escort carriers, southern units of the same force Kurita's ships had encountered a little to the north. At least three escort carriers were damaged by these sentient missiles.

431

Another successful special attack this same morning was led by Lieutenant Seki. Escorted by four fighter planes, his unit of five special attack planes left Mabalacat soon after sunrise seeking targets against which to make their sacrifice. One of the escorting pilots furnished a report of the action.

> Sighting an enemy force of four carriers and six other ships at 1040, distant 90 miles, bearing 85 degrees from Tacloban, Lieutenant Seki banked his plane vigorously to the right and left as a signal and then dived headlong into one of the carriers, which he rammed successfully. A colleague followed directly after him and crashed into the same ship, from which there rose a great column of smoke. Successful hits were also scored by two more pilots, one on another flattop, the other on a light cruiser.

A total of ninety-three fighters and fifty-seven bombers were flown in conventional attacks on this day, inflicting no damage on the enemy. The superiority of special attacks was manifest, and Admiral Ohnishi's belief was proven true. Hundreds of planes making orthodox attacks could not inflict as much damage on the enemy as a mere handful of kamikazes.

News of the successes scored by Lieutenant Seki's unit flashed throughout the navy to inspire men at home as well as those in the Philippine theater. But even the mighty power of such attacks was not enough to stem the tide of war. The situation was now so grave that Admiral Ohnishi, who had originally urged the use of special attacks only for the initial stage of the *Sho* Operation, was convinced that further and extended employment of these inhuman tactics was unavoidable. He pressed this opinion on Vice Admiral Fukudome, commander in chief of the Second Air Fleet, saying, "Nothing short of all-out use of special attacks can save us. It is time for your air fleet to adopt these tactics."

Fukudome considered this advice, deliberated with his staff, and on 23 October announced that his air fleet would carry out kamikaze attacks. At this same time the decision was made to facilitate operations by combining the First and Second Air Fleets. Admiral Fukudome was named to command the combined forces, Admiral Ohnishi serving as his chief of staff.

As October ended it was apparent that it would take more than a miracle to save Japan from impending disaster. Admiral Kurita's force, after making a successful approach to Leyte Gulf and then fortuitously getting an inferior enemy force within gunfire range, mysteriously failed to press home its attack and withdrew from the trembling enemy. The Ozawa ships served to good purpose as a decoy force but were almost completely annihilated in the process. All available planes of the army and naval air forces had been mobilized to carry out conventional attacks on the enemy, but, like all our other efforts, this too was a failure. The invader had firmly established his bridgehead on Leyte Island by the end of the month.

It thus came about that kamikaze tactics were given full play, and young men volunteered freely for the opportunity to add to the intensity of the "divine wind." Reinforcements poured to the front from the homeland to crash in turn upon enemy warships. And each new pilot was as calm and composed as his predecessor.

If a pilot returned to his base unable for some reason to make an attack, he was always ready and eager to try again the next day. One such officer, a unit commander, came back to Cebu alone, having refrained from trying to crash his plane because the enemy ships had not been reached until after dark. He wrote a report to his commanding officer in which he said, "I think it advisable to launch special attacks at dawn, with Cebu as the last staging base. Please tell those who follow never to lose patience and attempt an attack under adverse conditions." He extolled the virtue and bravery of his subordinates, describing how they had gone unflinchingly to their death.

The last seconds of a kamikaze attack were fast and furious. This plane, engine dead, heads for destruction on a U.S. cruiser.

Before dawn the next morning he took off alone from Cebu field to fulfill his destiny by crash-diving into a ship at Leyte Gulf.

Day by day the situation around Leyte Island became more desperate and hopeless. But as the tempo of the enemy invasion increased, so too did the intensity and volume of kami-

434

kaze attacks. One after another the brave young volunteers had planes assigned to them, made a few practice flights, and then received orders for their target and time of takeoff. Fighter pilots who served as escorts until their comrades reached the attack point returned to make reports and to take their place in subsequent attacks.

Impressive yet typical was the performance of Lieutenant S. Kanaya, who came to the Philippines in late December as leader of the last kamikaze reinforcement echelon to arrive that year. Irresistible Allied forces had already swept through the central Philippines and the fate of Luzon was inevitable. Kanaya's attitude was calm but completely detached, and he evinced interest in only one subject—that his plane make an effective hit. He practiced at making speedy takeoffs until his timing was perfect to the split second. This was important in view of the constant threat of enemy air raids which might come at any time, often thwarting special attacks before they even got started. Every day he was first in practice, approaching his plane at a run, in full flying gear, despite the sultry Philippines weather. Each time that he was asked to submit a list of names from his unit for the next attack, his name headed the list. It was not until 5 January that his chance came and he led a unit of fifteen fighter-bombers in the last large-scale suicide attack upon the enemy invasion forces at Lingayen Gulf. Observers reported that one cruiser and four transports were hit and damaged.

The last kamikaze flights from Philippine bases had been scheduled for 5 January and the dwindling supply of planes had been allocated accordingly. On that date the last operational planes took off on their deadly missions; only remnants of damaged planes remained, and they were to be destroyed. But energetic maintenance crews worked throughout that night patching and repairing so that by early morning of 6 January five extra fighter planes were ready for flight. The base commander had the difficult task of selecting five pilots from the more than thirty who remained, all having volunteered for this final special attack from a Philippines base. The men selected showed their gratitude at having been thus honored by saluting solemnly as they taxied past the commander for takeoff. They circled the field once before disappearing into the northern sky.

Further Japanese defeats followed quickly after the fall of the Philippines. The mighty enemy invaded Iwo Jima in February and Okinawa in April, trapping Japan in a grip of death, which inspired desperation tactics on an unprecedented scale. The decision was made to throw every possible plane into repelling the enemy at Okinawa. Convinced that kamikaze attacks were the only means at their command that might prove effective against so powerful an enemy, headquarters ordered that they be exploited to the fullest extent. Even training planes were mobilized for the effort.

A new suicide weapon was introduced in 1945 consisting of a rocket-powered 1,800-kilogram missile. It was attached to a "mother" bomber for delivery to within sight of a target. There it would be released and a volunteer suicide pilot would fly it in to crash an enemy ship. This ingenious device was developed and promoted by a naval aviator who had been organizing and training a special unit since September 1944. This group was called *Jinrai Butai* (divine thunderbolt unit), but "*Baka* (foolish) bomb" was the notorious nickname it earned among the Allies.

This weapon was first employed in battle on 21 March, when an enemy task force built around three carriers was sighted bearing 145 degrees, distant 320 miles from the southeastern tip of Kyushu. A flight of eighteen medium bombers, all but two carrying human bombs, was reluctantly ordered to attack by Vice Admiral Ugaki, who, as commander in chief of the Fifth Air Fleet, was in charge of air operations for the area. Ugaki hesitated about ordering this attack because of the scarcity of fighter planes to act as escorts. His doubts proved to be well founded when this unit was ambushed and completely destroyed by a vastly superior

436

group of enemy fighters, fifty miles short of the task force position.

One of the largest air attacks against the invaders at Okinawa was made on 12 April. Some *"Baka* bombs" were used in this attack, and one of them scored the first hit for this type of weapon. The successful pilot, a higher normal school graduate, was a reserve sublieutenant, and very conscientious in everything he did. One of his subsidiary duties at the Kanoya air base had been to supervise the junior officers' billet, which was located in a shabby primary school. His last words before climbing into the mother bomber were, "Keep an eye out for the new straw mats I ordered for the billet; fifteen of them are supposed to arrive today." Such was his composure that he napped peacefully during the flight toward Okinawa and had to be awakened when the time came to board his flight to eternity. Upon release from the mother ship, the bomb sped down and away at great speed, soon disappearing from sight of the bomber crew. The big plane had turned and was heading back to base when, after several minutes of anxiety, her crew was relieved to see a huge column of black smoke reaching skyward—silent evidence that a "divine thunderbolt" had found its mark.

There were a few volunteers for the suicide missions who tended to become morose during the wait for their call to action. This was especially true during the Okinawa campaign, in which there were more than 1,800 special attack flights and pilots, requiring involved planning and causing extended delays in many cases. By the time of Japan's surrender, a total of 2,519 men and officers of the navy had futilely sacrificed themselves in the mad eddy of the divine wind. This does not include volunteer suicide army pilots, nor does it include a small group of naval pilots who took off on suicide flights but were not counted as kamikaze attacks because their sortie was made after the imperial rescript proclamation of 15 August 1945, calling for immediate cessation of the war.

Santaro Iwata's "Departure of Special Air Attack Corps, Kamikaze, from Base on Home Airfield." *U.S. Army photograph*

At noon of that day the emperor's voice had gone out to his people by radio with the words of the rescript, an event without precedent in Japan's history. A few hours later the Fifth Air Fleet commander, Admiral Ugaki, spoke to his assembled officers and men. "Our air fleet has long been of the conviction that every man would fight to the finish, but we have come to a sorry day. I am going to take off for a crash attack upon the enemy at Okinawa. Those who wish to follow me are requested to raise their hands."

Sensing the imminent surrender, Ugaki had determined early that morning to die crashing an enemy ship at Okinawa, where he had sent so many pilots to their death in suicide attacks. He ordered his staff duty officer to prepare dive-bombers for takeoff. Close friends and members of his staff tried to dissuade the admiral from his plan, but, true to his

438

reputation for imperturbability, his blunt answer was that he "must have a place to die."

Cautious and thorough as ever, Admiral Ugaki stripped the insignia of rank from his uniform, and carried only a short samurai sword. His enthusiastic pilots responded eagerly to the admiral's query about followers. There were more volunteers than there were planes available to follow the commander. The eleven planes finally took off and, although four of them were forced to drop out or turn back along the way, seven planes, including Admiral Ugaki's, sent back their "time of diving on target."

Japan's surrender found another sponsor of the kamikaze corps in the important post of vice chief of the Naval General Staff in Tokyo. Admiral Ohnishi had been ordered to Taiwan when the fall of the Philippines appeared inevitable in early January and remained there until ordered to Tokyo in June. On 15 August came the proclamation of Japan's surrender, and that evening Ohnishi summoned staff officers to his official residence for a discussion that lasted late into the night. On their departure he penned a note: "To the souls of my late subordinates I express the greatest appreciation for their valiant deeds. In death I wish to apologize to the souls of these brave men and their families."

Upon completing this last testament in the early morning of 16 August, he plunged a samurai sword into one side of his abdomen and drew it across to the other in complete satisfaction of the harakiri tradition. When told of this, his secretary rushed to the dying man, only to be ordered, "Do not try to help me." Thus, refusing both medical aid and a coup de grâce, he lingered on in agony until six o'clock that evening. His choice to endure prolonged suffering was obviously made in expiation for his part in the most diabolical tactic of war the world has ever seen.

14

Japanese Submarine Tactics and the *Kaiten*

KENNOSUKE
TORISU,
assisted by
MASATAKA
CHIHAYA

To Western observers, one of the most curious features of Japan's naval war is her failure to use submarines more aggressively. Samuel Eliot Morison, writing of German U-boats, contended that "the submarine was the greatest threat to Allied victory over the Axis."[1] The German submarine fleet sank over 2,500 merchant ships totaling over 14,000,000 tons. The Japanese, by contrast, sank only 171 vessels, including warships, for a total of less than 1,000,000 tons. Partly this is a reflection of the smaller scale of the Japanese submarine force. During the war the Japanese employed a total of 187 boats, the Germans almost 1,200.

The following article, while by no means a complete survey of the submarine war, suggests the major reasons for Japanese passivity. Before the war, both the United States and Japan planned to use submarines to attack enemy warships. After Pearl Harbor, U.S. boats quickly undertook a war against the empire's merchant marine. Japanese naval leaders, however, held to the doctrine that submarines

440

should be used as auxiliaries in main fleet actions to reconnoiter and attack enemy ships of the line. When reverses were met in the Solomons, the high command gave submarines the added mission of resupplying island garrisons. Submariners themselves attempted to modify standard doctrine after their operations in the Gilberts. In November 1943 a force of nine submarines tried to break up U.S. landing forces at Makin and Tarawa; only three came back, and they were heavily damaged. Members of the Sixth (submarine) Fleet staff and boat commanders forcefully advocated a switch of tactics to interdiction of enemy supply lines. But they were ignored as preparations went forward for later decisive battles, first of the Philippine Sea and then of Leyte Gulf. Until almost the end of the war, submarines continued to serve as fleet auxiliaries or engaged in futile attacks against well-defended U.S. amphibious operations.

Japanese doctrine is, of course, only one half of the story. The other is the antisubmarine warfare of the Americans. The author seems to consider radar the key, but there was more. It has long been known that an increased role for aircraft and the development of hunter-killer groups dramatically improved U.S. antisubmarine warfare starting in 1943. Recently the important role of communications intelligence has been recognized. In *Double-Edged Secrets*, W. J. Holmes explains how intercepted enemy transmissions helped the *England*, DE 635, sink five submarines on the "*Na* line" before the Battle of the Philippine Sea.[2]

The author focuses on efforts of the human torpedo, or *kaiten*, forces to bring about a reversal of Japan's fortunes in late 1944 and 1945. Although he makes it appear that concern with "special" operations developed late in the war, a sacrificial attitude was very strong in the submarine arm from the start, as exemplified by the actions of the midget submarines at Pearl Harbor (see Chapter 1). A popular novel by Toyo Iwata called *Kaigun* (The Navy) appeared serially in the *Asahi* newspaper in 1942 extolling the "nine brave warriors" who died in submarines at Pearl. It represented the spirit of the navy and in particular that of the underwater service as one of joyful self-immolation.

The author's own commitment to the suicide weapon probably grew out of frustration with the navy's antiquated submarine doctrine. Yet as he points out, even *kaiten* were first expended wastefully against well-protected U.S. anchorages; only at the end of the war were they freed to attack convoys at sea. Saddest of all in light of the sacrifices the *kaiten* entailed was their utter failure as weapons of war. In *Axis Submarine Successes 1939–1945*, Jürgen Rohwer documents fifty-one *kaiten* attacks.[3] In all they sank only an oiler and a destroyer and damaged three other vessels. The cruiser *Indianapolis*, America's great loss at the end of the war, was sunk by a conventional torpedo attack. The author and some other Japanese sources, notably the semiofficial history of the submarine service that appeared in Japan recently, are reluctant to speak of the *kaiten*'s ineffectiveness.[4] They are perhaps motivated by respect for the young men who gave their lives in the *kaiten* campaign.

ONE OF THE most interesting questions having to do with Japanese submarine operations in World War II concerns the sinking of the cruiser USS *Indianapolis* by the *I-58*. How did it happen that the submarine found herself in such an advantageous position on 29 July 1945?

In *Abandon Ship! Death of the U.S.S. Indianapolis*, Richard F. Newcomb briefly touched on this point. He wrote that the submarine commander "seems to have known of the impending fate of the cruiser."[5] Actually, the meeting of the two vessels was coincidental. It can be said, however, that the *I-58* was on station at the point where a line joining Okinawa and Palau crosses a line from Guam to Leyte in accordance with a specific operation order. As a staff officer of the Sixth

Fleet, which was the sole submarine fleet of the Japanese navy at that time, I was responsible for drafting that order.

The dispatch of the *I-58* to a point where no submarines had ever been sent before was not planned overnight. To explain why and how she was ordered there needs, I think, some discussion of the development of the Japanese navy's submarine operations up to that time. Perhaps that can best be done in terms of my own experience.

Before I joined the staff of the Sixth Fleet in March 1944, I had been commanding officer of two submarines, the *RO-64*, an obsolete 996-ton craft, and the *I-165*, a more modern vessel displacing 1,705 tons.

My first contact with the enemy was made on 25 August 1942 about three hundred miles southwest of Colombo, Ceylon, where I sank a British merchantman with two torpedo hits. After the war, I learned she was the *Hermonides*.

My withdrawal from the scene of battle, however, was not so successful as my attack. When I surfaced the ship after dark, we were suddenly lighted up by flares dropped from a plane. I dove. Terrifying indeed was the ensuing struggle between the hunters and the hunted. Only a few hours were left before dawn, when I managed to shake off the two or three enemy destroyers.

This experience in my first encounter with an enemy brought home to me the fact that because of radar, the cloak of darkness was no longer sufficient protection for the submarine. It also began to make me doubt the wisdom of employing underwater craft solely in a battlefront area.

From the outbreak of war, the Japanese navy had stuck to its long-cherished "one-big-battle" idea, in which all naval arms—surface, air, and underwater—were to be used once and for all. The employment of the underwater arm was not excepted, even after the loss of Guadalcanal turned the tide against us.

As the defense perimeter had to be pulled back toward the homeland, all the forces of the empire were fanatically thrown into the fight regardless of losses. Many submarines

Japanese war art: *Kaidai* Type 6 submarines in heavy seas. *U.S. Army photograph*

were ordered to attack Allied landing forces or to transport a small amount of badly needed supplies to hard-pressed, isolated islands. Fifteen submarines were lost by the summer of 1943.

Submarine crews were opposed to such deployment. They strongly advocated using their ships to intercept enemy communications lines instead, but they were overruled or ignored by the high command, which deemed it imperative to give "the last-minute shot" to half-starved troops trapped on tropical islands for the sake of getting cooperation from the army.

This blunder in submarine employment was hard to remedy. As the mistake was repeated again and again, the loss of Japanese submarines increased. Six of them were lost following the Allied invasion of the Gilbert Islands. Of thirty-eight

submarines deployed to the Marianas area when those islands were invaded, eighteen were lost. Eight submarines went missing during the Philippine campaign in the fall of 1944.

In the meantime, strenuous studies and efforts had been made in the homeland on how to save the ever-deteriorating submarine situation. Typical among them was a human-torpedo project, which was originally advocated by two young submarine officers, Lieutenant Hiroshi Kuroki and Sublieutenant Sekio Nishina.

Kuroki and Nishina, both graduates of the naval academy, hated to see the deterioration of the submarine fleet, and they decided to do what they could by volunteering to man a large torpedo themselves and ram an enemy ship.

The concept that the empire could only be saved by sacrificing blood had gradually been appearing elsewhere in the armed forces.

Early in the summer of 1944, both officers came to see me,

for by that time I was an operations officer on the Sixth Fleet staff. The more they advocated their cherished plan for the use of manned torpedoes, the more I was impressed by them. Just a short time before, we had experienced our heavy losses in the Marianas. That action had convinced me that our submarines were no match for Allied warships, which were well equipped with sonar and radar.

I thought this weapon proposed by Kuroki and Nishina could and should be used in raiding enemy communications lines. It seemed likely to me that a manned torpedo could be released from a submarine and carry out its attack far enough away from the submarine to allow the releasing vessel to remain undetected—in contrast to my own experience off Ceylon. But I believed at the same time that this new weapon should not be employed until a sufficient number became available for operation.

My voice, however, was not yet strong enough to persuade other staff members to share my idea of employing manned torpedoes in raiding operations at sea. As soon as a dozen of the weapons were readied, it was decided to launch the first torpedo attack on Ulithi atoll.

The submarines *I-36* and *I-47*, each carrying four manned torpedoes on deck, approached the entrance to Ulithi in the early hours of 20 November 1944 and launched one and four manned torpedoes respectively. These weapons were designated *kaiten,* meaning "make a big change like turning Heaven." Some of them successfully penetrated the Ulithi lagoon through the gate, which had not been closed after the exit of three cruisers and four destroyers bound for Saipan, and hit a target, the fleet oiler *Mississinewa*. All of the *kaiten* crews, of course, perished, while both submarines returned safely to their home port, Kure in the Inland Sea.

On the other hand, the submarine *I-37*, which headed for the nearby Kossol Passage, met with bad luck. On 19 November, the day before the designated date of attack, this submarine was discovered at the west entrance of the passage and was sunk with her four *kaiten* by two escort destroyers.

446

As to the damage inflicted upon the enemy by this first human-torpedo attack, the Japanese navy repeated an often-committed error in overestimating that five carriers and battleships were sunk.

I hoped that this first human-torpedo attack would put an end to our usual tactic of employing submarines against a well-guarded enemy area. To try to bring this about, I took advantage of a Naval General Staff conference held by the Combined Fleet and the Sixth Fleet in early December on board the *Tsukushi Maru,* the flagship of the Sixth Fleet, by bringing up for discussion the submarine operations to be undertaken in the future.

I proposed that the news of the first *kaiten* attacks be released on 1 January 1945. My reasoning was: 1) the enemy was believed to know about our human torpedoes, 2) similar subsequent attacks had less prospect of success against an enemy now on the alert for them, and 3) the loyal deed of those who had perished should be made known to their kin as soon as permissible.

My real purpose with this proposal was to discourage further attacks of this nature by making public the details of the first one. But, to my great regret, no one dared support my view. To my conservative colleagues, it was out of the question to employ *kaiten* in raiding operations at sea. The press release was, of course, postponed.

My disappointment was increased by my position, because as a staff officer for submarine operations, I had to help launch the second *kaiten* attack on American bases then presumed to be ready to defend themselves against an attack of this nature. This time, six submarines and twenty-four *kaiten* were gathered to attack Ulithi, the Kossol Passage, Seeadler Harbor in the Admiralty Islands, Guam, and Hollandia. On 12 January 1945 all six submarines released their manned torpedoes as planned, but apparently little damage was inflicted upon the enemy. One of the six submarines failed to return.

In the meantime, I had informally contacted Lieutenant

Commander Mitsuma Itakura, who was the commanding officer of the *kaiten* training center at Otsujima. Itakura was a veteran submarine officer with a great deal of battle experience, and he shared my views on how to employ submarines.

Complying with my informal request to train *kaiten* to attack a moving target, Itakura had vigorously pushed ahead such training, while informing me constantly of its development. As training progressed, it became possible to attack slow convoys with a good chance of success.

On the other hand, time was running out very quickly on the hard-pressed inner perimeter of the empire. When Iwo Jima was invaded by the Americans on 19 February 1945, the submarines *I-368, I-370,* and *I-40* were hurriedly ordered to launch a determined *kaiten* attack there. This attempt spelled another failure, however, for two of the three submarines were lost, and no enemy ships were sunk.

Iwo Jima was not the last graveyard of Japanese submarines. Greater losses came about one month later, when the mighty forces of the Allies seized Okinawa. With the grimmest determination, the Japanese navy did not hesitate in sending against the landing force almost all the air, surface, and underwater forces it had. The desperate attempt to save the island was in vain.

Four submarines, carrying twenty *kaiten,* and five conventional submarines were ordered to attack the invading enemy. All but two of the nine failed to make port again. The only survivors were the *I-58,* which never got through the enemy alert zone around the besieged island, and the *I-47,* which had been damaged by air attack soon after her sortie from the homeland. The *I-58* was destined to attack the *Indianapolis* about four months later.

The heavy losses in the Okinawa campaign left the fast-shrinking Japanese navy only four large attack submarines and six transport submarines. There were also several obsolete boats, available for training purposes only. In addition, four 3,500-ton submarines, a dozen 1,000-ton, high-speed

The *I-58,* which sank the *Indianapolis.*

boats, and several 320-ton coastal submarines were nearing completion.

There was no reason to doubt that all of the remaining submarines in operating condition would be expended in the desperate campaign around Okinawa. I believed that the time was long overdue to make a big change in the nature of submarine operations, as the name *kaiten* indicated.

I made a final attempt to persuade my superiors to accept my theory that the *kaiten* should be used to intercept Allied sea communications lines. My plea was at first bluntly rejected by the chief of staff, who further informed me that the commander in chief was of the same view. I then asked the chief of staff to relieve me from my post as a staff officer for operations, if my view on operations was to be entirely ignored. At this request, the chief of staff suggested I see the commander in chief of the Sixth Fleet, Vice Admiral Shige-yoshi Miwa, and personally express my view to him.

My recommendation to Admiral Miwa was made in an operations room of the headquarters, with the chief of staff and other staff members also attending. I described in detail how futile the Okinawa campaign had been, and tried to show the uselessness of sending more of our submarines into the well-guarded sea around Okinawa. I stressed that the only means of employing submarines usefully under the extremely adverse circumstances with which we were faced was in raiding operations with *kaiten* against enemy convoys. In a recent

449

experiment, *kaiten* had proved practical for such operations, I explained.

Finally, I added that my view on this new employment of submarines was shared by almost all the submarine skippers and crews, and also that all preparations necessary for conducting raiding operations at sea had already been completed.

By that time, the empire was hard pressed on all sides. Its outer perimeter in the Solomons, Gilberts, Marshalls, Marianas, New Guinea, and the Philippines had long since collapsed, while its inner stronghold had just been punctured at Iwo Jima and Okinawa. Clearly, desperate measures were called for.

Admiral Miwa listened very attentively to my suggestions on the new employment of the remnant of his submarine force. Seemingly, he had some difficulty in making a decision, but he finally approved the use of two submarines scheduled for the next operation, the *I-36* and *I-47*, in a raiding operation at sea.

This decision was reported immediately to higher command in Tokyo. The Combined Fleet Command gave ready approval to the submarine fleet's decision, but the Naval General Staff was harder to crack. It was only after a long, argumentative telephone conversation that its staff in charge of operations finally gave in, on the condition that this operation would not be repeated.

The submarine *I-47* left Kure on 20 April 1945, and the *I-36* sortied two days later. Each carried six *kaiten* on deck, assigned to the new mission of attacking enemy ships at sea.

The *I-47*'s patrol station was between Ulithi and Okinawa, and the *I-36* was to operate between Saipan and Okinawa. Until then, Japanese submarines had never been used to interrupt the enemy's line of communication between a newly invaded point and his rear bases.

While submerged at dawn on 27 April, the *I-36* discovered on the brightening horizon far to the south a group of ships that soon turned out to be over thirty vessels apparently heading for Okinawa.

450

Immediately, orders for preparing a *kaiten* attack were given. Out of six human torpedoes, two were found to be inoperable.

When the submarine had closed to a point some 7,000 meters forward of the beam of the enemy convoy, four *kaiten* were released. There was no indication that the *I-36* had been detected. Ten minutes after launch time, four big explosions were heard. The submarine was not subjected to counterattack by the enemy, but she failed to confirm the result of her *kaiten* attack. How much damage this first *kaiten* attack on ships at sea inflicted was unknown to us.

In the meantime, the *I-47* had been patrolling between Okinawa and Ulithi. After dark on 1 May, her newly installed radar picked up a target, and the submarine closed the range in a rough sea. At 10,000 meters, the *I-47* dove without having gained visual contact.

About twenty-five minutes after submerging, the ship was in a favorable position, some 4,000 meters forward of the beam of the target, and she fired four ordinary torpedoes. Through the periscope, the skipper confirmed three hits.

The unexpected good luck of the *I-47* had not ended. At 0930 on the following morning, a sonar contact was gained, which soon turned out to be two transports and two escort ships. Two *kaiten* were ordered to attack them, and two big explosions shook the submarine twenty-one minutes and twenty-five minutes respectively after they were released. Taking advantage of this success, the *I-47* released one more *kaiten* soon afterward to attack the two escort ships. This time, an explosion was heard forty-eight minutes later. The skipper of the *I-47* believed most of the attacks she delivered were successful, although they were unconfirmed.

The *I-47* shifted station to a point between Okinawa and Guam soon after this successful attack. At 1100 on 6 May, the submarine picked up what seemed to be a cruiser. Twenty-four minutes after a *kaiten* was released, a big explosion convinced the crew that the enemy cruiser had been sunk by the *kaiten*.

How much damage these *kaiten* attacks inflicted on the enemy was unknown to us, but their reported results, though unconfirmed, sufficed to convince our commanders and staff that this new tactic of employing submarines in raiding operations was far more effective than the previous tactic of sending them into well-guarded areas around bases.

A striking contrast to the sea raiding operations was the fact that out of twelve submarines that had been deployed in the vicinity of Iwo Jima and Okinawa, eight failed to make port again. No longer were there any grounds to stick to the past policy, which had proved a failure.

The operational policy of the Sixth Fleet was then switched entirely to raiding operations at sea. As the second attempt, the *I-367* made a sortie on 5 May to patrol on the line connecting Okinawa and Saipan, where she destroyed the USS *Gilligan*, a destroyer, with two *kaiten*.

In the final attempt, this time with six submarines—the *I-47*, *I-53*, *I-58*, *I-363*, *I-366*, and *I-367*—the *I-53* was assigned an area between Okinawa and Leyte, and the *I-58* went to a station between Leyte and Guam.

The *I-53* was first to bag game. On 21 July she destroyed the transport *Marathon*, and three days later she sank the destroyer escort *Underhill*.

The *I-58* made her first contact on 28 July, when she discovered a large tanker. The oiler was believed to have been sunk by two *kaiten*.[6]

After this attack, the *I-58* proceeded to the point where the Okinawa-Palau line crosses the Guam-Leyte line, the point where she met the USS *Indianapolis* on 29 July.

The contacting and sinking of that vessel, from our viewpoint, was a fortune of war that showed our newly adopted submarine tactics to be correct. To the Americans, the loss of this vessel with so many of her officers and men, so near the end of the war, was undoubtedly a most painful misfortune.

452

15

Kamikazes in the Okinawa Campaign

TOSHIYUKI
YOKOI

The long, arduous Allied advance across the Pacific was intended to culminate in a massive invasion of the Japanese homeland that would bring the war to an end. Okinawa in the Ryukyus was selected as a suitable site for an advanced base to support the final assault, and Operation Iceberg was mounted to capture the island. Forming part of the inner ring of the Japanese defense perimeter, Okinawa was defended by well-entrenched, dedicated troops and by planes based on not-too-distant airfields.

The complex Allied plan incorporated all of the experience gained in the previous two years of fighting. Carrier-based aircraft succeeded in temporarily neutralizing many of the adjacent airfields, and heavy naval bombardment preceded the initial landings, which encountered surprisingly little resistance. The Allied force was deployed to prevent interference or reinforcement by Japanese surface forces, and radar picket ships were stationed to warn of approaching enemy aircraft. The need for these precautions became clear

453

as the stubborn resistance anticipated by the Allies soon materialized.

In what amounted to a last-ditch stand to defend the island, the Japanese troops in elaborately prepared installations bitterly contested every foot of ground. Simultaneously, hordes of kamikazes struck the Allied surface vessels in an effort to destroy the cordon protecting and supporting the amphibious operation. How close this desperate venture came to succeeding will never be known, but U.S. losses totaled twenty-one ships sunk and sixty-six damaged as some seven thousand sorties were flown by Japanese navy and army aircraft.

The following article, although critical of the decision to employ kamikaze tactics, presents the factors that motivated the high command and reveals the progress of the battle for Okinawa as perceived by the Japanese. In this account are also found those shortcomings which plagued Japanese operations throughout the war: specifically, inaccurate information and an absence of unity of command. But what the author calls "the vanity of heroism" was the rule rather than the exception on both sides in this savage last great battle of the Pacific War.

JAPAN'S special air attack units (kamikaze) were initially organized under very particular circumstances and with limited operational objectives in the Philippines late in 1944. In the first stage Admiral Ohnishi certainly did not conceive of either allocating more than twenty-four planes for such suicide attacks or continuing this type of operation indefinitely, because there are serious basic defects in this type of attack. First, the expenditure of life and materiel is great. It takes several years to train one good pilot, yet in kamikaze operations he, as well as his plane, will be expended in a single sortie. This runs counter to the most important problem of an operations staff, which is to attain objectives with the least possible expenditure of life and materiel. Second, the striking velocity of a plane is not great enough to penetrate the decks of fleet carriers or battleships and cause critical damage below. A suicide attack on a carrier deck will not strike a vital blow unless the deck is full of planes. Third, operational command of kamikaze planes is difficult because results cannot be evaluated with any accuracy. When his subordinates' lives are sacrificed, a commander will naturally tend to overestimate the results achieved. When such overestimates are compounded, a totally erroneous picture will be presented to the high command, whose judgment and decisions in turn will be falsely influenced.

These factors provide substantial reason why wise commanders were opposed to suicide air attacks, and yet the early reports of the kamikazes' amazing success caught the fancy of military leaders as well as the public—and the craze was on. The fact that sunken U.S. escort carriers were reported as standard fleet carriers was completely unknown and unrecognized in the surge of enthusiasm that overrode all defects of the kamikaze attacks.

Another factor contributing to the situation was the vanity of heroism.

Thus came the age of suicide air attacks.

Imperial General Headquarters was so fully convinced that it issued an outrageous and unprecedented order to the effect that *all* armed forces should resort to suicide attack. This proved that the high command, utterly confused by a succession of defeats, had lost all wisdom of cool judgment and had degenerated to the point of indulging in wild gambling. The order was nothing less than a national death sentence. Like every military order, it was issued in the name of the emperor and was, therefore, no matter how outrageous, not open to question or criticism. Obedience was imperative; there was

A final salute by his comrades sends a kamikaze pilot on his last flight.

no alternative. Critics of the kamikaze attacks should distinguish the completely volunteer flights of October 1944 from those made after this imperial order.

Once the Philippines were lost, the Japanese navy expected the next enemy thrust to be made at Okinawa. Here there were anchorages adequate for a large fleet and sites to accommodate a group of large airfields.

Okinawa is 1,000 miles from Leyte and 1,200 miles from the Marianas, too great a range for land planes to operate, so the U.S. Navy would probably have to commit all of its carrier striking force in order to cover the landings. On the other hand, it should be comparatively easy for the defending Japanese to maintain supply lines to the Japanese mainland, only 350 miles distant, especially since there were operational airfields on the intervening islands of Kikai and Minami Daito. These circumstances promised a good opportunity to bring air power to bear in striking a serious blow at the enemy task forces.

In early November 1944 I was given command of the Twenty-fifth Air Flotilla, which was based at Kanoya in southern Kyushu. A study of recent Japanese defeats had convinced me that the ineffectiveness of our land-based air strength was attributable, in the main, to poor defense measures and the inexperience of the pilots. I felt firmly that carrier-based aircraft were no match for land-based planes properly employed. In the Marianas, the Philippines, and Taiwan, our planes had been defeated easily because of inadequate patrol systems and improper defensive tactics generally. Successful operation of land bases demanded improved patrol methods, elimination of surprise by the enemy, and effective measures to protect ground installations so that fighting strength would not be interrupted. If these could be achieved, our shorter lines of communication would provide a supply advantage that would enable us to await an enemy blunder that might lay him open to a fatal blow.

In anticipation of the enemy attack on Okinawa, I concentrated on building up airfield defenses in southern Kyushu. It was fortunate that most of these bases were located on tablelands where tunnels could easily be dug in the sandy earth. Materials and manpower were insufficient for the preparation of underground hangars, but most of the other important installations, such as the command communications system, telegraph stations, ammunition dumps, repair shops, and living quarters, were dug in. The planes were to be concealed in the surrounding forests and hills. Terrain permitting, runways were to be camouflaged to resemble ordinary roads. Emptied barracks and hangars were left above ground as a decoy to absorb enemy attacks. In carrying out these plans I encouraged and supervised the construction crews and also

457

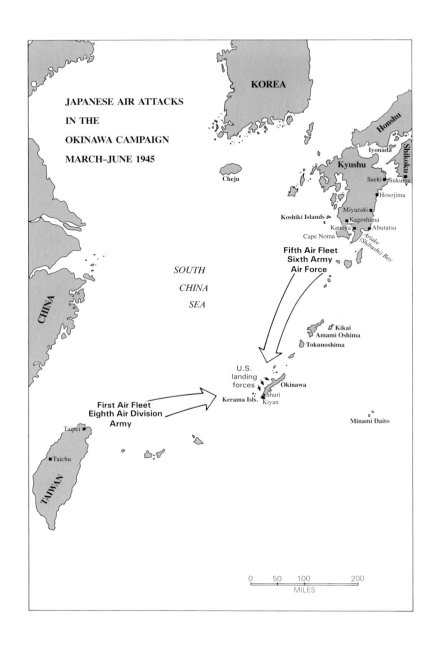

JAPANESE AIR ATTACKS
IN THE
OKINAWA CAMPAIGN
MARCH–JUNE 1945

KOREA

Honshu

Shikoku

Iyonada

Kyushu

Saeki Sukuma

Hosojima

Cheju

Miyazaki

Koshiki Islands

Kagoshima

Kanoya Aburatsu

Cape Noma

Ariake (Shibushi) Bay

Fifth Air Fleet
Sixth Army
Air Force

SOUTH

CHINA

SEA

CHINA

Kikai
Amami Oshima

Tokunoshima

U.S.
landing
forces

Okinawa

Kerama Isls. Shuri
Kiyan

First Air Fleet
Eighth Air Division
Army

Minami Daito

Taipei

Taichu

TAIWAN

0   50   100   200

MILES

458

urged off-duty aviation personnel to assist them, so that by early February 1945 great progress had been made in the earthworks and I felt confidence in our position.

On 9 February I received orders to report to the Naval General Staff as soon as possible. I left Kanoya immediately in a bomber plane that took me to Atsugi, but it was dark when I reached the residence of the chief of the Naval General Staff. There Vice Admiral Seiichi Ito, the vice chief, greeted me with the information that I was to be appointed chief of staff to the Fifth Air Fleet Commander, Vice Admiral Matome Ugaki, the man who had been chief of staff of the Combined Fleet under the famous Admiral Isoroku Yamamoto at the time of Pearl Harbor.

"What is the mission of this command?" I asked.

"The Fifth Air Fleet will be composed of approximately six hundred planes comprising the eight élite aviation units remaining in the Japanese navy. Its area of operation will extend from Okinawa eastward to a north-south line through the middle of the Japanese home islands. Your mission will be to break up enemy carrier striking forces by concentrating all power in suicide air attacks."

Since I had never believed in the soundness of such tactics, the words "concentrating all power in suicide air attacks" were especially disagreeable to me. Accordingly, I frankly expressed my opinions concerning air operations and asked permission to decline this post, which would call for carrying out assignments in which I did not believe. Admiral Ito went to consult with his chief and returned shortly to say that I was still requested to take the post. Thereupon I accepted with the understanding that implementation of the attacks should be left to the decision of the Fifth Air Fleet commander. I insisted on this condition to ensure that the Fifth Air Fleet could determine how and when each of its units would be employed. I knew that two of the eight units were practically untrained and so were not fit for anything but suicide duty. The others, capable of any kind of operation, should be kept flexible as to their employment as long as possible. The air-fields of northern Kyushu and Shikoku were designated for training or rear area purposes, while the ones in southern Kyushu were to be operational bases.

Our new headquarters were established at Kanoya on 13 February, and the direction of operations was begun. The headquarters office was located in a new barracks building set unobtrusively beside the airfield. This temporary structure was not even adequate to keep out the cold winter wind, and charcoal braziers were our only form of heating apparatus. But the approach of spring was soon heralded by white plum blossoms in the trees, delicate violets peeking from the weeds, and nightingales warbling in bushes outside the barracks windows.

On 14 March a reconnaissance plane from Truk reported the departure of an enemy task force from Ulithi. On 17 March at 2300 the alarm in the headquarters of the Fifth Air Fleet rang loudly to announce a report from one of our planes patrolling in waters to the south. It had made radar contact with a northbound fleet of enemy ships. Our planes, alerted since early afternoon, were ready and waiting to launch an attack on any enemy ships that might appear in our area of operations. This was the golden opportunity.

At 0350 the next morning fifty torpedo planes took off from fields at Miyazaki and Kanoya, the night attack units followed directly by dawn attack units, in accordance with Battle Plan No. 1. And most of the night attack units succeeded in locating the enemy and launching their torpedoes.

Enemy planes in turn struck the Kanoya base at about 0500 and maintained incessant attacks for almost five hours, but these raids were so weak and disordered that it appeared we might have upset their assault plan. From dawn reconnaissance reports it was estimated that the enemy force was built around fifteen carriers, one of which had been set afire.[1] Starting at 0600 our fighters and bombers took advantage of

460

every interval between enemy attacks on the field to get into the air and assault the enemy ships.

From a hilltop vantage point I observed that most of the enemy attacks concentrated on empty hangar and barracks buildings from which our colors waved enticingly in the breeze. There was no real damage done at Kanoya during the first day except for a few men injured by bomb fragments, but the battle raged day and night.

Reconnaissance planes sent out in the morning of 19 March reported that the enemy had only eleven carriers. This was encouraging, but communication wires at our land bases had now been severed by the bombardment, and radio channels were so crowded and confused that planes returning from combat were landing everywhere on Kyushu, Shikoku, and Chugoku.[2] It was impossible for commanders to know how many planes they had or where they were, and directing the operations became extremely difficult.

On 19 March there were no enemy attacks in southern Kyushu, and at 1030 the next morning the enemy task force was found to be withdrawing to the east. An immediate order for all units to pursue brought out more planes than I had counted on to continue the attack, and the day's reports indicated that three more enemy carriers had been bombed.[3] Following night and dawn sorties by our planes on 21 March, the enemy was spotted about three hundred miles southeast of Kanoya. In an effort to take advantage of this opportunity, eighteen bombers were ordered to take off at 1330, each bomber loaded with a 4,700-pound *Oka* (cherry blossom) bomb.[4]

This cumbersome cargo deprived a bomber of all maneuverability and made it a sitting duck for enemy fighter planes. Hence these bombers should have had plenty of escort planes for such a mission, but the fatigue after several successive days of battle left only thirty fighters to accompany the bombers. This force approached to within some sixty miles from the enemy fleet when it was intercepted and engaged by about

461

fifty Grumman fighters. In ten minutes of combat the entire Japanese force was destroyed.

In three days of battle the Fifth Air Fleet lost 161 planes. Aerial reconnaissance indicated that five enemy carriers had been withdrawn from the battle line because of damage. These results were less than had been anticipated, but I was satisfied that the fighting flexibility of the Fifth Air Fleet had been maintained.

It did not seem that the enemy had even had time enough to regroup his fleet for another offensive, when, on 23 March, raids were made on Okinawa and Minami Daito islands, followed by naval shellings the next day. On 25 March the enemy landed on the nearby Kerama Islands preliminary to invading Okinawa. Having earlier placed the Third and Tenth Air Fleets under the Fifth Air Fleet, the commander in chief of the Combined Fleet now ordered that the combined force attack enemy forces around Okinawa. Our combined naval air strength amounted to about 1,815 planes, including 540 special attack planes, and the Sixth Army Air Force had been ordered to cooperate with us. Preparations were being made for this all-out effort when the enemy, on the first day of April, made his first landings on Okinawa. It had been settled with the army that their planes would attack transports while our navy planes would be responsible for the warships. Thus, target allocations had been made, but the only planes and pilots capable of attacking anything stronger than a transport were those of the original Fifth Air Fleet and a few elements of the Third.

Full preparations were completed and our first general attack was launched on 6 April. In the early morning reconnaissance planes had spotted four U.S. task forces in the water south of Amami Oshima. From surrounding air bases we sent thirty dive-bombers, forty fighter-bombers, and fifty fighters to assault this enemy. The only indication of results came from the intelligence section at Kanoya, which judged, from

A crippled Frances bomber passes over an escort carrier somewhere near Okinawa, April 1945. The antiaircraft gunners ignore the plane as they train outboard for other possible suicide attacks. *Official U.S. Navy photograph*

enemy radio interceptions, that at least four carriers had been hit by bombs. Another thirty fighters from Kanoya took off at noon and flew directly to Okinawa. Their approach was coordinated with planes from other bases, all timed to catch the enemy fighters just after they had landed. A total of about a hundred of our fighters charged upon Okinawa in this effort to gain control of the air. Paced with their approach, three reconnaissance planes scattered counter-radar "window" to the east of Okinawa, successfully deceiving the enemy, who took Minami Daito Island to be our main base and attacked it with most of his force. Seizing this opportunity, some 110 naval suicide planes and 90 army planes pulled a surprise

463

attack from the west on U.S. warships and transports in the vicinity of Okinawa. The First Air Fleet and the Eighth Air Division from Formosa also contributed to this assault, which set fire to many ships and so filled the sky with smoke that reconnaissance planes could not see enough to make a clear report of the situation. The Thirty-second Army, which was defending Okinawa, reported that more than thirty ships were observed sinking, and more than twenty burning.[5]

In the early morning of 7 April a scout plane found three carriers moving southeastward at slow speed and trailing oil. Of thirty planes dispatched promptly to attack them, nineteen were reported to have plunged into the carriers. This same day saw seventy planes crash into enemy transports. And again intercepted enemy radio messages indicated that a great deal of damage had been done.[6]

This day saw another form of suicide venture by the Japanese navy that failed completely. The battleship *Yamato* was sunk, along with the light cruiser and three destroyers of her nine escorting warships, by enemy air attack. This force had sortied from the homeland the day before, heading for Okinawa. Its mission was to approach the enemy-besieged island and shell the landing areas with the *Yamato*'s long-range 18.1-inch guns. It was felt that the massed firepower of these ten ships could wreak profitable damage on the enemy aircraft they were bound to attract, and that at the same time Japanese suicide planes would have increased success in striking their targets without aerial competition, as a result of the American fighter protection being lured to the *Yamato*. Japanese resignation to the sacrifice of the *Yamato* in this mission was apparent from the fact that on her departure from Japan she was provided with only enough fuel for a one-way run to Okinawa. As it turned out, this was more than enough, for after two hours of intense air attack she sank at 1430 of the day following her sortie, a full day before reaching her bombardment position off Okinawa.

However, we at Fifth Air Fleet headquarters received an

464

encouraging message on 9 April, as follows: "In view of the impact your heavy assaults are having on the enemy, the Naval General Staff expects you to continue general attacks at all cost." Accordingly, a second general attack consisting of 100 suicide planes and 150 fighters was launched on 12 April. On the same day another detachment of twenty planes attacked an enemy task force cruising in the waters east of Okinawa, and that night forty-five torpedo planes made still another attack in which five warships were reported set afire.[7]

A report from our naval attaché in Portugal announced the serious losses sustained by the U.S. Navy and indicated that if the rate of attrition continued, the operation would result in disaster for the enemy. This inspired a third general attack by 220 army and navy planes on the night of 15–16 April, while a separate detachment of 110 planes assaulted enemy task groups southeast of Kikai Island.[8]

By this time it was obvious that our operations were making some progress, but, as might be expected of such tactics, they were also taking a terrific toll of our own air strength. It was estimated that two thousand naval planes were involved in combat operations between 23 March and 16 April, and some six hundred of these were destroyed. As aircraft complements became depleted and replacements were not immediately available, we were compelled to suspend operations for a short time. While the navy took the attitude that these were last-ditch operations and devoted its entire energy to them, the army regarded the Okinawa campaign as a mere preliminary to decisive battles in Japan proper, and so kept most of its strength in reserve. There was little, if any, unity of idea between the two services on this point.

On 17 April the Tenth Air Fleet was withdrawn from our command, leaving us only 610 planes, of which a mere 370 were operational. In addition our forces had been fighting day and night and everyone was beginning to show signs of fatigue. Under such circumstances, despite the urgency and our own eagerness, we were unable to launch continuous and

465

The carrier *Bunker Hill,* hit by kamikazes off Okinawa on 11 May 1945. *Official U.S. Navy photograph*

successive attacks as before, but had to be content with sporadic air actions. A fourth general attack was finally launched on 28 April, but fewer than sixty planes could be mustered for the event.[9]

Meanwhile the army's situation on Okinawa was in serious jeopardy under the enemy's overwhelming firepower. The fresh green of the mountains north of Shuri had been transformed into a scorched brown. The Thirty-second Army's elaborately-worked-out positions were reduced one after the other as the enemy moved steadily southward. This irritated the army command into pressing a courageous and determined offensive on 4 May in which the navy joined by carrying out a fifth general attack with 280 planes.[10] As a result, we were pleased to receive a message of thanks from the Thirty-second Army which reported that the offensive had made good progress. But our joy was fleeting, as the army called off the offensive after suffering almost seven thousand casualties.

Our sixth general attack was executed on 11 May and the

466

240 participating planes achieved some results.[11] A night patrol plane spotted an approaching enemy task force at 0300 on 14 May, but its report was delayed owing to a communication failure, and no planes were sent to intercept. From early morning until mid-afternoon, therefore, the air bases of southern Kyushu were raided by about 450 planes, but again our casualties were insignificant. With great patience our air units bided their time throughout the day and made preparations for a night attack. In our midnight attack a carrier was set on fire, but a sudden rain prevented our following up this opportunity.[12]

On the night of 24 May a seventh general attack was made in cooperation with the army, who had decided to make air attacks on Allied airfields on Okinawa.[13] By this time we had been forced to include *shiragiku* (white chrysanthemum) units in our operations. These units were made up of old training planes whose combat capabilities were practically nil, but they were used anyhow to fill the many gaps in our decimated organization. I had to smile, therefore, on reading an intercepted message from an enemy destroyer, "We are being pursued by a Jap plane making eighty-five knots."

Two final efforts were made on 27 May and 7 June when we executed our eighth and ninth general attacks, but so few planes were available each time that we were obliged to acknowledge the failure of these attempts.[14] The Thirty-second Army continued its reluctant southward retreat in the latter part of May, withdrawing from the Shuri redoubt to the Kiyan area at the southern tip of Okinawa. It was greatly hampered by the seasonal rains, which also interrupted our feeble efforts to help. Rejecting an enemy order to surrender, the commander, Lieutenant General Ushijima, and his chief of staff committed suicide at their command post on 23 June, and eighty days of fierce battle on Okinawa came to an end.

In these operations, in which a total of three thousand planes took part and more than seven hundred were lost, the Japanese navy utterly exhausted itself. The battle for Okinawa proved conclusively the defects of suicide air attacks. Such operations cannot be successful where materiel and trained manpower are limited. It would have been far wiser for the sadly depleted Japanese military to have conserved its manpower instead of squandering it as was done. It is not strange that this unrealistic aerial tactic ended in failure. Even the physical destructive power of the weapon itself was not sufficient for the task for which it had been designed. While it might deal a fatal blow to small warships or transports, the enemy aircraft carriers, which were meant to be primary targets, were sometimes able to survive attacks in which they were hit several times. Setting aside Admiral Ohnishi's original concept of adopting suicide attacks for the limited purpose of inactivating carrier decks for a week, the whole concept of suicide attacks to annihilate enemy task forces was more than unreasonable, it was sheer lunacy. Once the order had been issued by headquarters for these suicide attacks, they lost their volunteer aspect and became, instead, "murder attacks," and humanity was lost sight of.

As might have been expected, these attacks created many command problems. Early in the Okinawa campaign pilots could go to their death with some hope that their country might realize some benefit from their sacrifice. But toward the last, the doomed pilots had good reason for doubting the validity of the cause in which they were told to die. The difficulties became especially apparent when men in aviation training were peremptorily ordered to the front and to death. When it came time for their takeoff, the pilots' attitudes ranged from the despair of sheep headed for slaughter to open expressions of contempt for their superior officers. There were frequent and obvious cases of pilots returning from sorties claiming that they could not locate any enemy ships, and one pilot even strafed his commanding officer's quarters as he took off. When planes did not return there was seldom any way of knowing the results of their sacrifice. There was no conclusive means of determining if they had crashed into a target. Even with reconnaissance planes accompanying, there was no assurance of a valid report because observers were usually kept too busy avoiding enemy fighters. After a careful examination of all reports I estimated that only a total of five enemy carriers had been damaged by Kyushu-based planes. Yet a single unit commander gave me absolute assurance that his men alone had damaged eight carriers, and he continued, "If the results achieved are going to be so underestimated, there is no justification for the deaths of my men. If headquarters will not acknowledge these achievements at full value I must commit harakiri as an expression of my disapproval and by way of apology."

Upon conclusion of the Okinawa campaign the Japanese Naval General Staff produced an estimate of the situation, which summed up prospective moves of the enemy.

First, Allied forces would attempt to seize the southwestern home islands of Tokunoshima, Kikai, and Amami Oshima. At the same time his air forces at Okinawa and Iwo Jima, and in the Marianas would increase their bombing operations against Japan so as to lower morale, destroy airfields, and disrupt land and sea communications.

Second, just before invading the homeland, Allied task forces would concentrate on smashing the Japanese fleet and air bases. The most likely points of invasion were in southern Kyushu and in the Kanto Plain area which surrounds Tokyo, but there was a strong probability that landings would also be made at Cheju (Quelpart Island, Saishuto), south of Korea, in order to sever communications between Korea, Manchuria, and Japan. Landings in southern Kyushu would take place after August and would be attempted by 15–20 divisions. When a foothold had been established there, an invasion of the Kanto Plain by some thirty to forty divisions would follow, sometime after September.

A further breakdown of enemy capabilities and intentions was made with predictions that one division would hit the

Koshiki Islands, off Kyushu, to set up a base; no fewer than six divisions would assault the western coast, north of Cape Noma; and when a bridgehead was established there, the main force of at least eight divisions would land at Ariake (Shibushi) Bay, on the eastern coast of Miyazaki. In the east a minimum of eight divisions would lead off by striking at Oshima, Kujukurihama, and the Kashima coast, followed by about twelve divisions on the Boso Peninsula, and then the main force would land at Sagami Bay and sweep over the Kanto Plain.

It was indicated that the Allies would have the following naval forces available to carry out these operations:

	United States	British
Aircraft carriers	25–26	4
Escort carriers	70–74	8
Battleships	23–24	6
Cruisers	35–36	
Destroyers	244–254	

To oppose these forces, in August 1945, Japan's principal strength lay in its four naval air fleets, which contained a total of 5,044 planes, in categories as follows:

Fighters	1,170
Night fighters	125
Light bombers	636
Medium bombers	352
Reconnaissance	70
Seaplanes	398
Trainers	2,218
Others	75

Of ships and naval craft Japan had the following:

Aircraft carriers	5	(all damaged)
Battleships	4	(all damaged)
Cruisers	2	
Destroyers	23	

470

Submarines	46
Midget submarines	400 (*Koryu* and *Kairyu*)
Manned torpedoes	120 (*Kaiten*)
Charge-laden motor- boats	2,000 (*Shinyo*)

For the benefit of readers unfamiliar with craft of the last three categories, salient specifications of each are given.

Pocket Submarines

	Displace- ment tonnage	Length	Width	Height	Safe submerged depth	Explosive	Crew
Koryu	59.3	86'	6'8½"	9'8½"	330	2 18" torps (in tubes)	5
Kairyu	19.3	57'	4'3"	4'3"	650	2 18" torps (external) or 1 1,300-lb warhead	2

Manned Torpedoes (*Kaiten*)

Type	Length	Diameter	Range	Explosive	Crew
I	48'	39"	78 mi. at 12 knots 23 mi. at 30 knots	3,200-lb	1
II (IV)	54'	52"	83 (62) mi. at 20 knots 25 (27) mi. at 40 knots	over 3,200-lb	2

The charge-laden motorboats (*shinyo*) were 16½ feet in length, weighed 2,800 pounds, had a top speed of 23 knots, a cruising radius of 250 miles, and carried a 550-pound explosive charge in the bow.

A careful study of the situation led the Naval General Staff to conclude that all Japanese surface forces should be meticulously conserved until the enemy actually began landing. To this end all warships were ordered into concealment at various Inland Sea islands north of Iyonada. And, following the pattern I had established earlier in southern Kyushu, a system

471

of airfield defense was instituted throughout the country.

It was determined that special attack units, both air and submarine, should seize every opportunity to hit enemy ships at advanced bases before their task forces sortied. Careful and thorough patrols were flown day and night by some 140 planes, which covered the sea to a distance of six hundred miles from each of the anticipated landing points. Coastal waters were patrolled by small and medium submarines.

As soon as the enemy's intended landing points were indicated, almost all Japanese air and sea forces would immediately be concentrated in the battle area. There were 150 specially equipped torpedo planes set up in night attack groups to strike warships bombarding our coast, and 330 top-notch planes and pilots constituted élite units that were assigned to engage approaching enemy task forces. Another group of planes—a hundred transports—were designated to carry 1,200 airborne troops to Okinawa airfields, where they would destroy planes and fuel dumps at the critical moment. Most of the air forces were disposed in the southwestern part of the homeland, while the surface and underwater suicide units were distributed about equally between the eastern and western areas as follows:

		Kairyu	*Kaiten*	*Shinyo*
Kyushu	Hosojima	20	12	325
	Aburatsu	20	34	125
	Kagoshima	20		500
	Saeki	20		
Shikoku	Sukumo	12	14	50
	Sunosaki	12	24	175
Kanto Plain area		180	36	775
Total		284	120	1,950

As enemy convoys finally approached their assault destinations, all suicide forces were to launch day and night attacks which would be sustained for at least ten days. It was

472

expected that 3,725 naval planes (more than half of them trainers), and 2,500 army planes would be available to carry out these attacks. At the same time a squadron composed of one cruiser and nineteen destroyers was to make night attacks on the ships once they had anchored. It was calculated that these combined efforts would succeed in sinking half of the anticipated ships in the enemy invasion fleet.

But this whole scheme was conceived in futility and prepared for in despair. So critical was the situation by August 1945 that Japan's shortage of fuel alone was enough to banish confidence. The contemplated ten-day aerial effort would have drained every drop of fuel from every plane and storage tank in Japan. The only commodity to survive the pinch of Japan's wartime economy was hope, and that was rapidly disappearing.

An official announcement by Combined Fleet Headquarters said that 2,409 kamikaze pilots were killed in performance of their duty during World War II. It was a real scourge of Japan's military forces that permitted human life to be treated so lightly through a misinterpretation of the true spirit of *bushido*.

Japan's suicide air operations mark the Pacific War with two scars that will remain forever in the annals of battle: one, of shame at the mistaken way of command; the other, of valor at the self-sacrificing spirit of young men who died for their beloved country.

16

The Sinking of the *Yamato*

MITSURU
YOSHIDA

Throughout much of history, control of the sea has
been determined by fleet action. In the late nineteenth century a controversy arose among naval authorities over the
respective merits of raiding commerce and of a single major
engagement as the decisive method of exerting sea power.
Japan, in keeping with her program of westernization, emu-
lated Great Britain and the United States in embracing the
fleet concept with the battleship as the ultimate arbiter.
After denouncing the naval limitation treaties, Japan embarked on a building program that included the construction of the most formidable warships ever to sail the seas.
The *Yamato* was the pride of the surface Japanese Imperial
Navy. No effort had been spared to incorporate every com-
ponent to make her the mightiest engine of destruction
afloat, and her survival of the battles of Midway, the Philippine Sea, and Leyte Gulf encouraged a belief that she could
follow up the kamikaze attacks on the Allied naval forces at
Okinawa and wipe out the remaining surface vessels.

In the following article one senses the feeling of impend-

474

ing doom as the majestic ship sailed forth on its desperate mission. Subjected to repeated and relentless air strikes, she finally capsized and sank. With her passing, wrote Samuel Eliot Morison, "five centuries of naval warfare ended," and her loss symbolized the demise of Japanese naval power.

O N 1 APRIL 1945 we were moored to No. 26 buoy floating in the outermost border of Kure Naval Port, waiting our turn to enter the dock for quick repairs and overhaul. I was the junior radar officer on board the super-dreadnought *Yamato*.

Suddenly the ship's loudspeaker filled the stillness of the morning air: "Commence sailing preparations from 0815; weighing anchor at 1000!"

U.S. forces had landed at Okinawa!

Would we pass through Shimonoseki-Moji Channel and fuel at Sasebo or Pusan and then proceed directly south? Or would we sail straight through Bungo Channel? Where was the sea battle to be? What ships would consort with the *Yamato*? Was this to be the decisive battle for supremacy of the South Sea area?

Once again the loudspeaker reverberated throughout the ship: "All divisions, bring inflammables topside! Stow all personal belongings. Secure all watertight compartments! . . . Last boat to shore at 0831! . . . All division officers, check watertight integrity!"

I was in charge of the last launch to shore and soon headed for No. 1 pier. Thin clouds curtained the sky; the sea was misty in the dreamy naval port of Kure. After arriving at the pier and finishing the business at hand, roll call was taken to assure that nobody was left behind. (If a man missed his ship's sailing for action, he would face a firing squad.)

As we glided toward the *Yamato*, preparations were made for hoisting our launch as soon as we came alongside. Painted silvery gray, the *Yamato* lay in the sea like a gigantic rock commanding all around her. Anchored nearby, the cruiser *Yahagi* easily read our flashing signal lights, "Preparations for sortie completed. . . ."

At 1000 the *Yamato* started out to sea, the only ship leaving that day. To the last man on board our hearts were filled with gaiety and pride. Hundreds of eyes from other vessels at anchor focused upon the slowly gliding *Yamato*. It was a silent send-off, profoundly touching! Stealthy but majestic was our departure.

As we sailed toward the Suo-nada Sea, the captain and his staff on the bridge discussed the operation plan. A detailed chart of the waters surrounding Okinawa was spread on the chart table. Above the island extended an arc whose focal point was the beach where the enemy had landed; the radius of this arc was forty kilometers, the firing range of the *Yamato*'s big guns.

At dusk the *Yamato* lay anchored off the shore of Mitajiri. Several destroyers had arrived before us and had entered Kyo Channel, which was impassable to our ship. Our mooring was a temporary anchorage where all the ships could assemble, having left Kure independently to preserve utmost secrecy. No shore leaves were granted, and so the only thing left to do was await the "Go" sign.

Meanwhile all personnel had been ordered to gather on the deck. Dressed in fighting khakis, 3,000 of us stood at silent attention as Captain Kosaku Ariga explained our mission and objective and expressed an ardent hope that we would do our best. Then Captain Jiro Nomura, the executive officer, shouted—"*Kamikaze Yamato*, be truly a *kamikaze!*"

Reports that a U.S. task force was in the area and likely to launch an air strike at any time put us all on the alert. As we got under way for maneuvers the next day, an early morning report informed us that enemy planes were headed in our direction. We stood fast at battle stations all day, but only

The end of the line for the *Yamato,* 7 April 1945. Under attack by
U.S. Navy carrier aircraft, the ship trails oil from ruptured tanks.
The destroyer in the foreground tries to fight off attackers. *Official
U.S. Navy photograph*

one B-29 was sighted. He blindly dropped one medium
bomb, which inflicted no damage, but he must have taken
aerial photographs and this thought disrupted our hopes for
secrecy of movement. In the afternoon, reports came pouring
in that many areas of Japan were suffering heavy air raids.
This news stirred our emotions, and we thought bitterly,
"Wait—just wait! —until we sortie!"

By sunset we had returned to the anchorage. A launch
came alongside carrying fifty proud midshipmen, who
quickly scrambled on board for a tour of the ship. In the
meantime our radio had picked up an enemy message: "U.S.
task forces will raid all areas tomorrow." The time to strike
our decisive blow was imminent.

On 4 April a morning report announced the approach of
U.S. planes. Without losing a moment, all ships began to leave

port and disperse on the open sea, until the threat of attack was gone and we could return to the anchorage.

The following day a message from Imperial General Headquarters indicated that the tempo of battle in the Okinawa area was increasing. A yearning for immediate action was kindled in our hearts and souls.

In the gunnery room, young officers exchanged heated words on the question of battleships versus aircraft. No one seemed to have a good word for battleships—they are doomed in an encounter with aircraft!

About 1730 the loudspeaker squeaked out a succession of orders: "All midshipmen, prepare to leave ship! . . . Each division, get ready for your *sake* ration! . . . Open the canteen!"

Each announcement brought closer the moment for our sortie. The midshipmen assembled for immediate debarkation but were invited to join in a final toast. When the navigation officer raised his *sake* cup, it slipped from his trembling fingers and fell to the floor. As it shattered, scornful eyes converged upon his ashamedly downcast head. Every man present knew that death was coming eventually—and probably soon. And when it did, each one of us must greet it determinedly, lightheartedly.

So in each division of the ship, drinking jamborees were held in solemn gaiety. At 2300 the executive officer issued an order resolutely but with a little friendly touch. "It has been good to see all of you enjoying this day. Now our time is up. To your quarters and duty stations!" Then, with one destroyer on either side of the *Yamato,* all hands went into action to unload the nonessential goods and load the oil. It was a beautiful moonlit night, and the tense atmosphere of departure filled every corner of the ship.

In the first hour of 6 April a B-29 was heard roaring overhead. "All hands to duty stations!" came an immediate order. The plane, however, flew so high that we did not fire our antiaircraft guns. The enemy's pertinacity in scouting made us grind our teeth in vexation.

At about 0200 the midshipmen boarded a waiting destroyer and went ashore. They were so young and enthusiastic. To have served on the *Yamato* must have been their most cherished desire. It was touching to see them leave the ship, their dreams shattered like the glass dropped on the floor.

All men who had been ordered to other vessels took this occasion to leave. Serious hospital cases, unable to withstand combat, were removed from the ship. We junior officers implored the skipper to also excuse those men past the forty-year mark, but following a conference of the senior officers, only a few were permitted to leave the ship.

Combat preparations were rapidly being concluded. As the fueling was finished, the destroyers were cut loose. However much oil they might have held, it was not nearly enough to fill the *Yamato*'s big tanks. All this, every move, every step taken this day, was observed by U.S. aircraft.

With the advent of morning, the loudspeakers came to life: "Sailing at 1600; general assembly at 1800 on foredeck!" Watertight compartments were inspected over and over. The length and breadth of the ship was packed with tension, finally broken by the loudspeaker: "Mails closing 1000!"

Mails closing? Closing for what? For the last letter this hand of mine will scribble? There was little heart for it, but comrades persuaded one another to write, knowing full well that this was to be a last will and testament. I wrote: "Please dispose of all my things. Take good care of yourselves and give the best in whatever you do to the last! That and that only I pray of you!" Dropping this letter into the mailbox severed my last tie with home. . . . This was the beginning of the end of everything.

Gathered in our quarters, we received an offering of His Majesty's cigarettes and other things from the canteen. Those who had the duty left first to return to their stations. These men stood at attention at the door, each one holding a white bundle containing a clean uniform. Each had a sword swinging from his side as he bowed in silence, and left the room to

479

the mumbled greeting of his comrades. As war comrades we were now so intimately related that mere glances spoke volumes.

By afternoon sortie preparations were completed. The *Yamato*'s battle flag fluttered in the air. All weapons and equipment were in perfect readiness.

At 1600 the last of the once grand Japanese Fleet set sail for the front. The mighty *Yamato*, flying the Second Fleet flag, was escorted by the *Yahagi* and the destroyers *Fuyutsuki, Suzutsuki, Yukikaze, Kasumi, Isokaze, Hamakaze, Hatsushimo,* and *Asashio.* Cruising at twelve knots, we glided through Bungo Channel. Twang! the final arrow was shot from the bow!

On the bridge my duty was to receive lookouts' reports, brief them, and relay them to the captain and his aides. To my left was Vice Admiral Seiichi Ito, the force commander, and his chief of staff, Rear Admiral Nobuei Morishita, stood on my right. I felt lucky then, and very proud.

At 1800 a final assembly was ordered, but since the captain could not leave his post, the executive officer read the solemn lines addressed to us by the commander in chief of the Combined Fleet: "Render this operation the turning point of the war!"

Then *"Kimigayo"* (the national anthem) rang out, followed by martial airs, and finally three cheers for His Imperial Majesty. Knifing through the waves, the *Yamato* pressed on as wakes from the escorts splashed to the right and left of her.

On duty, I overheard the talk of our leaders. Our strike was to be coordinated with that of kamikaze planes against the enemy in the Okinawa area. Counterattacks of the superior U.S. fighter planes against our clumsy suicide craft, heavily overloaded with explosives, had been overpowering. It became necessary therefore to decoy the enemy planes away so that our "special attack" planes could operate more effectively. This project called for something that would attract a maximum number of enemy planes and withstand their attacks for as long as possible. The *Yamato* was the most likely bait, and the nine escorts were intended to prolong her life. Thus with our fleet absorbing the bulk of the pressure from enemy forces, the way would be open for our suicide planes to make tremendous scores. If we survived this diversionary phase of our assignment, we were to advance straight into the midst of the enemy and effect maximum destruction. To this end the *Yamato* was filled to capacity with ammunition for every weapon she carried. Her tanks, however, were loaded with only enough fuel for a *one-way* passage to Okinawa! This was not bravery, but suicide; a suicide born of desperation.

In the history of sea battles, how striking and unprecedented this operation would be! How would it all turn out? The officers exchanged heated words as to the real value of this sortie.

"How is our air power? It must be near the zero mark!" ..."Have you seen the reports on the magnitude of U.S. forces at Okinawa? Our forces must be as nothing in comparison." ..."It surely is a murky situation, like groping through the inky night with a lantern." ..."We may fall victim to submarine attacks in Bungo Channel." ..."Halfway to our goal, we may fall prey to the enemy's aerial torpedoes." (This last prediction had many advocates among the young officers ... and how right it proved to be!)

Meanwhile the vanguard of our advancing flotilla was passing the midpoint of Bungo Channel. This was the line of demarcation between friendly and hostile waters.

Suddenly the detector spotted what seemed to be a submarine. Quickly the equipment was focused in that direction. There was still only faint registration, but torpedo attacks were certain and we had to be ready for them. Because of the night, we had to rely entirely on the underwater sound-detector.

We intercepted enemy messages that gave our exact course and speed. Minute by minute they were keeping track of our position.

It was now 2345. In fifteen minutes I was due on the bridge for lookout duty. Opening the curtains to the radar room, I started up the ladder to the bridge. Like a piece of paper my body was pressed by the wind against the iron rungs.

I was alone. There was no telling when another such opportunity might arise. From our course I estimated the direction and faced toward my home. Grasping the iron rail tightly, I lowered my head in a brief prayer. This done, I was soon up the ladder.

On the darkened bridge not a soul was moving. The vague silhouettes of some twenty men silently engrossed in their work came into my sight. To distinguish one from the other in the dark, the highest-ranking officers wore fluorescent initials on the back of their caps. The sight of these caps glowing eerily in the blackness was encouraging.

At daybreak on 7 April our fleet passed through Osumi Channel and proceeded southwesterly. One of the *Yamato*'s reconnaissance seaplanes winged from its catapult. This plane could serve no purpose by going to the bottom of the sea with us, so it was returning to the haven of Kagoshima Naval Air Base.

Not a single escorting plane could be seen; nor was one to be seen from this time on. We were literally abandoned. But then no matter how many fighter planes we might have been able to have as air cover, it would have been but a drop in the bucket before the overwhelming number of hostile planes that could be brought to bear.

With the approach of dawn, the submarines quit trailing us, and in their stead two Martin patrol planes appeared. They circled just beyond the range of our antiaircraft guns, which still cut loose from time to time. The planes dodged the shells adroitly. Our aircraft radar was practically useless because of the weather. Clouds were hanging very low and visibility was poor. How dexterous the planes were! They darted in and out of the clouds and continued to shadow us.

On our right flank the *Hatsushimo* began dropping back. Her flag hoist signaled "Engine trouble!" and we received a radio message that she was undergoing emergency repairs.

Despite great activity on the *Yamato*'s bridge, absolute silence prevailed. The deep lull before the storm!

The southern tip of Kyushu had already vanished. The distance between us and our homes widened steadily with every tick of the clock.

While on a course of 250 degrees, we came across several small transports. They flashed, "Good luck! Wish you success!" as a farewell encouragement to the sanguine crew of the *Yamato*.

The *Hatsushimo* lagged farther and farther behind. Enemy planes were certain to attack a lone ship, so we turned back to let her rejoin, after which we returned to course.

About 0900 I went to the upper radar room. While the *Yamato* was not on patrol duty (the ships were divided into two groups that engaged in radar patrolling duties alternately), the men sat around enjoying cigarettes from His Imperial Majesty and liquor from pocket flasks that were passed around.

An orderly came along and exclaimed gleefully "Ensign Yoshida, tonight's refreshment will be *shiruko!*" (a red-bean soup sweetened with sugar, to which rice cakes are added). His broad smile showed his pleasure at being able to spread this news.

Lowering heavy clouds were followed by an outburst of rain, which limited visibility severely and further increased the difficulties of our search duty.

Our noonday meal was simple and miserable in every respect; yet the polished white rice tasted good. It was followed by hot black tea, which we drank until our stomachs bulged. In our hearts something was smarting with every sip of tea. I went to my duty station on the bridge little dreaming that this would be my last watch in the battleship *Yamato*.

At 1200 the fleet reached the halfway mark of the expedition. The commander in chief smiled broadly and said, "During the morning watches all was well, wasn't it?"

Twenty minutes later the radar detected a formation of

483

On trial runs in 1941, the *Yamato* shows her main battery of nine 18.1-inch guns. At full load, she displaced over 70,000 tons. *Courtesy of Shizuo Fukui*

aircraft. From the after radar room the hoarse voice of the monitor could be heard reporting on the distance and direction of the approaching planes. This was so much like our routine drills that it was difficult to believe actual combat was at hand.

The targets were confirmed. Alerts were flashed to the other ships at the same time as our loudspeakers announced the emergency. Tension mounted and every lookout strained in the direction of the oncoming planes.

"Two Grummans, 25 degrees to the left, altitude 8 degrees, distance 4,000 meters, advancing to the right!" shouted the gruff voice of the No. 2 lookout. Now the planes could be seen with the naked eye.

"The target is now five planes—over ten—over thirty!" continued the lookout with mounting excitement, as a great formation of planes roared out of the clouds and circled widely in a clockwise direction.

"Over one hundred hostile planes are heading for us!" shouted the navigator.

The captain's order "Open fire!" was followed by the rattling crash of 24 antiaircraft and 150 machine guns, which burst forth simultaneously from the *Yamato* and were joined by the main batteries of her escorting destroyers.

Amid the deafening din of explosions a man nearby was struck dead by a shell fragment. I heard the dull thud of his skull striking the wall and sniffed fresh blood in the pall of smoke rising from the shellfire.

On our left flank, the *Hamakaze* had been hit and was beginning to sink. Her stern protruded high in the air. Within thirty seconds she plunged into the sea, leaving only a circle of swirling white foam.

Silvery streaks of torpedoes could be seen silently converging on us from all directions. Their distances and angles were estimated, and the *Yamato* was brought parallel to them just in time to dodge their deadly blow. All-important now were the sightings, calculations, and decisions.

Grinding along at top speed of twenty-six knots, we zigzagged desperately through the water. The rolling and vibrations were terrific! By now bombs and machine gun bullets from the planes were showering the bridge.

Time after time we avoided torpedoes, often by hairbreadths, until 1245, when a hit was scored forward on the port side. Next we took two bomb hits aft, but the ship remained on an even keel. At this point the first wave of the enemy withdrew. These planes were F6Fs and TBFs and they had used 250-kilogram bombs.

The chief of staff remarked, "Judging from their skill and bravery, these must be the enemy's finest pilots!"

"So at last a torpedo got us, eh?" said the navigator with a complacent smile. There was, however, neither reply nor smile from the others present. His arms folded, the admiral was silent as three corpses were carried from the bridge on stretchers. These were victims of machine gun bullets.

An order from the division officer was handed to me: "Radar room on aft deck damaged by bombs; inspect and report on damage at once!"

The after radar room damaged by bombs! Quickly the faces of Lieutenant JG Omori, Petty Officer Hasegawa, and the others appeared before my eyes. Naturally I would have been with them had it not been my turn for patrolling duty.

Into the haze of smoke I dashed toward the after deck. The ladder to the radar room was missing, so I lowered a rope and slid down. Despite its heavy steel walls, this solid room had been split in two and its upper half blown to pieces. There was no trace of the delicate instruments, the bombs having played havoc with everything in the room. A human torso was blown against one bulkhead and other fragments were scattered here and there. But these gruesome remnants were all that was left of eight human beings! The rest must have been pulverized into thin air by the bombs.

A roaring noise pushed closer and closer and the deck vibrated uncannily beneath my feet. Looking up, I saw the second wave of hostile planes approaching with horrifying rapidity. I thought, "This is not where I should die. My duty is on the bridge." Head down, I ran desperately back toward my station.

I was about to scramble onto the ladder beneath the foremast when a blast caused me to blink for a split second. I opened my eyes to find only a pall of white smoke rising from where the machine gun fire-control tower should have been.

Dazedly I began to climb the ladder, repeating aloud my report on the radar room, "All personnel killed in action—equipment completely destroyed—use impossible!" Machine gun bullets were striking in rapid succession against the steel plates beside me. I finally reached the ladder top and gave my report to the division officer.

During bombing and torpedo runs a certain amount of straight flying by the attacking planes is essential. These enemy planes, however, managed to maintain such a vulnerable position for only the briefest interval and then immediately shifted to zigzag flying. This was most disconcerting for our gunners, whose peaceful firing practice against sham targets had been quite different. Here were incessant explosions, blinding flashes of light, thunderous noises, and crushing weights of blast pressure!

Most of the planes in this second attack carried torpedoes.

Three scored direct hits on our port side near the after mast. Even the invulnerable *Yamato* was unable to withstand such overwhelming attacks, and our tremendous firepower seemed all but useless. As soon as the planes had dropped their deadly loads, they would turn in a lateral direction to avoid our fire, and then they would machine-gun the bridge. As though the very breath of the hostile planes were being puffed against us, the misty smoke of the explosions, the roar of the bursting shells, and the pillars of flashing flames all converged against the bridge windows with terrific force.

Now and then a hostile plane was shot down and plunged flaming into the sea, but its mission of dropping torpedoes or bombs had already been accomplished. Not a single enemy plane was rash enough to carry out a crash-dive attack on us. That these pilots repeated their attacks with such accuracy and coolness was a sheer display of the unfathomable, undreamt-of strength of our foes! There was nothing for us to do but conserve our fighting power, wait for their exhaustion, and avoid as much damage as possible.

One after another the *Yamato*'s machine-gun turrets were blown high into the air by direct hits. Our electrically operated turrets were another cause for concern. Loss of power made them inoperable, and blind firing meant decreased accuracy. Soon there were signs of unrest and shirking among the enlisted men.

White smoke was now trailing from the *Yamato*'s aircraft deck. Near misses ahead and on our bows exploded into rows of great pillars of water through which we forged. Bitten by an inexpressible feeling, I wiped the sea-drenched chart table dry with a piece of cloth. I was soaked to the skin as the second attack wave withdrew. In the twinkling of an eye the third wave came at us like a driving thunderstorm, scoring five direct hits on our port side, and the clinometer began to register a slight list.

There were so many casualties among damage-control personnel that it became impossible to maintain our watertight integrity. But the most serious problem confronting us was the damage to the control room, which made it difficult to counterflood our starboard compartments.

"All hands to work to trim ship!" ordered the captain over the loudspeaker. We had to correct the listing no matter what the sacrifices might be. The order was given to pump sea water into the starboard engine and boiler rooms. These were the largest and lowest ones in the ship, and their flooding should produce optimum results toward correcting the list. I hastily phoned these rooms to warn the occupants of the flooding order, but it was too late. Water, from both the torpedo hits and the flood valves, rushed into these compartments and snuffed out the lives of the men at their posts, several hundred in all. Caught between cold sea water and steam and boiling water from the damaged boilers, they simply melted away—a thankless end to all their days of toil in the scorching heat and deafening noise of their laborious duty.

The sacrifice of the engine room personnel scarcely affected the ship's list. We were dependent on one screw for propulsion and were losing speed rapidly. The needle of the speedometer swung crazily.

The fourth attack wave now approached on our port bow. More than 150 planes!

Here and there torpedoes pierced new holes in the port side, while more than ten bombs hit on the mizzenmast and quarter deck. On the bridge, casualties from machine gun bullets were mounting, and shrapnel flew all around. We were completely at the mercy of the hot, relentless steel.

All of a sudden, a heavy pressure fell upon me from three sides. Three men standing near me had been struck simultaneously. I managed to shake them off, and they crumpled limply to the deck. Two of them had been killed instantly. The third, Ensign Nishio, rose up on his left knee trying desperately to bandage his right thigh with a blood-soaked towel. I shouted for a stretcher, but even as we placed him on it his

face turned ghastly pale, he opened his lips as if to say something, smiled slightly, and fell back dead. His fleeting smile
changed into a distorted grimace.

One orderly, a youth of eighteen, stood trembling, his lips
quivering as he looked upon this scene of destruction. So
transfixed was he with shock that I had to strike him on the
jaw to bring him to his senses. His face flushed with a childish
look.

Casualties on the bridge were becoming grievous. Already
reduced by half, those remaining now had room to move
around much more readily.

Entering the upper radar room, I saw a pile of instruments
destroyed beyond repair from continuous hits as well as the
recoil from our own big guns. The radar personnel were
huddled together for protection. I heard afterward that they
all went down with the ship in that nestled position. This
often happens to men who have had no designated duties in
combat.

The wireless room, noted for its watertight construction,
was completely flooded. Here we lost the valuable services of
the communication officer and his subordinates, forcing the
Yamato to rely entirely on flag and light signals. What could
such a modern giant do deprived of modern ears and mouth?

Some 3,000 meters ahead of the *Yamato*, the light cruiser
Yahagi was now dead in the water, signaling the destroyer
Isokaze to come alongside. Noticing this, one group of planes
preparing to dive at the *Yamato* reversed course and headed
for these two ships. The *Yahagi* was honeycombed by more
than ten torpedoes, and gray spumes swirled about her as she
went to the bottom of the sea. The *Isokaze*, also at a standstill, was emitting a pall of black smoke.

The *Fuyuzuki* to port and the *Yukikaze* to starboard signaled, "All is well with us!" as the *Yamato* surged sluggishly
ahead through the mountainous waves. These two ships were
all that remained intact of our nine escorts. The other seven
were at a standstill, listing awkwardly, or sunk.

489

The *Yamato* under air attack in an earlier action, probably the Battle off Samar, 25 October 1944. *Courtesy of the National Archives*

With no hostile planes overhead, this was the first prolonged interval of quiet since battle had been joined. Bombs, bullets, and torpedoes had reduced the *Yamato* to a state of complete confusion. Communications were disrupted beyond any hope of repair and the chain of command was in utter disorder.

On the quarterdeck men could be seen desperately trying to extinguish a blazing fire. The desolate decks were reduced to shambles, with nothing but cracked and twisted steel plates remaining. Shell holes pock-marked the entire upper deck. All of the big guns were inoperable because of the increasing list, and only a few machine guns were intact.

There was not enough time to report all the dead and wounded. Many bullets had found targets below the bridge, and one devastating blast in the emergency dispensary had killed all its occupants including the medical officers and corpsmen. The casualties were so numerous by this time that my mind was confused as to who was alive and who was dead.

490

My feeling of exhaustion had passed and I was hungry. Both pockets of my raincoat were filled with biscuits, which I now munched, keeping my eyes riveted on the clinometer. The biscuits tasted delicious.

Once again waves of enemy planes roared over us in rapid succession. Taking advantage of our reduced speed, their attacks were concentrated against our rudder. Unable to evade them, we could do nothing but wring our perspiring hands in desperation and wait for the inevitable stern explosion.

The voice of the chief quartermaster could be heard sputtering over the telephone, giving reports on the flooded condition of the next compartment and repeating the steering orders one by one. All of a sudden an excited report came over the phone, "Flooding imminent! Flooding imminent!" as a split-second detonation aft reverberated throughout the ship; and the reports were ended.

The *Yamato*'s distress flag was hoisted, accompanied by the code signal, "Our rudder in trouble!"

This was the last flag to fly above the great *Yamato*. Emitting pillars of flame, her stern seemed to protrude high in the air for a moment. The sub-rudder had been turned fully to the left when the steering room became flooded. Now the main rudder was swung full right, but the big ship failed to respond. The main rudder steering room was gradually flooding and she was forced to turn in a counterclockwise direction. Death's paralysis had taken over her movements!

From near the funnel, black smoke was rising in great puffs. There was a sudden increase in our list, and speed fell off to only seven knots! Now we were easy prey for the planes.

As if we did not have enough trouble, the destroyer *Kasumi* came dashing headlong for us on our starboard bow, flying the distress flag. Her rudder must have been damaged too. In our helplessness there seemed to be no way to avoid a collision. At the last instant she skimmed past us so closely that she all but scraped our paint.

Our list had now reached 35 degrees! As though awaiting

this moment, the enemy came plunging through the clouds to deliver the coup de grâce. This attack against the impotent *Yamato* was certain of success.

It was impossible to evade the bombs; all scored direct hits. Lying flat on the deck, I braced myself to withstand the shocks.

I could hear the captain vainly shouting, "Hold on, men! Hold on, men!" But how many could even hear his words? All electric power was wiped out; the loudspeaker was silent. Great columns of water suddenly rose high into the air on the port side amidships. We were almost swept off our feet by the cascading water as it fell.

We had suffered terrific punishment, and now the clinometer registered a rapid increase in our list. My position was not uncomfortable, for by this time the canting deck provided a good backrest. I managed to crawl along the deck.

Suddenly there was an odd emptiness in the air above us— not a single hostile plane was in the sky! Had we won survival after all? Comparative tranquility settled over the ship. But still the needle of the clinometer continued its stealthy advance.

I heard the executive officer report to the captain in a heartbroken voice, "Correction of listing hopeless!" I repeated this information throughout the bridge at the top of my voice.

Men were jumbled together in disorder on the deck, but a group of staff officers squirmed out of the pile and crawled over to the commander in chief for a final conference, after which he struggled to his feet. His chief of staff then arose and saluted. A prolonged silence followed, during which they regarded each other solemnly.

The commander in chief looked around, shook hands deliberately with his staff officers, and then went resolutely into his cabin. This was the last that was seen of the Second Fleet commander, Vice Admiral Seiichi Ito.

Of the bridge personnel there were fewer than ten surviving at this time. The deadly silence was broken at last by new destructive explosions. On the deck below, a group of men hastily tried to abandon ship and were lost. I heard the captain say, "What has become of His Imperial Majesty's portrait?" The officer in charge of the portrait reported that he was guarding it with his life.

We saw the navigator and his assistant tying themselves to the binnacle to prevent the disgrace of surviving when the ship went down. We started to do the same.

"Hey! What are you doing? Into the water and swim—all you young men!" thundered the chief of staff with an angry voice. Plunging among us, he swung a good sound blow at each man to move us to immediate action. Slowly we dropped our ropes to comply with his order.

Several points had been settled in that final conference. Fighting was to be stopped immediately, all personnel were to be rescued, and the ship was to be abandoned without a moment's loss. We had not received this information, but the escorting ships had been notified by signal. Emergency signals atop our mainmast were desperately flashing to the destroyers, "Approach nearer, approach nearer!" They dared not come alongside the *Yamato* lest the explosions and the downward pressure of the whirlpool prove fatal to them.

The horizon seemed to take on a mad new angle. Dark waves splattered and reached for us as the stricken ship heeled to the incredible list of 80 degrees!

The captain's orderly carried a further command to all sections of the superstructure: "All hands to the upper deck!" It was obviously too late to save the men below, but the captain was resolved to rescue as many as possible.

Somewhere from above, two code books dropped beside me. I stowed them in the chart table from force of habit. I was at a loss whether to abandon my post or remain with the ship as the senior officers were doing. There was no assignment left for me, so, moving warily, I reached for the lookout port in an effort to pull myself through and escape. I tumbled to the deck with a cry of pain when the man ahead stepped abruptly on my hands. I quickly scrambled upright again and crawled out through the port.

Stubbornly refusing all help, the navigator and his assistant had lashed themselves tightly together. As the ship rolled over they merely stared at the onrushing waves. On the protruding starboard bilge keel, now well out of the water, a row of survivors gave three cheers for His Imperial Majesty.

The deck was nearly vertical and the *Yamato*'s battle flag was almost touching the billowing waves. Below the flag a young sailor clung unwaveringly. Willingly he had volunteered to stand guard in this honorable duty. What a proud thing it was to die such a death!

The waves began to dash against the deck. Instead of being swallowed up, men on board were flipped and flung far out into the water. But suddenly a cone fifty meters deep opened into the sea. Some men disappeared into this whirlpool; others were just tossed about. A kaleidoscopic pattern of human beings was imprinted in this resplendent watery cone.

The *Yamato* now lay flat on her beam ends—a list of ninety degrees. Shells of the big guns skidded and bumped across the deck of the ammunition room, crashing against the bulkhead and kindling the first of a series of explosions. It was unthinkable that anyone could survive.

Then the ship slid under completely. Down we went with some two thousand rounds of armor-piercing and antiaircraft shells. With the sinking came the blast, rumble, and shock of compartments bursting from air pressure and exploding magazines already submerged.

Bursting for air, I was heaved up, down, tossed about, and pounded flat. Strangling, I kicked and fought toward the only light I could see—a gray, greenish glow in a weird and watery world. And then I was amazingly spewed out into daylight.

As the capsized ship submerged, huge fingers of flame went flashing and skyrocketing into the dark clouds above. (According to a destroyer officer, these flames leaped six thousand meters into the sky. They were clearly visible from Kagoshima in Kyushu.)

The swirling water pulled me down once more beneath the surface. A few seconds later an explosion blasted me up again. Many men were engulfed by the dreadful suction of the ship's funnel. Had I been ten feet nearer, I would have been another victim. Oil from the ruptured fuel tanks made my eyes smart as I floated on the surface. I wiped my face and gasped for air. Around me were clusters of swimmers, floating bodies, and occasional patches of splintered and charred debris. This was all that remained of the world's mightiest battleship after just two hours of antiaircraft battle.

A misty rain fell as one battle ended and another began—this time against bleeding wounds, smarting oil, cold, and sharks. Some men cheered themselves with songs; others went mad and sank to the bottom. Still others with deep wounds were groaning in pain, although the black oil served to retard bleeding. The enemy carrier planes were devoting their full attention to the remaining destroyers, so at least we had relief from the relentless rain of hot steel.

I heard the assistant gunnery officer shouting, "All officers, gather men together around you!" and the need for prompt action brought me out of my daze. I began to gather the men closest to me, giving words of encouragement and cautioning them to conserve their strength.

Rafts were needed for the seriously wounded who were still afloat. Here and there were a few charred sticks, but we could find no wood suitable for building rafts. How could there be any sizable timbers anyway! I turned away to search for other drifting articles and saw that the cold water was rapidly taking its toll of the men.

Suddenly a destroyer headed toward us at top speed. At the last moment it swung its stern wide to the left, narrowly missing my group, who, fortunately, were merely buffeted about by the wake. But the miserable men nearer to the rushing craft were drawn into the powerful screws.

On board the destroyer somebody was waving signal flags at us reading, "Wait awhile!" Its guns were still hammering vainly at the swooping enemy planes. I silenced the shouting men and urged them to wait patiently for the next move.

Still desperately countering the attacking planes, the de-

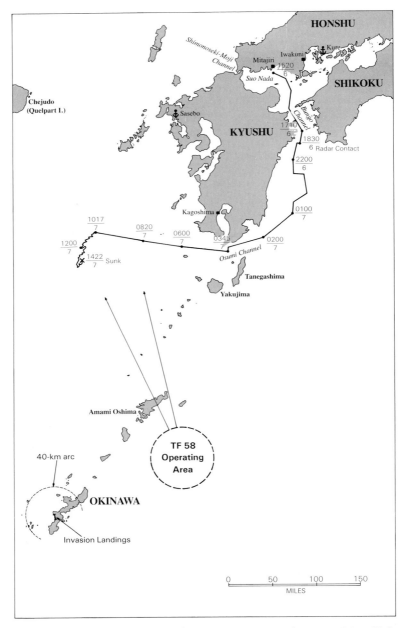

Approximate Track Chart of the *Yamato,* April 6–7, 1945: U.S. records indicate the ship sank at lat. 30°22′N, long. 128°04′E. A Japanese search team found and photographed the wreck at lat. 30°43′17″N, long. 128°04′E in July 1985. This map, compiled from Japanese sources, shows the real location of the sinking.

stroyer came to a standstill some two hundred meters away. All those men who were excited and eager to be first were encouraged to take it easy and swim forward with the aid of floating pieces of debris. It was clear that haste would sap the men's strength and prevent their reaching the ship. In the long struggle to our destination the black oil felt as thick as melted caramels.

As we neared the destroyer, a clamor of voices could be heard on all sides. Suddenly with the lifeline from the deck dangling before us, the bitter truth of man's selfishness burst upon us. The first two men to reach the rope grasped eagerly, but no sooner had they clenched it than both slipped back into the water, never to appear again. Another man was being pulled up by the rope when a frantic shipmate in the water sought to hang onto his shoes, with the result that both of them slid into the oily sea forever. As one man was being lifted up, I saw a long arm reach out to grab him, and I knocked the arm aside quickly. All of us in the water were desperate, and I was trying to rescue as many men as possible. It was, therefore, a great shock for me to suddenly find myself alone in the water. Where were they? How many had been rescued? Only four? The majority of them had vanished help-lessly beneath the waves.

From the deck above voices shouted, "Hurry up!" as the ship began to move. I saw a rope ladder hanging down crazily from the ship's side, but it was near the stern, where the screws were churning the water to a froth. This, however, was my only chance. I lunged forward and hooked my hands onto the ladder, which went taut with the weight of my body. It felt like I was being torn apart by the drag of the waves. My hands started to slip. Desperately and stubbornly I braced myself and hung on.

Smeared with blood and oil, I dangled precariously from the ladder, which was gradually raised until two men on board could grasp my hands. On the deck I lay prostrate, too exhausted even to lift my head. Men removed my uniform

497

and thrust fingers down my throat, forcing me to vomit the oil I had swallowed. They asked if my clothes contained any valuables. How in the world could I have thought of valuables? Then they wrapped me in a blanket and said, "Your head is wounded, sir. Hurry to the dispensary." I had been unaware of any wounds, and though they mentioned a wide gash in my scalp, I felt no pain whatsoever.

Stumbling now and then, I weaved my way into the corpse-filled dispensary of the destroyer *Fuyutsuki.*

Two medical officers, their white headbands smeared with blood, were attending the wounded. Several stitches were taken in my scalp and the oil was washed out of my eyes. The ship was filled with the dreadful smell of death: a rankling, intolerable odor.

The *Yamato*'s vain sortie was over. We were on our way home.

According to the *Yamato*'s chief lookout, Captain Ariga had gone down gallantly with his ship. I also learned that the executive officer, Captain Nomura, had been rescued by the destroyer *Yukikaze.* It is a wonder that he was saved, for he had been stationed below decks. No sooner had the after guns of the *Yamato* been silenced than he made his way to the main deck, where he distributed candies, biscuits, and His Majesty's brand cigarettes to the men. He seemed, however, to have forgotten something. He suddenly remembered that it was "the call of nature," and ordered the men to stand in a row and urinate at will. Afterward, when the ship went down, he had been blown clear and was saved.

When I awakened on the morning of 8 April, sleep had restored my strength. On the deck of the ship I washed my face, and the spring sun poured into my eyes, which still smarted, seemingly as a reminder that I was one of the few who had survived. Soon the contour of the mountains came into sight. Their beauty took my breath away and I sighed with joy in spite of myself.

To be alive is wonderful after all!

498

17

Thoughts on Japan's Naval Defeat

TOSHIYUKI
YOKOI

It is appropriate that the final article in this volume provides an overview of the naval war from the broadest perspective. The author examines the institutions of government and the modes of thinking that lay behind Japan's debacle. He argues that army-navy rivalry and military domination of policymaking prevented the development of a grand strategy. At the start of the war, Japan and the other Axis powers appeared awesomely monolithic and single-minded. But as we see in the case of Japan, this was an illusion fostered by the momentum of early victories. In the long run, rigid thinking at the top meant that Japan was less able than her opponents to respond to changing circumstances—that is, to formulate effective strategies as the war progressed.

The outmoded doctrine of victory through a main fleet action governed the navy. This theme, repeatedly sounded in earlier articles in this book, is here given full development. The outlook of the high command is reminiscent of the Royal Navy's offensive mentality in World War I, which delayed adoption of the convoy system as a response to the

German U-boat threat. In that war, however, British naval forces were ultimately successful in protecting sea lanes and denying their use to the enemy despite the lack of a decisive naval battle. The Japanese navy remained a prisoner of the battleship mentality, however, and had no such success.

Although this author's treatment of the war is very broad, it only hints at one or two ultimate issues. Even if the navy had developed an effective strategy for prosecuting a war of attrition, could it have prevailed? Certainly it could have extracted an even higher price for Allied victory. But the nation's ambitions clearly outran its capabilities, and even if unity of leadership within the government had been achieved, only a grand strategy that limited these ambitions, it seems, could have kept Japan from catastrophe.

THERE HAS BEEN a tendency among Western writers and students of national military policies to give Japan more credit than is due for her prewar and World War II strategic planning. Unfamiliarity with the language, a paucity of books and articles on the subject, and an official reluctance to allow research in official Japanese records in past years have prevented interested parties from analyzing correctly the status of Japanese naval strategic thinking. Thus, some writers have considered Japanese naval planning to have been "concrete" and "directed against specific enemies and territories" since the Sino-Japanese War of 1894–1895. Such conclusions result from the assumption that there was unity of thought and planning at the highest levels in the Japanese government. Unfortunately for Japan, this was not so.

In April 1907 Marshal Yamagata made a report to the emperor entitled "Imperial Defense Policy." It included desired levels of army and navy armaments and operation plans;

it specified Russia as the major hypothetical enemy. Later, the Bolshevik revolution and ensuing international tensions, particularly between America and Japan, made it necessary for Japan to change and enlarge the list of hypothetical enemies to include the United States, Soviet Russia, and China, in that order. As the Soviet Union increased its national power, there occurred frequent Russo-Japanese disputes, which forced the Japanese army to increase its armaments, placing Russia as her first hypothetical enemy and consequently burying Yamagata's Imperial Defense Policy in the dead file.

One may say that in Japan, up to the Russo-Japanese War, the objective of the national policy was in accord with military and naval armaments. After the war, however, the Japanese navy and army started to make frantic efforts to increase their respective armaments, each selecting a different hypothetical enemy in its operational planning.

In the meantime, the cabinets that took power one after another were too busy with their own interparty strife to carry out their responsibilities of deciding overall national policies. The Japanese armed forces took every advantage of the nation's unique system, the so-called "independence of supreme command," that was originally designed to prevent the influence of party politics and their attendant evils. Under such a system, politicians knew little about delicate military matters and were tactfully kept away even if they tried to show their interest in military affairs. The professional soldiers lacked knowledge of both political and economic affairs. Hence, there was virtually nobody qualified to establish overall state policy in Japan.

From the time of the Russo-Japanese War to late 1941, Japanese military leaders pointed out the immediate necessity of continental expansion and a southward advance. The former was chiefly voiced by the army circles and the latter by the navy. Of course neither objective could be interpreted as a simple indication of patriotism. From the most cynical point of view, the army tried to show its predominance over the navy, and vice versa. In this way, discord between the two services eventually developed into a very serious situation. Neither wished to be subordinate to the other, and this attitude directly prevented coordination of objectives.

Strategy has two meanings, one broad, the other narrow. In the broad sense it implies the best method of using all of the resources of a nation to achieve the national objective and should be consistent with that policy. Thus, grand strategy includes all the important factors of politics, economics, diplomacy, and military affairs. In prewar days Japan had *Kikaku-In* (the Planning Board) under the direct control of the Cabinet. The board was responsible for carrying out the duty outlined above. However, the evils of party politics, together with the army-navy disputes, completely paralyzed the expected function of the Planning Board.

Strategy in a narrow sense—that is, military strategy—is primarily concerned with military affairs only. Nowadays, however, military strategy cannot be independent of politics, economics, and diplomacy. What are the necessary forces? How can they be used? How can they be prepared in peacetime? All these problems should be considered on the basis of grand strategy in order to be in line with the national objectives. Therefore, naval strategy should naturally follow the unified and direct line of grand and military strategies and cannot by any means be independent.

Nevertheless, in Japan there was nothing that could be called grand or military strategy until a short time before the outbreak of World War II. There was little correlation between her national defense theory and the strategic plans of the army and navy. In this author's opinion, an institutional defect was the main cause of this situation, which eventually resulted in the calamity of Japan entering into her disastrous war.

The Japanese counterpart of the American Joint Chiefs of Staff was called *Dai-hon'ei,* the Imperial General Headquarters, composed of ministers of the two services, the chiefs of staff of the army and navy, and their high-ranking assistants. Imperial General Headquarters enjoyed the special privilege of allowing no governmental interference in command affairs. The government, therefore, found it imperative to establish *Dai-hon'ei seifu renraku kaigi*, or the Imperial Headquarters–Government Liaison Conference. This group directed the war in a manner considered appropriate and desirable for both state affairs and supreme command. The council was attended by the prime minister, the foreign minister, the chiefs of the general staffs, and, in case of need, other ministers concerned and the deputy chiefs of the general staffs.

The Imperial General Headquarters did not exist in peacetime, but functioned solely during the period of hostilities. This was the main difference from the function of the Joint Chiefs of Staff of America in the post–World War II period. Because of this fact, Japan lacked an institution that could study and prepare grand strategy or overall military strategy. The Army and Naval General Staffs, respectively, were responsible for the planning of army and navy strategies. But there existed no unified grand and overall strategies on a national scale. Actually, the two general staffs were too weak to be entrusted with the fate of the nation.

On 28 June 1941 the Imperial Headquarters–Government Liaison Conference decided upon an "Outline of National Policies in View of the Changing Situation." It aimed at "the establishment of the Greater East Asia Co-prosperity Sphere" and continuation of efforts "to effect a settlement of the China Incident" involving "steps to advance south. . . ." [1]

On 7 September the conference, in the presence of the emperor, confirmed the above principles. In order to fulfill these objectives, the conference held to the resolution that Japan would not avoid hostilities against America, England, and Holland, if and when necessary. Toward the end of October, the conference decided to continue war preparations. If and when the diplomatic negotiations failed, the conference agreed to approve the war automatically.

In mid-October the Tojo Cabinet was formed. To the new prime minister, the emperor gave the order to reexamine entirely the decision of 7 September in view of the then-existing world situation. At the conference meeting held on 15 November, Tojo obtained approval of a document entitled "Draft Proposal for Hastening the End of the War Against the United States, Great Britain, the Netherlands, and Chiang Kai-shek." This title created a strange impression with its reference to "the End of the War," particularly since this policy was being enunciated well before the start of the war in question. However, this was the sole grand strategy ever made before the war began.

This strategy in brief was:

> *Policy:* 1) We will endeavor to quickly destroy American, British, and Dutch bases in the Far East. . . . We will endeavor at the same time to hasten the fall of the Chiang regime . . . , to work for the surrender of Great Britain in cooperation with Germany and Italy, and to destroy the will of the United States to continue the war. . . .
>
> *Summary:* 1) Our empire will engage in a quick war, and will destroy American and British bases in eastern Asia and in the southwest Pacific region. At the same time that it secures a strategically powerful position, it will control those areas producing vital materials, as well as important transportation routes, and thereby prepare for a protracted period of self-sufficiency. At the appropriate time, we will endeavor by various means to lure the main fleet of the United States [near Japan] and destroy it.
>
> 2) First of all, Japan, Germany, and Italy will cooperate and work for the surrender of Great Britain. . . . The connection between Australia and India and the British mother country will be broken by means of political pressure and the destruction of commerce, and their separation will be achieved; the independence of Burma will be promoted, and this will be used to stimulate the independence of India.
>
> 3) Japan, Germany, and Italy will cooperate and en-

deavor to deal with Great Britain, and at the same time endeavor to destroy the will of the United States to fight. . . . In dealing with the Philippines, for the time being the present policy will be continued, and thought will be given to how it can hasten the end of the war. An all-out attempt will be made to disrupt commerce to the United States. . . . Strategic propaganda against the United States will be stepped up. . . . Attempts will be made to break the ties between the United States and Australia.

4) In China we will stop support going to Chiang. . . .

5) The empire will endeavor to the utmost to prevent the outbreak of war with the Soviet Union while we are engaged in military operations in the south.[2]

These plans were hastily drawn up in only one month. Consequently, their improvised contents were extremely general. General Suzuki, then president of the Planning Board, was alleged to have changed his estimates on Japan's war capability several times before the beginning of war. This would clearly indicate the unsoundness of Japan's war plans that had lacked peacetime preparation. Even assuming these plans were the best available at the time, what could Japan have prepared in less than a month prior to the outbreak of war?

It was relatively late when Japan was ranked among the world's modern navies, and her naval service had not been an institution of long tradition. The founder of the Japanese navy is commonly believed to have been Kaishu Katsu. At the time of the Meiji Restoration in 1868, he did not change his loyalty toward the doomed Tokugawa Shogunate, but put forth every ounce of his energies to maintain the house of Tokugawa. But his achievement remains only in the records treasured in the library of the former Navy Department and did not materially influence the modern Japanese navy. On the other hand, the Japanese navy later showed much interest in the life and achievements of Admiral Nelson and Mahan's

The Influence of Sea Power upon History. Orthodox concepts of the Anglo-American navies were adopted by Japan.

The Japanese navy was always haunted by a poverty complex. At the time of the Sino-Japanese War in 1894–1895, Japan had no big warships comparable to the *Ting Yüan* and *Chen Yüan* class of the Chinese fleet. Japan then hastened to construct the three warships, the *Matsushima, Itsukushima,* and *Hashidate,* each of 4,278 tons and with one twelve-inch gun.

The victory of the Yellow Sea was attributable to the strength and characteristics of these new ships and Admiral Ito's tactical abilities in taking advantage of his superiority in speed and quick firing.

After this battle, the perspicacious Meiji emperor decided upon an epoch-making naval expansion. The result was a fleet composed of six battleships and six armored cruisers. This "6-6 Fleet," however, was still inferior in numbers to the Russian fleet, the greatest naval menace to Japan at that time.

It was quite natural for the Japanese navy to follow the same view held by the Anglo-American navies, that the annihilation of the enemy fleet was the only way to gain the command of the sea. Nevertheless, the Japanese navy still was destined to fight against heavy odds. To cope with this situation, the only means to attain the Japanese navy's objective seemed to be the strategy of the "offensive defense," or lying in wait near home waters, without resorting to the all-out offensive operations adopted by the Anglo-American admirals. This was further confirmed by the victory of Tsushima.

After the Russo-Japanese War, the Japanese navy compiled the *Kaisen yomurei,* or the Regulations of Naval Warfare, a drill book on naval strategy and tactics. This book has since exerted tremendous influence on the strategic thinking of Japanese naval officers. On general principles it notes:

"Battle is the sole means of victory. So everything should satisfy what the battle demands. . . . The keys of victory lie in initiative and concentration. Even when forced to stand on the defensive, one should always be alert in grasping the first opportunity of regaining the initiative. . . ." All of these concepts apparently indicate the high priority in which naval officers held the decisive battle, an esteem paralleling that of Clausewitz and Mahan.

World War I brought the concept of total war into Japan's strategic thinking. But it was limited to the area of philosophic matters as in Ludendorff's *Total War*. This new concept had not yet matured into the more modern strategic one that required the concentration of all national resources for the achievement of national objectives.

At the same time, one might imagine that the German Navy's "unrestricted submarine warfare" should have had a strong influence on Japanese naval officers because geographically and economically, the Japanese nation was in a position quite similar to that of Great Britain. Nevertheless, they were, curiously enough, little impressed by this German submarine strategy. Japanese naval officers well realized that their fate depended upon command of the sea. But they were probably too absorbed in other problems, particularly the one that would decide how an inferior naval force could obtain command of the sea.

This trend in naval thought was further intensified by the Washington and London conferences. World strategists had then established the theory that the ocean-crossing offensive fleet should outnumber the enemy by an approximate ratio of 10:7. In other words, seventy percent of the enemy's naval strength was considered to be the minimum requirement of Japan's national defense. Nevertheless, Japan was forced to accept the ratio of sixty percent in capital ships and seventy percent in auxiliary warships. This was the most serious problem for all Japanese naval officers. How could they carry out their national defense responsibility with such relatively inferior forces?

Answers to this question were: a) the so-called "whittling-down" operation against an attacking hostile fleet, b) empha-

507

sis on night operations, and c) the construction of fleets that were superior in armament and speed.

The first countermeasure proposed successive surprise attacks against and the gradual bit-by-bit diminution of the enemy's strength. In this way Japan hoped to create the opportunity for a decisive battle against any enemy fleets that might come across the ocean. In this operation, submarines and aircraft were expected to play the most important roles. From this point of view, submarine operations consisted of watching, shadowing, and making surprise attacks on the enemy fleets, while only secondary significance was placed on operations against the enemy's maritime communication lines.

Night operations were looked upon as the most suitable strategy for the Japanese fleet, while still inferior in number. In such operations the final tactical and strategic results would be less influenced by the number of Japanese ships than in case of day battles. Furthermore, fighting strength at night probably would depend mainly upon previous training. Thus, the Japanese navy started a series of night operational training exercises that appeared to be even more realistic and difficult than actual wartime night combat. The considerable number of losses in ships and personnel that occurred during these exercises never changed the course of training.

The idea of building ships superior in speed was not aimed at "avoiding battles." It was rather a logical conclusion from emphasis on the maneuver of intercepting invading fleets near home waters by utilizing the advantage of speed superiority.

The second Shanghai Incident of 1937 (the start of navy involvement in the China war) marked a new era in the development of Japanese naval aviation. Up to this time, the naval air force had been considered only an auxiliary of the fleet. Consequently, it was expected to perform the minor roles of reconnaissance, gunnery observation, aerial attack, and cover in the decisive battle. However, the remarkable achievements that Type 96 medium bombers and Zero fighters accomplished in China tremendously encouraged the self-confidence and pride of Japanese naval aviators. They began to feel that Japan's main naval strength was shifting from battleships to aircraft.

From this time on, there arose a heated controversy between battleship and aircraft proponents. Unfortunately, however, the ruling circle then in control of the Japanese navy was too possessed of a "battleship superiority complex" to pay serious attention to the results of the China war and its ensuing debates. Some important naval leaders believed the power of a new weapon was apt to be overestimated. Some even argued that it was not fair to compare ever-progressing aircraft with battleships that had been delayed in their progress since the Washington Conference. All of these absurd arguments, however, were accepted by the majority of the Japanese navy, with the consequent loss of an excellent opportunity to change a basic concept of naval warfare.

On 31 December 1936 both the Washington and London treaties expired. America instantly started naval construction programs, following the Vinson First, Second, and Third Naval Expansion Bills. Despite this, Japan could not mobilize her limited national resources into a desperate effort to overtake American naval expansion. In 1938 and 1939 the Japanese navy set up the so-called Zero 3 and Zero 4 naval expansion programs for building a total of eighty-eight ships of 542,000 tons, including four *Yamato*-class superbattleships, three carriers, six cruisers, thirty-seven destroyers, and thirty-eight submarines. Zero 5 of 1940 included the construction of eighteen carriers and 361 small vessels. All this effort to prevent the decline of Japan's relative naval power was planned and carried out in vain.

To cope with this disadvantageous situation, the ship construction programs were detailed as follows:

a) Every ship should exceed the corresponding American warship in its armament and maneuverability. The *Yamato* class was the obvious manifestation of this idea when it was designed as the world's largest battleship with a full-load displacement of 72,800 tons, nine 46-centimeter guns, and speed of 27 knots. The relative power of the *Yamato* class, as compared with the *North Carolina* of the U.S. Navy, of contemporary design and construction, was as follows:

	Yamato	*North Carolina*
Tonnage	62,315	35,000
Length	256 meters	216.5 meters
Beam	38.9 meters	32.9 meters
Armament	9 46-cm.	9 40-cm.
Speed	27 knots	27 knots

In addition, moreover, the Japanese navy planned the construction of two even larger battleships, numbers 798 and 799, which were designed to mount six 50-centimeter guns, as well as super-heavy cruisers of 32,000 tons, six 36-centimeter guns, and 33 knots.

b) As to the carriers, the Japanese navy adopted the principle of many small carriers instead of a few big ones. Following this principle, the *Hiryu* class of 17,300 tons was regarded as the most suitable type for fleet action. But the defensive vulnerability of this type made it inevitable gradually to expand carrier size to the *Shokaku* class of 25,675 tons, the *Taiho* class of 29,300 tons, the No. 5021 class of 30,360 tons, and finally to the *Shinano*'s 62,000 tons.

c) As to the cruisers and destroyers, considerable emphasis was placed on increased torpedo armament and power, with the introduction of Type 93 oxygen torpedoes.

d) Submarines were to be built for fleet actions; consequently they were of larger size but fewer in number.

As is apparent from the ship construction programs listed above, the strategic concept of the Japanese navy was undoubtedly based upon the doctrine of annihilating the enemy in a decisive battle, with battleships the backbone of the Japanese fleet. Since this concept prevailed so widely and strongly among the Japanese naval officers, there was virtually no one who paid proper attention to the valuable lesson of World War I that had clearly indicated the importance of maritime communications lines, both as to defending one's own and interrupting those of an adversary. If any emphasis was to be placed on the destruction of enemy maritime communication lines, Japanese naval authorities should have demanded medium-sized submarines in great quantity. If Japan had decided that the use and protection of her maritime lanes were paramount, this should have been implemented by the construction of many escort vessels.

In Japan's ship construction program, therefore, there appeared no indication of the strategic importance of maritime communication lines, either offensively or defensively. As a Japanese naval officer, I spent nearly half of my career on the sea, but I never saw exercises dealing with warfare either against or in defense of maritime communication lines. Over these years the Japanese navy went through training period after training period for the decisive fleet battle. Of course this training emphasis on surface action did contribute something to Japan's readiness for many of the actual Pacific battles of World War II.

On 10 April 1942, four months after the outbreak of war, Japan's first escort squadron was organized, with only twenty-four ships, including over-age destroyers, torpedo boats, and auxiliary gunboats. These twenty-four ships were assigned to safeguard Japan's vastly extended maritime communication lines, the artery of her war economy. Because of their small number and limited efficiency, Japanese escorts and their convoys were at the mercy of the relatively few American submarines.

The strategic concept of the Japanese navy can be further observed by the way in which special or midget submarines, which displaced only fifty tons with sixteen- to nineteen-knot underwater speed, were used. As their operational range ex-

511

tended only three hundred to one thousand miles, they should have been used mainly or solely for coastal defense. Nevertheless, they were actually employed in attacking enemy ships lying at anchor inside such protected anchorages as Pearl Harbor and Sydney. Furthermore, the Japanese navy initially had planned to use these midget submarines for fleet actions. Two seaplane tenders, the *Chitose* and *Chiyoda*, which were later converted into aircraft carriers, were designed to carry twelve of these midget submarines to the decisive battle theaters.

In short, the strategic concept of the Japanese navy was directed solely toward gaining command of the sea by the decisive surface battle. In other words, the Japanese navy had well-planned tactics, but not strategies. The *Kaisen yomurei* established definitions of strategy and tactics which, from an international point of view, tended to confuse the two terms and label one usually accepted strategic term as tactics and another as strategy.

For example, the *yomurei* stated that "tactics is the art of using forces while keeping contact with enemy forces; strategy is the art of using forces while keeping distance from the enemy."

The modern development of industry had entirely changed the characteristics of naval warfare from war of annihilation to war of attrition. For instance, the American navy constructed sixteen *Essex*-class carriers, nine *Independence*-class ships, and fifty-three escort carriers during the war. Japan constructed or converted fifteen carriers during the same period. The war of attrition became the problem not only of the army and air force, but of the Japanese navy as well, though it still clung to its anachronistic strategy of annihilation. This misconception doubtless led Japan into the total defeat that started from the collapse of its naval forces.

The aforementioned controversy of "battleship or airplane" that arose after the second Shanghai Incident finally developed into an actual bombing test at the Kashima Bombing Range in 1939, when a life-sized model of the *Saratoga* was successfully test-bombed. Torpedo tests against models of American battleships were also carried out at Yokosuka naval base. These efforts later contributed to initial Japanese success at Hawaii and Malaya at the start of the Pacific War.

These results, however, did not succeed in breaking the illusions of Japanese naval leaders, who still ordered the use of stereotyped battle plans in the annual maneuvers of the Combined Fleet. Observation of enemy ports by Japanese submarines; shadowing oncoming hostile fleets by planes and submarines; whittling-down operations by surprise surface forces; night attacks by light forces; and finally the decisive engagement between main surface fleets were the routine of strategically stultified Japanese Combined Fleet maneuvers.

The battles of Hawaii and Malaya completely altered battleship doctrine. The U.S. Navy was wise enough to develop carrier task forces as the backbone of their sea forces, although, of course, the damage to their battleships at Pearl Harbor made this progressive step even more obvious. Nevertheless, the obstinate Japanese naval authorities still hesitated to cast away their conventional battleship doctrine until they were completely defeated at the Battle of Midway. Here they realized they were not only wrong but too late.

In this battle, most of the Japanese battleships were under the direct command of Admiral Yamamoto. They maintained their location three hundred miles behind the carrier task forces and achieved nothing but retirement at full speed once Japanese carrier forces were given a fatal blow. Right after the battle, Japanese fleet organization was changed to the task force formation where the battleships were assigned the duty of carrier escort. However, this change was a fatal six months late.

Fleet organization or naval tactics are relatively easy to change, but naval armament can seldom be prepared in a short time. The tremendous waste of limited resources that

513

had been poured into the construction of useless giant ships now turned out to be the most adverse blow to stubborn Japanese naval leaders. Naval air forces that should have been the core of the new organization were maintaining strikingly short reserves. It was not the loss of four carriers but of skilled airmen, who could not easily be replaced, that made the Battle of Midway a milestone on the road to the eventual defeat of Japan. From this time on, the Allied offensive increased its intensity, while Japan's naval air force, because of a lack of reserve strength, could not even keep up its normal fighting capability. New pilots that were assigned to fill the gaps caused by the loss of skilled airmen were too inexperienced to carry out their missions.

The fall of Guadalcanal in February 1943 was the turning point of the Pacific War. Japan's naval offensive strategy was forced to the defensive. In this new situation, land-based air forces inevitably were regarded as the main defensive bastion. Admiral Koga, who succeeded Fleet Admiral Yamamoto after the latter's death, ordered the organization of a defensive zone of air bases against expected Allied lines of assault. This idea originated from the concept of the war of position exercised in military operations. In intent, Japan hoped to form a zone of air bases sufficient in depth to give flexible operational capacity to land-based air forces and to continue determined resistance against the superior air strength of Allied task forces. In carrying out this plan, as we know, Japanese lines of communication were completely cut to pieces by hostile submarines and aircraft. It became impossible to transport construction and other basic materials for air bases and their defense.

On 15 June 1944 American task forces attacked the Marianas. Japan's carrier task forces, barely reequipped and reorganized, took a last chance by staking everything they had in this battle off the Mariana Islands. The result was predictable. There was little Japan could do with such an inferior number of unskilled airmen. After this battle there disappeared all possibility of averting the defeat of Japan's navy and nation. Suicide attacks were the last means left for the Japanese navy and they too were fruitless.

To summarize Japan's naval strategy before and during World War II, the Japanese navy had no strong or effective national or grand strategy to augment it. It had long been plagued by obstinate leaders who adhered to the outdated strategy of annihilation and battleship doctrine. Japan's naval concepts had been based on old, obsolete concepts from the days of Nelson and the Russo-Japanese War, notwithstanding tri-elemental technological progress in maritime warfare. The Japanese navy could do little in defense of her exposed and necessary maritime communications lines. The severance of these lines quickly and steadily weakened her war potentialities to the point of final collapse.

There was no well-considered strategy in the Japanese navy. Accordingly, defeat was inevitable at the hands of opponents more skilled and powerful in strategy, as well as stronger in the other elements of national power. The defeat of Japan's navy in World War II remains an unenviable monument to obstinate, outdated naval strategists.

Notes

INTRODUCTION

1. Stephen Roskill, *Naval Policy Between the Wars: The Period of Anglo-American Antagonism, 1919–1929* (London, 1968).
2. Chester A. Nimitz, handwritten letter displayed in the library of the Naval War College, Newport, Rhode Island.
3. Roskill, op. cit.
4. John Creswell, *Sea Warfare, 1939–1945* (Berkeley, Calif.: University of California Press, 1967).

CHAPTER 1: THE HAWAII OPERATION

1. Nimitz, op. cit.
2. Samuel Eliot Morison, *History of United States Naval Operations in World War II.* Vol. 3, *The Rising Sun in the Pacific, 1931–April 1942* (Boston: Little, Brown, 1948), p. 132. This and the following quotes from Morison in this article are not verbatim but apparently retranslations from Japanese versions of Morison's text.
3. Ibid., p. 125.
4. Ibid., p. 132.
5. The author's reference to "A Sure Hit with Human-Piloted Torpedo" is unclear, as is the source of the quotation that fol-

lows it. Neither of these appears in his *Shikan Shinjuwan kogeki* [A historical view of the Pearl Harbor attack] (Tokyo: Jiyu Ajia Sha, 1955).

A good deal of uncertainty surrounds the origin of the midget submarine. Its true father was apparently Captain Kaneji Kishimoto, chief of the torpedo section (First Department, Second Section) of the Bureau of Ships, or *Kansei hombu*. In late 1931 and early 1932 his section discussed a document entitled *Gyorai nikko an* [Proposal for human torpedo attacks]. The probable author of the document was Captain Yokoo, then retired, who met with Captain Kishimoto's section to argue for the practicability of "human torpedoes." In 1904 Captain Yokoo had himself taken part in a heroic attempt to fire torpedoes from a raft against Russian ships at Port Arthur. Captain Kishimoto eventually adopted a plan for a small submarine with a crew of two and armament of two torpedoes. The submarine would be released from a mother ship of about ten thousand tons. See Ryuichi Kurihara, *Ko hyoteki* [Target A] (Tokyo: Nami Shobo, 1974), pp. 10–11, and Hirokazu Sano, *Tokushu senkotei* [Midget submarines] (Tokyo: Tosho Shuppansha, 1975), pp. 21–23.

CHAPTER 3: THE OPENING AIR OFFENSIVE AGAINST THE PHILIPPINES

1. The first news of the attack on Pearl Harbor reached Manila at 0300 on 8 December. At Clark Field nearly all planes were airborne by 0830 in answer to a general alarm, but they returned following an all clear at 1000, with the result that only two U.S. planes were aloft in the vicinity of Manila at about 1245 when the Japanese attacked. See Wesley Frank Craven and James Lea Cate, eds., *The Army Air Forces in World War II*. Vol. 1, *Plans and Early Operations, January 1939 to August 1942* (Chicago: University of Chicago Press, 1948), pp. 203–13.

2. Shore-based Japanese naval aircraft sank the *Prince of Wales* and *Repulse* in the afternoon (Philippine time) of 10 December. See Arthur J. Marder, *Old Friends, New Enemies: The Royal Navy and the Imperial Japanese Navy—Strategic Illusions, 1936–41* (New York: Oxford University Press, 1981), Chapter XIV.

3. Stefan T. Possony, *Strategic Air Power: The Pattern of Dynamic*

Security (Washington, D.C.: Infantry Journal Press, 1949), p. 186.

CHAPTER 4: JAPANESE OPERATIONS IN THE INDIAN OCEAN

1. H. P. Willmott, *Empires in the Balance: Japanese and Allied Pacific Strategies to April 1942* (Annapolis, Maryland: Naval Institute Press, 1982), p. 438.

2. Strictly speaking, *junsen,* or "submarine-cruisers," were boats of over 2,000 tons designed for reconnaissance and pursuit far removed from base. Another type of large boat, the *kaidai,* was built originally for fleet actions. By the start of the Pacific War there were no great differences between fleet boats and submarine-cruisers. Submarine-cruisers were simply large, independently operating boats.

CHAPTER 5: THE BATTLE OF MIDWAY

1. These were probably the seaplane tenders *Thornton* (AVD-11) and *Ballard* (AVD-10), which had been stationed at French Frigate Shoals.

2. Probable, but not actual. This transmission was not picked up by the Americans.

3. W. J. Holmes, *Double-Edged Secrets: U.S. Naval Intelligence Operations in the Pacific During World War II* (Annapolis, Maryland: Naval Institute Press, 1979), p. 54.

CHAPTER 6: THE STRUGGLE FOR GUADALCANAL

1. Also known as the Battle of Savo Island. The U.S. cruisers *Quincy* (CA-39), *Vincennes* (CA-44), and *Astoria* (CA-34) and the Australian cruiser *Canberra* were sunk; the heavy cruiser *Chicago* (CA-29) and the destroyers *Ralph Talbot* (DD-390) and *Patterson* (DD-392) were damaged. Damage to Japanese ships was negligible.

2. By the submarine *Growler* (SS-215) on 5 July.

3. The former destroyers *Shimakaze, Nadakaze, Suzuki,* and *Tsuta,* converted like the U.S. Navy's APDs.

4. These planes were based at Espiritu Santo.

5. The destroyer *Blue* (DD-387) was actually damaged by tor-

pedo attack on 22 August but was scuttled by U.S. forces the next day, latitude 09°17'S, longitude 160°02'E.

6. There was slight bomb damage to the field, but no U.S. planes were shot down.

7. Vice Admiral Frank Jack Fletcher's Task Force 61, which was made up of the carriers *Saratoga* (CV-3), *Enterprise* (CV-6), and *Wasp* (CV-7); the battleship *North Carolina* (BB-55); and seven cruisers and eighteen destroyers.

8. But by this time Task Group 18 (the carrier *Wasp*, three cruisers, and seven destroyers) had been sent south to refuel and was not part of the Japanese targets.

9. The *Enterprise* was the only U.S. ship damaged by aerial attack on this date.

10. Actually under escort of the *Suzukaze*.

11. Severely damaged by the *I-19*'s torpedo in position latitude 12°25'S, longitude 164°08'E, the *Wasp* was sunk by U.S. forces the same day.

12. Actual losses were the *Salt Lake City* (CA-25), *Boise* (CL-47), *Duncan* (DD-485), and *Farenholt* (DD-491) damaged on 11 October; the *Duncan* sank on the twelfth.

13. At this time and place the *I-176* reported "direct hits on a *Texas*-class ship causing two induced explosions after two minutes. Did not stay to see sinking." Headquarters Record of Meritorious Service, National Archives document number 12065 (WDC 161701).

14. The heavy cruiser *Chester* (CA-27) was damaged on 20 October 1942 by submarine torpedo in position latitude 13°31'S, longitude 163°17'E, but did not sink.

15. U.S. Navy casualties as a result of the Battle of Santa Cruz were the carrier *Hornet* (CV-8) sunk at latitude 08°38'S, longitude 166°43'E; damaged were the carrier *Enterprise*, the battleship *South Dakota* (BB-57), the cruiser *San Juan* (CL-54), and the destroyers *Smith* (DD-378), *Hughes* (DD-410), and *Porter* (DD-356). The last-named ship was disposed of by U.S. gunfire at latitude 08°32'S, longitude 167°17'E.

16. The cruisers *Atlanta* (CL-51) and *Juneau* (CL-52, victim of a submarine torpedo an hour before noon) and the destroyers *Cushing* (DD-376), *Monssen* (DD-436), *Laffey* (DD-459), and *Barton* (DD-599) were sunk; and three cruisers and three destroyers

were damaged. Of the thirteen U.S. warships engaged, only the *Fletcher* (DD-445), last in the column, was unscathed in this battle of Friday the thirteenth.

17. The *Sado Maru* managed to limp back to the Shortland anchorage.

18. The *Kinugawa Maru, Yamatsuki Maru, Hirokawa Maru,* and *Yamaura Maru.*

19. The *Preston* (DD-379), *Walke* (DD-416), and *Benham* (DD-397) were sunk. The *South Dakota* and *Gwin* (DD-433) were damaged.

20. Not quite so. Two of eight torpedoes fired by the *Oyashio* shortly before midnight found their mark in the *Northampton* (CA-26), injuring her fatally, but not until just after 0300 the next morning did the heavy cruiser sink in position latitude 09°12′S, longitude 159°50′E.

21. U.S. losses were the three heavy cruisers—*Pensacola* (CA-24), *New Orleans* (CA-32), and *Minneapolis* (CA-36)—damaged, in addition to the loss of the *Northampton*.

22. Good fortune, yes. But there was more, and it has best been said by Morison. "Nimitz, ever magnanimous to the enemy as generous to his task force commanders, praised Japanese gunfire, torpedo technique, 'energy, persistence, and courage.' It is always some consolation to reflect that the enemy who defeats you is really good, and Rear Admiral Tanaka was better than that—he was superb. Without his trusted flagship *Jintsu*, his decks cluttered with supplies, he sank a heavy cruiser and put three others out of action for nearly a year, at the cost of one destroyer. In many actions of the war, mistakes on the American side were cancelled by those of the enemy; but despite the brief confusion of his destroyers, Tanaka made no mistakes at Tassafaronga." Morison, op. cit., Vol. 5, *The Struggle for Guadalcanal, August 1942–February 1943* (1954), p. 315.

CHAPTER 7: THE BATTLE OF SAVO ISLAND

1. Operation WATCHTOWER, as the Allied offensive was termed, employed one battleship, three carriers, fourteen cruisers, thirty-one destroyers, twenty-three transports, six submarines, and lesser craft for a grand total of eighty-nine.

2. The initial American landing on Guadalcanal consisted of 11,000 U.S. Marines from sixteen transports.

3. The times given in this article are Zone minus 9, which was the Rabaul time kept by the Japanese. Allied forces were using Zone minus 11 time. Accordingly, the main action opened at 2337 Japanese time and two hours later by Allied time.

4. This ship was the U.S. destroyer *Blue.*

5. The U.S. destroyer *Ralph Talbot.*

6. Four cruisers (the USS *Astoria, Quincy,* and *Vincennes* and the Australian *Canberra*) were sunk, over a thousand Allied naval personnel killed, and the *Chicago* and *Ralph Talbot* severely damaged.

Chapter 8: The Withdrawal from Kiska

1. East longitude dates and local times are used. The time of 0800 and date of 29 July listed above correspond to 1000, 28 July for the Allied forces.

2. A small fleet of "S-boats" based at Dutch Harbor patrolled the Aleutians in the summer of 1943, but no record exists of the encounter described here, to judge from such a detailed and complete work as Clay Blair, Jr.'s, *Silent Victory: The U.S. Submarine War Against Japan* (Philadelphia: J. B. Lippincott, 1975).

3. See Bruce McCandless, "The Battle of the Pips," U.S. Naval Institute *Proceedings* 84 (February 1958), pp. 48–56. It describes the "phantom battle" of the U.S. North Pacific Force with a radar mirage in the early morning hours of 26 July.

4. Author's interview with Ray Champagne, a corporal at the time of his participation in the Kiska operation.

5. The author has relied on Morison, op. cit., Vol. 7, *Aleutians, Gilberts and Marshalls, June 1942–April 1944* (1951), pp. 61–65, for details concerning the American side of the operation.

Chapter 9: Ozawa in the Pacific

1. Disregarding damaged ships, Allied losses were actually much smaller; only one destroyer and four auxiliaries were ultimately sunk. About twenty-five aircraft were destroyed. See Morison, op. cit., Vol. 6, *Breaking the Bismarcks Barrier, 22 July 1942–1 May 1944* (1950), p. 127.

2. See for example Hiroyuki Agawa, *The Reluctant Admiral: Yamamoto and the Imperial Navy* (New York: Kodansha International, 1979), p. 345.

3. Yamamoto was killed on the morning of 18 April, when the plane in which he was flying was shot down near Buin by P-38s from Henderson Field.

4. Yamamoto's body was cremated at Buin on 21 April. Agawa, op. cit., p. 363.

5. The Special Duty Section (*Tokumuhan*) of the Naval General Staff was established on 15 November 1940 to plan for and carry out communications intelligence.

6. From *Dai ichi kido kantai sento shoho* [First mobile fleet detailed battle report], appearing in Japan Defense Agency, War History Section, *Mariana oki kaisen* [The naval battle off the Marianas], Vol. 12, Senshi Sosho series (Tokyo: Asagumo Shimbunsha, 1968), p. 572.

7. "A" Force of the Main Body was the First Carrier Division under Ozawa; "B" Force was the Second under Joshima. "FHHOO" in this message represents a grid designation actually in characters of the Japanese syllabary, that is, *he, chi, chi,* followed by two zeros; "FHHOO" is the equivalent in Roman letters.

8. Genda was being critical of the "outranging" tactic. In Japanese fencing with bamboo swords (*kendo*) one seeks to win with a single concentrated blow carried out with feet firmly planted. When one strikes one is close to the opponent. Genda meant that Ozawa's mode of attack involved repeated lunges forward beyond normal reach, holding the opponent as far away from one's own body as possible, as in Western fencing.

9. By this time General Tojo was not only prime minister and army minister; he was also chief of the Army General Staff.

10. A lieutenant had three small stars on his collar as a badge of rank.

11. On 29 May 1945 Ozawa became chief of the All Navy Command (*Kaigun sotai*), which replaced the Combined Fleet as the navy's largest unit of operating forces. But he remained a vice admiral.

Chapter 10: The Air Battle off Taiwan

1. The author is mistaken in designating this aircraft as the Ki-81. According to Commander Akihiko Yoshida of the Japanese Maritime Self Defense Force, an authority on World War II,

the aircraft is probably the Ki-67, Mitsubishi Type 4 heavy bomber, known as *Hiryu*, or in Allied parlance as "Peggy."

Chapter 11: The Battle of Leyte Gulf

1. The existence of the dispatch in question has been confirmed by later research. See Japan Defense Agency, War History Section, *Kaigun Shogo Sakusen Fuirippin oki kaisen, ni* [The navy *Sho* operation, naval battles off the Philippines, no. 2], Vol. 30, Senshi Sosho series (Tokyo: Asagumo Shimbunsha, 1970), pp. 353–94.

2. United States Strategic Bombing Survey, Pacific, Naval Analysis Division, *Interrogations of Japanese Officials*, 2 vols. (Washington, D.C.: U.S. Government Printing Office, 1946), 1: 147–52 records the author's interview of 24 October 1945 in which he said that the American force was reckoned to be "five or six carriers, a few battleships, and a few cruisers." The survey considered the author a "reliable witness" (2: 556).

Chapter 12: Why Japan's Antisubmarine Warfare Failed

1. Theodore Roscoe, *United States Submarine Operations in World War II* (Annapolis, Maryland: U.S. Naval Institute, 1949); Transportation Division of the United States Strategic Bombing Survey, *The War Against Japanese Transportation, 1941–1945* (Washington, D.C.: U.S. Government Printing Office, 1946).

2. Morison, op. cit., Vol. 1, *The Battle of the Atlantic, September 1939–May 1943* (1947); see chapters X–XII.

3. Roscoe, op. cit., pp. 332–34.

4. Fielding Eliot, "How to Lose a War," U.S. Naval Institute *Proceedings* 76 (July 1950), p. 707.

Chapter 14: Japanese Submarine Tactics and the *Kaiten*

1. Samuel Eliot Morison, *The Two-Ocean War: A Short History of the United States Navy in the Second World War* (Boston: Atlantic Monthly Press, 1963), p. 563.

2. Holmes, op. cit., pp. 171–72.

3. Jürgen Rohwer, *Axis Submarine Successes 1939–1945* (Annapolis, Maryland: Naval Institute Press, 1983), pp. 286–91.

4. Japan Defense Agency, War History Section, *Sensuikan shi*

[History of submarines], Vol. 98, Senshi Sosho series (Tokyo: Asagumo Shimbunsha, 1979) sets forth the facts regarding *kaiten* attacks but in its concluding sections is conspicuously silent about their failure.

5. Richard F. Newcomb, *Abandon Ship! Death of the U.S.S. Indianapolis* (New York: Henry Holt, 1958). This quotation does not appear in the book, though p. 230 stresses the "nearly miraculous combination of circumstances" that allowed the *I-58* to make its kill.

6. Only a few of the successes claimed for the *kaiten* have been substantiated by later research. *Kaiten* from the *I-47* sank the *Mississinewa* (AO-59) at Ulithi. The *I-53* released *kaiten* that blew apart the *Underhill* (DE-682) in the Philippine Sea. Aside from these two vessels sunk, results were meager. The destroyer escort *Gilligan* (DE-508) was damaged by *kaiten,* as were the repair ship *Endymion* (ARL-9), the attack transport *Marathon* (APA-200), and possibly the destroyer *Lowry* (DD-770). See Rohwer, op. cit., pp. 286–91. As Rohwer notes on p. xii, "The real cause of the large overestimates of success was the difficulty the U-boats had in getting the necessary data following an attack. . . . The U-boat captains were prone to classify almost all torpedo detonations heard as hits, and all manner of acoustic noise as 'sinking' sounds."

CHAPTER 15: KAMIKAZES IN THE OKINAWA CAMPAIGN

1. The USS *Intrepid* (CV-11), an *Essex*-class carrier, was damaged when hit by a suicide plane on this date.

2. Chugoku is the western end of Honshu Island, roughly from Okayama to Shimonoseki.

3. Only the destroyer *Halsey Powell* (DD-686) and the submarine *Devilfish* (SS-292) are recorded as having been damaged by suicide attacks on this date.

4. This was the piloted, rocket-powered bomb described in Chapter 13, called the "*Baka* bomb" by the Americans. The weight of the explosive charge in the nose was 2,650 pounds.

5. Records show U.S. losses around Okinawa on this date to have been two destroyers, one minesweeper, and one tank landing ship sunk, with eleven destroyers, two destroyer escorts, and seven minesweepers damaged.

525

6. No sinkings are recorded, but six ships, including the *Maryland* (BB-46) and *Hancock* (CV-19), were damaged by suicide planes. On 8 April a destroyer and a transport were damaged by suicide boats.

7. On 12 April off Okinawa, the destroyer *Mannert L. Abele* (DD-733) was sunk by a *Baka* bomb and LCSL (3)-33 by a suicide plane. Damaged ships included the *Idaho* (BB-42), *Tennessee* (BB-43), four destroyers, four destroyer escorts, one minesweeper, two minelayers, and two landing craft.

8. On 16 April attacks by suicide planes sank the destroyer *Pringle* (DD-477) and damaged the *Missouri* (BB-63), the *Intrepid*, three destroyers, one destroyer escort, one oiler, two minesweepers, and three landing ships.

9. No ships were sunk by kamikazes in the attack of 28 April, but four destroyers, a hospital ship, a minesweeper, and a landing craft were hit and damaged.

10. On 4 May the destroyers *Luce* (DD-522) and *Morrison* (DD-560) along with three landing ships were sunk in the vicinity of Okinawa. The light carrier *Sangamon* (CVE-26), the cruiser *Birmingham* (CL-62), four destroyers, five minesweepers, two minelayers, and a landing ship were damaged.

11. The *Bunker Hill* (CV-17) was damaged in this 11 May raid, as were the destroyers *Evans* (DD-552) and *Hugh W. Hadley* (DD-774), the latter by a *Baka* bomb.

12. Both the *Enterprise* and the *Bataan* (CVL-29) were damaged by kamikazes on 14 May.

13. Three transports were sunk and three destroyer escorts, two minesweepers, and two transports were damaged.

14. On 27 May the destroyer *Drexler* (DD-741) was sunk and two destroyers, a destroyer escort, a minesweeper, a surveying ship, three transports, three landing ships, and two smaller ships were damaged.

Chapter 17: Thoughts on Japan's Naval Defeat

1. Nobutaka Ike, trans. and ed., *Japan's Decision for War: Records of the 1941 Policy Conferences* (Stanford, California: Stanford University Press, 1967), pp. 68–70, 78.

2. Ibid., pp. 247–48.

Sources

Chapter 1: "Hawaii Operation," U.S. Naval Institute *Proceedings* 81 (December 1955): 1314–31.

Chapter 2: "I Led the Air Attack on Pearl Harbor," U.S. Naval Institute *Proceedings* 78 (September 1952): 939–52.

Chapter 3: "Japanese Naval Air Operations in the Philippine Invasion," U.S. Naval Institute *Proceedings* 81 (January 1955): 1–17, 1048–49.

Chapter 4: "Die japanischen Operationen im Bereich des Indischen Ozeans," *Marine Rundschau* 55 (April 1958): 49–54.

Chapter 5: "Prelude to Midway," U.S. Naval Institute *Proceedings* 81 (May 1955): 505–13; "Five Fateful Minutes at Midway," U.S. Naval Institute *Proceedings* 81 (June 1955): 660–65; and "America Deciphered Our Code," U.S. Naval Institute *Proceedings* 105 (June 1979): 98–100.

Chapter 6: "Japan's Losing Struggle for Guadalcanal," U.S. Naval Institute *Proceedings* 82 (July 1956): 687–99, 83 (August 1956): 815–31.

Chapter 7: "The Battle of Savo Island," U.S. Naval Institute *Proceedings* 83 (December 1957): 1262–78.

Chapter 8: "Mysterious Withdrawal from Kiska," U.S. Naval Institute *Proceedings* 84 (February 1958): 30–47.

Chapter 9: "Ozawa Jisaburō no kidōbutai to Torakku kanshō" [Jisaburo Ozawa's mobile fleet and Truk atoll] and "Gunreibu sakusenshitsu kara miru Mariana oki kaisen no Ozawa kantai" [The Ozawa fleet in the battle off the Marianas as viewed from the operations room of the Naval General Staff] in Minoru Nomura, *Rekishi no naka no Nihon kaigun* [The Japanese navy in history] (Tokyo: Hara Shobō, 1980), pp. 134–88.

Chapter 10: "Strategic Aspects of the Battle off Formosa," U.S. Naval Institute *Proceedings* 78 (December 1952): 1285–93.

Chapter 11: "With Kurita in the Battle for Leyte Gulf," U.S. Naval Institute *Proceedings* 79 (February 1953): 119–33.

Chapter 12: "Why Japan's Anti-Submarine Warfare Failed," U.S. Naval Institute *Proceedings* 78 (June 1952): 587–601.

Chapter 13: "The Kamikaze Attack Corps," U.S. Naval Institute *Proceedings* 79 (September 1953): 933–45.

Chapter 14: "Japanese Submarine Tactics," U.S. Naval Institute *Proceedings* 87 (February 1961): 78–83.

Chapter 15: "Kamikazes in the Okinawa Campaign," U.S. Naval Institute *Proceedings* 80 (May 1954): 505–13.

Chapter 16: "The End of the *Yamato*," U.S. Naval Institute *Proceedings* (February 1952): 116–29.

Chapter 17: "Thoughts on Japan's Naval Defeat," U.S. Naval Institute *Proceedings* 86 (October 1960): 68–75.

Contributors

MASATAKA CHIHAYA, born in Taiwan of a Kagoshima family, graduated from the Naval Academy in 1930. As a lieutenant he attended gunnery school; later he served on the destroyer *Asagumo*, the cruiser *Chikuma*, and the battleships *Fuso* and *Nagato*. During the war he was chief antiaircraft officer on the battleship *Musashi*, attended the Naval War College, and held a number of staff posts. He ended the war as a commander on the Combined Fleet staff. Since 1951 he has been with the English-language journals *Shipping and Trade News* and *Zosen*, first as managing editor (1958–1965) and then as editor (1965–1975) of both publications. He continues to serve as senior adviser to them. He has contributed frequently to the U.S. Naval Institute *Proceedings* as both author and translator, has written several books in Japanese on the Japanese navy in World War II, and has been very active as a translator of American books on the subject.

MASARU CHIKUAMI was born in Hawaii. He graduated from Hilo High School in 1932 and was doing graduate work in Japan when the war began, at which time he performed duty as a shortwave radio monitor.

529

DAVID C. EVANS was educated at Stanford University, from which he received his master's degree in Japanese in 1969 and his Ph.D. in history in 1978. He served as an ensign and lieutenant, junior grade, USNR, 1963–1966. He has lived in Japan and is currently associate professor of history at the University of Richmond in Richmond, Virginia, where he teaches Asian history.

MITSUO FUCHIDA (1902–1976), a native of Kashiwara, Nara Prefecture, graduated from the Naval Academy in 1924. He underwent his first aviation training at Kasumigaura in 1928; by the time the war started he was a seasoned pilot with three thousand hours of flight time. He was also an air officer of considerable stature, having attended the Naval War College and attained the rank of commander. He commanded the air groups of Carrier Division 1 during the Pearl Harbor attack. At Midway, recovering from an appendectomy, he was unable to take part in the action but was wounded nevertheless. After a year's convalescence he took up a series of staff posts. At the end of the war he was air operations officer of the Combined Fleet with the rank of captain. He wrote two books in Japanese on his wartime experiences and also was co-author, with Masatake Okumiya, of *Midway, the Battle That Doomed Japan* (Annapolis, Maryland: Naval Institute Press, 1955).

SHIGERU FUKUDOME (1891–1971) grew up in Tottori Prefecture. He graduated from the Naval Academy in 1912 and after a series of shipboard assignments attended the Naval War College in 1924–1926. His career then developed in the direction of administrative and staff positions rather than sea duty, with special assignments to Europe and the United States in 1932–1933. He held a series of staff posts with the Combined Fleet and the Naval General Staff, commanded the battleship *Nagato,* earned flag rank (1939), and was chief of staff to Admiral Yamamoto when the Pearl Harbor attack was planned. He was chief of the plans and operations section of the Naval General Staff from April 1941 to May 1943. Then he again became chief of staff of the Combined Fleet. Later in the war he commanded the Second Air Fleet and the Sixth Base Air Force in defense of the Philippines and Taiwan. At the war's end he was serving concurrently as commander of the first South Sea Fleet, Tenth Area Fleet, and Thirteenth Area Fleet. After the surrender he wrote *Kaigun no hansei* [Reflections on the navy] (1951) and *Shikan Shinjuwan kogeki* [A historical view of the Pearl Harbor attack] (1955). His experience made him one of the foremost authorities on high-level planning and direction of operations throughout the Pacific War.

RIKIHEI INOGUCHI (1903–1983), born in Tottori Prefecture, graduated from the Naval Academy in 1924 and attended the Naval War College, 1934–1936, before serving as gunnery officer on the cruisers *Kinu* and *Iwate*. When the Pacific War began he was in the Personnel Bureau of the Navy Ministry. Although not himself a flier, he spent the last year of the war in aviation activities. He became senior staff officer of the First Air Fleet in August 1944 and joined the staff of the Tenth Air Fleet in March 1945. At the war's end he was a captain at Imperial General Headquarters. He wrote *The Divine Wind* (Annapolis, Maryland: U.S. Naval Institute, 1958) with Tadashi Nakajima.

CLARK KAWAKAMI graduated from Harvard University and spent several years in Japan as a news correspondent before World War II. During the war he was a first lieutenant in the U.S. Army, with military intelligence units in the China-Burma-India theater. From 1947 to 1950 he was chief American historian with occupation authorities for the project of studying Japanese military operations during World War II. Subsequently he did research on Japanese naval history for the U.S. Naval War College. He later served in the U.S. Information Agency in Washington, D.C., in various capacities, capping off his career as editor of the periodical *Problems of Communism*. He retired in 1976 and died in 1985.

TOMIJI KOYANAGI (1893–1983) was reared in Niigata Prefecture and graduated from the Naval Academy in 1914. He attended torpedo school and the Naval War College. He served on destroyers and destroyer division staffs and taught at various naval schools. In 1936 he was promoted to captain; at the start of the war he was commanding officer of the battleship *Kongo*. During the Battle of Leyte Gulf he was a rear admiral and chief of staff of the First Strike Force on the battleship *Yamato*. He finished the war as a vice admiral. He wrote *Kurita kantai* [The Kurita fleet] (1956).

TADASHI NAKAJIMA, from Kumamoto Prefecture, graduated from the Naval Academy in 1930. He had been a navy flier for eleven years when, in 1944, he took command of the 201st Air Group, the first to launch kamikaze attacks, in the Philippines. He served on the staff of the Fifth Air Fleet during the Okinawa campaign. After the war he entered the Japan Air Self-Defense Force, attaining the rank of major general before leaving the service in 1960. He served as aviation materials consultant and executive in the Yokohama Rubber Company until his retirement in 1974. With Rikihei Inoguchi, he is the author of *The Divine Wind* (Annapolis, Maryland: U.S. Naval Institute, 1958).

MINORU NOMURA graduated from the Naval Academy in 1942. After service on the battleship *Musashi,* the carrier *Zuikaku,* and the Naval General Staff, he taught at the Naval Academy. During the U.S. occupation he worked in the Navy Demobilization Bureau. In 1956 he joined the Defense Agency. He played a leading role in production of the War History Section's War History Series on World War II (*Senshi sosho*), authoring volumes dealing with the Naval Section of Imperial General Headquarters. He is now Professor of Defense Studies at the National Defense Academy, where he teaches naval history.

RAYMOND O'CONNOR has been emeritus professor of history at the University of Miami since 1980 and is visiting scholar at Stanford University. A native of St. Louis, he served in the U.S. Navy during World War II on the light cruiser *Trenton* and in the Bureau of Naval Personnel. He received his M.A. degree from American University in 1948 and his Ph.D. in history from Stanford in 1957. He has taught at Stanford, the University of Kansas, and Temple University in addition to the University of Miami. During 1967–1968 he held the Ernest J. King Chair of

Maritime History at the U.S. Naval War College. He has written widely on American military policy and arms control.

TOSHIKAZU OHMAE (1902–1978), a Naval Academy graduate of 1922, attended torpedo school and served on a number of ships as a junior officer. He took the Naval War College course from 1932 to 1934 and was on special detached duty in the United States from 1935 to 1937. After commanding the destroyer *Kikuzuki*, he took up a series of administrative and staff posts. When the war broke out he was a captain in the Military Affairs Bureau of the Navy Ministry. He was chief of the operations section of the Naval General Staff in August 1945. During the U.S. occupation he became chief of the Historical Research Section of the Navy Demobilization Bureau.

ATSUSHI OI, a native of Yamagata Prefecture, graduated from the Naval Academy in 1923. From 1928 to 1930 he underwent special training in the English language; during his stay in the United States, 1930–1932, he attended the University of Virginia and Northwestern University. After studying at the Naval War College from 1934 to 1936 he served on a number of fleet staffs and the Naval General Staff. In 1940 he became operations officer with the Second China Fleet and in 1941 was appointed to the Personnel Bureau of the Navy Ministry. Later he served as executive officer of the Special Base Force 21 on Java, a member of the operations and plans section, Naval General Staff, and operations officer of Grand Escort Command Headquarters. At the end of the war he was a captain. During the U.S. occupation he did research on the Pacific War for the historical section of GHQ, Supreme Commander Allied Powers. He has written the standard work on Japanese merchant shipping during the war. Its most recent edition is *Kaijo goei sen* [The sea escort war] (Tokyo: Asahi Sonorama, 1983).

MASATAKE OKUMIYA is a native of Kochi Prefecture. He graduated from the Naval Academy in 1930 and began flight training in 1933. After duty in the China war during 1937, he was a test pilot for dive-bombers until September 1938, when he suffered

533

a serious aircraft accident. Just before the war, as a lieutenant commander, he joined the staff of the Eleventh Air Fleet. During the Aleutian operation he served under Rear Admiral Kakuji Kakuta on the carrier *Ryujo* as staff officer of the Fourth Air Fleet; he was also with Kakuta on the *Junyo* during the Battle of the Santa Cruz Islands and other fighting in the Solomons. He saw duty at Wewak in December 1942, in the Guadalcanal withdrawal of early 1943, and at Rabaul in early 1944. In June 1944 he was air staff officer under Rear Admiral Takaji Joshima on the *Junyo* in the Battle of the Philippine Sea. At the conclusion of hostilities he was a commander on the Naval General Staff. As a member of the Navy Demobilization Bureau after the war, he had access to what naval records remained. He entered the Japan Air Self-Defense Force after the U.S. occupation and retired with the rank of lieutenant general in 1964. Since then he has served as a consultant to Matsushita Electric and the PHP Institute. He has written on current defense issues as well as Japanese military history. With Mitsuo Fuchida he wrote *Midway, the Battle That Doomed Japan* (Annapolis, Maryland: Naval Institute Press, 1955).

ROGER PINEAU, Captain, USNR, Ret., graduated from the University of Michigan in 1942 and from the U.S. Navy Japanese Language School in 1943. As a lieutenant, he worked for the U.S. Strategic Bombing Survey in Japan just after the war. Later he assisted Samuel Eliot Morison in the preparation of the *History of U.S. Naval Operations in World War II.* He worked for the Department of State in the 1950s and early 1960s. In 1966 he became editor of the Smithsonian Institution Press and in 1972 became director of the Navy Memorial Museum in Washington, D.C. He has translated and edited numerous works on the Japanese navy in World War II. Recently retired, he has just completed work on the posthumous memoirs of Rear Admiral Edwin T. Layton, *"And I Was There": Pearl Harbor and Midway— Breaking the Secrets* (New York: Morrow, 1985).

KOICHI SHIMADA, a Naval Academy graduate of 1927, became an aviator as a sublieutenant in 1931. He attended the Naval War

College in 1940 and, after a number of air assignments, was assigned to the staff of the Eleventh Air Fleet for operations against the Philippines at the start of the war. He held a succession of air staff appointments, ending the war as a commander. After the U.S. occupation he joined the Japan Air Self-Defense Force and rose to the rank of brigadier general.

RAIZO TANAKA (1892–1969), a native of Yamaguchi Prefecture, graduated from the Naval Academy in 1913. He attended torpedo school in 1920 and served on destroyers as a torpedo specialist. At the war's inception he was a rear admiral and commanded the Second Destroyer Squadron. He fought at the Coral Sea and Midway, and he became Japan's foremost destroyer squadron commander during the battles in the Solomons. Later he commanded the marine detachment at Maizuru and at the war's conclusion was a vice admiral.

KENNOSUKE TORISU, a native of Fukuoka, graduated from the Naval Academy in 1930. Before the Pacific War he served on four different submarines as gunnery and torpedo officer. After the outbreak of hostilities he commanded two submarines as noted in the text. He attended the Naval War College in 1943–1944 and subsequently became operations officer on the staff of the Sixth Fleet, the submarine force. Since the war he has made an extensive study of the navy's submarine operations, writing and editing several books on the subject and establishing himself as the foremost authority on *kaiten*. His latest work is *Ningen gyorai: Tokko heiki "kaiten" to wakodotachi* [Human torpedoes: The special-attack weapon *kaiten* and the young men (who manned them)] (Tokyo: Shinchosha, 1983).

TOSHIYUKI YOKOI (1897–1969) graduated from the Naval Academy in 1918. He entered flight training in 1922, attended the Naval War College, and became a flight instructor. He was a captain on the staff of an air group when the war began. He was wounded while in command of the carrier *Hiyo* in 1944. When the kamikaze corps was formed later that year, he was commander of the Twenty-fifth Air Flotilla with the rank of rear admiral. He served as chief of staff of the Fifth Air Fleet in the Okinawa campaign. At the time hostilities ended he was a vice admiral.

Mɪᴛsᴜʀᴜ Yᴏsʜɪᴅᴀ (1923–1979) was in his third year at Tokyo Imperial University when picked by the student draft of December 1943. He entered the navy and was trained in electronics. In December 1944 he was assigned to the *Yamato* as a radar officer with the rank of ensign. After the war he had a successful career with the Bank of Japan and wrote several books on naval subjects including a biography of the fleet commander who went to his death on the *Yamato*, Seiichi Ito. The article by Yoshida that appears in this book is an abridgment of his *Senkan Yamato no saigo* [The end of the battleship *Yamato*], now considered one of the few classics of war literature to come out of World War II on the Japanese side. The complete version, excellently translated by Richard Minear, recently appeared as *Requiem for Battleship Yamato* (Seattle: University of Washington Press and Kodansha International, 1985).

536

Index

537

Cape Esperance, Battle of, 171,
180, 196
Caroline Islands, 4, 31, 310, 344,
409
Carrier Striking Force: in Hawaii
Operation, 90; at Battle of Mid-
way, 132, 154
Carrier Task Force (Third Fleet): at
Truk, 160; in Solomons, 165
Case (U.S. destroyer), 47
Catalina patrol plane, 275
Cavalla (U.S. submarine), 320
Cavite Harbor, Luzon, Philippines,
101
Cavite Naval Base, Luzon, Philip-
pines, 96
Cebu air base, Philippines, 426,
428
Celebes Sea, 309
Celebes, the, 103, 157
Center Force (Kurita), Battle of
Leyte Gulf. *See* First Striking
Force
Central Pacific Area Fleet, 314
Ceylon, 108, 109, 110, 113, 114,
115, 116, 117, 215, 394
Champagne, Ray, 522ch8n4
Cheju Island, Korea, 469
Chen Yüan (Chinese armorclad
turret ship), 506
Chester (U.S. cruiser), 520n14
Chiang Kai-shek regime, China,
504
Chicago (U.S. cruiser), 519ch6n1,
522ch7n6
Chicago-class cruisers, 49
Chikuma (cruiser), 26, 42, 53, 58,
135, 137, 184, 215, 252, 283,
296, 298
China, 76, 99, 342, 508–9
China Incident (Sino-Japanese
War, 1937–1945), xiii, 20, 94,
210. *See also* China
China Seas Fleet: sea area of, re-
sponsibility of GEHQ, 401
Chinio, Camp (airfield, Luzon,
Philippines), 80

Chinkai Minor Naval Station, 390
Chitose (seaplane tender, 1936),
33, 512; (light carrier, 1944),
298, 322
Chiyoda (seaplane tender, 1937),
512; (light carrier, 1943), 298
Chokai (*Chōkai*, cruiser), 159,
182, 187, 191, 204, 220, photo
221, 225, 226, 227, 235, 236,
237, 239, 240, 242, 298
Choshu (Chōshū), army air base,
Taiwan, 80, 89
Chugoku (Chūgoku), western
Honshu, 461, 525ch15n2
Chungking (Nationalist Chinese
regime), 107, 393
Clark Field, air base, Luzon, Phil-
ippines, 80, 86, 87, 90, 91, 100,
416, 518n1
"Claude" fighter, 89
Clausewitz, Carl von, 507
"Climb Mount Niitaka" (coded
message), 28
Cocos Islands, Indian Ocean, 394
Code Book D, 154
Code Breakers, The (book), 155
Colombo, Ceylon, 106, 111, 135,
443
Combat information center (U.S.),
329
Combined Chiefs of Staff (Anglo-
American), xvi, xviii, 117
Combined Fleet: air attacks at
1940 maneuvers of, 7; and air
offensive against Philippines,
101–2; and Indian Ocean operations, 108, 109–10, 114, 116;
and Midway operation, 121,
125, 132–33; and Solomons
battles, 165, 169, 172, 190, 194,
209, 241; planned further conquests in 1942, 213–14; and
Saipan, 279, 332; Aleutian
battle plan of, 289; and Operations Y and Z, 292; and Operation RO, 294; forward base of,
shifted, early 1944, 296, 410;

"Imperial Defense Policy": formulated, 388–89; of 1907, 500; became outmoded, 501

Imperial General Headquarters (*Dai-hon'ei*): establishment and composition, 19; issued navy order for war, 42; breach of security by, 86–87; and Indian Ocean operations, 105; Army Section of, called meeting about India, 108; Navy Section of, favored further conquests in early 1942, 213; Navy Section of, opposed Midway operation, 214; radio intelligence from Special Duty Group of, 222; sent reinforcements to Attu, 250; and Guadalcanal withdrawal, 252; and Kiska evacuation, 252, 290; planned Aleutian effort, 289; T Attack Force attached to, 338; made situation estimate after loss of Saipan, 344; and air battle off Taiwan, 351; and kamikaze operations, 417; adopted general suicide tactics, 455; was counterpart to U.S. Joint Chiefs, 502–3

Imperial Headquarters–Government Liaison Conference. *See* Liaison Conference

Imperial Naval General Staff Order No. 1, 20–21

Imperial Navy Directive No. 86, 16 April 1942, 214

Incredible Victory (book), 155

Independence-class ships, 512

India, 394, 504

Indian Ocean, 292, 393

Indianapolis (U.S. cruiser), 316, 442, 448, 449

Indispensable Strait, Solomons, 241

Influence of Sea Power upon History (book), 506

Inland Sea, 158, 282, 289, 296, 312, 471

Inoue, Shigeyoshi (Inoue Shigeyoshi), 216, 220, 333

International Military Tribunal for the Far East, 21–24

Intrepid (U.S. carrier), 525ch15n1, 526n8

Isokaze (destroyer), 26, 42, 151, 167, 170, 171, 172, 174, 480, 489

Isuzu (cruiser), 180, 181, 182, 187, 191

Itakura, Mitsuma (Itakura Mitsuma), 448

Italy, 400

Itaya, Lieutenant Commander (Itaya Shigeru), 55, 135

Ito, Seiichi (Itō Seiichi), 322, 326, 330, 398, 459, 480, 492

Itsukushima (protected cruiser, 1889), 506

Iwakuni, Honshu, 297

Iwata, Toyo (Iwata Tōyō), 441

Iwo Jima (Iōjima, Iō Tō), Volcano Islands, 326, 391, 448, 450, 469

Iyonada, Inland Sea, 471

"Jake" Type O reconnaissance seaplane, 317

Japan, Sea of, 406

Japan Defense Agency, War History Office, 121, 290

Jarvis (U.S. destroyer), 47

Java, 110, 114, 180

Java Sea, xix

Java Sea, Battle of, xviii, 105, 196

Jellicoe, Admiral (Sir John Jellicoe), 401

"Jill" torpedo plane, 300, photo 301, 302, 305, 306, 316, 317

Jinrai butai (divine thunderbolt unit): kamikaze operations, 436

Jintsu (*Jintsū*, cruiser), 158, 160, 161, 162, photo 168, 169

Jo, Eiichiro (Jō Eiichirō), 425

Johnston Island, 50

Johore Bharu, Malaya, 307